MODERN EUROPEAN HISTORY

Birdsall S. Viault, Ph.D.
Winthrop College

An American BookWorks Corporation Project

McGraw-Hill, Inc.

New York   St. Louis   San Francisco   Auckland   Bogotá   Caracas
Lisbon   London   Madrid   Mexico   Milan   Montreal   New Delhi
Paris   San Juan   Singapore   Sydney   Tokyo   Toronto

For those who guided me in the study of European history:
Robert Ernst, Chester L. Barrows, Hans Rothfels, John S. Curtiss,
E. Malcolm Carroll, Harold T. Parker

Birdsall S. Viault is Professor of History at Winthrop University, Rock Hill, South Carolina. He received his B.S. degree from Adelphi University and an M.A. degree in secondary education from the same institution. Further graduate work at Duke University led to an M.A. and Ph.D. in history.

Prior to joining the faculty at Winthrop University, Professor Viault taught at Adelphi University. He is the author of several other volumes in McGraw-Hill's College Core Books series. His articles and reviews have appeared in journals in the United States and Europe, and for a number of years he wrote on subjects related to history and current affairs in a weekly column, ''Perspective,'' which appeared in over thirty South Carolina newspapers.

Editor: Tyler Deierhoi, Ph.D., University of Tennessee at Chattanooga

The maps were executed by Jean Paul Tremblay, Francis & Shaw, Inc., Dyno Lowenstein, and Vantage Art, Inc.

Modern European History

Copyright © 1990 by McGraw-Hill, Inc. All rights reserved. Printed in the United States of America. Except as permitted under the Copyright Act of 1976, no part of this publication may be reproduced or distributed in any form or by any means, or stored in a data base or retrieval system, without the prior written permission of the publisher.

21 22 23 24 DOC DOC 0 9 8 7

ISBN 0-07-067453-1 (Formerly published under ISBN 0-07-067433-7.)

Library of Congress Cataloging-in-Publication Data

Viault, Birdsall S.
     Modern European History / Birdsall S. Viault.
         p.   cm. — (McGraw-Hill's core books)
     "An American BookWorks Corporation project."
     Includes index.
     ISBN 0-07-067433-7
     1. Europe—History—1492– . I.Title.   II. Series
D209.V49   1991   91-14195
940.2—dc20   CIP

Map Acknowledgments

The maps on pages 19, 50, 202, 297, 303, 363, 367, 508, 553, and 561 were reproduced from John B. Harrison, Richard E. Sulllivan, and Dennis Sherman, *A Short History of Western Civilization*, 7th ed., McGraw-Hill, New York, 1990. The maps on pages 71, 111, and 558 were reproduced from the 6th edition, 1985.

The maps on pages 126, 142, 211, 390, and 397 were reproduced from Mortimer Chambers, et al., *The Western Experience*, 4th ed., Knopf, 1987.

Preface

This volume presents the history of Europe since the Late Middle Ages, focusing on the great movements, ideas, events, and personalities that shaped Europe's development. It is designed to be used in two ways: as a textbook in its own right and as a supplement to any of the standard college texts.

To enhance comprehension and retention of historical material, each chapter contains a time line, an overview and a summary, and a system of clearly related subheads. Dates of birth and death are given for most individuals cited. For monarchs and popes, the dates refer to their reigns and are indicated as "r."

No attempt has been made to cover the major interpretive or historical debates relating to the history of modern Europe. Rather the reader is encouraged to consult the recommended reading sections that appear at the end of each chapter. Here the reader will find detailed studies of subjects considered in the chapter. In selecting books to be included, emphasis has been placed on recent scholarship and classic works.

Acknowledgments

It is a pleasure for me to acknowledge the constributions of those who have done so much to make this book possible.

Greg Dobbins assisted with the research, while Judy Lassiter, Denise Cody, and David Turner helped with the preparation of the manuscript. The content editor, Professor Tyler Deierhoi of the University of Tennessee at Chattanooga, reviewed the manuscript with a keen eye and made recommendations that have improved the final product. My colleague and friend Jason Silverman also reviewed part of the manuscript, making a number of useful suggestions. The staff of the Dacus Library of Winthrop College, especially Susan Silverman and Nancy Davidson, provided me with considerable help, while Fred Grayson offered encouragement and support throughout the project.

I must also express my appreciation to the hundreds of students in my classes in European history over the past thirty years. From them I have learned much about how to make history understandable and meaningful.

I owe my greatest gratitude to my wife, Sally, for her support, encouragement, and enthusiasm. She also proofread the manuscript with great skill.

Birdsall S. Viault
Rock Hill, SC
September 1989

Contents

Maps

CHAPTER 1

The Emergence of Modern Europe

Time Line

1302	Pope Boniface VIII issues the bull *Unam Sanctam*
1305–1378	The popes reside in Avignon during the Babylonian Captivity of the Papacy
1347	The Black Death sweeps through Italy
1356	The Golden Bull establishes a system for the election of the Holy Roman emperor
1378–1417	During the Great Schism, there are two, and even three, rival claimants to the papacy

1415	John Hus is burned at the stake
1417	The election of Pope Martin V ends the Great Schism
1453	The Hundred Years' War ends
1455–1485	England is torn by the Wars of the Roses
1461	Louis XI becomes king of France
1469	Ferdinand of Aragon marries Isabella of Castile
1485	Henry Tudor becomes King Henry VII of England
1492	The Spanish government orders the country's Jews either to convert to Christianity or leave
	The Spanish reconquer Granada from the Moors
1519	Charles V becomes Holy Roman emperor
1556	Charles V begins the process of abdication

During the fourteenth century, a series of crises undermined the civilization of medieval Western Europe, the civilization that had developed and matured following the collapse of the Roman Empire during the fifth century A.D. The Babylonian Captivity of the Papacy and the Great Schism weakened the prestige and authority of the Roman Catholic Church. Great Britain and France became embroiled in the Hundred Years' War, which threatened the authority of the monarchy in both countries. In Central Europe, the Holy Roman Empire was disintegrating into an array of virtually independent princely states. To compound Europe's problems, the Black Death suddenly swept out of the East, claiming the lives of a quarter to a third of Europe's population.

Signs of improvement appeared during the fifteenth century, however. The Great Schism ended, although the Roman Catholic Church continued to face serious problems. While the decline of the Holy Roman Empire continued, in England, France, and Spain, strong na-

tional monarchies emerged. The civilization of modern Europe was taking shape.

The Decline of the Roman Catholic Church

Philip the Fair and Boniface VIII

The declining power and prestige of the papacy signified momentous change in Europe during the Late Middle Ages.

Clericos Laicos

During the late thirteenth century, there were already some signs of an erosion of papal authority. Then, as the century drew to a close, a bitter conflict erupted between King Philip IV (r. 1285–1314) of France, known as Philip the Fair, and Pope Boniface VIII (r. 1294–1303). In need of money to finance his war against England, Philip demanded, in 1296, that the French clergy pay taxes. Boniface responded with the bull *Clericos Laicos* (1296), prohibiting the taxation of the clergy without papal approval.

Unam Sanctam

Both the king and the pope refused to give way, and the conflict intensified. In the bull *Unam Sanctam* (1302), Boniface VIII stated his claim to papal supremacy in uncompromising terms, insisting that resistance to the will of the pope was resistance to the will of God. Enraged, Philip the Fair sent agents to Italy in search of the pope. In September 1303, the French found Boniface at his summer home in Anagni and took him prisoner, although he was soon set free. Not long after this "Crime of Anagni," as it became known, Boniface died. The new pope, Benedict XI (r. 1303–1304), carefully avoided further conflict with Philip.

The Babylonian Captivity of the Papacy

Following the death of Benedict XI, Bertrand de Got, the bishop of Bordeaux in France, was elected pope, becoming Pope Clement V (r. 1305–1314). In order to avoid the anarchy then prevalent in Rome, Clement took up residence in Avignon, a papal possession in southern

France. A succession of French popes resided in Avignon for almost seventy years. During this period, known as the Babylonian Captivity of the Papacy (1305–1378), the popes were subject to a substantial degree of control by the French monarchy. While not noted for the quality of its spiritual leadership, the Avignon papacy was marked by considerable administrative and financial efficiency.

The Great Schism

In 1377, Pope Gregory XI (r. 1370–1378) decided to move back to Rome. Following Gregory's death in 1378, the cardinals, who feared the Roman mob, elected an Italian pope, Urban VI (r. 1378–1389). A group of French cardinals then declared that Urban's election had taken place under duress and was thus invalid. They elected a Frenchman as pope, who became Clement VII (r. 1378–1394). Clement took up residence in Avignon.

The election of Clement VII began the Great Schism. For the next four decades, from 1378 to 1417, there were two popes, one at Rome and the other at Avignon, each claiming to be the true vicar of Christ on earth.

France and its allies, including Scotland and the Spanish kingdoms of Castile, Navarre, and Aragon, supported the Avignon papacy. France's enemy, England, as well as the Holy Roman Empire, Portugal, and Italy, backed the Roman pontiff.

The Council of Pisa

The Great Schism had a negative impact on the religious life of Catholic Europe. In an effort to end the split, a council of some five hundred bishops and other churchmen met in Pisa in 1409. The council deposed both Gregory XII (Rome) and Benedict XIII (Avignon) and elected a new pope, Alexander V. But neither Gregory nor Benedict would give way, so now there were three popes.

The Council of Constance

The Council of Constance, which met from 1414 to 1418, ended the Great Schism. In 1417, the council elected Pope Martin V (r. 1417–1431), who won recognition from all factions. Martin V took up residence in Rome.

During the fifteenth century, the popes became actively involved in the political and cultural life of Renaissance Italy (see Chapter 2) and did little to deal with the much-needed reform of the Roman Catholic Church. This failure contributed to the Protestant Reformation of the sixteenth century.

Heresy

The problems of the church in the Late Middle Ages were compounded by the emergence of heresies. A heresy, by definition, is a teaching contrary to the accepted orthodox doctrine.

Wycliffe

In England, John Wycliffe (c. 1328–1384), a scholar who taught at Oxford University, insisted that the Bible was the only source of Christian doctrine. To make the Bible more accessible to literate Englishmen, he translated it into English. Wycliffe rejected the authority of the papacy and the hierarchy of the church, regarding them as both unscriptural and unnecessary, and he denounced the wealth and corruption of the clergy. He also rejected the Roman Catholic doctrine regarding the Eucharist, which taught that the consecrated bread and wine were miraculously transformed into the body and blood of Christ.

Wycliffe won a number of followers, known as Lollards, especially among the lower classes. The church, with the support of the English government, suppressed the movement.

Hus

In Bohemia, John Hus (c. 1369–1415), a teacher at the university in Prague, embraced Wycliffe's ideas. Hus and his followers, the Hussites, represented both a religious and national revolt, winning support among the Czechs of Bohemia, who objected to German domination of their homeland. Hus appeared before the Council of Constance to respond to charges of heresy. Although he had been promised safe conduct, he was tried, condemned by the council as a heretic, and burned at the stake in 1415. Despite Hus's death, the Hussite Wars between his followers and the papal forces continued in Bohemia for several years.

The thought of Wycliffe and Hus foreshadowed the ideas of the Protestant reformers of the sixteenth century.

The Black Death

The Black Death was an epidemic of the bubonic plague that devastated Europe in the mid-fourteenth century.

Early in the century, the bubonic plague swept through parts of China. It then spread along the trade routes and was carried to Europe on rat-infested ships. Fleas from infected rats transmitted the plague bacteria to humans.

In 1347, the bubonic plague appeared in Sicily and in the Italian port cities of Venice, Genoa, and Pisa. Sweeping through Italy, the disease spread within months to Switzerland, Germany, and Eastern Europe. It hit France in 1348 and moved on into Spain and England.

The Mortality Figures

The death toll was highest in thickly populated urban areas. While there are no statistics recording the loss of life, it is likely that somewhere between 35 and 65 percent of the urban population died. The toll in rural areas was less. The Black Death hit hardest at the poor, whose crowded living conditions encouraged the spread of disease. The wealthy benefited from being better housed and fed and from their ability to escape to the countryside. In subsequent years, the bubonic plague became endemic in Europe, with additional serious outbreaks occurring during the fourteenth century and later.

Economic Effects

The loss of population produced a temporary economic decline and also hastened an economic revolution, promoting a decline of serfdom and the manorial system. The serious labor shortage forced landowners to make concessions to the peasants, who gradually won freedom from the bonds of serfdom. In much of Western Europe, a free peasantry came into being, although the peasants had to pay rent and taxes for their use of the land. In the towns, the decrease in the supply of labor resulted in substantially higher wages for skilled artisans.

Psychological Effects

The Black Death also provoked an intensification of superstition and hysteria in European society. Religious fanatics known as flagellants beat their bodies in the belief that this mortification of the flesh would lead God to intervene on humanity's behalf. The witchcraft delusion became widespread, and civil and church authorities joined to persecute those accused of practicing black magic. In addition, the Black Death led to increased persecution of the Jews. Jews had long been the victims of persecution by Christians, and now they were blamed for causing the plague. In a number of areas there were anti-Jewish riots, known as pogroms, and many Jews were massacred.

The Rise of National Monarchy: England

Effects of the Hundred Years' War

The Hundred Years' War (1337–1453), a disastrous conflict between England and France, ended with the English loss of all of their territorial holdings in France, except the port of Calais on the English Channel. The war weakened the authority of the monarchy in both France and England.

The Wars of the Roses (1455–1485)

In 1455, a civil war broke out in England. Known as the Wars of the Roses, this vicious conflict lasted for thirty years. The chief antagonists were the house of Lancaster, whose symbol was a red rose, and the house of York, symbolized by a white rose. The Wars of the Roses were, above all, a struggle among members of the nobility and landed gentry, who sided with the contending houses primarily for reasons of their own selfish interests.

In 1461, King Edward IV (r. 1461–1483), a Yorkist, seized the throne from the Lancastrian king Henry VI (r. 1422–1461), who was murdered in the Tower of London. A capable military leader and administrator, Edward IV succeeded in restoring at least some limited order to the kingdom.

Following Edward IV's sudden death at the age of forty-one, his brother, the duke of Gloucester, became King Richard III (r. 1483–1485). Richard III's two young nephews, the sons of Edward IV, were murdered in the Tower of London. One of the boys was the lawful king, Edward V; his brother, Richard, was duke of York. Richard III's role in the murders has remained a subject of historical controversy.

Henry Tudor, an illegitimate Lancastrian, challenged Richard III. The two met in 1485 in the Battle of Bosworth Field, where Richard lost his life. The Wars of the Roses thus came to an end with a Lancastrian victory.

King Henry VII (r. 1485–1509)

The victor of Bosworth Field became King Henry VII, the first of England's Tudor monarchs. Henry moved quickly to consolidate his position by marrying a Yorkist princess, Elizabeth, the eldest daughter of King Edward IV, and by securing Parliament's endorsement of his position as king.

Henry VII achieved a remarkable success in restoring order and stability to England, and he passed on a strong monarchy to his successor.

Domestic Affairs

Henry strove to restore the authority of the English monarchy. In order to reduce the power and influence of the nobility, he chose his ministers mainly from the prosperous middle class. The king's active encouragement of trade also helped win middle class support.

Henry managed government affairs well, balancing the budget and building up a sizable surplus in the royal treasury. The king's frugality freed him from dependence on Parliament for grants of money. As a result, the power of Parliament declined. Parliament met only five times during Henry's reign and only once during its final twelve years.

Foreign Affairs

While Henry VII used force effectively to suppress several rebellions and to defeat rival claimants to the throne, in his conduct of foreign affairs he preferred diplomacy to expensive wars. In order to improve relations with Scotland, which had supported France during the Hundred Years' War, he arranged for his daughter to marry the Scottish king. To maintain good relations with the Hapsburgs, he arranged the marriage of his eldest son, Arthur, to Catherine of Aragon, the aunt of the future Holy Roman emperor Charles V. When Arthur died, Henry arranged for Catherine to marry his younger son, who became King Henry VIII (r. 1509–1547).

The Rise of National Monarchy: France

King Louis XI (r. 1461–1483)

During the reign of King Louis XI, France recovered from the devastation of the Hundred Years' War and regained its position as the leading power in Europe. By the time of Louis XI's death, France was a strong state with a population of 16 million, compared to 5 million in England, and was well on its way to becoming an absolute monarchy.

Domestic Affairs

Like Henry VII in England, Louis XI faced the problem of reestablishing royal authority at the expense of the nobility. Like Henry, Louis chose many of his advisers from the upper middle class. The consultative assembly, the Estates General, met only once during his reign, in 1468. Louis made laws and levied taxes by decree. The king also worked to organize an efficient centralized bureaucracy and succeeded in establishing royal control over the judicial system. These actions increased the power of the crown and also resulted in a substantial increase in royal income.

Foreign Affairs

Louis XI created an effective army, which he used to suppress revolts of the nobility. However, in foreign affairs, he preferred diplomacy to force. Louis wove such intricate webs of political and diplomatic intrigue that he won the nickname the Universal Spider.

As a continental country, however, France could not avoid war as readily as England could. The Duchy of Burgundy, lying between France and the Holy Roman Empire, presented the greatest threat to Louis's authority and French unity. The dukes of Burgundy ruled not only the Duchy of Burgundy itself, but also the Franche-Comté (the

Free County of Burgundy) and most of the Netherlands. Louis XI fought against two dukes of Burgundy, Philip the Good (r. 1419–1467) and Charles the Bold (r. 1467–1477). After Charles the Bold was killed in battle, Louis acquired the Duchy of Burgundy, as well as Picardy. He also succeeded in adding the provinces of Anjou, Maine, and Provence to the French royal domain.

French Conflict with the Hapsburgs

In 1491, King Charles VIII (r. 1483–1498) acquired Brittany by marriage, but he wasted the financial resources of the French monarchy by invading Italy in 1494. King Louis XII (r. 1498–1515), a cousin of Charles VIII, continued the unsuccessful Italian war. These French incursions into Italy were the opening round in the long conflict between the Valois kings of France and the Hapsburgs.

King Francis I (r. 1515–1547)

King Francis I increased the centralization of royal administration and finances and strengthened the army. His failure to summon the Estates General into session (it had last met in 1468) further increased royal authority, as did the Concordat of Bologna, concluded with Pope Leo X (r. 1513–1521) in 1516. The concordat authorized the king to nominate bishops and other high officials of the Catholic Church in France, thereby giving the monarch administrative control over the church.

Like his immediate predecessors, however, Francis I squandered much of his resources in unsuccessful foreign wars. In particular, France continued its costly intervention in Italy, where Francis I faced the powerful Charles V, the Hapsburg who was both Holy Roman emperor and king of Spain.

The Rise of National Monarchy: Spain

The Unification of Aragon and Castile

During the Middle Ages, the Spanish Christians carried out the reconquest (*Reconquista*) of Spain from the Moslems, creating several Christian states in the Iberian peninsula.

In 1469, the future king Ferdinand (r. 1479–1516) of Aragon married the future queen Isabella (r. 1474–1504) of Castile, thereby creating the basis for the union of their kingdoms. As rulers, Ferdinand and Isabella strove to increase royal power at the expense of the nobility and the towns. Toward that end, they called the Cortes (the traditional consultative assemblies representing the nobility, the towns, and the clergy) into session as infrequently as possible.

Under Ferdinand and Isabella, the Spanish army became one of Europe's best. Also during their reign, Christopher Columbus discovered the New World (see Chapter 6).

The Spanish Inquisition

Ferdinand and Isabella gained control over the Catholic Church in Spain and used the church as an instrument of royal power. As a result of the efforts of Queen Isabella and Tomás de Torquemada (1420–1498), a Dominican priest and the queen's confessor, the Spanish Inquisition was established. With Torquemada as inquisitor general, the Inquisition became an important instrument of royal authority. While Isabella and Torquemada were evidently motivated primarily by religious concerns, Ferdinand viewed the Inquisition as a useful weapon against rebellious nobles and churchmen.

The Inquisition began operating in Castile in 1480 and in Aragon seven years later, using torture in its investigations and confiscating the property of its victims. The Inquisition announced its sentences at an elaborate public ceremony called an *auto-da-fé* (act of faith). Executions, usually by burning at the stake, were not a part of the auto-da-fé itself but took place sometime later. During the fifteen years that Torquemada served as inquisitor general, at least two thousand people were burned at the stake.

The Jews

Like many other rulers of their time, Ferdinand and Isabella believed that religious unity was a prerequisite for political unity. In 1492, the government ordered all Spanish Jews either to adopt Christianity or to leave the country. As many as 200,000 Jews left, with many going to North Africa, Italy, the Ottoman Empire, Poland, and Russia.

The Spanish Jews who accepted Christianity were known as Marranos. The Inquisition charged that many Marranos continued to practice the Jewish religion in secret. The Marranos were persecuted, and many were expelled from the country.

The Moslems

In 1492, the Spanish reconquered Granada, the last remaining Moslem state in the Iberian peninsula. The government promised religious freedom to the Moors, as the Spanish Moslems were known, but this promise was revoked following a revolt of the Moors in 1501. The government then sought to force the Moors to convert to Christianity. Many left Spain, while those who remained and adopted Christianity were known as Moriscos.

Many of the Moriscos continued to practice Islam secretly, which resulted in their being persecuted by the Inquisition. The Moriscos were finally expelled from Spain in 1609.

The Holy Roman Empire

While strong national monarchies emerged in England, France, and Spain, in the German lands of Central Europe, the Holy Roman Empire experienced continuing disintegration as the nobility increased its power at the expense of the emperor.

The Golden Bull of 1356 provided that the Holy Roman emperor would be chosen by seven princes of the Holy Roman Empire, who were designated as electors. There were three ecclesiastical and four secular electors. The ecclesiastical electors were the archbishops of Cologne, Trier, and Mainz, while the secular electors included the king of Bohemia, the duke of Saxony, the margrave of Brandenburg, and the count palatine of the Rhine. In effect, the Golden Bull made the princes of the empire virtually independent rulers of their own domains.

Beginning in the early fifteenth century, the imperial title was customarily conferred on members of the Hapsburg dynasty.

Charles V: King and Emperor

Following the death of King Ferdinand of Spain in 1516, the Spanish crown passed to his grandson, who became King Charles I (r. 1516–1556). Charles was also the Hapsburg heir to the throne of the Holy Roman Empire, becoming Emperor Charles V (r. 1519–1556). While the title of Holy Roman emperor brought with it little power, Charles V's personal domains made him an extraordinarily powerful ruler.

The Domains of Charles V

From Emperor Maximilian I (r. 1493–1519), his paternal grandfather, Charles V inherited the Hapsburg domains in Central Europe, customarily referred to as Austria. Charles expanded these domains by acquiring part of Hungary, Bohemia and Moravia, and Silesia. From Mary of Burgundy (r. 1457–1482), his paternal grandmother, he inherited the Burgundian holdings, including the Franche-Comté and the Netherlands. In addition, Charles claimed the Duchy of Burgundy, as well as Picardy, which had been acquired by King Louis XI of France in the late fifteenth century. From his maternal grandparents Ferdinand and Isabella, Charles inherited Spain and the Spanish Empire, as well as Naples, Sicily, and Sardinia.

Wars of Charles V

The Hapsburg Emperor Charles V became involved in a bitter struggle with the Valois King Francis I of France. The two rulers fought over the Burgundian lands, as well as over their conflicting claims in Italy. While Charles V failed to win a decisive victory over the French, he succeeded in warding off the French threat to Naples and in acquiring the Duchy of Milan.

In addition to his war with France, Charles V also faced the challenge of Martin Luther's Reformation in Germany (see Chapter 4).

Successors of Charles V

In 1556, Charles V began the process of abdication, dividing his domains between the Austrian and Spanish Hapsburgs. Charles's son became King Philip II of Spain (r. 1556–1598), while his younger brother became Holy Roman Emperor Ferdinand I (r. 1558–1564).

The fourteenth and fifteenth centuries were a time of transition in Europe. The continuing problems of the Roman Catholic Church reduced the power and influence of what had been the central institution in European life during the Middle Ages. Strong national monarchies developed in England, France, and Spain. While the Holy Roman Empire continued its process of disintegration, the Hapsburg emperors found a substantial power base in their personal domains.

What historians call Modern Europe was beginning to take shape. The emergence of Modern Europe involved other factors, as well, among them the Renaissance, the Reformation, the revival of capitalism, and the age of exploration.

Recommended Reading

Aston, Margaret. *The Fifteenth Century: The Prospect of Europe* (1968).

Barraclough, Geoffrey. *The Origins of Modern Germany* (1946).

Bowsky, William M., ed. *The Black Death: A Turning Point in History?* (1971).

Cheyney, Edward P. *The Dawn of a New Era, 1250–1453* (1936).

Chrimes, S. B. *Henry VII* (1972).

Elliott, John H. *Imperial Spain, 1469–1716* (1963).

Elton, G. R. *England Under the Tudors* (2nd ed., 1974).

Ferguson, Wallace K. *Europe in Transition, 1300–1520* (1962).

Gottfried, Robert S. *The Black Death: Natural and Human Disaster in Medieval Europe* (1983).

Hay, Denys. *Europe in the Fourteenth and Fifteenth Centuries* (2nd ed., 1989).

Holmes, George. *Europe: Hierarchy and Revolt, 1320–1450* (1975).

Huizinga, Johan. *The Waning of the Middle Ages* (1924).

Kendall, Paul M. *Louis XI: The Universal Spider* (1970).

Lander, J. R. *The Wars of the Roses* (1966).

Lerner, Robert E. *The Age of Adversity: The Fourteenth Century* (1968).

McFarlane, K. B. *John Wycliffe and the Beginnings of English Nonconformity* (1952).

Myers, A. R. *England in the Late Middle Ages* (1952).

Ozment, Steven E. *The Age of Reform, 1250–1550: An Intellectual and Religious History of Late Medieval and Reformation Europe* (1980).

Perroy, Edouard. *The Hundred Years' War* (1952).

Renouvard, Yves. *The Avignon Papacy, 1305–1403* (1970).

Rice, Eugene F., Jr. *The Foundations of Early Modern Europe, 1460–1559* (1970).

Spinka, Matthew. *John Hus and the Czech Reform* (1941).

Spinka, Matthew. *John Hus at the Council of Constance* (1965).

Tuchman, Barbara W. *A Distant Mirror: The Calamitous 14th Century* (1978).

Ullmann, Walter. *The Origins of the Great Schism* (1948).

Wood, Charles T. *Philip the Fair and Boniface VIII: State vs. Papacy* (2nd ed., 1971).

CHAPTER 2

The Italian Renaissance

Time Line

c. 1304	Giotto begins work on his frescoes in the Arena Chapel in Padua
1348–1353	Giovanni Boccaccio writes the *Decameron*
1378	Gian Galeazzo Visconti becomes the ruler of Milan
1425	Masaccio paints *The Holy Trinity*
1434	Cosimo de' Medici becomes the ruler of Florence
1450	Francesco Sforza becomes the ruler of Milan
1469	Lorenzo de' Medici becomes the ruler of Florence

1480	Ludovico il Moro becomes the ruler of Milan
c. 1480	Sandro Botticelli paints *The Birth of Venus*
c. 1485	Giovanni Bellini paints *St. Francis in Ecstasy*
1494	Savonarola takes power in Florence
c. 1495–1498	Leonardo da Vinci paints *The Last Supper*
1501–1504	Michelangelo completes his statue of *David*
c. 1502	Leonardo da Vinci paints the *Mona Lisa*
c. 1505	Giorgione paints the *Tempesta*
1508–1512	Michelangelo paints the ceiling of the Sistine Chapel
1510–1511	Raphael paints *The School of Athens*
1513	Niccolò Machiavelli writes *The Prince*
1518	Baldassare Castiglione writes *The Book of the Courtier*
	Titian paints the altarpiece of *The Assumption of the Virgin*
1548	Tintoretto paints *The Miracle of St. Mark*
1558–1562	Benvenuto Cellini writes his *Autobiography*

The term "renaissance" ("rebirth" in French) was introduced by Giorgio Vasari (1511–1574), an Italian art historian who wrote of the rebirth (riniscità) of art in Italy during the fifteenth and sixteenth centuries. The concept of the Renaissance was then applied more broadly to describe a dramatic rebirth of civilization in Western Europe. This view of the Renaissance involves two erroneous concepts. First, there is the idea that the Middle Ages had few cultural accomplishments to their credit. Second, there is the idea that, sometime around 1350, a sudden rebirth of literature, art, and scholarship began in Italy.

These views overlook the accomplishments of medieval European civilization, especially those of the High Middle Ages from about 1000 to 1300. During this period, Romanesque and Gothic architecture emerged, the first universities were established, and scholastic philosophy developed.

What occurred in Italy beginning in the fourteenth century was not, therefore, a sudden rebirth but rather a continuation of what had been underway for several centuries, although there were some significant shifts in emphases. Above all, the Italian Renaissance involved an intensification of interest in the classical civilizations of ancient Greece and Rome, especially in classical literature, thought, art, and architecture. In addition, the Italian Renaissance brought an intensification of the secular spirit in Western European civilization. This meant an increasing concern with the things of this world rather than with eternity and a new emphasis on the individual and individual accomplishment.

The Italian States

Urban Civilization

The civilization of the Italian Renaissance was urban, centered on towns that had become prosperous from manufacturing, trade, and banking. Italians had acquired considerable wealth, and some of this wealth was used to support writers, scholars, and artists.

During the Renaissance, Italy remained divided politically. In northern Italy, the city-states of Florence, Milan, and Venice became major centers of Renaissance civilization. Rome dominated the Papal States of central Italy, while the Kingdom of the Two Sicilies embraced most of southern Italy.

Florence

During the fourteenth century, Florence emerged as a major center of handicraft industry, specializing in textiles, especially woolens. In addition, Florence became an important banking center. An independent republic, Florence was ruled by a small oligarchy.

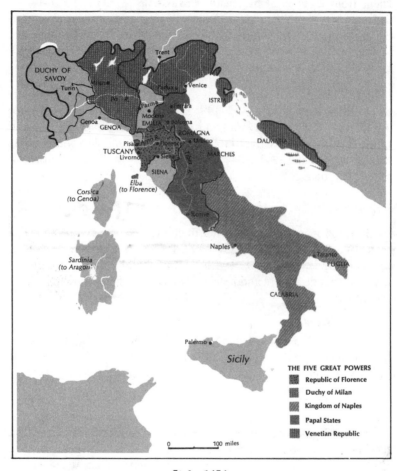

Italy, 1454

The Medici

During most of the fifteenth century, the Medici family dominated Florence. The Medici had extensive interests in industry, trade, and especially banking. The first of the Medici to gain an influential role in the politics of the city was Giovanni di Bicci de' Medici (1360–1429).

Then, from 1434 until his death, Cosimo de' Medici (1389–1464), Giovanni's son, ruled the city. Cosimo was succeeded by his son Piero (1416–1469), but the most famous of the Medici was Lorenzo the Magnificent (1449–1492), Cosimo's grandson, who ruled Florence from 1469 until his death.

Decline of Florence

In 1494, Savonarola (1452–1498), a Franciscan friar, gained power in Florence, exercising a strict and puritanical rule over the city. In 1498, the Florentines overthrew the dictator, and Savonarola was burned at the stake. After Savonarola's death, the Medici returned to power, but the great age of Florence had passed.

Milan

Located in northern Italy, the duchy of Milan was an important center of the overland trade between Italy's seaports, especially Venice, and Northern Europe, on the other side of the Alps. Milan also gained wealth from agriculture and industry, especially the production of silk and armor.

The Visconti

From 1227 to 1447, members of the Visconti family ruled Milan. In particular, Gian Galeazzo Visconti (c. 1351–1402), who became Milan's ruler in 1378, furthered the city's development as a commercial center.

The Sforzas

Following the death of the last of the Visconti, Milan was briefly a republic, from 1447 to 1450. In the latter year, Francesco Sforza (1401–1466), the son-in-law of the last Visconti ruler, became duke and established himself as Milan's despotic ruler. Sforza was the son of a *condottiere*, a professional soldier of fortune who commanded mercenaries. Ludovico (1479–1508) was the most famous of the Sforzas. Known as Ludovico il Moro (Ludovico the Moor), he dominated Milan from 1480 to 1499. Like Francesco, he was an enthusiastic patron of the arts.

Decline of Milan

In the early sixteenth century, Milan experienced a substantial political and economic decline. The city became part of the Spanish empire in 1535.

Venice

The great commercial city of Venice was reputed to have one of the most effective governments in Europe.

Government

Venice was an oligarchy. Political power was the exclusive preserve of the male descendants of the wealthy merchants who had served as the councillors of the city-state prior to 1297 and whose names were inscribed in the Golden Book. The oligarchy comprised the Great Council, which elected the doge (duke), the chief executive of Venice, for a lifetime term. In practice, the doge was largely a figurehead ruler, subject to the control of the inner circle of the oligarchy who comprised the Council of Ten.

Trade

Located at the northern end of the Adriatic Sea, the prosperity of Venice was based on trade, particularly with the largely Moslem-controlled lands at the eastern end of the Mediterranean Sea. By the fifteenth century, Venice held a near-monopoly on the sale of spices and luxury goods from the East to the rest of Europe.

The Renaissance Popes in Rome

The Great Schism (see Chapter 1) ended with the election of Pope Martin V (r. 1417–1431). He and his immediate successor, Pope Eugenius IV (r. 1431–1447) reestablished papal control over Rome and the Papal States of central Italy.

As the fifteenth century progressed, the popes became increasingly involved in secular affairs and Renaissance culture, actively promoting learning and the arts. However, the secular involvements of the Renaissance popes reduced their effectiveness and undermined their prestige as the administrative and spiritual leaders of the Roman Catholic Church in Western Europe.

Nicholas V

Pope Nicholas V (r. 1447–1455) had previously served the Medici family of Florence as a librarian. As pope, he established the Vatican Library with its original collection of 1,200 volumes.

Pius II

Pope Pius II (r. 1458–1464) had earlier achieved note as a humanist scholar under the latinized name of Aeneas Silvius. He devoted himself to efforts to preserve ancient Roman structures that had fallen into ruin.

Sixtus IV

Pope Sixtus IV (r. 1471–1484) became active in the tumultuous politics of Renaissance Italy, hoping both to make the Papal States more powerful and to advance his family's political fortunes. His interest in cultural affairs led him to expand the Vatican Library.

Alexander VI

Pope Alexander VI (r. 1492–1503), a member of the Spanish Borgia family, also sought to promote the interests of his family. He spent large sums to support the army of his son Cesare Borgia (c. 1476–1507), who was trying to create a family domain in central Italy.

Julius II

Pope Julius II (r. 1503–1513), the nephew of Sixtus IV, became known as the Warrior Pope. He personally led the papal armies into battle against both the French and the Venetians.

Leo X

Pope Leo X (r. 1513–1521), a Medici, used papal money to help his family in the domestic and external struggles of Florence. He was pope at the beginning of Martin Luther's Reformation (see Chapter 4).

The Kingdom of the Two Sicilies

Until the early fifteenth century, the French House of Anjou ruled Naples, while Sicily was controlled by the Spanish Kingdom of Aragon.

In 1442, Aragon acquired Naples. The combination of Sicily and Naples became known as the Kingdom of the Two Sicilies. The new kingdom included about half of the Italian peninsula, but it never became powerful enough to threaten the independence of the other Italian states.

Literature

The Tuscan Triumvirate

During the Italian Renaissance, serious literary works began to be written in Italian, the vernacular language, instead of Latin. The first three major writers—Dante, Petrarch, and Boccaccio—of the Italian Renaissance are known as the Tuscan Triumvirate because of their association with Florence, the major city of the region of Tuscany. Their work helped make the Tuscan dialect the standard form of the Italian language.

Dante

Dante Alighieri (1265–1321) was in many ways a writer of the Middle Ages, but he can also be regarded as the first author of the Italian Renaissance. He is best known for the *Divine Comedy,* an epic poem written in Italian. Divided into three parts, the *Divine Comedy* tells of Dante's journey through Inferno (hell), Purgatory, and Paradise (heaven). The Latin poet Virgil serves as Dante's guide through Inferno and Purgatory, while Beatrice, Dante's idealized woman, is his guide through Paradise. Virgil represents reason and the values of classical civilization, while Beatrice represents love, faith, and divine revelation.

Petrarch

Francesco Petrarca, known as Petrarch (1304–1374), is renowned for his love lyrics, in the form of sonnets, addressed to Laura. Petrarch developed the Italian sonnet, a poem of fourteen lines, divided into a group of eight and a group of six, with each group having its own rhyme scheme.

Petrarch became an important figure in the movement of literary humanism, which involved the search for long-lost or forgotten Latin manuscripts, and the effort to write in Latin in imitation of the ancient authors. Petrarch's original work in Italian was of greater literary merit than his imitative writings in Latin, however.

Boccaccio

Giovanni Boccaccio (1313–1375) is best known for his *Decameron* (1348–1353), a collection of witty and often bawdy tales told over a period of ten days by a group of ten young people fleeing Florence at the time of the Black Death in 1348. Petrarch interested him in the search for ancient manuscripts, and Boccaccio learned Greek, which Petrarch had not done.

Other Renaissance Writers

Machiavelli

Niccolò Machiavelli (1469–1527) was the most important writer on politics to emerge during the Italian Renaissance. In *The Prince* (1513), Machiavelli rejected the traditional Christian view that the state is subject to divine law. Instead, he adopted a totally secular and amoral view of politics. In Machiavelli's view, the state existed for its own sake. The ruler should be concerned, above all, with the preservation of his authority. Toward that end, the ruler was justified in using any means.

Castiglione

Baldassare Castiglione (1478–1529), a humanist and papal diplomat, wrote *The Book of the Courtier* (1518), in which he presented rules of gentlemanly behavior. He believed a gentleman should know both Greek and Latin and should have a fluent writing style in both the classical languages and the vernacular. Castiglione was an important advocate of a humanistic education that emphasized the study of classical languages and literature.

Cellini

Benvenuto Cellini (1500–1571) was both a famed goldsmith and silversmith and an important writer. An unabashed egotist, he wrote a revealing *Autobiography* (1558–1562), characterized by a remarkable frankness about his sexual and other exploits.

Valla

Lorenzo Valla (c. 1405–1457) was an important Renaissance scholar. He applied the methods of linguistic and historical analysis to demonstrate that the Donation of Constantine, a document supposedly written in the fourth century, was in fact an eighth-century forgery. According to this document, the Roman Emperor Constantine had given to Pope Sylvester I the right to rule over central Italy. In reality, the pope's claim to central Italy was based on the Donation of Pepin, an eighth-century Frankish king.

Art and Architecture

Giotto (c. 1266–1337)

Giotto, a contemporary of Dante, is often regarded as the first artist of the Italian Renaissance. He was trained in the Byzantine style, which had dominated medieval Italian art. In this style, the subjects, usually Jesus, the Virgin Mary, and the saints, were portrayed in a highly stylized manner against solid backgrounds, often gold or black. Giotto departed significantly from this formula. While his work remained religious, he portrayed his subjects in a more truly human fashion and placed them in realistic settings, often landscapes. He also experimented with light and shade (chiaroscuro) in his paintings, which helped provide an illusion of depth. Giotto is most famous for his frescoes, including a series on the life of St. Francis of Assisi for the Basilica of St. Francis in Assisi. He also painted a noted series of frescoes in the Arena Chapel (begun c. 1304) in Padua. As the official architect of Florence during the last years of his life, Giotto designed the campanile (bell tower) of the city's cathedral.

Masaccio (1401-c. 1428)

For about a century after Giotto, there were few innovations in Italian art. Then, in the early fifteenth century, Masaccio, a Florentine painter, effectively used light and shade to create a greater sense of perspective. He demonstrated his mastery of perspective with especially dramatic effect in the painting of *The Holy Trinity* (1425), a fresco in the Dominican church of Santa Maria Novella in Florence. Masaccio's work had a powerful influence on other artists of the Italian Renaissance.

Sandro Botticelli (1444–1510)

Sandro Botticelli, a Florentine painter, is known for his graceful paintings marked by a use of vivid colors. Many of his best-known works were inspired by themes drawn from classical mythology. Among them are *The Birth of Venus* (c. 1480) and *Primavera,* an allegory representing the coming of spring. Botticelli also painted religious subject matter, including *The Adoration of the Magi.*

Leonardo da Vinci (1452–1519)

A native of Florence, Leonardo worked for many years in Milan and also spent several years in Rome. In his later life, he went to France to work for King Francis I and died there.

Paintings

Leonardo was the first Italian artist to use oil paints, which had been developed in Flanders (see Chapter 3). Among Leonardo's best-known paintings are the *Mona Lisa* (c. 1502), a haunting portrait of an Italian noblewoman, and a fresco of *The Last Supper* (c. 1495–1498), painted in the refectory of a Dominican friary in Milan. In *The Last Supper,* Leonardo portrayed the dramatic moment when Jesus told his apostles that one of them would betray him. Leonardo experimented with light and shadow in another famous painting, *The Virgin of the Rocks* (c. 1485). Like most Renaissance artists, Leonardo's work was mainly religious, but he dealt with this religious subject matter in a secular and humanized fashion.

Scientific Interests

Leonardo had very broad interests, including an intense interest in scientific subjects. His notebooks, filling more than 5000 pages, reveal that he was influenced by many sources, including classical authors, but Leonardo added his own bold imagination to what he learned from others. Studying fossils, he reached conclusions that were later confirmed by geologists. He acquired a considerable knowledge of anatomy by performing dissections. He prepared accurate drawings of most of the muscles of the human body, as well as sketches of the nerves and blood vessels. In addition, he provided the first accurate description of the human skeleton. Leonardo sketched all sorts of possibilities, including pumps and lathes, a diving helmet, a submarine, a parachute, an airplane, and a machine gun. For the most part, Leonardo's ideas remained on paper. Little was known about them during his lifetime. Following his death, most of his notebooks were dispersed, and few of his sketches were published prior to the nineteenth century.

Raphael (1483–1520)

During his short but highly productive life, Raphael Santi worked mainly in Florence and Rome. He is particularly well-known for his Madonnas, humanized portrayals of the Virgin Mary with the baby Jesus. One of the most famous is the brooding *Sistine Madonna.* Raphael also painted a series of frescoes on the walls of a number of rooms in the Vatican Palace, which became known as the Raphael Rooms (completed in 1511). Among these famous frescoes are *The School of Athens* and *The Triumph of Religion,* which reflect the artist's strong interest both in classical antiquity and the Christian religion. Raphael also painted a number of noteworthy portraits.

Michelangelo (1475–1564)

Michelangelo Buonarotti worked mainly in Florence and Rome. While he was a painter of great accomplishment, he believed himself to be primarily a sculptor.

As a young man, Michelangelo painted a series of frescoes on the ceiling of the Sistine Chapel in the Vatican (1508–1512). Over a period of four years, he painted nine scenes from the Old Testament dealing with the period from the Creation to the Flood. Later, he returned to the Sistine Chapel to paint his powerful *Last Judgment* (1534–1541) on the wall behind the altar.

As a sculptor, Michelangelo is famed for a number of works, including a nude statue of the Biblical king *David* (1501–1504) and a powerful portrayal of *Moses* (c. 1513–1515). This statue was intended to be a part of the tomb of Pope Julius II, which was never completed. Michelangelo also sculpted several pietàs (statues of Mary holding the body of the dead Jesus). The most famous *Pietà*, done when the sculptor was still in his twenties, is located in St. Peter's Basilica in Rome.

Sculpture

In addition to Michelangelo, the Italian Renaissance produced several noted sculptors.

Ghiberti

Lorenzo Ghiberti (1378–1455) is known for the bronze doors of the baptistery in Florence, depicting Old Testament scenes. This work made a powerful impression on Michelangelo, who described the doors as worthy of being the gates of paradise.

Donatello

Donatello (c. 1386–1466), a Florentine, studied classical sculpture. One of his best-known works is a bronze statue of *David* (c. 1430–1432), the first free-standing nude in European art since Roman times. Donatello also did a large bronze equestrian statue of the Venetian *condottiere* Gattamelata (1445–1450), which stands in a square in Padua. This was the first equestrian statue by a Western European artist since Roman times.

Architecture

Italian Renaissance architects revived the style of the ancient Romans, using columns, rounded arches, and domes.

Brunelleschi

Filippo Brunelleschi (1377–1446), the first major architect of the Italian Renaissance, designed several churches in Florence, including Santo Spirito and San Lorenzo, as well as the city's Pitti Palace. He is most famous, however, for the octagonal dome of the cathedral of Florence (begun in 1420).

Bramante

Donato Bramante (1444–1514) worked for Pope Julius II, who

gave him the task of rebuilding St. Peter's basilica. After Bramante's death, both Raphael and Michelangelo served for a time as architects of St. Peter's. While Michelangelo designed the dome of the new basilica, he did not live to see it completed.

The Later Renaissance: Venice

The Renaissance reached its height in Venice somewhat later than elsewhere in Italy. Since the city's damp climate quickly damaged frescoes, Venetian artists painted most frequently on canvas. They also usually worked with oil paints and are known for the richness of their colors.

The Bellini Brothers

The Bellini brothers, Gentile (1429–1507) and Giovanni (c. 1430–1516), were members of an illustrious family of painters. Giovanni Bellini's best-known paintings include *The Agony in the Garden* and *St. Francis in Ecstasy* (c. 1485), as well as a number of portraits.

Giorgione

Giorgione (c. 1478–1510) was a pupil of Giovanni Bellini. One of his most famous paintings is the *Tempesta* (c. 1505), a mysterious portrayal of a seminude woman in a stormy landscape.

Tintoretto

Tintoretto (1518–1594) was the nickname of Jacopo Robusti. The nickname means "little dyer," which was his father's trade. Among his major works are *The Miracle of St. Mark* (1548), devoted to the patron saint of Venice, and *Christ Before Pilate* (1566–1567).

Titian

Tiziano Vecellio, known as Titian (1477–1576), is the most famous of the Venetian painters of the Renaissance. He was extremely prolific, producing an average of one painting a month during his long career. Even among Venetian artists, Titian stands out for the richness of his colors, especially purple and above all, red. He did many religious paintings, including the great altarpiece of *The Assumption of the Virgin* (completed in 1518) in the Church of Santa Maria dei Frari in Venice, and works featuring the elaborate ceremonies of the church. In addition, he painted portraits of many of the great figures of the age, among them King Francis I of France, the Holy Roman Emperor Charles V, and King Philip II of Spain.

Palladio

Like other Renaissance architects, the Venetian architect Andrea Palladio (1508–1580) was influenced by the Roman style. He designed several churches and palaces in Venice, as well as a number of villas in the nearby countryside. The influence of Palladio can be seen in eighteenth-century Georgian architecture both in England and America.

The Italian Renaissance had a powerful impact on the civilization of Western Europe. The renewed emphasis on classical languages and literature influenced the development of European education over the next several centuries, while the revival of classical ideals in painting, sculpture, and architecture had an enduring influence on Western art.

In time, the achievements of the Italian Renaissance gradually spread beyond Italy, helping to produce a Renaissance in several other countries.

Recommended Reading

Artz, Frederick B. *Renaissance Humanism, 1300–1550* (1966).

Baxendall, Michael. *Painting and Experience in Fifteenth Century Italy* (1972).

Berenson, Bernard. *The Italian Painters of the Renaissance* (rev. ed., 1930).

Brucker, Gene A. *Renaissance Florence* (1969).

Burckhardt, Jacob. *The Civilization of the Renaissance in Italy* (many editions).

Chabod, Federico. *Machiavelli and the Renaissance* (1958).

Chambers, D. S. *The Imperial Age of Venice, 1380–1580* (1970).

Cheyney, Edward P. *The Dawn of a New Era, 1250–1453* (1936).

Clark, Kenneth. *Leonardo da Vinci* (rev. ed., 1989).

Ferguson, Wallace K. *The Renaissance* (1940).

Finlay, Robert. *Politics in Renaissance Venice* (1980).

Fusero, Clemente. *The Borgias* (1972).

Gilmore, Myron P. *The World of Humanism, 1453–1517* (1952).

Hale, J. R. *Florence and the Medici: The Pattern of Control* (1977).

Hay, Denys. *The Italian Renaissance in Its Historical Background* (2nd ed., 1977).

Holmes, George. *The Florentine Enlightenment, 1400–1450* (1969).

Lopez, Robert S. *The Three Ages of the Italian Renaissance* (1970).

Martinelli, Giuseppe, ed. *The World of Renaissance Florence* (1968).

Martines, Lauro. *Power and Imagination: City-States in Renaissance Italy* (1979).

Norwich, John Julius. *A History of Venice* (1982).

Partner, Peter. *The Lands of St. Peter: The Papal State in the Middle Ages and the Early Renaissance* (1972).

Partner, Peter. *Renaissance Rome, 1500–1559: A Portrait of a Society* (1976).

Plumb, J. H. *The Italian Renaissance: A Concise Survey of Its History and Culture* (1965).

Pullan, Brian S. *A History of Early Renaissance Italy* (1973).

Schevill, Ferdinand. *The Medici* (1949).

Smart, Alastair. *The Renaissance and Mannerism in Italy* (1971).

Trinkhaus, Charles. *The Scope of Renaissance Humanism* (1983).

CHAPTER 3

The Northern Renaissance

Time Line

c. 1427	Thomas à Kempis writes *The Imitation of Christ*
1432	Jan van Eyck completes *The Adoration of the Lamb*
c. 1456	Johannes Gutenberg prints an edition of the Bible
1495	Cardinal Francisco Ximénes de Cisneros becomes archbishop of Toledo
1500	Albrecht Dürer paints a *Self-portrait*
c. 1500	Hieronymus Bosch paints *The Garden of Earthly Delight*
1509	John Colet organizes St. Paul's School in London

c. 1509–1511	Matthias Grünewald paints the Isenheim altarpiece
1512	Erasmus publishes *Praise of Folly*
1516	Thomas More publishes *Utopia*
1532	François Rabelais publishes *Gargantua and Pantagruel*
1540	Hans Holbein the Younger paints his portrait of King Henry VIII
c. 1565	Pieter Brueghel paints the *Peasant Wedding*
1580	Michel de Montaigne publishes the first edition of his *Essays*
1605	Miguel de Cervantes publishes Part I of *Don Quixote*
1623	The First Folio, containing thirty-six of Shakespeare's thirty-eight plays, is published

---

The influence of the Italian Renaissance gradually spread northward across the Alps to the rest of Western Europe. The Northern Renaissance, as the Renaissance beyond Italy is known, differed from the Italian Renaissance in some respects. In particular, while the growing secular spirit had a powerful impact on the Northern Renaissance, there was a greater effort than had been the case in Italy to reconcile secular and Christian values and attitudes. The Northern Renaissance was thus infused with a more powerful Christian spirit than the Renaissance in Italy, where there had often been an almost open revolt against Christian ideals.

The Renaissance in Germany
and the Low Countries

The Development of Printing

One of the most important events in the Renaissance outside of Italy was the development of printing with movable type.

The Printing Press

Johannes Gutenberg (c. 1400–1468) of Mainz in the German Rhineland is generally credited with having set up the first practical printing press using movable metal type. About 1456, Gutenberg produced his superbly printed edition of the Bible.

Spread of Printing

The printing press won rapid acceptance. By 1480, there were over 380 printing presses operating in Western Europe. By 1500 there were more than 1000, and more than 25,000 separate editions had been printed. Books printed before 1501 are known as *incunabula* (literally, cradle works: that is, books printed when printing was still in its infancy).

The printing press had an immense impact on European civilization, enabling the rapid spread of new knowledge and ideas among the educated classes.

Humanism

During the Northern Renaissance, just as in Italy, humanist scholars studied and found inspiration in classical literature. Johann Reuchlin (1455–1522) visited Italy, where he developed a great enthusiasm for humanist studies. Returning to his native Germany, Reuchlin urged that the university curriculum be expanded to include the study of both Greek and Hebrew languages and literature.

Humanism in the Northern Renaissance is frequently referred to as Christian humanism because of the humanists' efforts to unite classical learning with the Christian faith. The Christian humanists rejected what they regarded as medieval Christianity's excessive emphasis on other-worldliness. They sought to achieve a balance of otherworldly and secular concerns and regarded the classics as legitimate guides in that quest. The Christian humanists also desired to bring their knowledge of the classical languages to bear in their effort to attain a deeper knowledge and understanding of the Christian faith.

The Brethren of the Common Life

The work of the Brethren of the Common Life contributed significantly to the development of Christian humanism. Founded by Gerard Groote (1340–1384) in Holland, the Brethren devoted themselves both to education based on classical learning and to inculcating among themselves and their pupils a deep spiritual relationship with Jesus Christ and a love of their fellow human beings.

Thomas à Kempis

Thomas à Kempis (1380–1471), a follower of the of the *devotio moderna,* as the religious and moral teachings of the Brethren were known, wrote *The Imitation of Christ* (c. 1427), one of the greatest of all works of Christian devotional literature.

Erasmus

Desiderius Erasmus (1466–1536) was probably the most outstanding of the Christian humanists and in fact, won the title of "Prince of the Humanists." Born in Rotterdam, Holland, he was educated in a school conducted by the Brethren of the Common Life, who introduced him to the Greek and Latin classics. Although he was ordained to the priesthood, Erasmus devoted his life primarily to classical studies.

In his first book, *Adages* (1500), which he wrote in Latin, Erasmus presented a collection of wise sayings from the classical authors, along with his own comments. He subsequently published several expanded editions of the *Adages.*

In the satirical *Praise of Folly* (1512), his most famous work, Erasmus ridiculed many attitudes of his own time, among them ignorance, superstition, and greed. His satire was especially sharp when it was directed against churchmen who manifested these qualities.

Erasmus also used his knowledge of the classical languages in an effort to achieve a deeper understanding of the Bible. In 1516, he published an annotated edition of the New Testament in Greek, which revealed several significant errors in the Latin Vulgate, the biblical text authorized by the Roman Catholic Church.

What is termed "Erasmian humanism" is based on Erasmus's belief that the Christian religion offered humanity sound guidelines for its moral conduct and that religion and learning were inextricably bound together. While Erasmus was a critic of abuses in the Roman Catholic Church, he was not a Protestant. Instead, he had a great faith in the ability of human beings to reform their institutions from within. He strongly opposed Martin Luther's Reformation and regarded Luther and other early Protestant reformers as even more doctrinaire and intolerant than the Roman Catholic leadership.

Painting

The greatest painters of the Northern Renaissance were Flemings (from Flanders, in what is today Belgium) and Germans.

The van Eycks

Jan van Eyck (c. 1390–1441) and his brother, Hubert (c. 1370–1426), worked mainly in the city of Ghent in Flanders. The van Eycks were the first major painters to develop and use oil paints successfully, and Italian artists, such as Leonardo da Vinci, learned about oils from them. The van Eycks' greatest work was *The Adoration of the Lamb*, an altarpiece in St. Bavon's cathedral in Ghent, which Jan van Eyck completed in 1432. Jan van Eyck also painted a number of portraits, including the well-known wedding picture of *Giovanni Arnolfini and His Bride* (1434). The van Eycks' work is marked by their attention to minute detail and their mastery of perspective.

Bosch

Hieronymus Bosch (c. 1450–1516), another Flemish painter, was one of the most unusual painters in the history of Western art. Bosch created a fantasy world inhabited by often nightmarish men and monsters. One of his most famous works is the highly symbolic *Garden of Earthly Delight* (c. 1500).

Brueghel

Pieter Brueghel (c. 1525–1569) was a Flemish painter who worked mainly in Antwerp and Brussels. While Brueghel painted both religious subjects and landscapes, he is best known for his earthy and lively paintings of the activities of ordinary people, especially peasants. Among his well-known works is the *Peasant Wedding* (c. 1565).

Dürer

Albrecht Dürer (1471–1528), a native of Nuremberg and one of the major German Renaissance artists, is most highly regarded for his woodcuts and engravings, which portray both religious and classical subjects. These works demonstrate his great technical mastery and power of expression. Dürer's paintings include a number of portraits, among them a noted *Self-portrait*.

Grünewald

Matthias Grünewald (c. 1475–1530) worked in the German Rhineland under the patronage of the powerful archbishop of Mainz. He painted primarily religious works, especially somber and awe-filled crucifixion scenes. The Isenheim altarpiece (c. 1509–1511) is probably his best-known work.

Holbein the Younger

Hans Holbein the Younger (c. 1497–1543) was the son of an important painter in the Gothic tradition of medieval German art. The younger Holbein may have studied in Italy; his work reveals considerable Italian influence. Particularly renowned as a portrait painter, he did several portraits of Erasmus and spent a number of years in England, where he painted portraits of King Henry VIII (1540) and his wives, King Edward VI, Mary Tudor, and Thomas More.

The Renaissance in France

Humanism

A number of French scholars studied in Italy, where they became enthusiastic humanists. During the late fifteenth century, Greek began to be studied in France. In 1529, King Francis I (r. 1515–1547) established the College de France in Paris, which encouraged the study of Hebrew, Greek, and Latin.

Vernacular Literature

The sixteenth-century writers François Rabelais (c. 1490–1553) and Michel de Montaigne (1533–1592) were among the first major authors to write in French.

Rabelais

Rabelais studied medicine and the classics and was ordained to the priesthood. Above all, however, he was an individualist and a rebel. He wrote *Gargantua* and *Pantagruel,* two satirical fantasies that were first published in 1532. Rabelais recounted the adventures of two giants who lived unrestrained lives, indulging in virtually every conceivable pleasure. Within the context of stories that have been described as coarse and lewd, Rabelais considered serious questions of philosophy, education, and politics, expressing his faith in individuals and their ability to lead good lives.

Montaigne

Montaigne was born into a wealthy family. His father was Catholic, while his mother was of Spanish Jewish descent. He studied law and served for a time as mayor of Bordeaux. Montaigne won fame as an essayist, publishing the first edition of his *Essays* in 1580. The mixed religious background of his parents may have contributed to his skepticism about religious beliefs. In religion and morality, Montaigne was a relativist. Since one could not know with absolute certainty, it was necessary to be tolerant.

Architecture

During the French Renaissance, there were a number of significant achievements in architecture. A number of chateaux were built, especially in the valley of the Loire River south of Paris. Unlike medieval castles, these chateaux were not fortified since the countryside had become more peaceful. The name of King Francis I is connected with a number of these chateaux, including those of Chambord and Blois. Francis I also built a chateau at Fontainebleau, closer to Paris, which served as his hunting lodge.

The Renaissance in England

Vernacular Literature

Geoffrey Chaucer (c. 1340–1400) was the first important figure in the development of literature during the English Renaissance. He was familiar with the works of the major Latin poets, although he was not a classical scholar, and he made at least two trips to Italy. He was clearly influenced by Italian Renaissance literature, and he may have met Boccaccio, the author of the *Decameron*.

Chaucer's most famous work is wholly English in subject as well as language. The *Canterbury Tales* is a collection of stories presented in poetic form, supposedly told by a diverse group of pilgrims journeying to the shrine of St. Thomas à Becket in Canterbury. The stories reveal Chaucer's profound insight into human nature and are strongly secular in spirit. Chaucer took particular delight in revealing the foibles and corruption of members of the clergy.

Humanism

During the fifteenth century, humanism began to take hold in England, and by the early sixteenth century, the study of Greek had been added to the curriculum at Oxford and Cambridge universities.

Colet

From 1497 to 1504, John Colet (c. 1467–1519) delivered a series of lectures at Oxford on the letters of St. Paul. While Colet knew little or no Greek, he brought a humanistic point of view to bear in these lectures. In 1505, Colet became dean of St. Paul's cathedral in London. He organized a new school at St. Paul's in 1509, which emphasized the study of Greek and Latin languages and literature. By the late sixteenth century, Greek was taught in many other English schools that prepared students for the universities.

More

Thomas More (1478–1535) was England's greatest humanist. After studying the classics at Oxford, he studied law at the Inns of Court in London. Entering the service of the monarchy, More became lord chancellor in 1529, during the reign of King Henry VIII (r. 1509–1547).

More's most famous work is *Utopia* (1516), which he wrote in Latin. *Utopia* (meaning "nowhere" in Greek) described an imaginary island where an ideal cooperative society flourished. In this society based on reason and tolerance, the citizens practiced a Christianity that was free of ignorance and superstition. There was no private property and no desire for profit, and there was no war, except in self-defense. More contrasted this society with the evils existing in his own society.

Elizabethan Literature

In the mid-sixteenth century, a great period began in the history of English literature. This Elizabethan period took its name from Queen Elizabeth I (r. 1558–1603). This was a time of great optimism and energy in English history, symbolized by the defeat of the Spanish Armada in 1588 (see Chapter 5).

Spenser

Edmund Spenser (c. 1552–1599) was regarded by his contemporaries as the leading poet of the age. The first six books of his unfinished masterpiece, the *Faerie Queen*, were published in 1596. This was a romantic epic, based on an Italian model.

Marlowe

Christopher Marlowe (1564–1593), a skilled playwright and poet, produced a number of outstanding works during his brief career. His major dramas include *Tamburlaine the Great, Doctor Faustus*, and *The Jew of Malta*.

Shakespeare

William Shakespeare (1564–1616) wrote lyric poetry but is best known for his dramas, both tragedies and comedies, which were produced on the London stage. Shakespeare's plays, which dealt with the entire range of the human experience, include *The Taming of the Shrew, A Midsummer Night's Dream, The Merchant of Venice, Romeo and Juliet, Julius Caesar, Hamlet, Othello, King Lear, Macbeth*, and

Antony and Cleopatra. Of his thirty-eight dramas, thirty-six were printed in the First Folio (1623), the first collected edition of his plays.

Jonson

Ben Jonson (1572–1637), a poet and dramatist, was the last major literary figure of the Elizabethan period. Jonson was a student of classical literature, and his plays remind the reader of Greek drama. *Volpone,* his best known play, was first produced in 1606.

The Spanish Renaissance

Humanism

The role of the Roman Catholic Church remained substantial in Spain. Thus, it is not surprising that the central figure in Spanish humanism was a churchman, Cardinal Francisco Ximénes (or Jiménez) de Cisneros (1436–1517), who became archbishop of Toledo in 1495. While he insisted on religious orthodoxy, Ximénes urged an improvement in the educational level of the Spanish clergy. Toward that end, he established the University of Alcala. He also sponsored the publication of the six-volume *Complutensian Polyglot Bible,* which presented the Hebrew, Greek, and Latin texts in parallel columns. As a Christian humanist, Ximénes believed that religious faith would be strengthened by a greater understanding of the sources of Christian revelation.

Literature

Cervantes

Miguel de Cervantes (1547–1616) was a contemporary of William Shakespeare; both men died in 1616 within a few days of one another. *Don Quixote* (Part I, 1605; Part II, 1615), his major work, is regarded by some literary critics as the greatest novel ever written. In this gentle satire of medieval chivalry, Cervantes told the story of a Spanish nobleman who traveled about the countryside in search of romantic adventures and his groom, Sancho Panza, whose common sense and prudence contrasted with the unrealism of his master. The novel presented characters of all types and classes, providing a good picture of Spanish life in the late sixteenth century, as well as a broader perspective on human nature.

Lope de Vega

Felix Lope de Vega (1562–1635) wrote in virtually every literary form, although he is best known as a dramatist. An extremely prolific playwright, he wrote more than 1,500 dramas, of which some 500 survive.

Painting and Architecture

A Greek, Domenicos Theotocopoulis, better known as El Greco (c. 1541–1614), was the greatest painter of the Spanish Renaissance. He studied in Italy with the Venetian painter Titian and worked in Rome before settling in Toledo in 1576. El Greco's paintings reflected his intense religious mysticism and were characterized by elongated and distorted figures and dramatic lighting effects.

The Escorial, built by King Philip II (r. 1556–1598) as a palace and mausoleum, stands as one of the greatest architectural monuments of the Spanish Renaissance.

The Northern Renaissance produced major achievements in humanistic scholarship, literature, and art. In some cases, scholars, writers, and artists were heavily influenced by the Italian Renaissance. In many other instances, however, they produced truly original works, many of which stand among the greatest of human achievements.

While the Renaissance brought an undeniable intensification of the secular spirit in Western European civilization, religious concerns continued to exert a powerful influence, as the Protestant and Catholic reformations demonstrated.

Recommended Reading

Bainton, Roland H. *Erasmus of Christendom* (1969).
Benesch, Otto. *The Art of the Renaissance in Northern Europe* (1945).
Bush, Douglas. *The Renaissance and English Humanism* (1939).
Caspari, Fritz. *Humanism and the Social Order in Tudor England* (1954).

Davies, R. Trevor. *The Golden Century in Spain, 1501–1627* (1937).

Duran, Manuel. *Cervantes* (1974).

Ferguson, Arthur B. *The Articulate Citizen and the English Renaissance* (1965).

Goldschmidt, Ernst P. *The Printed Book of the Renaissance* (1950).

Harbison, E. Harris. *The Christian Scholar in the Age of Reformation* (1956).

Huizinga, Johann. *Erasmus and the Age of Reformation* (1957).

Huizinga, Johann. *The Waning of the Middle Ages* (1924).

Marius, Richard. *Thomas More: A Biography* (1989).

Phillips, Margaret M. *Erasmus and the Northern Renaissance* (1950).

Scholderer, Victor. *Johann Gutenberg: The Inventor of Printing* (1963).

Smart, Alastair. *The Renaissance and Mannerism in Northern Europe and Spain* (1972).

Spitz, Lewis W. *The Religious Renaissance of the German Humanists* (1963).

CHAPTER 4

The Protestant Reformation

Time Line

1517	Martin Luther posts the Ninety-five Theses
1519	Ulrich Zwingli begins his reform of the church in Zurich
1520	Pope Leo X excommunicates Luther
1522	Luther begins his reform of the church in Saxony
1524–1525	The Peasants' Revolt takes place in Germany
1534–1535	John of Leyden heads an Anabaptist theocracy in Münster
1534	The English Parliament passes the Act of Supremacy

1536	John Calvin publishes *The Institutes of the Christian Religion*
1539	The English Parliament adopts the Six Articles
1549	The first *Book of Common Prayer* is published in England
1551	The Forty-two Articles reflect the growth of Calvinist influence in England
1555	Germany's Protestants and Catholics agree on the Peace of Augsburg
1559	The English Parliament passes a new Act of Supremacy and the Act of Uniformity
1560	Presbyterianism becomes the official religion of Scotland
1563	The Thirty-nine Articles are adopted in England

While the Renaissance promoted the growth of a secular spirit in the civilization of Western Europe, religious concerns remained important to Europeans. Abuses in the Roman Catholic Church led to growing demands for reform and resulted ultimately in the emergence of the Protestant Reformation.

The Reformation destroyed the religious unity of Western Europe, thereby ending what had been one of the central features of Western European civilization during the Middle Ages. The Reformation produced four major movements: Lutheranism, Calvinism, Anglicanism, and Anabaptism. These four movements led, in turn, to the development of virtually all of the Protestant denominations that exist today.

Lutheranism

Martin Luther: Early Life

Lutheranism was the first of the Reformation movements. Martin

Luther (1483–1546), its founder, was born in Saxony in central Germany. Although he originally planned to become a lawyer, he experienced a religious conversion and became an Augustinian monk in 1505. In 1508, he became a teacher of theology at the university at Wittenberg in Saxony.

Luther's Theology: Justification by Faith

Although he had become a monk, Luther remained troubled about the possibility of achieving salvation. In search of answers to his questions, he began to read the writings of the early Christian theologians, including St. Augustine, and the Bible. He found the answer he sought in St. Paul's Letter to the Romans (1:17), where Paul had written: "The just shall live by faith."

Luther concluded that the only path to salvation was through faith in the ultimate goodness and mercy of Jesus Christ. There was nothing the believer could do to earn salvation. Performing good works, participating in ecclesiastical rituals, and receiving the sacraments would not avail. A good Christian, of course, might do these things—indeed, should do them—but only Jesus Christ could grant the gift of salvation. Luther began to develop a system of theology based on what came to be called the doctrine of "salvation by faith alone" or "justification by faith."

The Beginning of Luther's Reformation

In 1517, Johann Tetzel (c. 1465–1519), a Dominican friar, began to sell indulgences in the area around Wittenberg. The doctrine of indulgences had been developed by medieval theologians, who taught that Jesus Christ and the saints, by their good works on earth, had accumulated a treasury of merit. By gaining indulgences, faithful Christians could draw from this treasury of merit to reduce the amount of time they or their deceased loved ones would remain in purgatory before entering heaven and the sight of God. An indulgence, according to the doctrine, did not bring forgiveness of sin (that came in the sacrament of penance) but rather a remission of temporal punishment due to sin.

By the Late Middle Ages, indulgences were often sold to raise money. The income from the indulgences sold by Tetzel was used to help pay the costs of the construction of the new St. Peter's basilica in Rome.

The Ninety-five Theses

Luther began to question the doctrine of indulgences, which appeared to be inconsistent with his doctrine of justification by faith. On October 31, 1517, he posted the Ninety-five Theses on the door of the castle church in Wittenberg. The Theses were intended to be a challenge to other scholars to debate the issue of indulgences.

Luther's rejection of indulgences quickly became more than an issue of theological debate. As Luther and his antagonists debated, the two sides sharpened their positions and became increasingly hostile to one another.

In 1519, Luther debated Johannes Eck (1486–1543), a noted theologian, in Leipzig. In this debate, Luther acknowledged that his views were essentially similar to those of John Hus, who had been condemned as a heretic a century earlier (see Chapter 1), and rejected the authority of the church's hierarchy.

When Pope Leo X (r. 1513–1521) issued a bull (1520) excommunicating Luther, the reformer responded by burning it.

The Diet of Worms

In 1521, the Holy Roman Emperor Charles V (r. 1519–1556) ordered Luther to appear before the Diet of the Holy Roman Empire at its meeting in Worms. When the Diet called on him to recant, Luther refused, declaring: "Here I stand. I cannot do otherwise."

When the emperor declared Luther an outlaw, Elector Frederick the Wise (1463–1525) of Saxony provided the reformer with refuge at the Wartburg Castle.

Acceptance of Luther's Reforms

In 1522, Luther returned to Wittenberg where, with the support of Frederick the Wise, he began to reform the local church in accordance with his ideas. Lutheranism won considerable public support and spread rapidly, especially in the northern and eastern German states.

The Doctrines of Lutheranism

In addition to the doctrine of justification by faith, Luther taught that the only valid source of Christian doctrine was the Bible. He thereby rejected the Roman Catholic view that Christian doctrine was revealed both in the Bible and in the traditions of the church, as defined by the councils of the church and the pope.

In Luther's view, only two sacraments—baptism and holy communion—had been established by Jesus Christ, as recorded in the New Testament. He thus rejected the Catholic teaching that there were seven sacraments (see Chapter 5).

Luther stressed the idea that the Christian church was not so much a formal organization as the whole body of the Christian faithful. He reemphasized the ancient Christian concept of the priesthood of all believers, recalling the words of the First Letter of St. Peter: "But you are a chosen race, a royal priesthood, a consecrated nation, a people set apart to sing the praises of God, who called you out of the darkness into his wonderful light."

In order to make the Bible more accessible to Christians, Luther prepared German translations of the New Testament (1522) and the Old Testament (1534). This translation of the Bible is regarded as one of the first great works of German literature.

Luther also abolished the monasteries and ended the requirement for celibacy of the clergy. The Lutheran service of worship was less elaborate than Catholic worship, although it was more formal than the worship service of the Calvinists.

Luther and the Peasants' Revolt

Peasants in the German states, as elsewhere in Europe, lived in poverty and were burdened by heavy taxes and obligations to the landowners. In 1524, a revolt against the landowners began among the peasants in southwestern Germany and spread further during 1525. The peasants sought to abolish serfdom and the manorial system.

While the peasants hoped for Luther's support, the religious reformer was a conservative on social and economic issues. He opposed the peasants and supported the princes in their suppression of the revolt.

The Spread of Lutheranism

Emperor Charles V remained concerned about Luther's movement, which threatened the unity of the Holy Roman Empire. However, the emperor faced other enemies, including the Turks and the French, and could not devote his full attention to events in Germany.

The Diet of Augsburg

In 1530, Luther appeared before Charles V at the Diet of Augsburg, where he presented a statement of his faith, which came to be known as the Confession of Augsburg. The Diet found it unacceptable. The Confession of Augsburg was written by Philipp Melanchthon (1497–1560), a prominent German humanist and theologian, who was a colleague of Luther's at the university in Wittenberg.

The Peace of Augsburg

Following the Diet of Augsburg, a number of German Lutheran princes and cities established the Schmalkaldic League (1531), a religious and military alliance directed against the Catholic Hapsburgs. As Germany became more sharply divided between Lutherans and Catholics, tension mounted. From 1546 to 1555, Germany was torn by a religious civil war.

In 1555, the contending forces reached a compromise agreement, the Peace of Augsburg. This gave to each German prince the right to determine the religion of his state, either Roman Catholicism or Lutheranism, on the basis of the principle set forth in the Latin formula *cuius regio, eius religio* (whose region, his religion). The Peace of Augsburg did not provide for the recognition of other religious groups, such as the Calvinists or Anabaptists.

Lutheranism became the predominant religion in much of Germany, especially the north and the east. Most of southern Germany, including Austria, and the Rhineland in the west remained Roman Catholic, as did the province of Silesia in the East.

Habsburg Dominions

Ottoman Empire

Boundary of the Holy Roman Empire

NORWAY

Bergen · · Oslo · Stockholm

EST

FINLAND

SCOTLAND

· Edinburgh

NORTH SEA

DENMARK

SWEDEN

· Copenhagen

BALTIC SEA

IRELAND

· Dublin

· York

ENGLAND

· London

Canterbury ·

· Hamburg

Danzig ·

BRANDENBURG · Berlin

Vistula R.

· Warsaw

DUTCH · Munster
NETH.

ATLANTIC OCEAN

· St. Malo

· Rouen

· Paris

· Antwerp
Brussels · BELG.
NETH.

· Cologne

· Wittenberg

SAXONY

SILESIA

· Breslau

Cracow ·

Leml

LUX.

· Trier

· Worms

Schmalkalden ·

BOHEMIA

· Prague

MORAVIA

· Orléans

· Bourges

Metz ·
PALATINATE · Ratisbon

Strasbourg · Augsburg

BAVARIA · Munich

Vienna ·

AUSTRIA

· Budapest

· Angoulême

FRANCE

FR.
COMTÉ · Basel

BURGUNDY

SWISS
CONFEDERATION

· Geneva

TYROL

· Trent

HUNGARY

· Bordeaux

DAUPHINE

SAVOY

· Milan

Parma ·

· Venice

VENETIAN
REPUBLIC

· Mohacs

· Belgrade

· Santiago

· Avignon

· Marseilles

· Genoa

DALMATIA

BOSNIA

PYRENEES

· Bayonne

· Oporto

Valladolid ·
· Burgos

NAVARRE

SPAIN
(Castile)

ARAGON

CATALONIA

· Barcelona

Corsica
(to Genoa)

Elba
(to Florence)

· Florence

PAPAL
STATES

Rome ·

MONTENEGRO

PORTUGAL

Escorial ·
Toledo ·
· Madrid

Valencia ·

Balearic I.

Sardinia
(to Aragon)

NAPLES
(Aragon)

Naples ·

ALBANIA

· Lisbon

· Cadiz

· Seville

· Granada

GRANADA

MEDITERRANEAN SEA

Palermo ·

Sicily
(to Aragon)

Ionian I.
(Venice)

Melilla (Spain) ·

Algiers ·

· Tunis

· Malta (Knights of St. John)

SULTANATE
OF FEZ

SULTANATE OF ALGIERS

SULTANATE OF
TUNIS

B A R B A R Y   S T A T E S

0   100   200   300 miles

Europe, 1526

Lutheranism Outside Germany

Lutheranism soon spread to Scandinavia, becoming the predominant religion in Denmark and Norway, which was then under Danish control, as well as in Sweden and in the Baltic area of Finland, Estonia, and Latvia, which Sweden ruled.

Calvinism

The Beginning of the Swiss Reformation: Zwingli

The story of the Swiss Reformation begins with Ulrich Zwingli (1484–1531). A humanist and a Catholic priest, Zwingli originally hoped that the Catholic Church would reform itself. In 1519, however, he led the church in Zurich in its break from Roman Catholicism.

Like Luther, Zwingli believed in the supremacy of the Bible. In contrast to the German reformer, however, Zwingli believed that baptism and holy communion were ceremonies symbolizing the believer's affiliation with the Christian church, rather than true sacraments. Zwingli rejected the celibacy of the clergy and emphasized simplicity in worship. In 1531, Zwingli was killed by Catholic forces during a civil war.

John Calvin: Early Life

Zwingli's death temporarily deprived the Swiss Protestants of a leader, but within a few years after Zwingli's death, they had embraced Calvinism.

Born in France, John Calvin (1509–1564) studied law and theology. Apparently influenced by the ideas of Luther, he became a Protestant and began to develop his own views on the Christian religion.

France remained a strongly Catholic country, and Calvin was forced into exile. He found his first refuge in the Swiss city of Basel, and then, in 1536, he settled in Geneva, where he quickly became the leader of that city's Reformation.

The Doctrines of Calvinism

John Calvin set forth his theology in *The Institutes of the Christian*

Religion (1536), the most important single work to emerge from the Protestant Reformation of the sixteenth century. Calvin agreed with Luther that the Bible was the only source of Christian doctrine and that there were only two sacraments, baptism and holy communion.

Unlike Luther, Calvin emphasized the doctrine of salvation by election, often called predestination. This belief was based on the contrast between the overwhelming power and majesty of God and the insignificance and depravity of human beings. According to this doctrine, at the beginning of creation, the all-powerful and all-knowing God had planned the whole universe to the end of time. For reasons of His own, which are beyond human comprehension, God determined those individuals who would be saved and those who would be condemned. Those destined for salvation were known as the elect. God had given to the elect a faith in Jesus Christ and a desire to live in accordance with Christian moral values, as well as a desire to labor to bring about the establishment of God's kingdom on earth.

Calvinism in Practice

Like Luther, Calvin ended both monasticism and the celibacy of the clergy. In worship, Calvin emphasized simplicity. Calvinist worship consisted of prayers, the singing of psalms, scripture readings, and a sermon. Calvinist churches, generally called Reformed churches on the European continent, were governed by laymen called elders, who were elected by the congregation.

Calvinism also emphasized a puritanical approach to life, which involved a renunciation of worldly pleasure. In addition to requiring church attendance, Calvinist puritanism banned card playing, gambling, dancing, theatergoing, the consumption of alcohol, and swearing.

Theocracy in Geneva

In Geneva, Calvin established a strict theocracy, with religious leaders dominating the city's government. Violators of the puritanical code of behavior suffered severe penalties, and religious dissenters were persecuted.

The most famous case of persecution involved the Spaniard Michael Servetus (1511–1553), who denied the divinity of Jesus Christ.

The Catholic Inquisition had convicted him of heresy and condemned him to death. Servetus fled to Geneva, where he was seized by the Calvinist authorities and burned at the stake. But while some people left Geneva in order to escape Calvinist rule, thousands of others found refuge there.

The Spread of Calvinism

The Calvinist Reformed Church became dominant in much of Switzerland, especially in the urban areas of Geneva, Zurich, Bern, and Basel.

In the mid-sixteenth century, Calvinism began to spread to France. The Huguenots, as the French Calvinists were known, received some support from members of the nobility who opposed the growing power of the French monarchy. France remained overwhelmingly Roman Catholic, however.

John Knox (c. 1514–1572), a disciple of Calvin, brought the new faith to Scotland. The Scottish Calvinists were known as Presbyterians, a term that refers to church government by ruling elders known as presbyters. In 1560, Scotland's parliament adopted Presbyterianism as the country's official religion.

In England, Calvinists known as Puritans sought to "purify" the English church of its remaining Catholic elements. The Puritans had a powerful impact on English politics and government during the seventeenth century (see Chapter 7).

Elsewhere, Calvinism won a considerable following in the Dutch Netherlands but made only limited gains in Germany. In Austria and Poland, Calvinism won a number of converts, but these gains were later wiped out by the Catholic Reformation.

Calvinism and Economic Development

The infuence of Calvinism on the economic development of Europe has been the subject of scholarly debate.

Max Weber (1864–1920), a German sociologist, was the first to propose the idea that Calvinism helped promote the development of capitalism in Europe. Calvinism, Weber noted, encouraged such capitalistic values as sobriety, thrift, and hard work and discouraged conspicuous consumption, which was economically unproductive. Those who succeeded in business often regarded that success as a sign that God had numbered them among the elect. While a number of Calvinist peoples, including the Swiss, the Scots, the Dutch, and later the New Englanders, proved to be successful in business, the Weber thesis has been challenged by many scholars.

Anglicanism

King Henry VIII (r. 1509–1547)

The Reformation in England led to the establishment of the state-controlled Church of England, also known as the Anglican Church. The present Episcopal churches in the United States and other countries trace their origins to the Church of England, while the Methodist denomination began as an offshoot of Anglicanism in the eighteenth century.

Conflict with the Papacy

The sequence of events that resulted in the English Reformation began with the desire of King Henry VIII to secure an annulment of his marriage to Catherine of Aragon (1485–1536). Catherine had borne only one surviving child, who became Queen Mary. Henry desired to have a male heir, however, and had also become infatuated with Anne Boleyn (1507–1536).

The king requested Pope Clement VII (r. 1523–1534) to grant him an annulment, contending that his marriage to Catherine was invalid. She was the widow of Henry's older brother, Arthur. According to canon law, a man was not permitted to marry his brother's widow. Pope Julius II (r. 1503–1513) had granted a dispensation to permit the marriage, but Henry now argued that the dispensation should not have been granted.

Not only did Pope Clement VII hesitate to reverse the decision of a predecessor, but his freedom of action was restricted by the fact that the Holy Roman Emperor Charles V, Catherine of Aragon's nephew, dominated Italy at the time.

Henry VIII became increasingly impatient. In 1529, he dismissed his lord chancellor, Cardinal Thomas Wolsey (c. 1475–1530), and replaced him with Thomas More (1478–1535; see Chapter 3). The new archbishop of Canterbury, Thomas Cranmer (1489–1556), granted the annulment in 1533. Henry now married Anne Boleyn, the second of his six wives.

Act of Supremacy

In 1534, Parliament passed the Act of Supremacy, which declared the king, rather than the pope, to be head of the English church. While England thus rejected papal supremacy, the English Church under Henry VIII remained fundamentally Catholic in its doctrine and practice. In 1539, Parliament approved the Six Articles, defining the doctrine of the English Church. On all major points, except papal supremacy, the Six Articles reaffirmed Catholic teaching and rejected Protestant beliefs.

Dissolution of Monasteries

Henry VIII did act against the English monasteries, which were regarded as strongholds of support for the papacy. An act of Parliament, passed in 1536, dissolved the smaller monasteries, while the larger ones were dissolved in 1539. The king, who needed money, sold most of the monastic lands to wealthy Englishmen.

Opposition to the Reformation

Henry VIII encountered some opposition to his break with Rome. Thomas More, the former lord chancellor, and John Fisher (1459–1535), the bishop of Rochester, refused to swear to support the Act of Supremacy and were executed in 1535. In 1536, a revolt, known as the Pilgrimage of Grace, broke out in conservative northern England, but Henry easily suppressed it.

Support of Subjects

Most Englishmen, however, supported their king. Many resented the great wealth of the Catholic Church, as well as the taxes and fees it levied. Furthermore, English hostility to the papacy had grown during the period of the "Babylonian Captivity" in the fourteenth century (see Chapter 1), when the papacy was dominated by France, England's traditional enemy. In addition, those who had bought monastic property strongly supported the king.

King Edward VI (r. 1547–1553)

King Edward VI, the son of Henry VIII and his third wife, Jane Seymour (1509–1537), succeeded his father at the age of ten. During Edward's reign, the English Church became more Protestant. The Six Articles were repealed and replaced with the Forty-two Articles of 1551, which reflected the increasing influence of Calvinist ideas. Furthermore, the English clergy were now permitted to marry.

Protestant ideas were also expressed in the worship of the Anglican Church, set forth in the majestic English of Archbishop Thomas Cranmer's *Book of Common Prayer* of 1549 (revised in 1553).

Queen Mary (r. 1553–1558)

Following Edward VI's death, Queen Mary, the daughter of Henry VIII and Catherine of Aragon, attempted to restore Roman Catholicism in England. This angered many of her subjects, as did her 1554 marriage to her cousin, an ardent Roman Catholic who became King Philip II (r. 1556–1598) of Spain.

Mary persecuted England's Protestants. During her reign, some three hundred people were burned at the stake, earning Mary the nickname of Bloody Mary. Among her victims was Thomas Cranmer, the former archbishop of Canterbury, who had been replaced by Cardinal Reginald Pole (1500–1558).

Queen Elizabeth I (r. 1558–1603)

Elizabeth I, the daughter of Henry VIII and Anne Boleyn, was the last of the Tudors to rule England. Concerned about the impact of religious discord on national unity, she sought a religious settlement that would satisfy the great majority of her subjects. In 1559, Parliament passed a new Act of Supremacy, which repealed the pro-Catholic laws of Mary's reign and once again established the monarch as head of the Anglican Church. The Act of Uniformity of 1559 adopted a modified version of the 1553 *Book of Common Prayer* and decreed its use in the country's churches.

In 1563, Parliament defined the teachings of the Anglican Church in the Thirty-nine Articles. While the church was generally Protestant, it continued to be governed by bishops. Above all, however, the Elizabethan religious settlement emphasized both compromise and ambiguity in wording in an attempt to unite as many as possible of the queen's subjects in the national church. By the time of Elizabeth's death in 1603, England was ranked among the Protestant powers of Europe.

Opposition to the Elizabethan Religious Settlement

Although the Elizabethan compromise won broad acceptance, many ardent Protestants opposed the settlement because it did not go far enough in making the Anglican Church truly Protestant. Some of these Protestants, known as the Puritans, wanted to purify the church of all remaining Catholic elements. In particular, many Puritans wanted to replace the bishops with the Presbyterian system of church government practiced in Scotland. Other Protestants, known as Separatists, wanted to leave the Anglican Church completely. The pilgrims who settled at Plymouth in 1620 were Separatists.

The Duke of Norfolk

Roman Catholics also rejected the Elizabethan compromise, and some of them plotted against the queen. In 1569, the Duke of Norfolk led an unsuccessful revolt against Elizabeth, which resulted in his execution. This and other Catholic plots led the government to take vigorous action against the Catholics. Some 200 to 300 people lost their lives as a result of religious persecution during Elizabeth's reign.

Mary Queen of Scots

Elizabeth I also faced a challenge from the Catholic Mary Stuart, better known as Mary Queen of Scots (1542–1587). In 1567, a revolt in Scotland resulted in her abdication in favor of her Protestant son, who became King James VI (r. 1567–1625). Mary fled to England in 1568. As a great-granddaughter of King Henry VII of England, she had a claim to succeed Elizabeth on the English throne. For almost twenty years,

Mary was involved in a series of Catholic plots against Elizabeth. In 1586, she supported Anthony Babington's (1561–1586) plot to assassinate the queen and was beheaded the following year.

Philip II

King Philip II of Spain also opposed Elizabeth. The English defeat of the Spanish Armada in 1588 (see Chapter 5) both eliminated this threat and gave a great boost to English patriotism.

Anabaptism

Anabaptist Beliefs

The Anabaptists were the radicals of the Protestant Reformation. Anabaptism became especially influential in western Germany, but Anabaptist groups also appeared in other countries, including the Netherlands, Austria, Hungary, Poland, Russia, and England.

While considerable variety existed among the Anabaptists, they were agreed in their rejection of infant baptism, insisting that the only real Christians were those who had undergone a conversion experience and had then been baptized. Many Anabaptists opposed the taking of oaths and the bearing of arms. In addition, they opposed the close relationship between religious and political authorities that generally existed in the sixteenth century. Instead, they believed that the church should be entirely separate from the state. In Germany, the Anabaptists were active in the Peasants' Revolt of 1524–1525.

Anabaptist Leaders

Münzer

Thomas Münzer (1489–1525), a German Anabaptist, preached not only a thorough religious reform but also the overthrow of the existing political and social order. He was captured and executed in 1525.

John of Leyden

From February 1534 until June 1535, John of Leyden (c. 1509–1536), a Dutch tailor, headed a theocratic government in the city of

Münster in Westphalia in western Germany. In this "new Zion," all property was held in common. Claiming to be directly inspired by God, John of Leyden endorsed polygamy and took four wives. After Münster was recaptured by its Catholic bishop, John of Leyden was executed in 1536.

Simons

Thomas Münzer and John of Leyden represent the extreme of the Anabaptist movement.   Menno Simons (1492–1559) was more moderate in his views. A Netherlander who had been a Roman Catholic priest, Simons became an Anabaptist in 1536, preaching simplicity in religious practice and in life generally. His teachings resulted in the establishment of the Mennonite movement, of which the Amish are an offshoot.

The Protestant Reformation inaugurated an era of bitter and often violent religious conflict. Catholics fought against Protestants, while the Protestant groups contended against one another. While the Reformation involved primarily religious issues, it paradoxically helped to promote the growth of secularism in Western European civilization since, in Protestant lands especially, the church came increasingly under the control of the state.

Recommended Reading

Bainton, Roland H. *Here I Stand: A Life of Martin Luther* (1950).

Bainton, Roland H. *The Reformation of the Sixteenth Century* (1952).

Bainton, Roland H. *Women of the Reformation*, 3 vols. (1971-1977).

Bindoff, S. T. *Tudor England* (1950).

Bouwsma, William J. *John Calvin: A Sixteenth-Century Portrait* (1988).

Chadwick, Owen. *The Reformation* (1964).

Clasen, Claus P. *Anabaptism: A Social History, 1525–1618* (1972).

Dickens, A. G. *The English Reformation* (rev. ed., 1967).

Donaldson, Gordon. *The Scottish Reformation* (1960).

Elton, G. R. *Reformation Europe, 1517–1559* (1966).

Erikson, Erik H. *Young Man Luther: A Study in Psychoanalysis and History* (1962).

Grimm, Harold J. *The Reformation Era, 1500–1650* (2nd ed., 1973).

Harbison, E. Harris. *The Age of Reformation* (1955).

Hillerbrand, Hans J. *The World of the Reformation* (1973).

Holborn, Hajo. *A History of Modern Germany: The Reformation* (1959).

Hughes, Philip. *A Popular History of the Reformation* (1957).

Jordan, Wilbur K. *Edward VI: The Young King* (1968).

Koenigsberger, H. G. and George L. Mosse. *Europe in the Sixteenth Century* (1968).

McGrath, Alister. *The Intellectual Origins of the European Reformation* (1987).

Manschreck, Clyde L. *Melanchthon: The Quiet Reformer* (1958).

Monter, E. William. *Calvin's Geneva* (1967).

Neale, J. E. *Queen Elizabeth* (1934).

O'Day, Rosemary. *The Debate on the English Reformation* (1986).

Reid, W. Stanford. *Trumpeter of God: A Biography of John Knox* (1974).

Ridley, Jaspar G. *Thomas Cranmer* (1962).

Scarisbrick, J. J. *Henry VIII* (1968).

Stephens, W. P. *The Theology of Huldrych Zwingli* (1986).

Tawney, R. H. *Religion and the Rise of Capitalism* (1947).

Weber, Max. *The Protestant Ethic and the Spirit of Capitalism* (1930).

CHAPTER 5

The Catholic Reformation and the Wars of Religion

Time Line

1540	Pope Paul III formally authorizes the Society of Jesus
1545	The Council of Trent opens its first session
1564	Pope Pius IV puts the decrees of the Council of Trent into effect
1567	King Philip II of Spain sends the Duke of Alva to suppress the revolt in the Netherlands
1571	Spain defeats the Turks in the Battle of Lepanto

1572	The St. Bartholemew's Day Massacre takes the lives of several thousand Huguenots
1588	England defeats the Spanish Armada
1589	Henry of Navarre becomes King Henry IV of France
1609	The Spanish agree to a twelve-year truce in their struggle against the Dutch
1618	A Calvinist revolt in Bohemia begins the Thirty Years' War
1625	Denmark intervenes in support of the Protestant cause in Germany
1630	Sweden intervenes in support of the Protestant cause in Germany
1632	King Gustavus Adolphus of Sweden dies at the Battle of Lützen
1635	The Treaty of Prague ends the Swedish period of the Thirty Years' War
	France intervenes directly in the Thirty Years' War
1648	The Peace of Westphalia ends the Thirty Years' War
1659	The Treaty of the Pyrenees ends France's war with Spain

The Catholic Reformation has often been called the Counter Reformation. Both terms have some validity. The term Catholic Reformation refers specifically to Roman Catholic efforts to bring a spirit of reform to the Catholic Church. This Catholic Reformation was, in fact, underway even before the beginning of the Protestant Reformation. Once the Protestant Reformation began, the Roman Catholics, in addition to continuing their efforts to reform the Catholic Church, initiated a campaign to combat the activities of the Protestants.

As religious emotions intensified and the lines of religious division became more sharply defined, Europeans became involved in the wars of religion. While these wars resulted in part from religious differences, it is important to realize that political issues also played a major role.

The Catholic Reformation

The Papacy and the Catholic Reformation

During the sixteenth century, the papacy played a central role in the renewal and reform of the Catholic Church.

Sixteenth-Century Popes

Pope Paul III (r. 1534–1549) had the longest pontificate of the sixteenth century. Serving during some of the most critical years of the Protestant Reformation, Paul III was a moderate reformer who appointed virtuous and capable men to high church offices, rather than individuals who were interested primarily in promoting their personal or family fortunes. He was, however, rather cautious in dealing with the challenge presented by the Reformation.

The cause of reform suffered a temporary setback during the papacy of Julius III (r. 1550–1555), a worldly pope who revived some of the worst practices of the Renaissance papacy (see Chapter 2).

The papacy became more strongly committed to reform during the pontificates of Paul IV (r. 1555–1559), Pius IV (r. 1559–1565), and Pius V (r. 1566–1572). These three popes were dedicated both to the reform of the Roman Catholic Church and to combatting the Protestant Reformation.

The Roman Inquisition

To assist in the campaign against what was regarded as heresy, the papacy established the Congregation of the Holy Office, known as the Roman Inquisition. The Inquisition used severe methods, including torture, secret witnesses, and the admission of hearsay and rumor as evidence, to secure the conviction of suspected heretics. In order to discourage the dissemination of views regarded as heretical, the Roman

Inquisition established a system of censorship that maintained an Index of Prohibited Books.

The Council of Trent

Pope Paul III summoned the Council of Trent, which met in three sessions, from 1545 to 1547, from 1551 to 1552, and from 1562 to 1563. The Council of Trent, an assembly of archbishops, bishops, and other church leaders, both defined Roman Catholic doctrine and initiated a program to eliminate abuses in the church.

Doctrinal Reaffirmation

In its consideration of doctrine, the Council of Trent rejected any possibility of compromise with the Protestants. Instead, the council strongly reaffirmed traditional Catholic teaching. The council declared, for example, that the sources of the Christian faith were to be found both in the Bible and in the traditions of the Church, thereby rejecting the Protestant belief in the supremacy of the Bible. The council also rejected Luther's doctrine of justification by faith and restated the doctrine of the seven sacraments, which included not only baptism and holy communion, but also confirmation, penance, matrimony, holy orders, and extreme unction (the anointing of the sick). The council also reaffirmed the validity of the invocation of the prayers of the saints and the veneration of relics and images, as well as the doctrines regarding purgatory and indulgences. Protestants generally rejected these practices and doctrines.

Reforms of Catholic Church

In its efforts to eliminate abuses in the church, the Council of Trent instructed archbishops and bishops to live in the areas they served. This was designed to eliminate the problem of absenteeism. Simony, the sale of church offices, was forbidden. The council instructed bishops to maintain seminaries for the education of the clergy. The council also decreed that indulgences should no longer be granted in exchange for financial contributions and that no fees should be levied for administering the sacraments.

While the Council of Trent retained the Latin language as the language of worship, the clergy were instructed to preach regularly in the vernacular.

Papal Authority

Finally, the Council of Trent strengthened the authority of the pope as head of the Catholic Church by decreeing that none of its decisions would become effective without papal approval. In this way, the council made it clear that the authority of the pope was superior to that of a council. In January 1564, Pope Pius IV issued a bull putting the decrees of the Council of Trent into effect.

The Jesuits

The establishment of new religious orders was a sign of the growing spirit of reform in the Catholic Church. The Society of Jesus, commonly known as the Jesuits, quickly became the most influential of the religious orders established during the sixteenth century.

Ignatius Loyola

The Society of Jesus was founded by St. Ignatius Loyola (1491–1556), a Basque from northern Spain. Serving in the Spanish army, Ignatius was wounded in a battle with the French. While he was recovering from his injuries, he experienced a religious conversion. Rather than fighting for the glory of the Spanish king, he would now fight for the greater glory of God.

In 1534, Ignatius and six followers took the vows of poverty and chastity. They were ordained to the priesthood in 1537. Three years later, Pope Paul III formally authorized the Society of Jesus. Ignatius wrote *The Spiritual Exercises*, setting forth a system of disciplined prayer and asceticism to guide the members of the society.

Organization of the Order

The Jesuits were organized along military lines, and the head of the society was known as the general. Emphasis was placed on obedience to authority. While the Jesuits have often been called "the first legion of the Lord," the militaristic aspects of the society can be overemphasized. These features should be understood primarily as metaphor, similar to the metaphor of the modern Christian hymn "Onward, Christian Soldiers" and similar, too, to the metaphor used by St. Paul in his Letter to the Ephesians. "Put on the whole armor of God," Paul declared, "that you may be able to stand against the wiles of the devil."

Activities of the Jesuits

The Jesuits dedicated themselves to combatting the spread of Protestantism. They have been credited with the recovery of Catholicism in Poland after that country had apparently been lost to Calvinism. The Jesuits also helped preserve the Catholic faith in Bavaria in southern Germany and in the southern Netherlands. They also ministered, at great personal risk, to Catholics in England during the reign of Queen Elizabeth I.

In addition, the Jesuits worked in the education of youth and in the foreign missions. The most famous of the early Jesuit missionaries was St. Francis Xavier (1506–1552), one of Loyola's original companions, who served as a missionary in India and Japan. Other Jesuit missionaries labored in Asia, Africa, and the New World.

Other New Religious Orders

In addition to the Jesuits, several other new religious orders emerged during the sixteenth century.

The Capuchins

Organized in central Italy, the Capuchins received papal approval in 1528. A reform of the Franciscan order, the Capuchins sought to return to the original principles of poverty and piety emphasized by St. Francis of Assisi in the thirteenth century. The Capuchins became known for their preaching and along with the Jesuits, did much to promote the recovery of Roman Catholicism in several areas of Europe where Protestantism originally seemed likely to triumph. The Capuchins also became active missionaries in Africa, Asia, and America.

The Oratorians

St. Philip Neri (1515–1595), who became known as the apostle of Rome, established a community of priests known as the Congregation of the Oratory. Receiving the approval of the papacy in 1575, the

Oratorians worked to promote the practice of religion in the areas they served through prayer, preaching, and the administration of the sacraments.

The Theatines

Founded in 1523, the Theatines were a society of priests whose mission was to improve the level of education and discipline among the clergy.

The Ursulines

The Ursulines, an order of nuns established in 1535, dedicated themselves to the education of girls.

The Discalced Carmelites

St. Theresa of Avila (1515–1582), a Spanish mystic, organized a convent of Discalced Carmelites (Barefoot Carmelites) at Avila in 1562. These cloistered nuns lived in strict observance of the Carmelite rule, which emphasized a life of poverty and simplicity devoted to prayer and contemplation. St. Theresa took the lead in organizing other convents of Discalced Carmelites, and she also assisted St. John of the Cross, another Spanish mystic, in organizing similar communities for men.

The Anti-Protestant Crusade of King Philip II

Spain remained a strongly Catholic country and made a major contribution to the Catholic struggle against the Protestant Reformation.

Domains of King Philip II

In the late sixteenth century, Spain was ruled by King Philip II (r. 1556–1598), the son of the Hapsburg Holy Roman Emperor Charles V (r. 1519–1556), who had also been King Charles I of Spain (r. 1516–1556). At this time, Spain was the world's strongest military and naval power.

Philip II's domains included not only Spain and the Spanish empire but also the Netherlands, the Free County of Burgundy (Franche

Comté), the Kingdom of the Two Sicilies, Sardinia, and the Balearic Islands in the western Mediterranean. In 1580, Philip II gained Portugal, thus securing control of the Portuguese empire.

Philip II hoped to use Spanish power in support of the Catholic cause against both the Protestants and the Moslem Turks. He became involved in war on several fronts, in the Netherlands, against England, and against the Turks.

The Dutch Revolt

In the Netherlands, Philip confronted a serious revolt against Spanish rule. Many Netherlanders resented foreign rule, and the northern provinces had adopted Calvinism. In addition, there was a widespread feeling among the Netherlanders that their industry and trade were being taxed too highly by the Spanish. The revolt in the Netherlands thus involved an explosive mixture of nationalism, religion, and money.

The Duke of Alva's Reign of Terror

In 1567, Philip sent the Duke of Alva (1508–1582) to the Netherlands with orders to suppress both the revolt against Spanish rule and Calvinism. The duke's reign of terror lasted for six years, resulting in the execution of several thousand rebels. Despite Spanish repression, the revolt continued.

Dutch Independence

In 1579, Spanish rule was restored in the ten southern provinces (modern Belgium), which had remained Catholic. The seven northern provinces, which were predominantly Calvinist, formed the Union of Utrecht (1579) and continued the struggle against Spain. The Dutch of the northern provinces found an effective leader in William of Orange (1533–1584), known as William the Silent.

In 1584, Spanish agents assassinated William the Silent, but the Dutch struggle for independence continued. Finally, in 1609, Spain agreed to a twelve-year truce. This represented a virtual Spanish acceptance of Dutch independence, which was formally recognized by the Peace of Westphalia of 1648.

The Battle of Lepanto

Encouraged by Pope Pius V, Philip II helped organize a combined Spanish, Genovese, and Venetian fleet to fight the Turks. This fleet, commanded by Philip II's half brother, Don Juan of Austria (1547–1578), destroyed a Turkish naval force at Lepanto in the Gulf of Corinth, Greece, in October 1571. The Battle of Lepanto was the last great Spanish naval victory. This and other Spanish victories over the Turks weakened, but did not destroy, Turkish power in the Mediterranean.

The Spanish Armada

At the beginning of his reign, Philip II was allied with England as a consequence of his marriage to Queen Mary (see Chapter 4), but this alliance ended with Mary's death and the accession of Queen Elizabeth I in 1558. The Spanish king hoped both to conquer England and to restore that country to the Roman Catholic fold. For several years, he encouraged conspiracies against Elizabeth. When these failed, he decided to take more direct action, launching the Spanish Armada against England in 1588.

The plan called for the Armada to join forces with a Spanish army near Dunkirk in the Netherlands and then to carry out an invasion of England.

Most of the English ships that fought the Armada were smaller than the Spanish vessels, but they were fast and easily maneuvered. In addition, they were armed with heavier long-range guns.

English Victory

On July 21, 1588, the Armada entered the English Channel, headed toward Dunkirk. For eight days, the English ships fought the Spanish, aided by a furious storm, which became known as the "Protestant wind." On July 28, the Armada was dispersed and fled to the north, around the tip of Scotland.

The Spanish Armada lost about forty ships, and many of those that made their way back to Spain were unfit for further service. Spanish deaths totaled in the thousands. The English lost no ships and about 100 men.

The defeat of the Spanish Armada dealt a serious blow to Spain's prestige and marked the first step in the long process of Spain's decline as a major power.

The French Wars of Religion

Conflict Between Catholics and Huguenots

France remained a predominantly Catholic country. Of a total population of about 16 million, some 1.2 million embraced Calvinism. However, a larger proportion of the French nobility became Calvinists, at least temporarily.

Conflict between Catholics and Calvinists, known as Huguenots, led to more than three decades of civil war. This conflict involved both religious and political issues, since some elements of the French nobility supported the Huguenot cause as a part of their struggle against the power of the monarchy.

King Henry II and His Heirs

From 1547 to 1589, France had the misfortune to be ruled by a series of ineffective rulers. King Henry II (r. 1547–1559) was physically robust but weak-willed.

Following Henry II's death, his widow, Catherine de' Medici (1519–1589), a member of the famous Florentine family, became the key figure during the reigns of her three sons, who succeeded in order of birth to the French throne: Francis II (r. 1559–1560), Charles IX (r. 1560–1574), and Henry III (r. 1574–1589). None of these three kings could cope effectively with the intensifying Catholic-Huguenot conflict, nor for that matter could the queen mother.

Open warfare between the Catholics and Huguenots broke out in 1562. The powerful Guise family led the Catholic cause, while the Bourbon family led the Huguenots. The first eight years of fighting ended indecisively, and an uneasy truce was concluded in 1570.

The St. Bartholemew's Day Massacre

Alarmed by the growing power of the Huguenots, Catherine de' Medici decided that they must be exterminated. At midnight on August

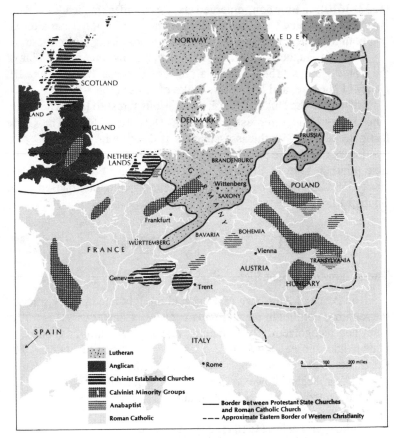

Religious Map of Europe, c. 1560

24, 1572, St. Bartholemew's Day, Catherine gave a signal from a Paris church tower which began the massacre of Huguenots in Paris. The massacre then spread to the provinces, taking the lives of several thousand Huguenots.

The War of the Three Henrys

Following the St. Bartholemew's Day Massacre, Henry of Navarre

(1553–1610), a Bourbon, emerged as the Huguenots' leader. King Henry III attempted to form a moderate Catholic faction as an alternative both to the Huguenots and to the uncompromising Guise faction.

Catholic-Huguenot conflict continued, culminating in the War of the Three Henrys (1585–1589), a conflict between King Henry III, Henry of Navarre, and Henry, the Duke of Guise (1550–1588).

Regarding the Duke of Guise as a serious threat to his own power, King Henry III had him assassinated in December 1588. The Guise faction retaliated with the assassination of the king in July 1589.

Henry of Navarre now became King Henry IV (r. 1589–1610), the first Bourbon king of France. Succeeding where others had failed, Henry IV made peace between the contending religious factions (see Chapter 8).

The Thirty Years' War

The Origins of the Conflict

The Peace of Augsburg of 1555 had brought a temporary truce in the religious conflict in the German states (see Chapter 4). This settlement had recognized only Lutherans and Roman Catholics, but Calvinism had subsequently made gains in a number of states. The Calvinists began to demand recognition of their rights. The Thirty Years' War began, however, as a direct result of a conflict in the Hapsburg-ruled Kingdom of Bohemia.

The Bohemian Period (1618–1625)

In 1617, the Bohemian Diet elected Ferdinand of Styria as king of Bohemia. Ferdinand, a member of the Hapsburg family, became Holy Roman emperor two years later, as Ferdinand II (r. 1619–1637). He was an ardent supporter of the Catholic cause.

Calvinist Revolt

Ferdinand's election alarmed Bohemian Calvinists, who feared the loss of their religious rights. In May 1618, the Calvinist revolt began when the rebels threw two Catholic members of the Bohemian royal council from a window some seventy feet above the ground. Both councillors fell into a pile of manure and suffered only minor injuries. This incident became known as the Defenestration of Prague.

Taking control of Prague, the rebels declared Ferdinand deposed and elected a new king, Frederick V (1596–1632), the elector of the Palatinate in western Germany and a Calvinist. The German Protestant Union, which Frederick headed, provided some aid to the Bohemian rebels.

Catholic Victory

Emperor Ferdinand II won the support of King Maximilian I (r. 1573–1651) of Bavaria, the leader of the Catholic League. Troops of the Holy Roman Empire and Bavaria, commanded by Baron Tilly (1559–1632), invaded Bohemia. In November 1620, Tilly won a decisive victory over the forces of Frederick V at the Battle of White Mountain, near Prague. Frederick, known derisively as the "Winter King," fled to Holland.

Emperor Ferdinand II regained the Bohemian throne, while King Maximilian of Bavaria acquired the Palatinate. The Bohemian period of the Thirty Years' War thus ended with a Hapsburg and Catholic victory. The Calvinist-led revolt in Bohemia had been suppressed, while in Germany, the Palatinate had been transferred from Protestant to Catholic control.

The Danish Period (1625–1629)

The Danish period of the conflict began when King Christian IV (r. 1588–1648), the Lutheran ruler of Denmark, intervened in 1625 to support the Protestant cause against Emperor Ferdinand II. King Christian was also the duke of Holstein and therefore a prince of the Holy Roman Empire.

Defeat of Protestant Forces

The emperor secured the assistance of Albrecht von Wallenstein (1583–1634), who raised an independent army of 50,000 men. The combined forces of Wallenstein and Tilly defeated Christian IV in August 1626 and then occupied the duchy of Holstein the following year.

End of Danish Period

The Treaty of Lübeck of 1629 restored Holstein to Christian IV, but the Danish king pledged not to intervene further in German affairs. The Danish period of the war, like the Bohemian period, thus ended with a Hapsburg and Catholic victory.

The Swedish Period (1630–1635)

The Catholic victories alarmed Protestants almost everywhere. Furthermore, the victories of the emperor endangered the independence of the German princes, while the French Bourbons were concerned about the growth of Hapsburg power.

Widening of the War

The Protestant cause soon found a new defender in King Gustavus Adolphus (r. 1611–1632) of Sweden. In the summer of 1630, the Swedes moved into Germany. Later in the year, France and Sweden signed an alliance, and France entered the war against the Hapsburgs.

The Thirty Years' War had begun primarily as a German conflict over religious issues. The conflict now became a wider European war, fought mainly over political issues, as Catholic France and Protestant Sweden joined forces against the Catholic Hapsburgs.

The Course of Battle

During the early stages of the conflict, the Swedes won several notable victories. Tilly, the imperial commander, fell in battle in 1632.

Frightened by his enemies' victories, Emperor Ferdinand II called on Wallenstein to form a new army. In November 1632, at the Battle of Lützen, the Swedes defeated Wallenstein, but Gustavus Adolphus was killed in the fighting.

When Wallenstein entered into secret negotiations with Sweden and France, Ferdinand II relieved him of his command in February 1634. The general was assassinated a few days later. In the autumn, the emperor's army decisively defeated the Swedes at Nördlingen in southern Germany.

The Treaty of Prague

The deaths of both Gustavus Adolphus and Wallenstein, together with the exhaustion of both the Holy Roman emperor and the German Protestant princes, brought an end to the Swedish period of the war. The Treaty of Prague, signed in 1635, generally strengthened the Hapsburgs and weakened the power of the German princes.

The French Period (1635–1648)

The settlement reached in the Treaty of Prague was wrecked by the French decision to intervene directly in the war. Cardinal Richelieu (1585–1642), the chief minister of King Louis XIII (r. 1610–1643) of France (see Chapter 8), wanted to weaken the power of the Hapsburgs and take the province of Alsace from the Holy Roman Empire. In addition, Richelieu had designs against Spain and its Hapsburg king, Philip IV (r. 1621–1665).

In Germany, the French could rely on support from the Swedes and a number of German princes in the struggle against the Hapsburg Holy Roman emperor, while France focused its attention on the war against Spain.

Both in Germany and in the Franco-Spanish conflict, the fortunes of war fluctuated. For a time, the forces of the Holy Roman emperor, aided by King Maximilian of Bavaria and other Catholic princes, more than held their own against the Swedes and German Protestants. France's success against Spain, however, enabled the French to send larger forces into Germany. This helped tip the balance in favor of the emperor's foes.

Emperor Ferdinand II died in 1637 and was succeeded by his son, Ferdinand III (r. 1637–1657). Peace negotiations began in 1641, but made little progress until the death of Cardinal Richelieu in 1642 and the French occupation of Bavaria in 1646.

The Peace of Westphalia (1648)

The Peace of Westphalia of 1648 ended the Thirty Years' War. Sweden, Brandenburg, and France all gained territory. Sweden acquired western Pomerania, while eastern Pomerania was assigned to Brandenburg. France annexed part of Alsace and some nearby territory. The settlement formally recognized the independence of the Dutch Republic and Switzerland and granted the German states the right to make treaties and alliances, thereby further weakening the authority of the Holy Roman emperor.

In religious affairs, the Peace of Westphalia expanded the Peace of Augsburg to include Calvinists, as well as Catholics and Lutherans.

The Peace of Westphalia ended the Holy Roman emperor's hope of restoring both his own power and the Catholic faith throughout the empire. The empire was now, more than ever, fragmented into a number of virtually independent states.

The end of the Thirty Years' War left Hapsburg Spain isolated. The French war against Spain continued until 1659, when the Treaty of the Pyrenees awarded France part of the Spanish Netherlands and some territory in northern Spain. King Philip IV of Spain agreed to the marriage of his daughter Maria Theresa to King Louis XIV (r. 1643–1715) of France.

Together, the Peace of Westphalia and the Treaty of the Pyrenees established France as the predominant power on the European continent.

The Catholic Reformation succeeded both in bringing a much-needed spirit of reform to the Roman Catholic Church and in stemming the tide of Protestant expansion in Western Europe. Nevertheless, the Roman Catholic Church was unable to regain the central position in Western European society it had held during the Middle Ages.

The wars of religion brought mixed results. While King Philip II of Spain succeeded in reducing the power of the Moslem Turks in the Mediterranean, he failed in his efforts to restore Roman Catholicism in England and lost control of the heavily Calvinist Dutch Netherlands. France remained a predominantly Catholic country, although it continued to have a significant Huguenot minority. In the Holy Roman Empire, the Hapsburgs failed to destroy Protestantism and in the process, suffered a further decrease of their own power. The power of the Spanish Hapsburgs declined, as well, and by the mid-seventeenth century, France had become the most powerful state on the European continent.

Recommended Reading

Bangert, William V. *A History of the Society of Jesus* (1972).

Braudel, Fernand. *The Mediterranean and the Mediterranean World in the Age of Philip II*, 2 vols. (1972-73).

Briggs, Robin. *Early Modern France, 1560–1715* (1977).

Davidson, N. S. *The Counter-Reformation* (1987).

Dudon, Paul. *St. Ignatius of Loyola* (1949).

Evennett, H. Outram. *The Spirit of the Counter-Reformation* (1968).

Mann, Golo. *Wallenstein: His Life Narrated* (1976).

Mattingly, Garrett. *The Armada* (1959).

Neale, J. E. *The Age of Catherine de' Medici* (1943).

O'Connell, Marvin R. *The Counter Reformation, 1559–1610* (1974).

Parker, Geoffrey. *The Dutch Revolt* (1977).

Parker, Geoffrey. *Spain and the Netherlands, 1559–1659* (1979).

Pearson, Hesketh. *Henry of Navarre: The King Who Dared* (1963).

Pierson, Peter. *Philip II of Spain* (1975).

Roberts, Michael. *Gustavus Adolphus and the Rise of Sweden* (1973).

Steinberg, S. H. *The Thirty Years' War and the Conflict for European Hegemony, 1600–1660* (1967).

Sutherland, N. M. *The Huguenot Struggle for Recognition* (1980).

Sutherland, N. M. *The Massacre of St. Bartholemew and the European Conflict, 1559–1572* (1973).

Wedgwood, C. V. *William the Silent* (1944).

CHAPTER 6

The Revival of Capitalism and the Expansion of Europe

Time Line

1419	Portugal's Prince Henry the Navigator establishes a school of seamanship and navigation
1427–1431	The Portuguese explore the Azores
1442	The Portuguese establish a slave-trading station in West Africa
1488	Bartholemew Diaz rounds the Cape of Good Hope
1492	Christopher Columbus discovers the New World

1493	Pope Alexander VI establishes the Papal Line of Demarcation
1497–1498	John Cabot explores the northeast coast of North America
1498	Vasco da Gama reaches Calicut on India's Malabar coast
1499–1500	Amerigo Vespucci makes two voyages of exploration along the Atlantic coast of South America
1500	Pedro Cabral claims Brazil for Portugal
1511	The Portuguese take Malacca on the Malay peninsula
1513	Ponce de Leon discovers Florida
	Vasco de Balboa crosses Panama to the Pacific Ocean
1519–1521	Hernan Cortés conquers the Aztec empire in Mexico
1519–1522	An expedition originally led by Ferdinand Magellan circumnavigates the globe
1524	Giovanni da Verrazano explores the coast of North America
1532	Francisco Pizarro conquers the Inca empire in Peru
1534	Jacques Cartier makes his first voyage to Canada
1542	The first Portuguese ship reaches Japan
1557	The Portuguese establish a trading station at Macao on the southern coast of China

The era of the Renaissance and Reformation was accompanied by the emergence of a modern capitalist economy and an age of exploration and expansion. The explorations of the late fifteenth and sixteenth centuries brought Europeans to Africa south of the Sahara and to Asia and resulted in the discovery of the two continents of the New World.

The Revival of Capitalism

Definition of Capitalism

The revival of capitalism was the most important economic development of early modern times. As defined in *The Random House College Dictionary,* capitalism is "an economic system in which investment in and ownership of the means of production, distribution, and exchange of wealth is made and maintained chiefly by private individuals or corporations." Those engaged in capitalistic enterprises are motivated primarily by their desire for profit.

Decline of Capitalism in Middle Ages

Capitalism had existed in ancient Greece and Rome, but it had declined following the collapse of the Roman Empire in the West. During the Early Middle Ages, the period from about 500 to about 1000 A.D., capitalism largely disappeared in Western Europe. Each community possessed virtual economic self-sufficiency. The manorial system promoted cooperation in agriculture, while the guild system emphasized cooperation in handicraft industry and trade. The quest for profits was discouraged, as the church insisted on the concept of the "just price," which involved the cost of materials plus labor. In addition, the church condemned the lending of money for interest as usury. The Jews were the only Europeans not bound by the laws of the church, and they practiced whatever small-scale money-lending there was.

Growth of Trade

Over the course of the Middle Ages, a gradual change occurred in the economy of Western Europe. The manorial system and the guild system both began to decay. Trade increased, and towns grew in size and number. The Crusades contributed significantly to the revival of trade by familiarizing Europeans with the spices and luxury goods of the East and creating a demand for these goods in Europe.

Italy

The Italian cities benefited most from the revival of trade. In the fourteenth century, Venice defeated Genoa, its major rival, and the Venetians gained a near monopoly on trade with the East. Milan prospered as a center for trade between Italy and Europe beyond the Alps.

Northern Europe

In Northern Europe, the Hanseatic League, which developed during the thirteenth century, dominated trade. At its height, the Hanseatic League included about eighty German towns on the North Sea and the Baltic Sea. The Hanseatic League dealt mainly in raw materials, including lumber, iron, tar, leather, and wood, along with food products such as salted fish and grain and some luxury goods. The league established trading posts in Russia, Scandinavia, the Netherlands, and England.

Elsewhere in Germany, other important commercial centers developed, including Cologne on the Rhine River and Nuremberg and Augsburg in southern Germany. London and Paris also became major trading centers, as did Amsterdam, Antwerp, and Bruges in the Netherlands.

Banking

As economic activity increased, so, too, did demands for capital. Despite the church's ban on usury, growing amounts of money were lent for interest. Some theologians began to argue that earning interest on money lent for useful and productive purposes was morally legitimate.

Italy

While Italy was a major center of trade, it also led the way in the development of banking. The Medici family and other Florentine bankers established branch operations elsewhere in Italy and in other parts of Europe, as well, while independent banking operations got under way in Venice, Milan, Genoa, and other cities.

Northern Europe

In Germany, the Fugger family of Augsburg became prominent in banking. During the fifteenth century, under the leadership of Jacob Fugger (1459–1525), known as Jacob the Rich, the Fugger family's wealth increased as a result of its development of silver mines in the Tyrol and copper mines in Hungary and its trade in wool, silk, and spices. The family also profited from loans made to the Holy Roman emperors and the popes.

The Beginning of European Exploration

Motives for Exploration

The desire of Europeans to bypass the Venetians and the Moslem middlemen in the Near East and gain direct access to the products of Asia provided a major motive for exploration. By the fifteenth century, the European demand for the spices and luxury goods of Asia far exceeded the supply, and there was a great potential for immense profits.

Religion also provided a powerful motive for exploration. Christianity had always been a missionary religion. During the Middle Ages, the Christian faith had been extended to virtually all of Europe, and the desire increased to bring the Christian gospel to other areas of the world.

Technological Advances

During the fourteenth and fifteenth centuries, a number of advances were made in ship construction and in aids to navigation. An improved compass, with a fixed dial and accurate pivoting needle, was introduced, while the astrolabe was used to determine latitude. It did not become possible to calculate longitude accurately, however, until the perfection of the chronometer in the eighteenth century.

Geographic Knowledge

The Europeans' knowledge of geography lagged behind their technological accomplishments. In the fifteenth century, maps and charts remained crude and inaccurate, and Europeans continued to accept the work of Ptolemy, a Greek astronomer and geographer of the second century A.D. Ptolemy's work on geography, usually referred to by its Arabic name, the *Almagest*, suffered from many inaccuracies.

Early Explorers

During the Middle Ages, a few Europeans had journeyed to Asia. Marco Polo (c. 1254-c. 1325), a Venetian, traveled overland to China in the late thirteenth century, and a few other Europeans also made their way to Asia. John of Monte Corvino, a monk, served for a time as a missionary in Persia and India and then went to China, settling in Peking. In the early fifteenth century, Niccolò de' Conti (c. 1395-1469), a Venetian merchant, visited India, Ceylon, and Burma, as well as the islands of Sumatra and Java in the East Indies. Nevertheless, European knowledge of geography remained severely limited.

Portugal: East by Sea to the Indies

Prince Henry the Navigator (1394–1460)

Prince Henry the Navigator, a son of Portugal's King John I (r. 1385–1433), developed an intense interest in Africa. In particular, he hoped to carry the Christian religion to Africa and to establish contact with the Christians of Abyssinia (Ethiopia). Reports of Abyssinian Christianity had reached Europe, exciting hopes that Abyssinia might be the land of the legendary Christian prince, Prester John. The legend of Prester John had first appeared in Europe in the twelfth century and continued to fascinate the European imagination.

Expeditions to Atlantic Islands

In 1419, Prince Henry established a school of seamanship and navigation, and expeditions he dispatched achieved considerable success. The Portuguese explored the Madeira Islands in 1420 and the

Azores In the period from 1427 to 1431. In 1460, Portuguese explorers discovered the Cape Verde Islands. Within a few years, the Portuguese developed the fishing industry in the Azores, while Portuguese settlers began to produce wine in the Madeiras. The Cape Verde Islands became a center of sugar production.

Enterprise in Africa

In the meantime, the Portuguese began the exploration of the west coast of Africa, rounding Cape Bojador in 1434. In 1441, the Portuguese reached Cape Blanco, south of the Tropic of Cancer. A slave-trading station was established on Arguim Island in Cape Blanco Bay in 1442. In addition to the slave trade, the Portuguese profited from African gold, ivory, and ebony. They also traded in exotic animals and birds, including monkeys and parrots, which became popular among wealthy Portuguese. Distracted by their profitable enterprises in Africa, the Portuguese lost interest for a time in further exploration.

The Portuguese Empire in Asia

Diaz

In 1487, King John II (r. 1455–1495) of Portugal dispatched an expedition led by Bartholemew Diaz (d. 1500), which made its way southward along the west coast of Africa. In 1488, Diaz rounded the Cape of Good Hope, at Africa's southern tip, and returned to Portugal to report his achievement.

Da Gama

In July 1497, Vasco da Gama (c. 1469–1524) left Portugal and sailed around the Cape of Good Hope. In East Africa, he secured the aid of an Arab pilot who directed him on the route to Calicut on the Malabar coast of India. Arriving in May 1498, da Gama loaded his ships with luxury goods to prove that he had reached the fabled Malabar coast. He returned to Lisbon in 1499.

Cabral

In 1500, Pedro Cabral (c. 1467– c. 1520) set out for India. Sailing far west of his course, he reached the coast of Brazil, which he claimed for Portugal.

Commercial Centers

Vasco da Gama's discovery of the route east by sea to the Indies opened the way to the development of a Portuguese commercial empire in Asia. In 1510, a Portuguese expedition led by Afonso de Albuquerque (1453–1515) took Goa on the Indian coast. Goa quickly became Portugal's main naval base and commercial center in Asia. Moving beyond India, Albuquerque took Malacca on the Malay peninsula in 1511. Malacca became the center for Portuguese trade with the East Indies, including the Moluccas, known as the Spice Islands. Also in 1511, the Portuguese gained a trade monopoly in the Chinese port of Canton. The first Portuguese ship reached Japan in 1542. In 1557, the Portuguese established a trading station at Macao on the southern coast of China, making Macao the oldest permanent European settlement in Asia.

Shift of Trade to the Atlantic

The Portuguese discoveries ended the Venetian and Moslem monopoly on trade with Asia. By dealing directly with Asian merchants, the Portuguese could considerably undercut the prices charged by the Venetians for spices and luxury goods. The center of European commerce now shifted away from the Mediterranean Sea toward the Atlantic Ocean. The decline of Italy as a trading center also had a negative impact on the commercial cities of southern Germany, which stood at the northern end of the transalpine trade routes. In addition, the shift of trade to the Atlantic reduced the economic importance of the Baltic Sea and led to a decline in the prosperity of the Hanseatic League.

Spain: West by Sea to the Indies

Christopher Columbus (1451–1506)

Christopher Columbus, a Genovese seaman, believed it was possible to sail west by sea to the Indies. By the fifteenth century, European geographers generally accepted the idea that the earth was round, although they considerably underestimated its circumference. Columbus calculated that the distance from Europe to what was called Zipangu

(Japan), sailing westward across the Atlantic Ocean, was only 3,000 miles.

Discovery of the New World

Columbus tried, without success, to interest the Portuguese in his project. He then turned to Queen Isabella (r. 1474–1504) of Spain, who was anxious to compete with her Portuguese neighbors. On August 3, 1492, Columbus left the Spanish port of Palos with his three small ships, the Niña, the Pinta, and the Santa Maria. On October 12, Columbus's expedition reached the island of San Salvador in the Bahamas. Columbus believed he had succeeded in reaching Asia. Continuing his exploration of the Caribbean area, Columbus sighted Cuba on October 27 and on December 5 reached the island of Hispaniola, where modern Haiti and the Dominican Republic are located.

Subsequent Voyages

Columbus made three subsequent voyages, in 1493–1496, 1498–1500, and 1502–1504. During these voyages, he established a base on the island of Hispaniola; discovered Trinidad, the Virgin Islands, Puerto Rico, Jamaica, and other Caribbean islands; and explored the coast of Central America and the mouth of the Orinoco River. Despite increasing evidence to the contrary, Columbus continued to insist that he had discovered a new sea route to Asia.

Lines of Demarcation

Shortly after Columbus returned to Spain from his first voyage, Pope Alexander VI (r. 1492–1503), a Spaniard, established the Papal Line of Demarcation of 1493. The line assigned to Spain all newly discovered lands one hundred leagues west of the Azores and the Cape Verde Islands. Newly discovered lands east of that line were assigned to Portugal.

The Portuguese protested the line drawn by the pope, and Portuguese-Spanish negotiations led to the signing of the Treaty of Tordesillas in 1494. The treaty established the line of demarcation at a point 370 leagues (about 1,100 miles) west of the Cape Verde Islands. Under the terms of this treaty, Brazil lay in the Portuguese sphere.

The Spanish Empire in America

During the early sixteenth century, the Spanish followed up on the voyages of Columbus.

Ponce de León and Balboa

In 1513, an expedition led by Ponce de León (c. 1460–1521) discovered Florida. In the same year, a party led by Vasco de Balboa (c. 1475–1519) made its way across Panama to the Pacific Ocean, which he called the South Sea.

Cortés and Pizarro

From 1519 to 1521, Hernan Cortés (1485–1547) conquered Montezuma's Aztec empire in Mexico, while Francisco Pizarro (c. 1476–1541) overran the Inca empire in Peru, ruled by Atahualpa, in 1532.

Coronado

From 1540 to 1542, Francisco de Coronado (c. 1510–1554) explored what became the southwest United States, traveling as far north as the present state of Kansas.

Government of Spanish America

In Central and 5outh America, the Spanish created an empire of settlement. The Indians became subjects of the Spanish king and were converted to Christianity. Spain governed its American empire through the Council of the Indies in Spain and viceroys in America. Spanish colonial government emphasized royal authority, and the American colonies gained few rights of self-government.

The Voyage of Magellan

In September 1519, Ferdinand Magellan (c. 1480–1521) set out on a voyage in search of the elusive route west by sea to Asia. He sailed along the east coast of South America and made his way through the straits that are still known as the Straits of Magellan. He called the ocean at the western end of the straits the Pacific because of its gentle winds.

Setting his course to the northwest, Magellan then sailed out of sight of land for nearly two months before reaching the Mariana Islands.

Sailing to the southwest, Magellan reached the islands that later came to be called the Philippines, in honor of King Philip II of Spain. Here, in April 1521, Magellan was killed.

Two of Magellan's ships, the *Trinidad* and the *Victoria,* continued the voyage, sailing to Borneo and the Molucca Islands. The *Trinidad* then set sail for Panama but was wrecked en route. The *Victoria* sailed through the Indian Ocean and around the Cape of Good Hope, arriving in Spain in September 1522. It had succeeded in circumnavigating the globe, thus removing any remaining doubts about whether the earth was truly round and demonstrating that the world was much larger than anyone had imagined.

The Naming of America

The New World acquired its name in the aftermath of voyages made by Amerigo Vespucci (1454–1512), a Florentine sailor. In 1499–1500, Vespucci explored the Atlantic coast of South America in the service of Spain, and he made a second voyage in 1501–1502 in the employ of the Portuguese. Vespucci's voyages confirmed that Columbus had not reached Asia but had in fact discovered a New World.

Vespucci's detailed reports received wide publicity, and when Martin Waldseemüller, a German geographer, published his map of the world in 1507, he labeled the southern part of the New World "America," the Latin form of Amerigo. While the term was applied at first only to South America, by the late sixteenth century all of the New World had come to be known as America.

English and French Explorations

Voyages of exploration conducted by the English and French in the late fifteenth and early sixteenth centuries were on a smaller scale than those of Portugal and Spain and produced less spectacular results.

Cabot

In 1497 and 1498, John Cabot (c. 1450– c. 1498), a Genovese sailor, perhaps accompanied by his son, Sebastian (c. 1483–1557), made two voyages along the northeast coast of North America.

Employed by King Henry VII (r. 1485–1509) of England, Cabot hoped to find a northwest passage leading to Asia. Henry soon lost interest in the undertaking, although English claims to North America were based on Cabot's voyages.

Verrazano

In 1524, Giovanni da Verrazano (c. 1480– c. 1527), an Italian sailing in the service of France, explored the North American coast. Verrazano may have been the first European to enter New York harbor.

Cartier

In 1534, the French explorer Jacques Cartier (1491–1557) began the first of his voyages to Canada in search of the northwest passage. During his second voyage, in 1535–1536, Cartier sailed up the St. Lawrence River as far as the present site of Quebec city. In 1541, he made another voyage to the same area. Cartier's voyages established France's claims to North America.

Despite these voyages, neither England nor France established permanent settlements in North America until the early seventeenth century.

The revival of trade and the development of capitalistic enterprise in Europe served as a powerful impetus for exploration. Within the space of a few generations, Europeans came to dominate much of the globe. In turn, exploration and discovery provided a further stimulus for Europe's continuing economic growth.

Recommended Reading

Ball, J. N. *Merchants and Merchandise: The Expansion of Trade in Europe, 1500–1630* (1977).

Boxer, C. R. *The Dutch Seaborne Empire, 1600–1800* (1965).

Boxer, C. R. *The Portuguese Seaborne Empire, 1415–1825* (1969).

Davis, David Brion. *The Problem of Slavery in Western Culture* (1966).

Davis, Ralph. *The Rise of the Atlantic Economies* (1973).

Dobb, Maurice. *Studies in the Development of Capitalism* (rev. ed., 1964).

Elliott, John H. *Imperial Spain, 1469–1716* (1963).

Elliott, John H. *The Old World and the New, 1492–1650* (1972).

Goodman, Edward J. *The Explorers of South America* (1972).

Hamilton, Earl J. *American Treasure and the Price Revolution in Spain, 1501–1650* (1934).

Haring, C. H. *The Spanish Empire in America* (1947).

Hemming, John. *The Conquest of the Incas* (1970).

Johnson, William W. *Cortés* (1975).

Landes, David S. *The Rise of Capitalism* (1966).

Morison, Samuel Eliot. *Admiral of the Ocean Sea: A Life of Christopher Columbus,* 2 vols. (1942).

Morison, Samuel Eliot. *The European Discovery of America: The Northern Voyages* (1971).

Morison, Samuel Eliot. *The European Discovery of America: The Southern Voyages* (1974).

Nowell, C. E. *The Great Discoveries and the First Colonial Empires* (1954).

Parr, Charles M. *Ferdinand Magellan: Circumnavigator* (2nd ed., 1964).

Parry, J. H. *The Age of Reconnaissance* (1963).

Parry, J. H. *The Spanish Seaborne Empire* (1966).

Rawley, James A. *The Trans-Atlantic Slave Trade: A History* (1981).

Roover, Raymond de. *The Rise and Decline of the Medici Bank, 1397–1494* (1963).

Strieder, Jacob. *Jacob Fugger the Rich: Merchant and Banker of Augsburg, 1459–1525* (1931).

CHAPTER 7

The Struggle for Constitutional Government in England

Time Line

1603	Death of Queen Elizabeth
1603–1625	Reign of King James I
1611	The King James Version of the Bible is published
1625–1649	Reign of King Charles I
1628	Parliament passes the Petition of Right
1629–1640	Charles I rules England without Parliament
1640	Charles I calls the Short Parliament into session
	The Long Parliament convenes

1642	The Civil War begins
1646	The Scots take Charles I prisoner
1648	"Pride's Purge" results in the creation of the Rump Parliament
1649	Charles I is executed
1649–1660	The Commonwealth and Protectorate
1653	Oliver Cromwell becomes lord protector
1660	The restoration of the monarchy
1660–1685	Reign of King Charles II
1661–1665	Parliament passes the Clarendon Code
1673	Parliament passes the Test Act
1685–1688	Reign of King James II
1688	The Glorious Revolution brings William and Mary to the throne
1689	Parliament passes the Bill of Rights
1701	Parliament passes the Act of Settlement
1702–1714	Reign of Queen Anne
1707	The Act of Union unites England and Scotland
1714–1727	Reign of King George I
1721–1742	Robert Walpole serves as prime minister
1727–1760	Reign of King George II
1760–1820	Reign of King George III

In early seventeenth-century England, the first two Stuart kings, James I and Charles I, sought to establish an absolute monarchy and to enforce their views on religion. These policies led to a revolt by Parliament, with the support of the Puritans, against Charles I. The English Civil

War of the 1640s ended with the victory of Parliament and the execution of the king.

During the period of the Commonwealth and Protectorate, the English conducted an unsuccessful experiment in republican government. In 1660, the monarchy was restored. The troublesome issues of the relationship between king and Parliament and the nature of the English church had not been resolved, however, and further conflict produced the Glorious Revolution of 1688. This revolution established a constitutional monarchy and confirmed the Church of England as the country's established church. During the eighteenth century, Parliament clearly established its ascendency over the crown.

King James I (r. 1603–1625)

Queen Elizabeth I, the last of England's Tudor monarchs, died in 1603. During the final years of her reign, Elizabeth had skillfully avoided conflict over two troublesome issues: the precise nature of the relationship between the crown and Parliament, and the challenge presented by the Calvinist Puritans to the established Church of England (the Anglican Church).

Under England's new king, James I, the unresolved problems quickly came to a head. James I was the son of Mary Queen of Scots (1542–1587), a cousin of Elizabeth I, and the first of the Stuart kings of England. He had been King James VI of Scotland and came to the English throne as a foreigner, unfamiliar with English traditions.

James I and Divine Right

James I insisted that he was king by divine right, thereby rejecting the English tradition of parliamentary government. In James's view, the king ruled by the will of God and was responsible only to God. He thus stood above the law, and his subjects had no legitimate right to question or resist his will.

James I and Parliament

Opposition to the king centered in Parliament, which consisted of two houses, the House of Lords and the House of Commons. The House of Lords, comprising the nobility and the bishops of the Church of England, generally supported the king, although opposition mounted in response to James's more extreme claims.

The House of Commons

Merchants, lawyers, and prosperous country gentlemen dominated the House of Commons. They were determined to defend what they regarded as Parliament's legitimate role in sharing in the government. In the early seventeenth century, the House of Commons was predominantly Anglican, but its membership included a growing number of Puritans who desired to "purify" the Church of England by eliminating elaborate ceremonies and establishing a representative form of church government to replace the bishops.

Conflict Between King and Parliament

In addition to being extravagant, James faced the problem of generally rising prices, which increased the cost of government. When James asked Parliament to approve new taxes, Parliament demanded that the king recognize its authority.

Rather than accede to Parliament's demands, James attempted to increase his income without seeking parliamentary approval. He imposed customs duties by proclamation and he compelled gentlemen to purchase knighthoods. Asserting its claims, Parliament adopted the Great Protestation in 1621.

James I and Religion

Although he had been king of Scotland, James I was an ardent Anglican, rather than a Presbyterian, which was the dominant religion in Scotland. The king distrusted Presbyterianism, regarding its representative system of church government as a threat to royal power. As king of England, James refused to make any concessions to the Puritans, who, like the Presbyterians, were Calvinists. Puritan opposition to the king increased, and some Puritans emigrated to New England.

The Gunpowder Plot

James also ran into trouble over the Catholic issue. At the beginning of his reign, the king relaxed restrictions on Roman Catholics.

Then, alarmed by a resurgence of Catholicism in England, he reimposed the restrictions. Several Catholic extremists, including Guy Fawkes (1570–1606), launched a plot to blow up Parliament when it met on November 5, 1605. The government uncovered the Gunpowder Plot before it could be carried out, and the plotters were executed. The plot intensified anti-Catholic feelings in England.

The King James Bible

The reign of James I provided one positive accomplishment in religion: the King James Version of the Bible, published in 1611. The magnificent language of this translation makes it one of the great works of English literature.

James I and Foreign Policy

James I sought to conduct foreign affairs without consulting Parliament and to establish an alliance with Catholic Spain. These policies evoked widespread opposition.

King Charles I (r. 1625–1649)

Charles I proved to be even more inflexible and inept than his father had been. When the unpopular Duke of Buckingham was assassinated in 1628, the king turned to Thomas Wentworth, a staunch supporter of royal power, who subsequently became the Earl of Strafford (1593–1641).

Charles I and Parliament—The Petition of Right

The antagonism between king and Parliament became even more intense during the reign of Charles I. In 1628, Parliament passed the Petition of Right. Insisting that the king was subject to the law, the Petition of Right provided that the king could not levy taxes without the approval of Parliament, impose forced loans on his subjects, declare martial law in peacetime, imprison citizens without trial, or quarter troops in private homes. Charles was so desperate for money that he agreed to sign the Petition of Right, although he never felt obliged to observe its limitations on his power.

The Personal Government of Charles I

For eleven years, from 1629 to 1640, Charles I ruled England without Parliament. The king engaged in an incessant search for new sources of income, employing methods that were either illegal or of questionable legality.

A particularly sharp controversy developed over the king's collection of ship money. In the past, even at the time of the Spanish Armada in 1588, ship money had been collected only in the coastal areas. Now, Charles collected ship money throughout the entire kingdom, insisting, against opposition, that it was legitimate to do so since the navy protected the whole country.

Charles I and Religion

Charles I's religious policy also evoked opposition. The king supported the efforts of William Laud (1573–1645), the archbishop of Canterbury, to enforce strict observance of Anglican doctrine, worship, and church organization and to drive the Puritans from the established church.

For their part, the Puritans continued to demand a purification of the Anglican church. In addition, they feared that Laud's policy might lead to a Catholic revival. This fear was strengthened by what the Puritans regarded as an increase of Catholic influence in the royal court. Charles I's wife, Henrietta Maria (1609–1669), the sister of King Louis XIII of France, was a Catholic, and laws against Catholics were not being strictly enforced.

Revolt in Scotland

The revolt against Charles I began in Scotland. In 1637, the English government ordered the use of the Anglican worship service in the Presbyterian churches of Scotland. In early 1638, thousands of Scots signed the Solemn League and Covenant, pledging to defend their Calvinist religion. The conflict was both religious and political, since Anglicanism was associated with the king's claims to absolute power. In 1639, the Scots rose in revolt.

The Short Parliament

Charles I desperately needed money in order to suppress the Scottish revolt, and he called Parliament into session in April 1640. This Short Parliament, which lasted only three weeks, demanded that the king make concessions. In particular, Parliament insisted that the king acknowledge that its approval was necessary for the levying of new taxes and that he agree to make the Anglican church more Protestant in character. Charles responded by dissolving Parliament in May.

The Long Parliament

In late August 1640, the Scots defeated Charles I's army at Newburn on the Tyne. In the Treaty of Ripon, signed on October 26, Charles agreed to pay the Scottish army £850 a day until a permanent settlement was reached. The king's need for money was now more desperate than ever, and he once again called Parliament into session.

This Parliament, which met for the first time on November 3, 1640, became the Long Parliament of the English Civil War. Although periodically reduced in size, it was not dissolved until 1653.

The king's opponents dominated the Long Parliament, and they quickly moved to impeach both the Earl of Strafford and Archbishop Laud. Strafford was condemned to death and executed in May 1641, while Laud was executed in 1645, during the Civil War.

Conflict with the King

In other actions, the Long Parliament barred the king from levying taxes without parliamentary approval. It also passed acts providing that Parliament should meet at least every three years and limiting the king's right to dissolve Parliament.

In the Grand Remonstrance, passed in November 1641, the Long Parliament summarized its political and religious grievances against the king. In January 1642, the angry Charles I went to Parliament with several hundred troops, planning to arrest five of its members. The five had been warned of the king's intentions and escaped.

Outbreak of the Civil War

The king left London and went to the north of England, where he was joined by some of his parliamentary supporters. The king's opponents remained in London. The two sides began to raise troops, and the English Civil War broke out in the summer of 1642.

The Civil War: Puritans and Roundheads

During the Civil War, the king's parliamentary opponents, known as the Roundheads, dominated London and southeastern England. These opponents included the lawyers and merchants, as well as the country gentry of the region. Many were Puritans. The royalists, known as the Cavaliers, controlled the more conservative north and west. The Cavaliers drew their support from the great noble families, ardent Anglicans, and the country gentry and peasants of the area.

In 1643, the Roundhead cause was strengthened by an alliance with the Scots. But even more important for the Roundheads was the creation of an effective army. Oliver Cromwell (1599–1658) organized the New Model Army, the Ironsides, which defeated the Cavaliers, first at Marston Moor in July 1644 and then at Naseby in June 1645. The Scots took Charles I prisoner in May 1646.

As the Civil War drew to an end, a conflict developed within Parliament between its more moderate and radical elements. The radicals soon gained the upper hand and in December 1648, Colonel Thomas Pride's (d. 1658) troops excluded ninety-six moderate Presbyterians from the House of Commons. "Pride's Purge" left some sixty members to comprise what came to be known as the Rump Parliament. The Rump Parliament voted to abolish the monarchy, the House of Lords, and the Anglican Church and ordered that Charles I be tried for treason. The king was executed in January 1649.

The Commonwealth and Protectorate— Oliver Cromwell

Following the execution of Charles I, England embarked on an eleven-year-long experiment in republican government. Under the Commonwealth, from 1649 to 1653, political power was in the hands of a one-house parliament, while the Council of State conducted the day-to-day affairs of the government.

Cromwell's Religious Policy

Led by Oliver Cromwell, the Commonwealth sought to reestablish order in England. Cromwell restricted the freedom of Anglicans and Catholics. An ardent Puritan, he enforced public morality, closing the theaters, prohibiting dancing, and requiring strict observance of the Sabbath.

Cromwell's Foreign Policy

Cromwell established English control over Scotland and crushed a revolt in Ireland. He also pursued an aggressive foreign policy designed to promote England's commercial interests. This led to war with Holland and Spain. The Dutch were defeated in 1654. In 1655, the English conquered the Spanish island of Jamaica in the West Indies.

Cromwell's Conflict with the Radicals

At home, conflict mounted as the lower classes demanded the satisfaction of their economic and social grievances. Cromwell now crushed the radicals much as he had earlier defeated the royalists. In April 1653, Cromwell dissolved both the Council of State and the Rump Parliament, replacing them with a new council and a Parliament of 140 members, the so-called Barebone's Parliament. In late 1653, Cromwell dissolved this parliament and took the title of lord protector. In effect, the Protectorate was one-man rule supported by the army.

The End of the Protectorate

When Cromwell died in September 1658, he was succeeded by his son, Richard (1626–1712), who possessed none of his father's ability and determination. Richard resigned in May 1659, and the army took power. Recognizing the failure of the experiment in republican government, General George Monk (1608–1670) moved to restore the monarchy.

King Charles II (r. 1660–1685)

The Restoration of 1660 brought Charles II, the eldest son of

Charles I, to the throne. In the wake of the tumultuous years after 1649, the Restoration proved popular. The question of the distribution of power between king and Parliament had not been resolved, however, nor had the conflicts over religion been settled. Charles wisely made no attempt to reestablish royal absolutism and generally avoided conflicts with Parliament.

Charles II and Religion

From 1661 to 1665, Parliament passed a series of laws known as the Clarendon Code, named for Charles II's chief adviser, the Earl of Clarendon (1609–1674). Reestablishing the Church of England, the Clarendon Code placed restrictions on Roman Catholics and non-Anglican Protestants, known as dissenters or Nonconformists.

Charles II and Foreign Policy

In 1666, the English suppressed a revolt in Scotland. From 1665 to 1667, Charles II fought a war against the Dutch, who inflicted a serious defeat on the English navy. When Parliament refused to vote sufficient taxes, the king accepted subsidies from King Louis XIV of France and in return supported the French in their war against the Dutch from 1672 to 1674.

The Question of the Succession

.   Charles II's alliance with the French increased fears of an attempt to restore Catholicism in England. These fears were already considerable, since both Charles's wife, Catherine of Braganza (1638–1705), and his brother, the Duke of York, were Roman Catholics. In 1672, the king issued a Declaration of Indulgence, removing the restrictions imposed on both Nonconformists and Catholics. Parliament forced the king to withdraw the declaration and passed the Test Act of 1673 requiring all officeholders to take oaths of allegiance to, and receive Holy Communion in, the Anglican Church. Charles was successful, however, in opposing efforts in Parliament to bar the Duke of York from the succession to the throne.

In 1678, the revelation of the Popish Plot, fabricated by Titus Oates

(1649–1705), intensified English fears of the Catholics. According to Oates, Catholics had formed a conspiracy to restore Catholicism in England. The testimony of Oates and others led to the execution of thirty-five innocent people.

King James II (r. 1685–1688)

In 1685, James II succeeded his brother, Charles II. James lacked his brother's moderation and attempted both to impose royal absolutism and to promote a restoration of Roman Catholicism. In 1687 the king issued the Declaration of Liberty of Conscience, granting freedom to all religious denominations. While this benefited Nonconformists as well as Catholics, the Protestants believed the declaration favored Roman Catholics.

The Glorious Revolution: William and Mary

In 1688, the birth of a son to James's Catholic second wife, Mary of Este (1658–1718), created a crisis, since the king would presumably have a Catholic successor. The leaders of the major political factions in Parliament, the Whigs and the Tories, joined in the Glorious Revolution to drive James from the throne. The Tories were, for the most part, royalists, landowners, and Anglicans and generally opposed the Whigs, who were largely supporters of parliamentary power, merchants, and Nonconformists. While the Tories did not share the Whigs' belief in parliamentary supremacy, they strongly supported the Anglican Church and opposed Catholicism. Some Tories remained loyal to James II and became known as Jacobites.

The king's opponents offered the crown to the Dutch ruler, William of Orange, the Protestant son-in-law of James II. William accepted the offer and invaded southwestern England in November 1688. The country demonstrated its support for William, and James fled to France in December without abdicating the throne, which Parliament then declared vacant.

The Revolution Settlement

Parliament awarded the English crown jointly to William of Orange, who now became William III (r. 1689–1702), and his wife Mary (r. 1689–1694), the daughter of James I by his first wife, a Protestant.

The Bill of Rights

In 1689, Parliament required William and Mary to accept the Bill of Rights, which established the claims that Parliament had set forth in its long conflict with the Stuarts. The Bill of Rights guaranteed members of Parliament freedom of speech and immunity from prosecution for statements made in parliamentary debate. The king was barred from levying taxes without Parliament's approval, maintaining a standing army in peacetime, and interfering in parliamentary elections. The right to trial by jury was guaranteed, and the king was barred from interfering with jurors. In addition, the Bill of Rights required frequent meetings of Parliament.

The Toleration Act

The Toleration Act, also adopted in 1689, granted some freedom of worship to Nonconformists, but the restrictions on office-holding imposed by the Test Act of 1673 technically remained in effect. After 1689, however, the Test Act was abrogated by Parliament's adoption of legislation legalizing the acts of officials who had not fulfilled the requirements of the Test Act. These officials were usually Nonconformists rather than Roman Catholics.

Provision for the Succession

Following Queen Mary's death in 1694, William III ruled alone until his death in 1702. The crown then passed to Anne (r. 1702–1714), another daughter of James II. Even before Anne's accession to the throne, it was evident that she would have no heirs. The Act of Settlement of 1701 excluded Catholics from the succession to the throne and provided that, on Anne's death, the crown would pass to Sophia, the electress of the German state of Hanover, and her heirs. Sophia was a Protestant granddaughter of James I. Under the terms of the Act of

Succession, George I, the first of the Hanoverians, became England's king in 1714.

The Development of Parliamentary Government

Under the terms of the Act of Union of 1707, England and Scotland were joined in a political union known as Great Britain. The act provided Scotland with substantial representation in the British Parliament, as well as guarantees for the established Presbyterian Church of Scotland.

The Cabinet

During most of the eighteenth century, the monarch ruled jointly with Parliament, although gradually the power of the crown declined. Following the Glorious Revolution, it was necessary for the crown to win parliamentary support for its policies. The monarchs thus began to depend increasingly on ministers who could command support in Parliament. Queen Anne and the first two Hanoverians, George I (r. 1714–1727) and George II (r. 1727–1760), relied on their ministers for developing policies and directing the conduct of government affairs.

The Prime Minister

Gradually, one member of the cabinet, the prime minister, emerged as its leader. Robert Walpole (1676–1745), who served under both George I and George II, was Britain's first real prime minister. A Whig member of Parliament, he became a member of George I's cabinet in 1721 and dominated the government until 1742.

The Cabinet's Responsibility to Parliament

Later in the eighteenth century, George III (r. 1760–1820) attempted to rule in association with ministers of his own choosing, who did not have the support of a parliamentary majority. George III ultimately failed in this effort, and by the end of the century, the principle of cabinet responsibility to the Parliament was clearly established in British political practice.

During the seventeenth century, England experienced a long conflict between Parliament and the Stuart monarchs. Following the Civil War of the 1640s and the execution of Charles I, England embarked on an abortive experiment in republican government. The Restoration of 1660, which returned the Stuarts to the throne in the person of Charles II, did not provide a resolution of the political and religious differences between king and Parliament. These issues quickly came to a head during the reign of James II, resulting in the Glorious Revolution of 1688.

The revolutionary settlement reaffirmed the established Church of England and placed restrictions on the power of the crown. During the eighteenth century, the power of Parliament continued to increase, while that of the crown declined. At the same time, the British constitutional monarchy became a model that reformers on the continent of Europe wished to emulate.

Recommended Reading

Ashley, Maurice. *England in the Seventeenth Century, 1603–1714* (1961).

Ashley, Maurice. *The Glorious Revolution of 1688* (1966).

Ashley, Maurice. *James II* (1977).

Aylmer, G. E. *Rebellion or Revolution: England, 1640–1660* (1987).

Aylmer, G. E. *A Short History of Seventeenth-Century England* (1963).

Cannon, John, ed. *The Whig Ascendancy* (1981).

Carlton, Charles. *Archbishop William Laud* (1987).

Fraser, Antonia. *Cromwell, the Lord Protector* (1973).

Fraser, Antonia. *King James VI of Scotland, I of England* (1975).

Fraser, Antonia. *Royal Charles: Charles II and the Restoration* (1979).

Haley, Kenneth H. D. *Politics in the Reign of Charles II* (1985).

Hill, Christopher. *The Century of Revolution, 1603–1714* (1961).

Hirst, Derek. *Authority and Conflict: England, 1603–1658* (1986).

Lockyer, Roger *Tudor and Stuart Britain, 1471–1714* (1964).

Plumb, J. H. *England in the Eighteenth Century, 1714–1815* (1950).

Sinclair-Stevenson, Christopher. *Blood Royal: The Illustrious House of Hanover* (1980).

Wedgwood, C. V. *The King's Peace, 1637–1641* (1955).

Wedgwood, C. V. *The King's War, 1641–1647* (1959).

Wedgwood, C. V. *Oliver Cromwell* (rev. ed., 1973).

CHAPTER 8

Absolute Monarchy in France

Time Line

1589	The Wars of Religion end; Henry of Navarre becomes King Henry IV
1589–1610	Reign of King Henry IV
1598	Henry IV issues the Edict of Nantes
1610–1643	Reign of King Louis XIII
1621	Cardinal Richelieu becomes Louis XIII's chief minister
1642	Richelieu dies; Cardinal Mazarin becomes chief minister.
1643–1715	Reign of King Louis XIV

1648	The Peace of Westphalia ends the Thirty Years' War
1648–1653	The Fronde threatens the power of the French monarchy
1659	The Treaty of the Pyrenees ends France's war with Spain
1661	Louis XIV's personal rule begins following Mazarin's death
1662	Jean-Baptiste Colbert becomes Louis XIV's chief minister
1667–1668	Louis XIV fights the War of Devolution
1672–1678	Louis XIV fights the Dutch War
1685	Louis XIV revokes the Edict of Nantes
1688–1697	Louis XIV fights the War of the League of Augsburg
1701–1714	Louis XIV fights the War of the Spanish Succession
1713–1714	The Peace of Utrecht and the Treaty of Rastatt and Baden end the War of the Spanish Succession
1715	Louis XIV dies

In the wake of the disastrous Wars of Religion in the late sixteenth century, King Henry IV, the first of the French Bourbon kings, began restoring the power of the French monarchy. Then, in the early seventeenth century, Cardinal Richelieu, the chief minister of King Louis XIII, raised the authority of the French monarchy to new heights and increased France's power in Europe.

Cardinal Mazarin continued Richelieu's work during the early years of the reign of King Louis XIV, further reducing the power of the nobility. After Louis XIV's personal rule began in 1661, the French absolute monarchy stood at the height of its power both in France and

Europe. The wars of Louis XIV proved extremely costly, however, and left France a burden of debt that would lead the French monarchy to collapse in the eighteenth century. Nevertheless, in the seventeenth century, France was the most powerful country in Europe.

King Henry IV (r. 1589–1610)

In 1589, at the end of the Wars of Religion, Henry of Navarre, the first Bourbon to wear the French crown, became king (see Chapter 5). As Henry IV, he began the process of reestablishing the power of the French monarchy. Henry had been a Protestant, but in 1593 he converted to Roman Catholicism, thereby embracing the faith of the overwhelming majority of his subjects.

In an effort to heal the wounds caused by the Wars of Religion, in 1598 Henry IV issued the Edict of Nantes, granting limited toleration to the more than one million French Protestants, the Huguenots.

The Duke of Sully (1560–1641)

The Duke of Sully served as Henry IV's finance minister and deserves the credit for much of the king's success. To increase the crown's income, Sully introduced sound accounting practices and sought to eliminate financial inefficiency and corruption. He did not, however, attempt any fundamental financial reforms, such as ending the tax-exempt status of the nobility and clergy. As a consequence, the tax burden borne by the bourgeoisie, peasantry, and working classes remained considerable.

While Sully tended to neglect industrial development, he promoted the construction of roads and canals. He also inaugurated the system of sending royal officials into the provinces to deal with many of the functions of local government, thereby reducing the nobility's influence in local affairs.

Sully's policies served to promote both the prosperity of the French economy and the political and financial strength of the monarchy.

King Louis XIII (r. 1610–1643)

In 1610, a Catholic fanatic assassinated Henry IV. During the more than a decade of political turmoil that followed the assassination, Henry IV's widow, Marie de Médicis (1573–1642), acted as regent for her son, King Louis XIII, who was only ten years old when he succeeded his father. The queen regent arranged for her son's later marriage to a Spanish princess. She also dismissed Sully, leaving France without strong leadership. The nobility and the Huguenots took advantage of the situation to press their own interests at the expense of royal authority.

Cardinal Richelieu (1585–1642)

In 1621, Armand-Jean du Plessis, the Cardinal-Duke of Richelieu, became Louis XIII's chief minister, remaining in that position until his death in 1642. With the strong support of the king, Richelieu developed and executed policies designed to reassert royal control over the nobility, destroy the political privileges of the Huguenots, and increase French power in Europe.

Richelieu and the Nobility

The French nobility had not yet been fully subordinated to the crown, and many noblemen routinely defied the king's authority. Aristocrats who held high offices in the government, the military, and the church often used their power to advance their own individual and class interests. Richelieu gradually reduced the influence of the nobility in the government. He extended the system established under Henry IV of sending royal officials into the provinces, establishing the office of *intendant*. These officials became important instruments in the process of centralizing political authority in the hands of the king's government. This reduced the power of the nobility, as did Richelieu's efforts to appoint more members of the middle class, especially lawyers, to the royal administration.

Richelieu and the Huguenots

The Edict of Nantes had not only granted limited religious toleration to the Huguenots but had also enabled them to establish centers of political power in their fortified towns. In 1625, several prominent Huguenot noblemen led a revolt against Richelieu. In 1627, Richelieu launched an assault against the Huguenot stronghold at LaRochelle on the Atlantic coast. Following a siege of fourteen months, his forces took the city in 1628. The next year, Richelieu deprived the Huguenots of the right to hold fortified cities, but he preserved their freedom to practice their religion. He thus succeeded in destroying the Huguenots' independent political power without initiating a policy of religious persecution that might have led to civil war.

Foreign Affairs Under Louis XIII and Richelieu

French power and prestige in Europe had declined during the years of domestic turmoil that followed the murder of Henry IV in 1610. In his effort to restore France's position in Europe, Richelieu revived the traditional French opposition to the Hapsburgs. During the Thirty Years' War (1618–1648), Catholic France joined with Protestant Sweden and the Protestant German states to fight the Catholic Hapsburgs (see Chapter 5). By the time the war ended with the signing of the Peace of Westphalia in 1648, France had become the most powerful country on the European continent.

King Louis XIV (r. 1643–1715)

The long reign of King Louis XIV had a powerful impact on France and Europe.

Cardinal Mazarin (1602–1661)

When Richelieu died in 1642, he was succeeded by Cardinal Mazarin, who remained in power following the accession of Louis XIV in 1643 until his own death in 1661. Louis XIV was only five when he became king, and Mazarin ruled with the queen regent, Anne of Austria (1601–1666), the king's mother.

Mazarin continued Richelieu's policies in both domestic and foreign affairs. Following the end of the Thirty Years' War in 1648, France remained at war with the Spanish Hapsburgs, acquiring part of

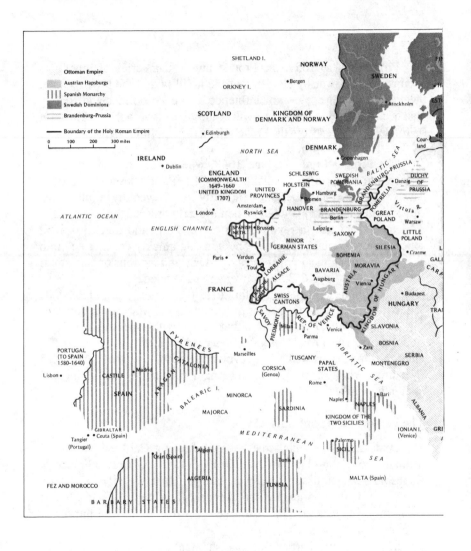

Europe, 1648

the Spanish Netherlands under the terms of the Treaty of the Pyrenees of 1659.

The Fronde

From 1648 to 1653, the Fronde involved a series of rebellions against royal power by elements of the nobility and the townspeople, whose traditional position of influence in French politics and society had been undermined by the growth of the crown's authority. (The term "Fronde" is derived from the French slang for the slingshot used by boys in the streets of Paris.)

The Fronde began in June 1648, when the Parlement of Paris objected to Mazarin's financial policy. (The Parlement was a court of law, comprised of members of the nobility and the wealthy middle class, rather than a legislative body.) When Mazarin ordered the arrest of the Parlement's leaders, a revolt broke out in Paris and quickly spread among the provincial nobility. The uprising quickly degenerated into infighting among the nobility, as individuals and factions pursued their own ambitions. By 1653, the movement had ended.

The Fronde represented a threat to the crown's power, and its failure demonstrated the success of Richelieu and Mazarin in developing strong political institutions that could withstand the nobility's opposition. The Fronde ultimately served to strengthen the crown, since the disorder created by the revolt convinced many that being ruled by a strong king was preferable to being dominated by competing and contentious noblemen.

The Personal Rule of Louis XIV

Louis XIV's personal rule began following Cardinal Mazarin's death in 1661. Until his own death in 1715, Louis XIV ruled France as an absolute monarch, supposedly declaring: *"L'état, c'est moi"* ("I am the state"). One important instrument of the king's absolute power was the *lettre de cachet,* an administrative order that authorized imprisonment or exile without trial.

In 1660, Louis married the Spanish infanta, Marie Thérèse (1638–1683), the daughter of King Philip IV of Spain, for political reasons.

Louis XIV and the Nobility

The experience of the Fronde taught Louis XIV to distrust the nobility, and he now sought to destroy whatever remained of their ability to oppose his will. He appointed to high office more men of middle-class origin, continuing the traditional practice of selling titles of nobility. The creation of hundreds of these new "nobles of the robe" served to undermine the prestige of the old "nobility of the sword."

Bishop Bossuet and Divine Right

The theory of the divine right of kings provided an intellectual justification for absolute monarchy. A French bishop, Jacques Bossuet (1627–1704), set forth this theory in the treatise *Politics Drawn From Holy Scripture,* published about 1670. Referring to the Bible as the authority for his arguments, Bossuet maintained that the king ruled by the will of God and was responsible only to God and not to any earthly power. Obedience to the will of the king was a religious obligation.

Versailles

Louis XIV spent immense sums on the construction of his vast and lavishly furnished palace at Versailles with its immense formal gardens. Located outside Paris, Versailles served as both the king's residence and the center of government.

At Versailles, the Sun King, as Louis was known, was surrounded by his servants and courtiers and a privileged group of French nobility, who, having lost their independence, were now reduced to fawning over the king.

Jean-Baptiste Colbert (1619–1683)

Colbert served Louis XIV as controller general of the finances from 1662 to 1683. A mercantilist, he sought to promote national economic prosperity by maximizing exports, limiting imports, and building up France's supply of gold and silver. He expanded the government's role in the economy, encouraging industry, reducing domestic customs barriers, and attempting to eliminate the ability of the nobility to interfere with trade. Colbert promoted the building of roads and canals and the expansion of France's merchant fleet. On the negative side, mercantilist regulations were often excessively restrictive, limiting innovation in industry and trade. As a consequence, progressive businessmen came increasingly to oppose mercantilist policies.

State Finances Under Louis XIV

Despite Colbert's policies, the government continued to depend on a haphazard financial system. The nobility and clergy remained exempt from most direct taxes; the wealthy middle class succeeded in evading many taxes. Thus, the main tax burden fell on the peasants and the lower middle class. The burden on the peasants was especially heavy, since they had to pay a substantial portion of their income in the form of taxes and other levies to the government, the church, and the landowners. The peasants were also subject to the *corvée* (forced labor on the roads).

The French government continued the traditional practice of farming out taxes to tax collectors who paid for the privilege. These tax collectors customarily forwarded only a small percentage of their receipts to the government.

While France was the richest and most powerful country on the European continent, the inadequacy of the government's financial system would become a major source of weakness for the monarchy.

Louis XIV and the Catholic Church

As an absolute monarch, Louis XIV wanted to extend his authority more completely over the Roman Catholic Church. Louis strongly defended the policy known as Gallicanism that had been established by his predecessors. Under this policy, the king exercised administrative control over the church in France while recognizing the pope's authority over faith and morals.

Louis XIV and the Jansenists

Although Louis XIV insisted on his right to control the administration of the French Catholic Church, he was devout in matters of faith and ardently opposed any teaching that deviated from orthodox

Catholic doctrine. This resulted in his campaigns against both the Jansenists and the Huguenots.

The Jansenists were followers of the teaching of Cornelius Jansen (1585–1638), a Flemish theologian. Jansen's writings on the theology of St. Augustine appeared in 1640, two years after his death. Jansenism resembled Calvinism in its emphasis on predestination and its insistence that God's grace comes as a gift, irrespective of any good works the believer may perform. In addition, like the Calvinists, the Jansenists insisted on a puritanical morality.

Both Pope Innocent X (r. 1644–1655) and Pope Clement XI (r. 1700–1721) condemned Jansenist teachings, and Louis XIV ordered the closing of the large Jansenist monastery at Port-Royal, near Versailles, in 1704.

Revocation of the Edict of Nantes

Although the Edict of Nantes had granted limited toleration to the Huguenots, France's overwhelming Catholic majority remained antagonistic to them. By the 1660s, the Huguenots constituted about 10 percent of the population.

Like most of his fellow rulers, Louis XIV believed that religious unity was a prerequisite for political unity. In October 1685, the king revoked the Edict of Nantes and initiated a campaign of active persecution.   Many Huguenots accepted forced conversion to Roman Catholicism, but others resisted. While they were not permitted to emigrate, some 200,000 Huguenots nevertheless fled, leaving their property behind. They found refuge in England, the Netherlands, Brandenburg and other Protestant German states, Switzerland, and the English and Dutch colonies in North America and South Africa. Many of these Huguenots were well-educated and industrious, and their departure deprived France of their knowledge and skills.

The Wars of Louis XIV

The Peace of Westphalia (1648) and the Treaty of the Pyrenees (1659) had broken the power of the Hapsburgs and created the possibility that France could establish its dominance over the European continent. The achievement of this ambition could be blocked only by an alliance of the other European powers.

France was at war during much of Louis XIV's reign, as the king sought to increase French power in Europe and advance France's frontiers in the northeast at the expense of the Spanish Netherlands and the Holy Roman Empire. He fought four major wars over the course of forty-six years.

The War of Devolution (1667–1668)

The War of Devolution began with a French invasion of the Spanish Netherlands (modern Belgium) and the Franche-Comté, also a Spanish possession, on France's eastern border. The Triple Alliance of England, Holland, and Sweden intervened in the war and forced Louis to withdraw. The Treaty of Aix-la-Chapelle (1668) awarded France several towns along the border of the Spanish Netherlands.

The Dutch War (1672–1678)

Louis XIV succeeded in breaking up the Triple Alliance by signing the Treaty of Dover with King Charles II of England in 1670. Louis then invaded Holland in 1672. William of Orange was able to defend his country only by opening the dikes, which resulted in the flooding of much of northern Holland. William also secured the support of the Holy Roman emperor, Brandenburg, and Spain. Under the terms of the Peace of Nijmegen of 1678-79, France gained the Franche-Comté and several additional towns along the border of the Spanish Netherlands.

The War of the League of Augsburg (1688–1697)

Also known as the Nine Years' War, the War of the League of Augsburg resulted from the efforts of Louis XIV to push France's frontier to the northeast into territory along the Rhine River. William of Orange, who became King William III of England in 1689, took the lead in forming a new alliance against the French. While the French made substantial conquests during the war, the Treaty of Ryswick of 1697 deprived Louis of most of his gains, although France retained Alsace, including the city of Strasbourg.

The War of the Spanish Succession (1701–1714)

The last of Louis XIV's wars, the War of the Spanish Succession, was both the longest and the hardest fought.

When the childless King Charles II (r. 1665–1700), the last Hapsburg king of Spain, died in 1700, he left the Spanish crown to Philip of Anjou, the grandson of Louis XIV. The Hapsburg Holy Roman emperor Leopold challenged the succession, claiming the Spanish crown for his son Charles. The stakes were great, since the victor would acquire not only Spain and its possessions in Europe but also Spain's overseas colonies with their vast wealth. The other powers of Europe could not permit France to acquire Spain and its domains and would accept a Bourbon as king of Spain only if he and his heirs were barred from ever holding the French crown as well. England, Holland, and the Holy Roman emperor joined forces to oppose the French.

England played a major role in the war against Louis XIV. The great English general, John Churchill, the Duke of Marlborough (1650–1722), joined with the Hapsburg commander, Prince Eugene of Savoy (1663–1736), to defeat the French in 1704 at Blenheim in southern Germany and in other battles. In 1704, England occupied Gibraltar, thereby acquiring an important naval base in the Mediterranean.

France signed peace treaties with her enemies, except the Hapsburgs, at Utrecht in 1713. The Treaty of Baden and Rastatt of 1714 ended the war with the Hapsburgs. The peace settlement recognized Philip of Anjou as King Philip V (r. 1700–1746) of Spain, but provided that neither he nor his successors could occupy the French throne. The Austrian Hapsburgs were compensated by the acquisition of the Spanish Netherlands and also received Naples, Sardinia, and Milan. Sicily was awarded to the Italian state of Savoy, which exchanged it in 1720 with the Austrian Hapsburgs for Sardinia. The French lost a number of colonies that the English had taken during the war, including Newfoundland, Acadia (Nova Scotia), and the Hudson Bay area, although France kept Quebec. The English retained Gibraltar and Minorca and also acquired the *Asiento,* a contract to supply slaves to Spanish America for thirty years. Finally, the elector of Brandenburg was recognized as king of Prussia.

From 1589 to the early 1640s, Kings Henry IV and Louis XIII and their chief ministers, the Duke of Sully and Cardinal Richelieu, established the foundations of the French absolute monarchy. In the mid-seventeenth century, Cardinal Mazarin's success in suppressing the Fronde marked the end of the nobility's efforts to reassert its independence of royal authority, although the nobles retained some of their traditional privileges.

During his long reign, King Louis XIV enjoyed virtually unchallenged authority. Nevertheless, his revocation of the Edict of Nantes was a blunder, while his wars proved to be enormously expensive. When Louis XIV died in 1715, he left a legacy of financial problems for his successors to deal with.

Recommended Reading

Barry, Joseph. *Passions and Politics: A Biography of Versailles* (1972).

Bergin, Joseph. *Cardinal Richelieu: Power and the Pursuit of Wealth* (1985).

Bernier, Olivier. *Louis XIV: A Royal Life* (1987).

Durant, Will and Ariel. *The Age of Louis XIV* (1963).

Goubert, Pierre. *The French Peasantry in the Seventeenth Century* (1986).

Goubert, Pierre. *Louis XIV and Twenty Million Frenchmen* (1970).

Hatton, Ragnhild. *Europe in the Age of Louis XIV* (1969).

Lewis, W. H. *The Splendid Century* (1954).

Ranum, Orest A. *Richelieu and the Great Nobility* (1963).

Scoville, Warren C. *The Persecution of the Huguenots and French Economic Development, 1680–1720* (1960).

Tapié, Victor-L. *France in the Age of Louis XIII and Richelieu* (1974).

Treasure, G. R. R. *Seventeenth Century France* (1966).

Wedgwood, C. V. *Richelieu and the French Monarchy* (1950).

Wolf, John B. *The Emergence of the Great Powers, 1685–1715* (1951).

CHAPTER 9

The Emergence of Austria, Prussia, and Russia

Time Line

1700–1721	Russia fights the Great Northern War against Sweden
1703	Peter the Great establishes St. Petersburg
1711–1740	Reign of the Hapsburg Charles VI
1713–1740	Reign of Frederick William I of Prussia
1740	Maria Theresa inherits the Hapsburg domains
1740–1786	Reign of Frederick the Great of Prussia
1740–1748	The War of the Austrian Succession
1765	Joseph II is elected Holy Roman emperor
1762–1796	Reign of Catherine the Great of Russia
1769–1774	Russo-Turkish War
1780	Maria Theresa dies; Joseph II begins his personal rule (to 1790)
1785	Catherine the Great issues the Charter of the Nobility
1790–1792	Reign of the Hapsburg Leopold II

In Central and Eastern Europe, the late seventeenth and early eighteenth centuries witnessed the emergence of three major powers: Austria, Prussia, and Russia.

In the late seventeenth century, the Hapsburg family continued to control the title of Holy Roman emperor. While the Holy Roman Empire contained within its borders most of the German lands of central Europe, it was a loose union of over three hundred virtually independent states. However, the Hapsburgs possessed a power base within their own personal domains, which included Austria, Bohemia, and Hungary. Hapsburg power and influence in Europe was based on these domains, rather than on their possession of the imperial title.

In northern Germany, the Hohenzollern family began to create a strong power base of its own in Brandenburg, one of the states of the

Holy Roman Empire. By the early eighteenth century, the Hohenzollerns had made Prussia into one of the major powers of Europe.

Farther to the east, in Russia, the Romanov dynasty came to power in 1613. Michael Romanov and his successors established a powerful monarchy, and by the time of Peter the Great, Russia had entered the ranks of the great powers of Europe.

The Emergence of Austria

The Austrian Hapsburgs faced many problems in consolidating power in their domains, which varied considerably in language and traditions. While Austria was inhabited primarily by Germans, the Czechs were the dominant nationality in Bohemia. The Magyars were predominant in Hungary. In addition, the Hapsburg domains included Slovaks, Croatians, Slovenes, Rumanians, Italians, and by the late eighteenth century, Poles.

Leopold I (r. 1657–1705)

In the late seventeenth century, Leopold I successfully resisted both the Ottoman Empire and King Louis XIV of France. In 1683, the Turks laid siege to Vienna. In September, following a two-months' siege, a force of imperial troops and a Polish army, led by Poland's king, John Sobieski (r. 1674–1696), came to the aid of Vienna, and the Turks were driven back. The Hapsburg army then took the offensive against the Turks, capturing Budapest, Hungary's capital, in 1686. Under the terms of the Treaty of Karlowitz (1699), Leopold acquired virtually all of Hungary. Leopold succeeded in imposing his authority over Hungary's Magyar aristocracy.

The war against the Turks marked the emergence of Prince Eugene of Savoy (1663–1736) as the Hapsburgs' most eminent general. In 1704, during the War of the Spanish Succession, Prince Eugene joined forces with the Duke of Marlborough, his English ally, to win a decisive victory over the French at the Battle of Blenheim. This victory, coming on the eve of Leopold I's death in 1705, confirmed Austria's position as one of the great powers of Europe.

Charles VI (r. 1711–1740) and the Pragmatic Sanction

At his death in 1705, Leopold I was succeeded by Joseph I (r. 1705–1711), who continued his predecessor's policies. Prince Eugene won additional victories over the French as the War of the Spanish Succession entered its final years.

In 1711, Charles VI succeeded his brother as Holy Roman emperor and ruler of Austria. Although the Hapsburgs failed in their effort to prevent a Bourbon from acquiring the Spanish throne, the peace settlement of 1713–1714 awarded the Hapsburgs the Spanish Netherlands and Spain's holdings in Italy as compensation.

Charles VI failed to produce a male heir and to avoid a conflict over the succession, sought to win the support of his nobility and the great powers of Europe for the Pragmatic Sanction of 1713. The Pragmatic Sanction provided for the inheritance of the Hapsburg holdings by his daughter, Maria Theresa. Following the death of Charles VI, however, Frederick the Great of Prussia invaded Austrian Silesia, beginning the War of the Austrian Succession.

Maria Theresa (r. 1740–1780)

During the War of the Austrian Succession from 1740 to 1748, Maria Theresa successfully defended her right to inherit the Austrian Hapsburg domains, although she lost Silesia to the Prussians. While her husband, Francis of Lorraine, received the title of Holy Roman Emperor Francis I (r. 1745–1765), he took relatively little interest in the government, leaving Maria Theresa in control.

The war convinced Maria Theresa of the need to extend her control more completely over her domains. Although she did not attempt to abolish the regional diets dominated by the local nobility, she succeeded in stripping them of most of their administrative functions, creating a centralized bureaucracy to control local affairs. German became the language of administration throughout Austria, and taxes were imposed on the nobility and clergy. Although Maria Theresa was personally devout, she established the state's control over the administration of the Roman Catholic Church.

Joseph II (r. 1765–1790)

Maria Theresa's son, Joseph II, was elected Holy Roman emperor on his father's death in 1765. His personal rule of Austria did not begin, however, until his mother's death in 1780.

As Austria's ruler, Joseph II sought to govern in the spirit of enlightened despotism, initiating a far-reaching program of reforms. His goal was to modernize his instruments of government in an effort to increase the crown's authority over the diverse Hapsburg domains and in particular, to establish royal power more firmly over the church and the nobility.

Joseph II and the Catholic Church

While Joseph II was a practicing Catholic, he granted limited religious toleration to his other Christian subjects and removed some of the restrictions on the Jews. He abolished several hundred monasteries and convents and confiscated much of the land of the church, arguing that the church's use of this land was unproductive. Revenues that had previously gone to the church now went into the state treasury, and the clergy became, in effect, employees of the state. He reduced the power of the papacy in Austria by requiring that all communications to and from Rome be forwarded through the government in Vienna. In addition, bishops and other high-ranking churchmen were required to swear obedience to the ruler.

Reforms of Joseph II

To promote trade, Joseph II eliminated many internal tariffs and encouraged road building and improvements in river transportation. He opposed serfdom, in the belief that, if the peasants were free, they would become more productive. A series of decrees issued in the early 1780s freed the serfs in Austria, Bohemia, Hungary, and Transylvania. In 1789, he abolished the *robot,* which obliged peasants to perform services for the landowning nobility. The service obligation was replaced with a tax. Only a part of the proceeds would go to the landowners; the state took the balance.

Leopold II (r. 1790–1792) and the End of Reform

The sweeping reforms of Joseph II came with little preparation and created much turmoil. In many areas, the peasants rose up in revolt to defend their new rights and to claim others, while the nobility protested reforms that worked to their disadvantage. Following Joseph II's death, the new emperor, Leopold II, repealed most of Joseph's reforms in an effort to conciliate the nobility. Serfdom and other feudal obligations, including the *robot*, remained in effect in most of the Hapsburg domains until 1848. Any hope for renewed reform were dashed by Leopold II's reactionary successor, who ruled first as Holy Roman Emperor Francis II (r. 1792–1806) and then, following Napoleon's abolition of the Holy Roman Empire, as the first emperor of Austria, Francis I (r. 1806–1835).

The Emergence of Prussia

In 1415, the Hohenzollern family began to rule as electors of Brandenburg in northern Germany. The Hohenzollerns gradually increased their holdings so that by the late seventeenth century their domains were second in size only to those of the Hapsburgs among the princes of the Holy Roman Empire. The Hohenzollerns now confronted the task of bringing their scattered lands together to form a single unified state.

Frederick William, the Great Elector (r. 1640–1688)

Frederick William, the Great Elector, began his rule at a time when the Hohenzollern domains had been devastated by the Thirty Years' War, which ended in 1648. Beginning the process of creating a modern state, the Great Elector reduced the autonomy of the Junkers (the nobility) and the estates (the nobles' assemblies). He established the civil service and the army as cornerstones of state power, compelling the nobility to pay taxes to support the army. He did not interfere, however, with the Junkers' complete control over the serfs who worked their land or with their dominance over the towns. Furthermore, the burden of taxes fell most heavily on the peasants and townspeople.

Alliance with the Junkers

The Great Elector recruited members of the nobility to serve in the civil service and as army officers. The Junkers came to dominate both the higher ranks of the civil service and the officer corps of the army. In this way, the power of the Hohenzollerns came to be based on the ruler's alliance with the aristocracy rather than on his opposition to it, as was the case in France and other countries.

Religious Toleration

In religious affairs, the Great Elector practiced a policy of toleration, welcoming to his domain some 20,000 French Huguenots, many Polish Jews, and other refugees from persecution.

Frederick I (r. 1688–1713)

Frederick I proved to be uncharacteristic of the Hohenzollerns, who typically focused their attention on the army and administration. A patron of the arts and learning, Frederick enjoyed living in luxury. He can, however, be credited with one major achievement in the development of Hohenzollern power. During the War of the Spanish Succession, he supported the Hapsburg Holy Roman emperor, who permitted him to assume the title King in Prussia. On his death in 1713, Frederick I passed the royal title to his son.

Frederick William I (r. 1713–1740)

Frederick William I replaced the extravagances of his father with a policy of austerity, imposing strict economies and practicing sound management in an effort to maximize Prussia's limited resources. This policy led to a substantial increase in the state's income.

Increase of Military Power

Known as the "Sergeant King," Frederick William more than doubled the size of the Prussian army from about 40,000 in 1713 to over 80,000 in 1740. Prussia thus came to have the third- or fourth-largest army in Europe, although it was thirteenth in the size of its population. The army officers increasingly became a privileged social class, and the officer corps attracted the most talented sons of the Junkers.

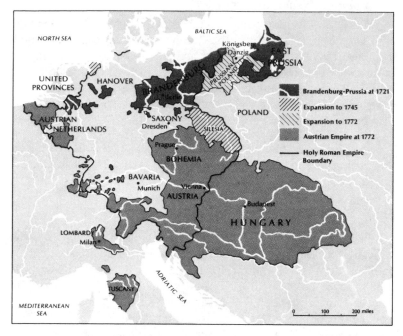

Prussia 1721–1772 and the Hapsburg Empire

While Frederick William was clearly a militarist, he sought to avoid war. The army was, above all, a sign of Prussian power rather than an instrument of aggression.

Frederick the Great (r. 1740–1786)

Frederick II, who became known as Frederick the Great, established Prussia's position among the great powers of Europe. Almost immediately after becoming king in 1740, he invaded Silesia, thereby beginning the War of the Austrian Succession (1740–1748). During the Seven Years' War (1756–1763), Frederick succeeded in retaining Silesia. Later in his reign, in 1772, he participated in the first partition of Poland (see Chapter 10).

Reform Program

A successful enlightened despot, Frederick the Great was familiar with the ideas of the eighteenth-century reformers and a friend of Voltaire. His reform program was designed above all to increase the power of the Prussian monarchy.

Modernizing his government, Frederick created a number of new agencies, including the bureaus of commerce and industry, excise and tolls, mines, and forestry. With the assistance of French experts, he reorganized the system of indirect taxes, which soon provided the state with more revenue than direct taxation on individuals. Frederick directed the codification of Prussian law and abolished the use of torture in legal proceedings.

Economic and Religious Policies

Frederick actively promoted economic development, encouraging the expansion of industry in Silesia and elsewhere. Tariffs were imposed to protect Prussia's young industries, while internal barriers to trade were reduced. The Bank of Berlin made credit available for economic development, and new canals were built. Swamps were drained to make more land available for agriculture. New crops were introduced, and for the first time, potatoes and turnips were grown extensively.

In religious policy, Frederick the Great permitted Catholics to settle in predominantly Lutheran areas and respected the rights of the predominantly Catholic population of Silesia.

The Emergence of Russia

In 1613, the boyars (Russian nobility) elected Michael Romanov (r. 1613–1654) as tsar. The Romanovs continued to rule Russia until the last tsar, Nicholas II, was overthrown in 1917. Michael Romanov and his successors reestablished stability following the turmoil of the Time of Troubles (1584–1613), although the boyars continued to challenge the tsar's authority, as did the *streltsi*, the guards of the Moscow garrison.

Peter the Great (r. 1682–1725)

Peter I, known to history as Peter the Great, became tsar at the age of ten, as coruler with his sickly half-brother, Ivan V (r. 1682–1696). Following Ivan V's death in 1696, Peter assumed full power.

As a young man, Peter was fascinated with Western Europe. In 1697, he became the first tsar ever to travel in the West, visiting Prussia, the Netherlands, and England, where he studied military organization, shipbuilding, commerce, and finance.

The *streltsi* took advantage of Peter's absence and rebelled in 1698. Rushing back to Russia, the tsar brutally suppressed the revolt. Some 1,200 rebels were executed, and their corpses were placed on display as a warning to other would-be rebels.

Peter's visit to Western Europe increased his determination to westernize and modernize his country. He moved to establish his control over the boyars, and he set out to promote economic development, strengthen Russia's armed forces, reorganize the central administration, and extend state control over the Russian Orthodox Church.

Peter the Great and the Boyars

Peter began his campaign for westernization by ordering the boyars to be clean shaven and to adopt Western dress. He also ended the traditional seclusion of upper-class Russian women and demanded that they participate in social functions with men.

Peter insisted that the nobility serve the state in either the civil service or the military. In 1722, he issued the Table of Ranks, which provided that social position and privileges be based on an individual's rank in the bureaucracy or the military, rather than on his noble status.

Peter the Great and Economic Development

To promote the modernization of Russia's economy, Peter ordered the boyars to send their sons to Western Europe to learn technical skills, and he encouraged Western European craftsmen and technicians to settle in Russia. He established schools and hospitals and founded the Russian Academy of Science.

Peter provided subsidies to assist the expansion of industry by private operators and established state mines and factories to insure adequate supplies for his military endeavors.

Peter's westernization program and his wars were expensive, forcing the tsar to use every available means to raise money. He established a head tax on every male, known as the soul tax, and collected the income from monopolies on a wide variety of products, including caviar and salt.

While westernization modernized Russia, it also divided the Russian people between the small, semiwesternized upper class and the mass of the people, who were primarily peasants living in poverty and ignorance.

Peter the Great and the Administration

In reorganizing his central administration, Peter followed the model of Sweden, where government departments were headed by colleges consisting of several individuals rather than a single minister. Peter created nine colleges of eleven members each to administer foreign affairs, the army, the navy, commerce, mines and manufactures, income, expenditures, justice, and control. He also established a Senate of nine members, with the authority to supervise the administration and direct its operations when the tsar was absent. In 1711, Peter took a new title: Emperor of All Russia.

Peter the Great and the Russian Orthodox Church

The Russian Orthodox Church was extremely conservative in both its theology and its attitudes toward westernization. To bring the church more completely under secular control, Peter abolished the office of patriarch. In place of the patriarchate, Peter established an agency that became known as the Holy Synod. The Holy Synod consisted of a committee of bishops, headed by a layman, the procurator-general.

The Wars of Peter the Great

In an attempt to gain territory on the Black Sea and the Baltic, Peter the Great fought wars against both the Ottoman Empire and Sweden. After going to war against the Turks in 1695, the Russians captured Azov on the Black Sea in 1696. In 1711, however, the Turks regained the port.

Peter was more successful in his war against Sweden, the Great

Northern War, which began in 1700. Sweden's King Charles XII (r. 1697–1718) quickly defeated the Russians at the Battle of Narva, but the Swedes failed to follow up this victory. In 1709, Peter won a major victory over the Swedes at the Battle of Poltava, but the war continued for several more years. The Peace of Nystad of 1721 confirmed Russia's acquisition of several Swedish provinces on the Baltic, including Karelia, Ingria, Estonia, and Livonia. While the war was still in progress, in 1703, Peter established his new capital of St. Petersburg on the Gulf of Finland. St. Petersburg served as Peter's "window on the West," a symbol of Russia's new Western orientation.

The Succession to Peter the Great

Peter the Great was hostile to his son, Alexis, and had him imprisoned in 1718. Alexis died in prison under mysterious circumstances. Prior to his own death in 1725, Peter failed to designate a successor. For the next generation, the army and the nobility controlled the succession. A series of rulers proved ineffective, and the power of the crown declined. In 1762, the weak and incompetent Peter III became tsar. After only a few months on the throne, he was overthrown and murdered with the approval of his wife, Catherine, a German princess from Pomerania.

Catherine the Great (r. 1762–1796)

Like Joseph II of Austria and Frederick the Great of Prussia, Catherine admired the reform ideas of the Enlightenment (see Chapter 12). She corresponded actively with Voltaire and other prominent eighteenth-century thinkers. Nevertheless, she did little to reform or modernize Russia. In 1767, Catherine established a Legislative Commission of over five hundred members to propose reforms in the legal system. The commission represented all classes in Russian society except the serfs, and in their deliberations, each faction seemed intent on promoting its own interests. The Legislative Commission accomplished little, and Catherine dismissed it in 1768.

In economic affairs, Catherine continued the program of development initiated by Peter the Great. She reduced internal barriers to trade, while Russia's exports of flax, furs, grain, and naval stores increased.

Catherine the Great and the Nobility

During the years following the death of Peter the Great, the nobility had escaped many of the restrictions that Peter had imposed on them. Their obligation to provide service to the state had been reduced, while their control over the serfs had been increased. Although Catherine desired to increase the crown's power, she owed her position to the nobility. She rewarded her supporters with grants of state lands inhabited by serfs who now became the property of the nobles.

From 1773 to 1775, Emelian Pugachev, a Don Cossack, led a great serf revolt in the Volga region. After Pugachev's capture and beheading, Catherine reorganized local government, creating fifty provinces in place of the twenty former provinces. The local nobility controlled the governments of the new provinces.

The Charter of the Nobility, issued in 1785, formally recognized the rights and privileges of the nobility, including exemption from taxes and military service and giving them total control over their estates and serfs.

The Wars of Catherine the Great

From 1769 to 1774, Russia fought a successful war against the Ottoman Empire. Under the terms of the Treaty of Kutchuk-Kainardji (1774), Russia acquired most of the Ottoman lands on the northern coast of the Black Sea, as well as full access to the Turkish Straits joining the Black and Aegean seas. The treaty recognized the independence of the Crimea, which Russia proceeded to annex in 1783. The treaty also contained a vague clause recognizing Russia as the protector of the Orthodox Christian subjects of the Ottoman sultan. This provided Russia with a pretext for later interventions in the Ottoman Empire. In its second war against the Turks from 1787 to 1792, Russia pushed its southwestern frontier to the Dniester River, acquiring the Turks' remaining lands along the northern Black Sea coast.

Catherine also participated with the Prussians and Austrians in the partitions of Poland (see Chapter 10).

By the late eighteenth century, the Austrian Hapsburgs, Prussian Hohenzollerns, and Russian Romanovs had developed their countries into great powers in Central and Eastern Europe.

Three monarchs—Joseph II of Austria, Frederick the Great of Prussia, and Catherine the Great of Russia—are often described as enlightened despots. The term suggests that these absolute monarchs sought to use their power to carry out reforms, making their governments more modern and more efficient, while at the same time making their own authority more absolute.

While the reforms of Joseph II were progressive, they failed to become a permanent feature of Austrian life because they lacked any real base of support.

Frederick the Great pursued enlightened policies, modernizing the structure of his government, promoting economic development, and practicing toleration in religious affairs. Nevertheless, Frederick's reforms were designed primarily to enhance his own power and that of the Prussian state, rather than to promote individual freedom.

Of the three enlightened despots, Catherine the Great is least deserving of the title. Despite her interest in Enlightenment ideas, Catherine's position depended on the support of the reactionary nobility, and she felt compelled to curry favor with them. In Russia, Peter the Great was far more an enlightened despot than Catherine.

Recommended Reading

Alexander, John T. *Catherine the Great: Life and Legend* (1989).

Anderson, M. S. *Europe in the Eighteenth Century, 1713–1783* (1961).

Beales, Derek E. D. *Joseph II* (1987).

Beloff, Max. *The Age of Absolutism, 1660–1815* (1954).

Bruun, Geoffrey. *The Enlightened Despots* (1967).

Craig, Gordon. *The Politics of the Prussian Army, 1640–1945* (1955).

Crankshaw, Edward. *Maria Theresa* (1970).

Ergang, Robert. *The Potsdam Führer: Frederick William I* (1941).

Haslip, Joan. *Catherine the Great: A Biography* (1977).

Holborn, Hajo. *A History of Modern Germany, 1648–1840* (1964).

Krieger, Leonard. *Kings and Philosophers, 1689–1789* (1970).

Lentin, A. *Russia in the Eighteenth Century* (1973).

Madariaga, Isabel de. *Russia in the Age of Catherine the Great* (1981).

Massie, Robert K. *Peter the Great: His Life and His World* (1980).

Mitchell, Otis. *A Concise History of Brandenburg-Prussia to 1786* (1980).

Raeff, Marc. *Imperial Russia, 1682–1825* (1971).

Ritter, Gerhard. *Frederick the Great: A Historical Profile* (1968).

Roider, Karl A. *Austria's Eastern Question, 1700–1790* (1982).

Schevill, Ferdinand. *The Great Elector* (1947).

Troyat, Henri. *Catherine the Great* (1980).

Wangermann, Ernst. *The Austrian Achievement, 1700–1800* (1973).

White, Reginald J. *Europe in the Eighteenth Century* (1965).

Wolf, John B. *The Emergence of the Great Powers, 1685–1715* (1951).

CHAPTER 10

The Eighteenth-Century Struggle for Power

Time Line

1713–1714	The end of the War of the Spanish Succession
1733–1735	The War of the Polish Succession
1740–1748	The War of the Austrian Succession
1756	The Diplomatic Revolution occurs, as Prussia forms an alliance with Great Britain, while Austria becomes allied with France
1756–1763	The Seven Years' War
1772	The first partition of Poland

1775	The American Revolution begins
1776	The Continental Congress approves the Declaration of Independence
1781	The Americans defeat Lord Cornwallis at Yorktown
1783	The Treaty of Paris confirms the independence of the thirteen colonies
1793	The second partition of Poland
1795	The third partition of Poland

The eighteenth century witnessed a great struggle for power, both on the European continent and in the colonial world. The War of the Polish Succession (1733–1735) ended with the installation on the Polish throne of the candidate favored by Russia and Austria, while the War of the Austrian Succession (1740–1748) confirmed Maria Theresa in her inheritance of the Hapsburg domains. The Seven Years' War (1756–1763) established Prussia as one of the great powers and gave Great Britain a predominant position in both North America and India. In the American Revolution (1775–1783), however, the thirteen British colonies along the Atlantic seaboard of North America made good their claim to independence from the mother country. Finally, the partitions of Poland from 1772 to 1795 ended Poland's existence as an independent state, with Prussia, Austria, and Russia dividing Poland's territory among themselves.

Great Power Rivalries in the Early Eighteenth Century

The Quadruple Alliance

The treaties signed in 1713–1714 concluding the War of the Spanish Succession brought an end to a long period of warfare among the European powers. Great Britain and France now formed an unusual alliance to help preserve peace. The Netherlands and Austria soon joined. This Quadruple Alliance remained in effect until 1733.

The War of the Polish Succession (1733–1735)

In 1733, the French arranged for the Polish nobility to elect Stanislas Leszczynski (1677–1766) as king. Stanislas was the father of Marie Leszczynska (1703–1768), the wife of France's King Louis XV (r. 1715–1744). Opposing the growth of French influence in Eastern Europe, Russia and Austria protested the election. The Russians sent an army to Poland, and a rump session of the Polish diet proceeded to elect a rival king, Augustus III (r. 1735–1763).

The War of the Polish Succession pitted Stanislas, France, and Spain, France's Bourbon ally, against Augustus III, Russia, and Austria. During the war, the French and Austrian armies fought their major battles far from Poland in northern Italy and in the Rhine valley. The peace settlement recognized Augustus III as king of Poland, thereby satisfying the demands of Russia and Austria.

The War of Jenkins's Ear

In 1739, war broke out between Great Britain and Spain as the result of a dispute over British trade with the Spanish colonies in America. The *Asiento* privilege, awarded to Great Britain by the Treaty of Utrecht (1713), gave the British a small share of this trade. In an effort to expand their trade with the Spanish colonies, British sea captains engaged in smuggling, which evoked a firm response from the Spanish. In 1738, one of these sea captains, Robert Jenkins, displayed his ear to the House of Commons, claiming that it had been cut off by the Spanish at Havana in 1731. The British declared war in October 1739. France soon entered the war in support of Spain.

The War of the Austrian Succession (1740–1748)

The War of Jenkins's Ear quickly became part of a general European war which began in the wake of the efforts of Prussia's new king, Frederick the Great (r. 1740–1786), to take Silesia from Maria Theresa (r. 1740–1780) of Austria.

During the War of the Austrian Succession, Prussia, France, Spain, Bavaria, and Saxony fought Austria, Great Britain, and the Netherlands.

In 1742, the anti-Austrian alliance collapsed when Prussia concluded a separate peace with Austria. Maria Theresa agreed to recognize Prussia's acquisition of Silesia. Then, when Austria began to win battles over her other enemies, Frederick the Great feared that Maria Theresa might attempt to regain Silesia and reentered the war. Compelling the Austrians once again to recognize his conquest of Silesia, Frederick dropped out of the war in December 1745.

Although Great Britain provided Austria with financial assistance, the British had little impact on the course of the war on the continent. Instead, the British focused their attention on the colonial war against France.

The Colonial War

The Anglo-French conflict in North America was known as King George's War. The French used their stronghold at Louisburg, at the mouth of the St. Lawrence River, as a base of operations for assaults on Nova Scotia and Massachusetts. In 1745, British troops and the Massachusetts militia counterattacked, capturing Louisburg. To the south, in the West Indies, British naval action disrupted France's profitable trade with her sugar islands.

The British navy also disrupted French trade in the Indian Ocean. In retaliation, Joseph François Dupleix (1697–1763), the governor of the French East India Company, took the British trading station at Madras in India in 1746.

The Peace of Aix-la-Chapelle (1748)

The War of the Austrian Succession ended in 1748 when the exhausted antagonists signed the Peace of Aix-la-Chapelle. The peace settlement attempted to restore the balance of power that had been established after the War of the Spanish Succession. Although Prussia retained Silesia, all other conquests, both in Europe and overseas, were restored to their former owners. In the New World, France regained Louisburg, while in India, Madras was returned to the British East India Company. In addition, Spain renewed the *Asiento* agreement with

Great Britain. The peace settlement recognized Maria Theresa's right to inherit the Hapsburg domains and confirmed her husband, Francis I (r. 1745–1765), as Holy Roman emperor. The peace settlement also recognized the rights of the House of Hanover, the British royal family, to its lands in northern Germany. While the Peace of Aix-la-Chapelle confirmed the emergence of Prussia as a European great power, it did not provide an enduring resolution of the colonial conflict between Great Britain and France.

The Diplomatic Revolution

As an uneasy peace prevailed in the years after 1748, a diplomatic revolution took place in Europe. Fearing a conflict between Russia and Prussia for control of the Baltic Sea and Poland, Prussia's King Frederick the Great decided to seek an alliance with the British. Under the terms of the Convention of Westminster, signed in January 1756, Frederick promised Great Britain that he would not move against Hanover.

The Austrians, for their part, hoped to retake Silesia from the Prussians. Seeking a more effective military ally than Great Britain, they concluded an alliance with France in May 1756, ending the traditional rivalry between France and the Hapsburgs. The Russians soon joined the Franco-Austrian alliance.

As a result of this diplomatic revolution, Great Britain and Prussia faced Austria, France, and Russia. Despite this reversal of alliances, however, the basic antagonisms remained: Prussia versus Austria and Great Britain versus France.

The Seven Years' War (1756–1763)

Like the earlier War of the Austrian Succession, the Seven Years' War involved both a continental war and a colonial conflict.

The War on the Continent

The continental war began in August 1756, when Frederick the Great of Prussia invaded Austria's ally, the kingdom of Saxony.

Frederick believed he was fighting a preventive war, attacking before his enemies could move against him. Confronting the powerful alliance of Austria, France, Russia, and Saxony, Frederick faced the greatest crisis of his career and suffered defeat in several battles. While the British could provide no direct military assistance to their Prussian ally, they did contribute substantial financial support. By strengthening Prussia, the British hoped to divert France's resources away from the colonial war overseas. Frederick also benefited from France's inability to fight both a continental and a colonial war simultaneously.

In 1762, the anti-Prussian alliance fell apart when Russia's new tsar, Peter III (r. 1762), who admired Frederick the Great, dropped out of the war. The Treaty of Hubertusburg, signed in February 1763, confirmed Prussia's possession of Silesia.

The Colonial War

In the colonial war against Great Britain, King Louis XV of France won the support of Spain. At first, the war went badly for the British. They quickly lost the Mediterranean island of Minorca, while in North America, where the war was known as the French and Indian War, they failed in their attempt to take Louisburg.

In India, the Anglo-French struggle resulted in a notorious event: The princely ruler of Bengal, an ally of the French, imprisoned 146 British captives in a small room. By morning, only 23 had survived what became known as the Black Hole of Calcutta.

The British finally found the war leader they needed in the person of William Pitt the Elder (1708–1778). From 1757 to 1761, Pitt's war ministry provided increased financial assistance to Frederick the Great and replaced incompetent military and naval commanders. The British also benefited from their control of the sea, making it impossible for the French to provide adequate reinforcements to their colonies.

The tide in the colonial war began to turn in Britain's favor. In India, British forces commanded by Robert Clive (1725–1774) defeated the French in the Battle of Plassey (June 1757). In the West Indies, the British seized the major French sugar islands. In North America, they took Fort Duquesne in western Pennsylvania in November 1758, renaming it Pittsburgh in honor of the prime minister. Further to the north,

General James Wolfe (1727–1759) took Louisburg in July 1758 and then advanced up the St. Lawrence River. In September 1759, both Wolfe and the French commander, Lt. General Louis Joseph Montcalm (1712–1759), were killed on the Plains of Abraham as the British moved to take Quebec. Montreal fell to the British in September 1760.

The Treaty of Paris (February 1763)

Under the terms of the Treaty of Paris, the British acquired French Canada and the land between the Appalachian Mountains and the Mississippi River. Little was left of the French empire in the New World apart from a few islands in the West Indies, including Martinique and Guadeloupe. In India, the British also established their dominance, although French trading stations remained at Pondichéry and Chandernagor. From Spain, France's ally, the British received Florida, including a strip of land along the Gulf of Mexico extending westward to the Mississippi River. As compensation, France turned over to Spain the city of New Orleans and the Louisiana territory west of the Mississippi River. The great colonial conflict had ended with the British winning a decisive victory over France.

The American Revolution (1775–1783)

The Origins of the Revolution

While the Seven Years' War resulted in a considerable expansion of the British Empire, Great Britain would soon lose an important part of that empire: the thirteen colonies along the Atlantic seaboard of North America.

The British conquest of French Canada had eliminated the American colonists' fear of French aggression, thereby reducing their need for British protection. At the same time, the colonists objected to a royal proclamation issued in October 1763, prohibiting them from establishing settlements in the newly acquired lands west of the Appalachian Mountains. While the British sought to avoid conflict with the Indians of the area, the colonists wanted to be free to exploit the new lands.

A number of other factors contributed to the growing conflict between the American colonists and Great Britain. The Seven Years' War had left the British with a substantial national debt, and the British government also had to bear the continuing costs of protecting the frontier in America. The colonists objected both to new taxes levied by the British and to Britain's mercantilist policies, which placed restrictions on trade conducted by the colonists.

The Struggle for Independence

The American Revolution began at Lexington and Concord, Massachusetts, in April 1775. Although the early stages of the war proved indecisive, the Continental Congress declared American independence in July 1776.

The turning point in the war came in October 1777 when the colonists defeated the British army commanded by General John Burgoyne (1722–1792) at Saratoga. The Americans then concluded an alliance with France, which soon secured the assistance of Spain in the war against Great Britain. The French supported the Americans in order to gain revenge against the British for the losses suffered in the Seven Years' War, although the cost of the war put further strains on French finances and thus contributed to the problems of the French monarchy that culminated in the French revolution of 1789.

In October 1781, Lord Cornwallis (1738–1805) lost the Battle of Yorktown to the Americans in large part because the French navy prevented reinforcements from reaching him.

The Treaty of Paris (September 1783)

In the Treaty of Paris, the British formally recognized the independence of the thirteen colonies. The British ceded Tobago in the West Indies and Senegal in Africa to France, while Spain acquired Florida and the Mediterranean island of Minorca.

The Partitions of Poland

During the course of the eighteenth century, the contentious Polish nobility proved increasingly incapable of regulating their own affairs

The Expansion of Russia and the Partition of Poland

and providing the country with effective leadership. In this situation, Poland became an object of intervention by the great powers.

In 1763, Catherine the Great (r. 1762–1796) of Russia secured the election of one of her former lovers, Stanislas Poniatowski (1732–1798), as king of Poland. In an effort to prevent the Russians from extending their control over Poland and to avert possible great-power conflict, Frederick the Great of Prussia intervened diplomatically, arranging the first of three partitions of Poland.

In this first partition, in 1772, Poland lost about half its population and a third of its territory, while Prussia acquired most of West Prussia, uniting Prussian-ruled East Prussia with Brandenburg, the center of

Prussian power. This was an important step in the consolidation of the Hohenzollern domains. Russia gained a large part of Belorussia (White Russia), while the Austrians took the province of Galicia.

In the second partition of Poland in 1793, Russia gained most of Lithuania and the western Ukraine, while Prussia took the area around the seaport of Danzig and additional territory in western Poland.

In 1794, a Polish national revolt broke out, led by Thaddeus Kosciuszko (1746–1817). In response, Prussia, Austria, and Russia carried out the third partition of Poland. Poland ceased to exist as an independent state. Prussia took the area around Warsaw, while Austria gained the Cracow region. The Russians took what remained of Lithuania and the Ukraine. While Russia's gains in Poland provided the Russians with buffer zones against their Prussian and Austrian neighbors, most of the Russians' millions of new Polish, Lithuanian, Belorussian, and Ukrainian subjects objected to being under Russian domination.

When the Seven Years' War ended in 1763, Great Britain, Prussia, and Russia were clearly established as the most powerful states in Europe. While France, Spain, and Austria survived, they did so as second-rate powers, although French power would reassert itself during the 1790s. The American colonists' victory over the British did not seriously weaken Great Britain's naval and imperial supremacy, and more than a century would pass before the United States became a significant factor in world affairs. While the partitions of Poland ended that country's independent existence until its re-creation following World War I, Poland's destruction had no significant impact on the international power balance since Poland had not played a major role in Eastern European affairs for several generations.

Recommended Reading

Alden, John R. *The American Revolution, 1775–1783* (1954).

Anderson, Matthew S. *Europe in the Eighteenth Century, 1713–1783* (1963).

Dorn, Walter L. *Competition for Empire, 1740–1763* (1940).

Krieger, Leonard. *Kings and Philosophers, 1689–1789* (1970).

Liss, Peggy. *Atlantic Empires: The Network of Trade and Revolution, 1713–1826* (1983).

McKay, Derek and H. M. Scott. *The Rise of the Great Powers, 1648–1815* (1983).

Morris, Richard B., *The Forging of the Union, 1781–1789* (1987).

Parry, J. H. *Trade and Dominion: The European Oversea Empires in the Eighteenth Century* (1971).

Roberts, Penfield. *The Quest for Security, 1715–1740* (1947).

Tucker, Robert W. and David C. Hendrickson. *The Fall of the First British Empire* (1982).

CHAPTER 11

The Scientific Revolution

Time Line

1543	Nicolaus Copernicus publishes *On the Revolution of the Heavenly Spheres*
	Vesalius publishes *The Structure of the Human Body*
1609	Johannes Kepler publishes his first two laws of planetary motion
1614	John Napier publishes a table of logarithms
1620	Bacon publishes the *Novum Organum*
1628	William Harvey publishes *On the Movement of the Heart and Blood in Animals*

c. 1630	The slide rule is invented
1632	Galileo publishes his *Dialogue on Two Chief Systems of the World*
1637	René Descartes publishes his *Discourse on Method*
1687	Sir Isaac Newton publishes the *Principia Mathematica*
1735	Carolus Linnaeus publishes the *Systema Naturae*
1749–1804	Buffon's 44-volume natural history is published
1789	Lavoisier publishes his *Elementary Treatise on Chemistry*
1795	James Hutton publishes *The Theory of the Earth*

While the attention of Europe had been focused on politics and war, great changes were occurring in the realm of ideas. By the early seventeenth century, exciting new developments were under way in astronomy and the physical sciences.

The heliocentric (sun-centered) theory of the universe, which Copernicus proposed in the mid-sixteenth century, gradually won acceptance, replacing the old geocentric (earth-centered) theory, first developed in ancient times. While Sir Isaac Newton developed the law of universal gravitation, other scientists laid the foundations for the scientific study of anatomy and physiology, chemistry, biology, physics, and geology. The methodology of science was debated, and scientific societies were established to promote further research and the spread of the new knowledge. The Scientific Revolution ultimately brought radical changes to people's understanding of the entire physical universe.

The Background of the Scientific Revolution

In the sixteenth century, Europeans' understanding of the universe was based on the conclusions of the ancient Greek philosopher Aristotle (fourth century B.C.) and the Hellenistic astronomer and mathematician Claudius Ptolemy (second century A.D.). According to the ancient geocentric view of the universe, the earth stood motionless at the center of the universe, while the moon, sun, planets, and stars revolved around the earth in a series of circular orbits. These heavenly bodies were composed of a substance different from that of the earth, and they were weightless. This was what made it possible for them to revolve around the earth. As the ancients understood motion, no heavy body could move without a mover. Since the earth was heavy, and since there was no mover, it remained motionless.

Problems with the Ancient View of the Universe

Although the ancient view of the physical universe had been accepted by Western Europeans during the Middle Ages, there were obvious problems with the Ptolemaic system. The most troublesome problem was that the planets could be observed moving in evidently noncircular patterns around the earth. Sometimes the planets even appeared to be moving backward.

To make these patterns of movement compatible with the geocentric theory of Ptolemy, medieval astronomers introduced the concept of epicycles. According to this concept, the planets made a second revolution in an orbit that was tangential to their primary orbit around the earth. The concept of epicycles greatly complicated the geocentric theory. Nevertheless, it won acceptance since it provided a satisfactory explanation of the motion of the planets as that motion was observed by human beings. It also helped shore up both the geocentric theory and the Christian belief that the earth stood at the very center of the universe that God had created.

The Revolution in Astronomy

Nicolaus Copernicus (1473–1543) and the Heliocentric Theory

In the sixteenth century, the Polish monk, mathematician, and astronomer Copernicus presented the first serious challenge in many centuries to the geocentric theory. He hypothesized that the sun stood at the center of the universe and that the earth moved in a circular orbit around the sun. For some twenty-five years, he worked on the development of this heliocentric theory. In 1543, the year of his death, Copernicus's treatise, *On the Revolution of the Heavenly Spheres,* was published. Other scientists and both Protestant and Catholic churchmen denounced Copernicus's theory, charging that it was illogical, unbiblical, and un-Christian.

Tycho Brahe (1546–1601) and Astronomical Discoveries

Brahe, a Danish astronomer, built Europe's most modern astronomical laboratory, where he and his associates collected a mass of accurate data about the stars and planets. These discoveries served to undermine the Ptolemaic view of the universe. Nevertheless, Brahe did not fully accept the heliocentric theory advanced by Copernicus, for he concluded that while the planets revolved around the sun, the earth remained stationary. Other astronomers, however, used the data collected by Brahe to support the view that the earth also circled around the sun.

Johannes Kepler (1571–1630) and the Laws of Planetary Motion

Kepler, a German astronomer who had worked as Brahe's assistant, accepted the fundamental validity of the heliocentric theory. He proceeded to develop the three laws of planetary motion, publishing the first two in 1609 and the third in 1619. According to the first law, the planets, including the earth, revolve around the sun in elliptical (rather than circular) orbits. The second law stated that the velocity of the planets varies according to their distance from the sun. A planet moves faster when it is closer to the sun than when it is farther away. The third law set forth a complex mathematical formula explaining the physical relationship among the moving planets.

Galileo Galilei (1564–1642) and Proof of the Heliocentric Theory

Galileo, an Italian mathematician, astronomer, and physicist, set out to demonstrate the validity of the heliocentric theory. The telescope had recently been invented in the Netherlands, and Galileo was the first to use a telescope for astronomical observations. With his telescope, Galileo could actually see what others had hypothesized: that the planets revolve around the sun. He discovered the mountains of the moon, the moons of Jupiter, the rings around Saturn, and sunspots. What mattered most, however, was that he provided decisive support for the heliocentric theory.

In 1632, Galileo published his *Dialogue on Two Chief Systems of the World* and promptly got into trouble with the authorities of the Catholic Church. While Galileo was personally devout in his religious faith, he contended that the Bible was not a reliable authority on scientific matters. The Church was prepared to tolerate the heliocentric theory if it was advanced as a hypothesis, rather than as established fact. In 1633, the Roman Inquisition condemned Galileo's work and placed it on the *Index* of prohibited books. Galileo was compelled to recant, although he is said to have muttered, referring to the earth, "And yet it does move."

Confined to house arrest in a comfortable villa, Galileo continued his scientific work, concentrating on less controversial subjects. His study of falling bodies disproved Aristotle's contention that objects fall at varying speeds, depending on their weights. Galileo also developed the theory of the pendulum and discovered the principle of inertia.

Sir Isaac Newton (1642–1727) and the Law of Universal Gravitation

The work of Copernicus, Kepler, and Galileo had left one great unanswered question: What is it that causes the planets, stars, and other heavenly bodies to move in an orderly fashion? Newton discovered the answer to this question.

The son of an English farmer, Newton's genius won him early recognition, and he became a professor of mathematics at Cambridge University while he was still in his twenties. Working independently of one another, both Newton and Gottfried Wilhelm von Leibniz (1646–1716), a German philosopher and mathematician, discovered differential and integral calculus.

Newton shared the conviction of other scientists that the physical universe was governed by natural laws. His research convinced him that all of the heavenly bodies moved as they did because of the operation of the law of gravity. In his *Principia Mathematica* (1687), Newton set forth the law of universal gravitation, which provided a mathematical explanation of the operation of gravity everywhere in the universe.

Scientific Methodology and the Promotion of Science

Francis Bacon (1561–1626) and the Inductive Method

Bacon, an English attorney and royal official, wrote extensively on history, ethics, and philosophy. While he was not a professional scientist, he did much to promote the inductive method of modern science. Bacon attacked the excessive reverence given to the work of ancient thinkers, including Aristotle. In particular, he challenged Aristotle's dependence on deductive reasoning.

Bacon insisted that valid conclusions about the physical universe could be reached only through the inductive method, which involves experimentation and the systematic collection and analysis of data. Generalizations can then be made on the basis of the collected and analyzed data. If scientists carefully examined the empirical evidence, he believed, they would develop new knowledge that would produce benefits for all of humanity. His major works include *The Advancement of Learning* (1605) and the *Novum Organum* (1620).

René Descartes (1596–1650) and the Deductive Method

While Bacon emphasized the inductive method, based on experiment and observation, the Frenchman Descartes promoted the deductive method, which involved reasoning out a general law from specific cases and then applying it broadly to cases that have not been specifically observed. Descartes set forth what came to be known as the Cartesian method in his *Discourse on Method* (1637).

Descartes began by doubting all authorities and all knowledge, both scientific and religious, until he was left with one thing he could not doubt: his own existence. *"Cogito, ergo sum"* ("I think, therefore I am"), he declared. He then proceeded to deduce the existence of God and the physical world.

Although the Cartesian method had a considerable influence on European thought, it was eventually replaced to a great extent by the inductive method.

A brilliant mathematician, Descartes developed analytical geometry.

Scientific Societies

As the interest in science mounted, scientific societies were organized in a number of countries to promote further research and the spread of scientific knowledge.

Galileo was a member of the scientific society established in Rome in 1603; the Medici family sponsored the establishment of the Academy of Experiments in Florence in 1657. In England, the Royal Society for Improving Natural Knowledge was founded in 1662. Four years later, the French Academy of Science was established. The Berlin Academy was founded in 1701.

Other Sciences and Mathematics

The Scientific Revolution ultimately gave rise to most of the fields of modern science.

Anatomy and Physiology

Research in human anatomy (the study of the structure of the human body) and physiology (the study of its functions) served to undermine the teachings of the ancient Hellenistic physician and anatomist, Galen (c. A.D. 130-201), whose conclusions had been unquestioned for centuries.

Vesalius

Andreas Vesalius (1514–1564), a Flemish-born professor of anatomy at the University of Padua in Italy, prepared the first textbook of human anatomy based on dissection, *The Structure of the Human Body* (1543).

Harvey

William Harvey (1578–1657), an English physician educated at Padua, did much to establish the foundations of modern medicine. He was the first to demonstrate the function of the heart and the circulation of the blood, publishing *On the Movement of the Heart and Blood in Animals* (1628).

Chemistry

Boyle

The title of the father of modern chemistry has been bestowed upon Robert Boyle (1627–1691), an Anglo-Irish chemist. He is most famous for Boyle's Law, which states that the volume of a gas under compression is inversely proportional to the amount of pressure. Boyle was the first to make a clear distinction between a chemical element and a chemical compound and to define clearly the nature of a chemical reaction.

Black

Joseph Black (1728–1799), a Scottish physician and chemist, proved that air was not a single element but instead consisted of several gasses.

Priestley and Lavoisier

In 1775, Joseph Priestley (1733–1804), an English Unitarian minister, published the results of his experiments isolating and identifying oxygen. A few years later, Antoine Lavoisier (1743–1794), a French chemist, demonstrated that water consisted of hydrogen and oxygen. He believed that water and other substances consisted of basic chemical elements, and he identified twenty-three of these elements. Lavoisier's book, *Elementary Treatise on Chemistry* (1789), contributed to the development of both organic and inorganic chemistry.

Biology

Although the study of biology had made some advances during the early stages of the Scientific Revolution, the systems of classification remained relatively primitive until the eighteenth century.

Linnaeus

Carolus Linnaeus (1707–1778), a Swedish botanist, developed a system for the classification of plants and animals by genus and species, which he presented in his *Systema Naturae* (1735). Linnaeus believed, however, that species remained constant, thus disregarding any concept of evolution. Linnaeus developed a botanical garden, and by the end of the eighteenth century, Europe boasted some 1600 botanical gardens.

Buffon

The Count of Buffon (1707–1788), a French zoologist, made important contributions to the classification of animal life. His 44-volume natural history was published between 1749 and 1804. Europeans organized a number of zoos, with the one at Versailles becoming particularly famous.

Physics

Galileo's study of motion and the work of Newton, including his study of optics, promoted the development of physics as a modern science.

Gilbert

Important discoveries were gradually made in the field of electricity. In 1600, William Gilbert (c. 1540–1603), the court physician to Queen Elizabeth I and King James I of England, described the presence of electric charges in many substances. His work won for him the title of the father of modern electricity.

Franklin and Volta

The experiments of Benjamin Franklin (1706–1790) identified the presence of electricity in lightning, and he invented the lightning rod. The Italian Alessandro Volta (1745–1827), a professor of physics, invented the storage battery, which made it possible to harness electricity. The unit of electrical measurement called the volt is named for him.

Geology

Gilbert

William Gilbert was also one of the pioneers in the field of geology, the study of the origins, development, and structure of the earth. In *De magnete* (1600), a study of magnetism, Gilbert suggested that the earth operated like a huge magnet.

Hutton

James Hutton (1726–1797), a Scotsman, developed theories about the origins of the earth and published *The Theory of the Earth* (1795). He concluded that the surface of the earth had been undergoing gradual changes over the course of many thousands of years.

Mathematics

There were other achievements in mathematics in addition to Descartes's invention of analytical geometry and the development of the system of calculus by Newton and Leibniz.

Logarithms

In 1614, John Napier (1550–1617), a Scottish mathematician, published a table of logarithms that provided a simplified method for multiplying and dividing large numbers and for finding square roots.

The Slide Rule

Using Napier's principle of the logarithm, William Oughtred and Edmund Wingate independently invented the slide rule about 1630.

The Scientific Revolution not only produced a vast amount of specific knowledge about the nature of the physical universe, it also demonstrated that all of nature operates in accordance with natural laws, which human beings are capable of discovering. These new ideas about the physical universe led, in turn, to the Enlightenment, the dominant intellectual movement of the eighteenth century. Applying the methods of science to the study of human affairs, the thinkers of the Enlightenment developed new and radical ideas about the nature of human beings and the organization of government and society.

Recommended Reading

Anderson, Fulton H. *Francis Bacon: His Career and Thought* (1978).

Boas, Marie. *The Scientific Renaissance, 1450–1630* (1962).

Bronowski, Jacob. *The Ascent of Man* (1974).

Caspar, Max. *Kepler* (1959).

Christianson, Gale E. *In the Presence of the Creator* (1984).

Clarke, Desmond. *Descartes' Philosophy of Science* (1982).

Cohen, Bernard I. *From Leonardo to Lavoisier* (1980).

Drake, Stillman. *Galileo* (1980).

Durant, Will and Ariel. *The Age of Reason Begins* (1961).

Frank, Robert Gregg. *Harvey and the Oxford Physiologists* (1980).

Fuller, Jean Overton. *Francis Bacon* (1981).

Geymonat, Ludovico. *Galileo Galilei* (1965).

Koyre, Alexander. *The Astronomical Revolution* (1973).

Ornstein, Mary. *The Role of Scientific Societies in the Seventeenth Century* (1975).

Ronan, Colin A. *Science: Its History and Development Among the World's Cultures* (1982).

Santillana, George de. *The Crime of Galileo* (1955).

Smith, Alan G. R. *Science and Society in the Sixteenth and Seventeenth Centuries* (1973).

Westfall, Richard S. *Never at Rest: A Biography of Isaac Newton* (1980).

CHAPTER 12

The Enlightenment

Time Line

1690	John Locke publishes the *Essay Concerning Human Understanding* and the *Second Treatise of Government*
1748	Montesquieu publishes *The Spirit of the Laws*
1751–1772	Twenty-eight volumes of the *Encyclopedia* are published
1759	Voltaire publishes *Candide*
1762	Rousseau publishes *Emile* and *The Social Contract*
1764	Cesare Beccaria publishes the *Essay on Crimes and Punishments*

1776   Adam Smith publishes *The Wealth of Nations*

1795   Condorcet's *Progress of the Human Mind* is
                  published

The Enlightenment, also known as the Age of Reason, was the dominant intellectual movement of the eighteenth century.

The achievements of the Scientific Revolution had revealed the ability of the human mind to penetrate the secrets of the physical universe. While the makers of the Scientific Revolution had used their intellectual powers to discover the natural laws that governed the operation of the physical universe, the thinkers of the Enlightenment sought through reasoning to discover the natural laws that governed the affairs of human beings and human society. They criticized the existing institutions of absolute monarchy and established church and proposed a broad range of reforms designed to eliminate abuses and to promote individual freedom.

The Philosophes

While the Enlightenment was a broad international movement, many of its leading thinkers were French. The Enlightenment thinkers are known collectively as *philosophes,* the French word for philosophers. In fact, the philosophes were not philosophers in the traditional sense. Instead, they were critics of the Old Regime who developed new ideas about government, economics, and religion and advanced proposals for the improvement of the human condition and the reform of society.

The philosophes shared the Enlightenment's faith in the supremacy of human reason, believing that people, through the use of their reason, could find answers to their questions and solutions to their problems. In particular, reason could be used to reveal the natural laws that regulated human affairs. Once these natural laws were discovered, the institutions of society could be reformed to bring them more in accordance with the natural order.

Condorcet and the Doctrine of Progress

In addition to their emphasis on rationalism, the philosophes believed in the progress of human beings and society toward a more perfect condition. In their view, human beings were basically good but had been corrupted by society. If the institutions of society were reformed, then this human goodness would prevail. The Enlightenment doctrine of progress was set forth most strongly by the Marquis de Condorcet (1743–1794) in the *Progress of the Human Mind* (1795). Condorcet traced the development of human history through nine eras, contending that in the tenth era peace, virtue, and justice would prevail.

John Locke (1632–1704)

The English thinker John Locke was one of the most widely read political philosophers during the Enlightenment. In two works published in 1690, Locke provided a vigorous defense of England's Glorious Revolution of 1688, which had resulted in the overthrow of King James II.

Knowledge from Experience

In his *Essay Concerning Human Understanding,* Locke advanced his theory of the *tabula rasa.* At birth, Locke argued, every human being's mind is a blank page, and all knowledge comes from experience. Rejecting the doctrine of innate ideas, Locke repudiated the view that human beings were born with a tendency to submit to authority.

The Social Contract and Natural Rights

Locke based his *Second Treatise of Government* on the social-contract theory. In Locke's view, people had come together in a social contract. By mutual consent, they had created a government to protect their natural rights to life, liberty, and property. The authority of government is thus derived from the consent of the governed. When government fails to protect the people's natural rights and instead, interferes with them by attempting to rule absolutely, the people have a right to rebel, as they had done in the Glorious Revolution. Locke supported the creation of a constitutional government that placed limits on the ruler's authority.

The thinkers of the Enlightenment accepted Locke's doctrine of the natural rights of human beings and his views on constitutional government. The doctrine of natural rights influenced Thomas Jefferson, for example, who wrote in the American Declaration of Independence about the right to "life, liberty, and the pursuit of happiness."

Voltaire (1694–1778)

François-Marie Arouet, better known as Voltaire, was a prolific and witty critic of the Old Regime, producing a host of essays, letters, stories, plays, and histories that helped popularize the ideas of the Enlightenment. The first collected edition of Voltaire's works, published from 1784 to 1789, totaled ninety-two volumes.

One of Voltaire's most famous works, the satirical tale *Candide* (1759), attacked superstition, religious persecution, war, and an uncritical optimism about the human condition.

Enlightened Despotism

In politics, Voltaire was a proponent of enlightened despotism and conducted a correspondence with Frederick the Great of Prussia and Catherine the Great of Russia (see Chapter 9). Enlightened despotism involved the idea that an absolute ruler would use his authority to promote reform. While some monarchs did in fact promote reforms designed to make their governments more efficient, even the most enlightened ruler could not contemplate, much less enact, any reforms that would serve to undermine his absolute authority. Beyond that, the outbreak of the French Revolution in 1789 brought terror to rulers in all lands, and they became adamant in their opposition to even moderate reforms, lest the floodgates of revolutionary upheaval be opened.

Deism

In religion, Voltaire was an advocate of deism, which many philosophes regarded as a more rational and natural approach to religion than the supernatural and mystical teachings of Christianity. The deists believed in a God who created the universe and set it in motion to operate in accordance with natural laws. This God, the prime mover, did not then interfere with the operation of his creation. He was not involved with people's daily lives and did not respond to prayer. Many deists believed in life after death, however, and believed further that God would reward and punish individuals according to their moral conduct during their lives. Nevertheless, the deists rejected the fundamental doctrines of the Christian faith.

Tolerance

After having been imprisoned briefly when some of his ideas offended the French authorities, Voltaire left France and lived in England from 1726 to 1729. There he came to admire England's spirit of tolerance in both politics and religion. Returning to France, he published *Letters on the English* (1733), expressing his admiration for England's constitutional government and criticizing the abuses of French absolutism.

Campaigning in support of tolerance, Voltaire defended Jean Calas, a Huguenot merchant from Toulouse, who was executed in 1762 for allegedly murdering his son in order to prevent his conversion to Catholicism. In his *Treatise on Tolerance* (1763), Voltaire contended that the case against Calas was groundless and that he had been convicted by a court dominated by anti-Protestant hysteria. Voltaire urged the authorities to conduct a new investigation, and the verdict convicting Calas was reversed in 1765.

Jean-Jacques Rousseau (1712–1778)

Born in Geneva, the son of a watchmaker, Rousseau rebelled against the restrictions imposed by the Calvinist tradition of the city. As a philosophe, he urged reforms in education and government.

Natural Education

Rousseau believed that people living in a state of nature had once been virtuous, free, equal, and happy. They had been corrupted by civilization. What they needed, therefore, was a natural education, free of the corruption and artificiality of society. Rousseau set forth his ideas on education in *Emile* (1762), which is part treatise and part novel. The story has two heroes: Rousseau, the teacher, and Emile, his pupil. In place of the formal schooling typical of the eighteenth century, Emile learned by direct experience, rather than from books. He was not forced to read at a young age, nor was he subjected to severe discipline.

The General Will

The Social Contract (1762), Rousseau's treatise on politics and government, opens with the words: "All men are born free, but everywhere they are in chains." Although government restricted individual freedom, it was nevertheless a necessary evil. There would be less evil, however, if government and individual liberty could be reconciled. In an effort to promote this reconciliation, Rousseau advocated a radical form of the contract theory of government. Rejecting the extreme individualism emphasized by many of his fellow philosophes, Rousseau stressed the role of the individual as a member of society. The social contract that he proposed was a contract in which the members of society agreed to be ruled by their general will. Although Rousseau never made it clear how the general will would operate in actual practice, he believed that all members of society would participate in the formulation of the general will, which would then be executed by a small group. Convinced that the general will is always right, Rousseau contended that obedience to the general will is an act of freedom.

Rousseau himself did not actually favor democracy, in the modern sense of the term, but his view of the general will—and particularly the idea that ultimately sovereignty resides with all the people—helped promote the development of the democratic ideology.

Baron de Montesquieu (1689–1755)

Charles-Louis de Secondat, Baron de Montesquieu, was a French attorney and philosopher. Montesquieu did not believe that there was any single ideal political system. Instead, different systems were appropriate for different peoples, depending on the size of the area to be governed, its population, its economic system, and its social and religious traditions. Nevertheless, he greatly admired the British political system and advocated the establishment of constitutional monarchy in France.

Separation of Powers

In *The Spirit of the Laws* (1748), Montesquieu set forth the concept of the separation of powers between the executive, legislative, and judicial branches of the government. This division of authority, with its checks and balances, would place effective limits on the power of the executive and thereby protect the rights of the individual citizens.

Montesquieu's ideas influenced the writers of the American Constitution, as well as of the French Constitution of 1791.

The Encylopedia

Virtually all of the important French philosophes, including Voltaire, Rousseau, and Montesquieu, were among the some 160 contributers to the *Encyclopedia,* edited by Denis Diderot (1713–17848) and Jean le Rond d'Alembert (1717–1783). The *Encyclopedia* was both a compendium of knowledge and a means for spreading the philosophes' often radical ideas on government, economics, religion, philosophy, and other subjects. Despite the opposition of state and church authorities, the first twenty-eight volumes of the *Encyclopedia* were published between 1751 and 1772, and five additional volumes appeared in 1776–1777.

Law and Justice

In their criticism of the Old Regime, the philosophes were particularly outspoken in their condemnation of outmoded and unjust laws and systems of justice, especially the use of torture and capital punishment.

In his *Essay on Crimes and Punishments* (1764), Cesare Beccaria, an Italian aristocrat, advanced his proposals for bringing law and justice into conformity with the rational laws of nature. Barbarous punishments, he believed, failed to deter crimes; the certainty of punishment was a far more effective deterrent than its severity. He believed further that justice should be swift and that punishment should focus on the rehabilitation of the criminal.

Economic Thought

In economics, the Enlightenment introduced the docrine of laissez-faire. The term is derived from the dictum of the French Physiocrats: *"Laissez faire, laissez passer"* ("Let do, let pass"). The advocates of laissez-faire believed that the economy should be left free to regulate itself by its own natural laws. In advancing this doctrine, they repudiated mercantilism, the prevailing economic doctrine and practice of the age, which emphasized state regulation of economic activity.

François Quesnay (1694–1774) and Physiocrat Theory

In France, the Physiocrats appeared as the main advocates of laissez-faire. Quesnay, the leading Physiocrat, was a biologist and surgeon who served as physician to King Louis XV and his mistress, Madame de Pompadour. Rejecting the mercantilist view that stressed the importance of a nation's accumulating gold and silver, Quesnay insisted that land was the only source of wealth. Instead of regulating trade, as the mercantilists urged, it should remain free of control. Rather than making goods more expensive by imposing tariffs and other taxes on them, the state should establish only one tax, on income derived from land.

Adam Smith (1723–1790) and Economic Self-interest

Smith, a Scottish economist, was the eighteenth century's most influential advocate of laissez-faire. In *The Wealth of Nations* (1776), Smith attacked mercantilist doctrine and practice. A nation's wealth, he contended, was based on its production of goods by its farmers, artisans, and factory workers. Mercantilist regulations interfered with production and thereby restricted the expansion of a nation's wealth. Smith believed that people should be free to pursue their own economic self-interest. Each individual's pursuit of economic self-interest in a free economy would promote the prosperity of the entire society. Instead of regulating economic activity, the government should restrict its role to protecting the life, liberty, and property of its citizens. The state should content itself with being a passive policeman.

The thinkers of the Enlightenment proposed a broad program for the reform of government and society. Although they often tended to oversimplify human nature and to exaggerate the supremacy of reason in human affairs, they offered forthright and often courageous criticisms of the inadequacies of the Old Regime. Their ideas had a powerful impact on the thought and action of the makers of the American and French revolutions and on advocates of reform generally in the Western world.

Recommended Reading

Baker, Keith M. *Condorcet* (1975).

Becker, Carl L. *The Heavenly City of the Eighteenth Century Philosophers* (1932).

Besterman, Theodore. *Voltaire* (1969).

Cobban, Alfred. *In Search of Humanity: The Role of the Enlightenment in Modern History* (1960).

Croprey, Joseph. *Polity and Economy: An Interpretation of Adam Smith* (1977).

Darnton, Robert W. *The Business of Enlightenment: A Publishing History of the Encyclopédie, 1775–1800* (1979).

Durant, Will and Ariel. *The Age of Voltaire* (1965).

Durant, Will and Ariel. *Rousseau and Revolution* (1967).

Fox-Genovese, Elizabeth. *The Origins of Physiocracy* (1976).

Gay, Peter. *The Enlightenment: An Interpretation,* 2 vols. (1966, 1969).

Hampson, Norman. *The Enlightenment* (1968).

Manuel, Frank E. *The Age of Reason* (1951).

Miller, James. *Rousseau: Dreamer of Democracy* (1984).

Rockwood, Raymond O., ed. *Carl Becker's Heavenly City Revisited* (1958).

Tully, James. *A Discourse on Property: John Locke and His Adversaries* (1980).

CHAPTER 13

Literature, Art, and Music in the Seventeenth and Eighteenth Centuries

Time Line

1607	Claudio Monteverdi's opera, *Orfeo*, is produced in Mantua
1608	Peter Paul Rubens begins painting in Antwerp
1624	Diego Velázquez becomes court painter to King Philip IV of Spain
1629	Giovanni Lorenzo Bernini becomes the architect of Rome's St. Peter's basilica

1637	Pierre Corneille publishes his tragic drama *Le Cid*
1664	Molière publishes his satirical drama *Le Tartuffe*
1667	John Milton publishes his epic poem *Paradise Lost*
1677	Jean Racine publishes his tragic drama *Phèdre*
	John Dryden's play *All for Love* is produced in London
1719	Daniel Defoe publishes *Robinson Crusoe*
1726	Jonathan Swift publishes *Gulliver's Travels*
1729	Johann Sebastian Bach composes the *St. Matthew Passion*
1734	Alexander Pope publishes his *Essay on Man*
1740	Samuel Richardson writes the novel *Pamela, or Virtue Rewarded*
1742	George Frederick Handel's *Messiah* has its first performance
1749	Henry Fielding publishes *Tom Jones*
1777	Richard Brinsley Sheridan writes *The School for Scandal*
1786	Wolfgang Amadeus Mozart's opera *The Marriage of Figaro* has its first performance
1791	Franz Joseph Haydn's *Surprise Symphony* has its first performance

During the seventeenth and eighteenth centuries, many Western European writers and artists were inspired by the literary and artistic achievements of ancient Greek and Roman civilizations and sought to pattern their work on classical models. Some artists, architects, and musicians, however, rebelled against the strict rules of classicism and developed a style known as baroque.

Both classicism and baroque were more immediately derived from the traditions of the Renaissance and disdained the cultural achievements of the Middle Ages. Although inspired by classical models, baroque did not accept classicism's insistence on restraint, order, harmony, and balance.

Seventeenth-Century French Literature

The seventeenth century was the classical period of French literature, sometimes called the Augustan period.

Pierre Corneille (1606–1684) and Jean Racine (1639–1699)

The classical tradition was reflected in the work of Corneille and Racine, who found inspiration in the heroes and heroines of ancient history and literature and wrote tragic dramas on the model of ancient Greek tragedy. Among Corneille's best-known works is *Le Cid* (1637), based on the legends of the medieval Spanish hero.

Focusing his attention on the problem of passion, especially in women, Racine's tragedies include *Andromaque* (1667), *Iphigenie en Aulide* (1674), and *Phèdre* (1677).

Molière (1622–1673)

Jean-Baptiste Poquelin, better known as Molière (1622–1673), wrote comedy and satire, and his work was less strictly governed by the rules of classicism. Molière delighted in exposing society's hypocrisies and follies. His many plays include *Le Tartuffe* (1644), *Le Misanthrope* (1666), *Le Bourgeois Gentilhomme* (1670), and *Les Femmes Savantes* (1672).

Madame de Sévigné (1626–1696) and the Duke of Saint-Simon (1675–1755)

Other important French writers of the period include Madame de Sévigné, who wrote more then 1,500 letters describing Paris society and life at her home in the Brittany countryside, and the Duke of Saint-Simon, who lived at the court of King Louis XIV and wrote memoirs covering the years 1694 to 1723.

Seventeenth- and Eighteenth-Century English Literature

John Milton (1608–1674)

The Puritan poet John Milton was seventeenth-century England's greatest literary figure. His most famous work, the epic poem *Paradise Lost* (1667), is based on the biblical tradition of Satan's revolt against God and the fall of Adam and Eve. *Paradise Regained* (1671), another poem in blank verse, tells of Jesus in the wilderness, overcoming the temptations of Satan.

John Dryden (1631–1700) and Alexander Pope (1688–1744)

The later English writers, Dryden and Pope, were, like Milton, thoroughly familiar with ancient Greek and Roman literature. A poet, dramatist, and critic, Dryden's best-known plays include the comedy *Marriage à la Mode* (1672) and *All for Love* (1677), a retelling of Shakespeare's *Antony and Cleopatra*.

Pope is generally recognized as England's greatest eighteenth-century poet. He is known for his translations into English of Homer's *Iliad* (1720) and *Odyssey* (1725-26), as well as for his original works. The *Rape of the Lock* (1714) is a mock-heroic poem poking fun at the fashionable society of the time. In a more serious vein, his *Essay on Criticism* (1711), written in heroic couplets, sets forth critical standards and tastes, while his *Essay on Man* (1734) is a summary, in poetic form, of eighteenth-century philosophical ideas.

Daniel Defoe (1659–1731)

England also produced several noted novelists. Defoe wrote *Robinson Crusoe* (1719), which some regard as the first true novel in English. *Robinson Crusoe* is the story of a man who meets the challenge of surviving on a desert island while maintaining his human integrity.

Another novel, *Moll Flanders* (1722), is the tale of a London prostitute and thief.

Jonathan Swift (1667–1745)

The Irish-born Swift is best known for *Gulliver's Travels* (1726), a biting political and social satire. Written in four parts, it is the story of Lemuel Gulliver's journey to Lilliput, a land of tiny inhabitants whose small size makes their pompous activities especially ridiculous, and to other mythical lands. Above all, *Gulliver's Travels* expresses Swift's disdain for his fellow human beings.

Samuel Richardson (1689–1761)

Richardson wrote the two-volume novel *Pamela, or Virtue Rewarded* (1740), the tale of a virtuous household servant who escapes the lecherous advances of her employer's son. He later wrote two additional volumes, as well as a novel in seven volumes, *Clarissa Harlowe* (1747–1748), the tragic story of a young woman who runs off with her seducer. An immensely popular writer in his own time, Richardson's novels are regarded today as excessively sentimental.

Henry Fielding (1707–1754)

A novelist and dramatist, Fielding is best known for *Tom Jones* (1749), a cheerful and often bawdy account of the wild adventures of its foundling hero.

Richard Brinsley Sheridan (1751–1816)

Sheridan, the manager of London's famed Drury Lane Theatre, wrote witty comedies, including *The Rivals* (1775), featuring the character of Mrs. Malaprop, and *The School for Scandal* (1777).

The Baroque Style

During the seventeenth century, European artists and architects developed a style known as baroque. While it was inspired by classical models and represented an outgrowth of the Renaissance style, baroque was more exuberant and flamboyant. The baroque style developed in the context of the Catholic Reformation and served as a symbol of the revived vigor and dynamism of the Roman Catholic Church.

Churches

Baroque buildings had a relatively simple exterior, but the interiors were elaborately decorated with dramatic paintings and sculpture. One of the first great baroque churches was the church of the Gesù (Jesus) in Rome, the mother church of the Society of Jesus. Outside Italy, many great baroque churches were built in Austria, Bohemia, southern Germany, and the Catholic cantons of Switzerland.

Baroque also had an impact on Protestant lands. Most notably, the English architect Christopher Wren (1632–1723) designed the new St. Paul's Cathedral (1675–1710) and a number of other churches in London.

Secular Architecture

Secular buildings were also constructed in the baroque style, among them King Louis XIV's great palace at Versailles. In 1715, Peter the Great of Russia began the construction of his baroque summer palace at Peterhof (Petrodvorets), located only a few miles from his new capital of St. Petersburg.

Giovanni Lorenzo Bernini (1598–1680)

Bernini was among the greatest of the baroque architects and sculptors. In 1629, he became the architect of St. Peter's basilica in Rome, designing the bronze canopy (baldachin) above the main altar and the great colonnade in the piazza. Bernini is also known for his dramatic statue of *The Ecstasy of St. Theresa*.

The Rococo Style

During the eighteenth century, the baroque style gradually gave way to the style known as rococo. Compared with baroque, rococo is lighter and even more ornate. Many great rococo churches were built in Austria and southern Germany. Among secular buildings, Maria Theresa's Schönbrunn palace in Vienna and Frederick the Great's Sans Souci palace at Potsdam outside Berlin are noted examples of rococo architecture.

The Venetian Giovanni Battista Tiepolo (1696–1770) was one of the most outstanding rococo painters. He decorated the interiors of a number of churches and palaces in northern Italy and the Residenz Palace in Würzburg in southern Germany.

Flemish Painting

Two Flemish painters, Peter Paul Rubens and his pupil, Anthony Van Dyck, are ranked among the major baroque artists. They presented classical themes, especially drawn from mythology, with a dramatic use of color. Both Rubens and Van Dyck are known for their portraits of aristocrats and rulers.

Peter Paul Rubens (1577–1640)

After studying in Italy, Rubens returned to his native Antwerp in 1608. In addition to his paintings based on mythology and portraits, the prolific Rubens is known for his religious paintings, landscapes, paintings of animals, and genre paintings (scenes of everyday life). His first major works, painted in Antwerp, include *The Raising of the Cross* and *Descent From the Cross*.

Anthony Van Dyck (1599–1641)

Like his teacher, Van Dyck studied in Italy. He worked for a time in England under the patronage of King James I and returned in 1632 to become court painter to King Charles I. In addition to his portraits, Van Dyck is known for his religious paintings.

Dutch Painting

While Flemish painters specialized in portraits of royalty and aristocracy, Dutch artists more often painted portraits of wealthy burghers, reflecting the differences in the nature of the two societies.

Rembrandt van Rijn (1606–1669)

Rembrandt is universally regarded as the greatest European painter of the seventeenth century. Working in Amsterdam, he became popular for his group and individual portraits, especially of the prosperous Dutch bourgeoisie. His major works include *The Anatomy Lesson of Dr. Tulp* (1632) and *The Nightwatch* (1642). In addition to his portraits, Rembrandt is noted for his paintings inspired by the Bible. Over the course of his career, Rembrandt painted almost one hundred self-portraits.

Frans Hals (c. 1580–1666)

Hals is known both for his individual and group portraits and his genre paintings. He spent most of his life in Haarlem.

French Painting

Nicolas Poussin (1594–1665)

Poussin was the leading French painter of the seventeenth century. His style evolved from baroque to become a major expression of French classicism. He is known for paintings based on classical themes, landscapes, and religious paintings.

Antoine Watteau (1684–1721)

The Flemish-born Watteau settled in Paris, where he won a reputation as a leading rococo artist, painting delicate fantasies in pastel tones.

François Boucher (1703–1770)

A rococo painter, influenced by Watteau, Boucher painted mainly scenes from classical mythology, pastoral scenes, and nudes. Boucher served as director both of the Gobelins tapestry factory and the French Academy.

Jean-Honoré Fragonard (1732–1806)

A student of Boucher, Fragonard became a popular court painter of portraits and landscapes.

Spanish Painting

Diego Velázquez (1599–1660)

In 1624, at the age of twenty-five, Velázquez became the court painter to King Philip IV of Spain. He is known for his portraits of members of the royal family and important court personages, as well as of dwarfs and buffoons.

Bartolomé Esteban Murillo (c. 1617–1682)

Murillo was a painter of portraits and religious subjects who spent most of his life in his native Seville. His works include a well-known series of paintings on the history of the Franciscans.

English Painting

The eighteenth century was the great age of English portraiture.

Sir Joshua Reynolds (1723–1792)

Reynolds produced over 2,000 historical paintings and portraits. In 1768, he became the first president of the Royal Academy.

Thomas Gainsborough (1727–1788)

Gainsborough painted both portraits and landscapes. One of his most famous works is the *Blue Boy*. A founding member of the Royal Academy, Gainsborough was a successful rival of Reynolds for commissions and royal favor.

Music

Opera

The emphasis of baroque on the dramatic helped promote the development of opera, which brought together the talents of singers, instrumentalists, dramatists, and painters to create a unified whole.

Monteverdi

One of the first major operatic composers was Claudio Monteverdi (1567–1643), who composed the opera *Orfeo* (1607) for his patron, the duke of Mantua. Within a few years operas were being performed in most of Italy's cities.

Scarlatti and Lully

Other major operatic composers of the seventeenth century include the Italian Alessandro Scarlatti (c. 1660–1725) and the Italian-born Frenchman Jean-Baptiste Lully (1632–1687).

Scarlatti wrote over one hundred operas, as well as church music and chamber cantatas. Lully composed many operas and ballets. He became very wealthy from producing his own works after he gained a monopoly of operatic production in France.

Johann Sebastian Bach (1685–1750) and George Frederick Handel (1685–1759)

Bach and Handel were the greatest European composers of the early eighteenth century. Both were born in the German kingdom of Saxony, although Handel lived in London for most of his life.

Known as an organist and a composer, Bach wrote both religious and secular compositions. His most famous works include the *St. John Passion* (1723), the *St. Matthew Passion* (1729), and the *Mass in B Minor* (1733–1738). He wrote over three hundred sacred cantatas. His orchestral compositions include the *Brandenburg Concertos* (1721).

Handel wrote close to fifty operas and developed the oratorio, a musical drama performed in concert form. The most famous of his more than thirty oratorios, *The Messiah*, received its first performance in

Dublin in 1742. Among his other well-known compositions are the *Water Music* (1717) and *Music for the Royal Fireworks* (1749).

Wolfgang Amadeus Mozart (1756–1791) and Franz Joseph Haydn (1732–1809)

During the late eighteenth century, Vienna became a great musical center. Mozart and Haydn were among the Austrian capital's leading composers in the classical style.

A child prodigy, Mozart produced more than six hundred compositions in virtually every musical form. He composed forty-one symphonies, over forty concertos, and several operas, including *The Marriage of Figaro* (1786), *Don Giovanni* (1787), and *The Magic Flute* (1791).

His unfinished *Requiem* was completed by another composer following his death at the age of thirty-five.

A prolific composer, Haydn wrote over eighty string quartets, more than fifty piano sonatas, and over one hundred symphonies, including the *Surprise Symphony* (1791) and the *Clock Symphony* (1794).

During the seventeenth and eighteenth centuries, European writers, artists, architects, and composers produced works of enduring significance. Their works, whether classical, baroque, or eluding easy classification, reflected the rational spirit of the age and the view of the orderly universe that the Scientific Revolution had produced. They appealed to the post-Renaissance tastes of the upper classes.

Recommended Reading

Brereton, Geoffrey. *A Short History of French Literature* (1954).

Busch, Harald and Bernd Lohse, eds. *Baroque Europe* (1962).

Durant, Will and Ariel. *The Age of Reason Begins* (1961).

Fleming, William. *Arts and Ideas* (7th ed., 1986).

Fosca, François. *The Eighteenth Century: Watteau to Tiepolo* (1952).

Friedrich, Carl J. *The Age of the Baroque, 1610–1660* (1952).

Grout, Donald Jay. *A History of Western Music* (3rd ed., 1980).

Held, Julius S. and Donald Posner. *Seventeenth and Eighteenth Century Art: Baroque Painting, Sculpture, Architecture* (1971).

Hibbard, Howard. *Bernini* (1965).

Humphreys, A. R. *The Augustan World: Society, Thought, and Letters in Eighteenth-Century England* (1954).

Schönberger, Arno and Halldor Soehner. *The Rococo Age: Art and Civilization of the 18th Century* (1960).

Ch: 14
Louis XV
Louis XVI
3 estates
Nat. Assem
Alliance
Republic
Constitution
Nat. Convention
Mountain
Jacobins
Robespierre
R. o. T.
C o. P. S.
Leg. assem
Treaty of T.
Directory

CHAPTER 14

The French Revolution

Time Line

1715–1774	Reign of King Louis XV
1743	Cardinal Fleury dies
1774–1792	Reign of King Louis XVI
1788	King Louis XVI summons the Estates General
(1789)	The Third Estate proclaims itself to be the National Assembly
	A Paris mob storms the Bastille
	The Great Fear sweeps the French countryside
	The National Assembly approves the Declaration of the Rights of Man and the Citizen

1790	The National Assembly enacts the Civil Constitution of the Clergy
1791	The Constitution of 1791 establishes a constitutional monarchy
	The Legislative Assembly convenes
1792	The Legislative Assembly deposes King Louis XVI and calls for the election of the National Convention
	The National Convention abolishes the monarchy
1792–1797	The War of the First Coalition is fought
1793	King Louis XVI is executed
	The Reign of Terror begins
1794	The Thermidorean Reaction ends the Reign of Terror
1795	The National Convention drafts the Constitution of 1795
	The Directory begins to rule France
1799	Napoleon Bonaparte seizes power.

When King Louis XIV died in 1715, he left France with a heavy burden of debt incurred during his wars of aggression. Although France was a prosperous country, the French monarchy was approaching bankruptcy, both in its finances and in its ability to provide the nation with effective leadership. Louis XIV's successors, Louis XV and Louis XVI, proved incapable of dealing with the government's financial and administrative problems.

The explosion came with the outbreak of revolution in 1789. During the next two years, the National Assembly, dominated by the reform-minded middle class, established a constitutional monarchy and reduced the power and privileges of the nobility and the Roman Catholic Church.

Under the Legislative Assembly (1791–1792) and the National Convention (1792–1795), the revolution entered a more radical phase. The monarchy was abolished, the king was executed, and the revolution passed through the Reign of Terror (1793–1794).

The Thermidorean Reaction of 1794 established a new government, the Directory, which failed to cope effectively with France's political and economic problems. This failure resulted in the establishment of Napoleon Bonaparte's military dictatorship in 1799.

The Old Regime: King Louis XV (r. 1715–1774)

In 1715, Louis XV, the great-grandson of Louis XIV, became king. In 1726, Cardinal André Hercule de Fleury (1653–1743), became chief minister. Fleury proved relatively successful in stabilizing the French currency and maintaining peace in Europe, although he did little to confront some of the more fundamental problems facing the French monarchy.

Following Fleury's death in 1743, Louis XV acted as his own chief minister, although he was lazy, possessed few skills, and remained generally unaware of his government's problems.

Financial and Administrative Problems

The financial problems of the French state persisted and became more serious in the aftermath of the Seven Years' War, which ended in 1763. To compound the government's problems, the royal administration was in near chaos. Various agencies had ill-defined and overlapping functions, which served to delay action on important issues. No strong figure emerged to provide a sense of order and direction.

Demands of the Nobility

The nobility agitated for a restoration of its traditional political rights, which had been lost as the kings moved to establish an absolute monarchy. The nobles wanted to create a system where they would share power with the king.

The Old Regime: King Louis XVI (r. 1774–1792)

In 1774, Louis XVI, the grandson of Louis XV, became king. His queen was Marie Antoinette (1755–1793), the daughter of Maria Theresa of Austria.

Jacques Turgot (1727–1781)

Louis XVI attempted to promote much-needed financial and economic reforms. In 1774, he named the physiocrat Turgot to the post of controller general of finances. Turgot sought to cut government expenditures and to abolish the trade guilds, which restricted the growth of the French economy. To relieve the peasants, he proposed ending the *corvée,* the requirement that the peasants perform labor on the roads. His efforts to reduce spending aroused considerable opposition, since a great many people benefited from government spending. Turgot's critics, especially the nobility, became increasingly outspoken in their attacks on his policies. In 1776, Louis XVI dismissed him only twenty months after his appointment to office. Turgot's dismissal served as a powerful symbol of the inability of the French monarchy to deal with its problems.

Jacques Necker (1732–1804)

financial advisor to Louis XVI

Necker, a Swiss banker who had lived in Paris for many years, succeeded Turgot. Instead of attempting to institute reforms to resolve the financial crisis, Necker resumed the traditional policy of borrowing money and increasing spending. Louis XVI dismissed Necker in 1781. The fiscal crisis intensified, and the increasingly more desperate king recalled Necker in 1788.

The Estates General

In July 1788, in an attempt to win popular support for new taxes, Louis XVI decided to summon into session the Estates General, a consultative assembly that had last met in 1614. The Estates General represented the three legally defined classes (estates).

Louis XVI summons estates gen 2
– C
– N
– comm.

The First Estate—The Clergy

The First Estate consisted of all of the clergy but was dominated by the higher clergy, the archbishops, bishops, and abbots who were drawn from the ranks of the nobility. The higher clergy enjoyed sizable incomes, while the ordinary parish priests were not much better off than the people they served.

The Second Estate—The Nobility

The nobility, numbering about 400,000 persons, comprised the Second Estate and held a virtual monopoly on the highest and best-paid positions in the state and church. The nobility owned about one-fifth of the land and like the clergy, was exempt from direct taxes.

The Third Estate—The Peasants, the Middle Class, and the Urban Workers

The Third Estate consisted of all who were not classified as clergy or nobility, primarily the peasants, the middle class (the bourgeoisie), and the urban workers (the proletariat), who totaled about 98 percent of the French population of 25 million.

Peasants

With few exceptions, the peasants were free of serfdom, and many owned the land they farmed. Others were tenants. However, the peasants were exploited by both the government and the nobility. They had to pay high taxes, including a salt tax (the *gabelle*). There were vestiges of the manorial system, which required the peasants to pay rent to noblemen who had once controlled the land and to perform the *corvée* and other services for them. The peasants were not particularly concerned with political rights but wanted relief from high taxes and an end to their manorial obligations.

The Middle Class

The middle-class townspeople were better off than the peasants, but they were even more discontented. The middle class desired an abolition of the economic restrictions imposed by mercantilist regulation, a fairer distribution to the tax burden, and a greater voice in public affairs.

Urban Workers

In the late eighteenth century, the urban working class was relatively small. In Paris, however, the workers were numerous enough to play an active and influential role during the revolution.

Elections for the Estates General

In calling for the election of the Estates General, the king declared that it should consist of 300 representatives of the clergy, 300 representatives of the nobility, and 600 representatives of the Third Estate.

The elections for the Estates General took place in an atmosphere of widespread discontent, which was intensified by the bad harvest of 1788. During the period of the elections, hundreds of pamphlets were published expressing the discontents and aspirations of various elements in the population. The electoral meetings not only elected representatives to the Estates General but also prepared written documents (*cahiers*) expressing the electors' grievances and proposals for reform. These pamphlets and *cahiers* provide an excellent picture of the attitudes of the French people on the eve of the revolution.

Demands on the Monarchy

At one end of the social scale, the nobility gave renewed expression to its demands for the establishment of a constitutional monarchy in which the aristocrats would exercise a substantial degree of control. The Third Estate called for an end to the special privileges enjoyed by the clergy and nobility. The peasants demanded the abolition of the *gabelle*, as well as of the *corvée* and other remnants of manorialism. The middle class called for an end to mercantilist restrictions on industry and trade, reform of the often corrupt courts of law, and the establishment of a constitutional monarchy with an elected parliament and guarantees of civil liberties.

Voting by Order

When the Estates General held its first meeting at Versailles on

May 5, 1789, Louis XVI ordered the estates to meet separately and to vote by order (by estates). The conservative First and Second Estates would thus outvote the representatives of the Third Estate, even though the clergy and nobility accounted for no more than 2 percent of the population.

The National Assembly (1789–1791)

On June 17, the increasingly rebellious Third Estate proclaimed itself to be the National Assembly and invited the members of the other two estates to join it.

3rd estate rising + joining w/ other estates

The Tennis Court Oath

On June 20, having been locked out of its usual meeting place, the National Assembly met in an indoor tennis court. In what came to be known as the Tennis Court Oath, the National Assembly pledged that it would not disband until it had given France a constitution. A number of aristocrats and a large part of the First Estate, especially parish priests, joined the National Assembly.

• locked out
• indoor tennis court
• not disband until constitution ← France

Louis XVI Versus the National Assembly

Break up 2 3 estates

The king continued to insist that the estates meet separately and ordered the National Assembly to disband. Under the leadership of the Comte de Mirabeau (1749–1791), the National Assembly defied the king. On June 27, Louis XVI gave way and ordered the first two estates to meet with the National Assembly. During this first period of the French Revolution, the period of the National Assembly, control was in the hands of moderates drawn from the middle class and the liberal nobility.

Louis XVI hoped to reassert his authority and began to mass Swiss and German mercenaries in the area of Paris and Versailles. Rumors spread that the king planned to use these mercenaries to disperse the National Assembly. On July 11, the king abruptly dismissed Necker. The rumors intensified and rioting broke out in Paris.

S + G mercenaries ⟶ N.A.

Paris mob
Bastille — prison

Storming of the Bastille

Necker → power
Lafeyette → National Guard

On July 14, a Paris mob stormed the Bastille, a fortress prison that stood as a hated symbol of the arbitrary rule of the Bourbons. In the aftermath of the taking of the Bastille, Necker was restored to power, Jean Bailly (1736–1793) became mayor of Paris, and the Marquis de Lafayette (1757–1834), a hero of the American Revolution, became commander of the newly created National Guard. The red, white, and blue tricolor flag of the revolution was adopted. As the revolution intensified, many aristocrats fled France.

The Great Fear

3rd estate rising + rebelling → end feudalism

During the summer of 1789, the Great Fear swept the provinces. Rumors reported an impending famine and told of bandits, in the pay of the king or the nobility, roaming the countryside attacking peasants. Revolutionary fervor spread among the peasants.

In an effort to halt the disorder in the countryside, the National Assembly, on August 4, ended the remnants of manorialism, including the *corvée*, and the privileges of the nobility. All French citizens now became equal in the eyes of the law.

Declaration of the Rights of Man

On August 27, 1789, the National Assembly approved the Declaration of the Rights of Man and the Citizen, which embodied many of the ideas that had been expressed by the Enlightenment. Representing in particular the aspirations of the middle class, the declaration proclaimed that all men were "born and remain free and equal in rights." These natural rights included the rights to "liberty, property, security, and resistance to oppression." More specifically, the declaration provided for freedom of speech and of the press, freedom of assembly and the right to petition the government, freedom of religion, and freedom from arbitrary arrest and imprisonment. The declaration also embraced the doctrine of popular sovereignty, providing that the "source of all sovereignty is essentially in the nation."

- Approved by Nat'll Assem.
- equality + freedom

Mob Action

*[handwritten: 1. King wants 2 restore power
2. Women mad abt ↑ bread $
↓ versailles
3. King confronts mob → Paris w/ wife]*

In the autumn of 1789, a new wave of rumors asserted that the king was planning to use military force in an effort to restore his authority. On the night of October 5–6, a Paris mob, composed largely of women who were angry about increases in the price of bread, marched out to Versailles. Confronted by the mob, the king and the royal family agreed to return to Paris and to take up residence in the Tuileries Palace in the heart of the city.

The Political Clubs

During the first months of the revolution, a number of political clubs emerged. These clubs consisted mostly of middle-class business and professional men who met to discuss the issues of the day. In time, the clubs came to exert a major influence on the course of the revolution.

The Jacobins

*[handwritten: - pol. club - abolish monarchy
- radical
↓ rep.]*

The Jacobin Club was the most famous. At first, the Jacobins were relatively moderate in their views, but they gradually became more radical, demanding the abolition of the monarchy and the establishment of a republic. Maximilien Robespierre (1758–1794) became one of the Jacobins' best-known leaders. *[handwritten: Robespierre]*

The Cordeliers

The Cordeliers were radicals who, like the Jacobins, favored the abolition of the monarchy and the creation of a republic. Leading Cordeliers included Georges-Jacques Danton (1759–1794), a lawyer; Camille Desmoulins (1760–1794), a journalist; and Jean-Paul Marat (1743–1793), a physician and journalist.

The Feuillants

The Feuillant Club was a more conservative organization that favored a limited monarchy, rather than a republic. Following the abolition of the monarchy, the Jacobins suppressed the Feuillants.

The Civil Constitution of the Clergy

In November 1789, in an attempt to deal with the financial crisis faced by the French state, the National Assembly confiscated the land owned by the Roman Catholic Church. The National Assembly then issued paper money, known as *assignats,* using the confiscated land as security. The assignats declined rapidly in value, however, and the government's financial problems persisted.

Deprived of its land, the church had lost its major source of income, and the French government now assumed the obligation of paying the salaries of the clergy.

The National Assembly proceeded to reorganize the administration of the church, adopting the Civil Constitution of the Clergy on July 12, 1790. Bishops and priests would now be elected by the people, and the clergy were required to swear an oath of allegiance to support the new arrangement. Over half of the clergy refused to do so. These nonjurors, as they were called from the French word *jurer* ("to swear"), became bitter opponents of the revolution, as did many faithful Catholic laypeople.

The Constitution of 1791

In a troubled situation, the National Assembly continued its efforts to draft a constitution for France.

In December 1790, Necker resigned after he lost favor with the National Assembly. Mirabeau now became the king's chief adviser, hoping to contribute to the establishment of a stable constitutional monarchy. Mirabeau's death on April 2, 1791, weakened the king's cause, as well as the cause of moderation.

On the night of June 20, 1791, the king and his immediate family fled from Paris, intending to leave France and secure foreign assistance against the revolutionaries. Captured in Varennes in northeastern France, the king and his family were compelled to return to the capital.

On September 14, 1791, Louis XVI accepted the new constitution. This Constitution of 1791 established a limited monarchy with separation of powers between the executive, legislative, and judicial branches. The king and his ministers constituted the executive, but their authority was limited by a one-house parliament, the Legislative Assembly.

Other Reforms of the National Assembly

The National Assembly abolished titles of nobility and also abolished the parlements and other courts of law that the nobility had dominated. A new system of courts was created, with elected judges and prosecutors. The use of torture was ended, and juries were introduced in the trial of criminal cases.

The National Assembly also reorganized local government. The old provinces were abolished, and France was divided for administrative purposes into eighty-three departments.

In the realm of economic policy, the National Assembly followed laissez-faire principles, abolishing the guilds and ending mercantilist restrictions on industry and trade. The old system of direct and indirect taxes was ended, and a tax on land was introduced, along with a tax on the profits of industry and trade. The practice of farming out taxes to private collectors was ended.

Mountain ← Jacobist radical group

The Legislative Assembly (1791–1792) *Girondists*

The newly elected Legislative Assembly held its first meeting on October 1, 1791, and remained in session for less than a year. The conservatives and moderates, who wanted to preserve the constitutional settlement of 1791, were weak and became weaker, while the influence of the radicals, who wanted to push the revolution further, increased. The radicals were divided into two main groups: the Girondists, whose leaders came from the area of Bordeaux in the department of the Gironde, and the Mountain, whose name came from the fact that its members occupied the highest seats on the left side of the meeting hall. The Mountain drew its main support from the Jacobin and Cordelier clubs.

Intervention of Foreign Powers

The Legislative Assembly faced a threat from foreign powers. In the Declaration of Pillnitz of August 27, 1791, Prussia and Austria declared their readiness to intervene if necessary to protect the French royal family and safeguard the monarchy. In February 1792, Prussia and Austria concluded an alliance.

P + A → French king alliance

(handwritten notes at top of page)

1st Coalition
LA War → Austria
Prussia

The Legislative Assembly responded by declaring war on Austria on April 20, 1792. The War of the First Coalition quickly got under way, as Prussia entered the war on Austria's side. Within a year, France was at war with most of Europe.

Radical Takeover

(handwritten: Paris mob → king → L.A. prisoner; elections for N.C.; const. ↓ F. ref.)

As the revolution moved in a more radical direction, the revolutionaries' watchword became "Liberty, Equality, Fraternity." On August 10, a Paris mob stormed the Tuileries Palace, massacring the king's Swiss Guards. The king fled to the Legislative Assembly, which took him prisoner. Voting to depose the king, the Legislative Assembly called for elections for a National Convention that would draft a constitution for a French republic.

The National Convention (1792–1795)

The National Convention held its first meeting on September 21, 1792. Proclaiming France a republic, the National Convention ruled the country for the next three years.

Radicals, once again known as the Mountain, dominated the National Convention under the leadership of Robespierre, Danton, Marat, and the Duke of Orleans (1747–1793), known as Philippe Egalité because of his support of democracy. The radicals had the support of the municipal government of Paris and the Paris mob, known as the *sans-culottes*. (The term means "without breeches," reflecting the fact that the workers wore long trousers rather than the knee breeches of aristocrats.)

Execution of Louis XVI

In December 1792, the National Convention found Louis XVI guilty of conspiracy against the liberty of the people and the security of the state. In January 1793, by a margin of one vote, the National Convention decided to execute the king. Louis XVI was beheaded on January 21, 1793.

The National Convention approved the draft of a constitution establishing a democratic republic, but then suspended it for the duration of the war. The constitution never went into effect.

Reforms Enacted by the National Convention

The National Convention also enacted a series of reforms. Slavery was abolished in the French colonies. Primogeniture, the practice under which property was inherited by the eldest son, was abolished. The metric system of weights and measures was established. Imprisonment for debt was abolished. The estates of the emigré nobility (the nobles who had left France) were confiscated, and the land was sold to peasants in small parcels of two or three acres. As a result, almost all the peasants of France became landowners.

Adopting a new calendar, the National Convention declared September 22, 1792, the first day of the year one of the French republic. A year of twelve months whose names were associated with the seasons and climate was established, and the week was extended to ten numbered days in order to eliminate Sunday.

Foreign and Domestic Threats

Prussia and Austria continued the war against France, and by early 1793 Great Britain, Holland, Spain, Portugal, Naples, and Sardinia had entered the conflict. Resuming the offensive, the Prussians drove the French out of the Austrian Netherlands (Belgium). As the crisis mounted in the spring of 1793, the National Convention ordered the conscription of 300,000 men.

Opposition to the National Convention mounted in a number of cities, as well as in rural areas. In March 1793, a major revolt broke out in the region of the Vendée, southwest of Paris. The National Convention now had to deal with the threat of a counterrevolution, as well as a foreign war.

The Reign of Terror

In an effort to combat the crisis, in April 1793, the National Convention established the Committee of Public Safety, which exercised dictatorial authority. Reorganized in July, its leading members included Danton, Robespierre, Marat, and Lazare Carnot (1753–1823), who specialized in military affairs.

When Danton urged a policy of moderation, he was removed from the Committee of Public Safety. The more radical Jacobins, led by Robespierre, established their full control over the government, and from the summer of 1793 to the summer of 1794, the Committee of Public Safety carried out an intensifying Reign of Terror. A revolutionary idealist, Robespierre hoped to create a republic of virtue where all citizens would possess high moral standards and be dedicated patriots. The most extreme violence was justified in order to achieve this noble end. A revolutionary tribunal was created to try those suspected of counterrevolution. The Reign of Terror ultimately claimed some 16,000 victims, including the former queen Marie Antoinette, Danton, Bailly, Desmoulins, and Philippe Egalité.

French Military Victories

As the war continued, Lazare Carnot ordered a *levée en masse,* the conscription of able-bodied men into the armies of the revolution, in August 1793. During 1793–1794, the French armies succeeded in defending the country against invasion. Then, during 1794–1795, they occupied the Low Countries, the Rhineland, parts of Spain, Switzerland, and Savoy. The treaties of Basel, signed in March and June 1795, ended the war against Prussia and Spain, respectively, although France remained at war with the Austrians and the British. In 1796, the French invaded Italy, occupying important areas of the country and forcing the Austrians out of the war. By 1797, the War of the First Coalition had ended, and only Great Britain remained at war against France.

The Thermidorean Reaction
and the Constitution of 1795

During early 1794, opposition mounted to Robespierre and his efforts to create a republic of virtue. On 9 Thermidor (July 27, 1794), a group of conspirators arrested Robespierre; he was beheaded the following day. A number of others who were responsible for the Reign of Terror were also executed. Power passed to the wealthy middle class, which took control of the National Convention and the Committee of Public Safety.

The National Convention prepared a new constitution, the Constitution of the Year III (the Constitution of 1795). The constitution created a two-house parliament consisting of the Council of Elders of 250 members and the Council of 500. Executive authority was exercised by five Directors who were elected by the Council of Elders. After completing the drafting of this new constitution, the National Convention was dissolved on October 26, 1795, and the Directory came into being.

[handwritten: Power → Wealthy Midd Class   N.C. → directory]

The Directory (1795–1799)

The new government of the Directory experienced great difficulty in dealing with France's severe financial crisis and other problems. Inflation was out of control, and there were serious food shortages. Corruption was rampant, and an atmosphere of exhaustion engulfed the country after years of turmoil. *[handwritten: 5 person executive gov by N.C.]*

As discontent mounted, the Directory came increasingly to rely on the army for support. Finally on 18 Brumaire (November 9, 1799), the popular general Napoleon Bonaparte overthrew the Directory and established a military dictatorship. *[handwritten: taken by N.B. → Mili. dic.]*

Napoleon's seizure of power marked the end of the revolutionary decade that had begun in 1789. The leaders of the French Revolution had failed to establish an orderly and workable system of government. Nevertheless, they had enacted some enduring reforms. The worst abuses of the Old Regime had been eliminated, including royal absolutism, the privileges of the nobility and the higher clergy, and the remnants of manorialism. The principles of freedom of religion and the equality of all citizens before the law had been introduced, and a number of other reforms had been established.

*[handwritten: economic prob ⊘ solved
· reforms
· equality + freedom]*

Recommended Reading

Behrens, C. B. *The Ancien Regime* (1967).

Bernier, Olivier. *Words of Fire, Deeds of Blood: The Mob, the Monarchy, and the French Revolution* (1989).

Brinton, Crane. *A Decade of Revolution, 1789–1799* (1934).

Bruenig, Charles. *The Age of Revolution and Reaction, 1789–1850* (2nd ed., 1977).

Cobban, Alfred. *A History of Modern France, vol. I, 1715–1815* (3rd ed., 1963).

Doyle, William. *Origins of the French Revolution* (1980).

Forrest, Alan I. *The French Revolution and the Poor* (1981).

Hampson, Norman. *The French Revolution: A Concise History* (1975).

Hampson, Norman. *The Life and Opinions of Maximilien Robespierre* (1974).

Hibbert, Christopher. *The Days of the French Revolution* (1981).

Kennedy, Michael L. *The Jacobin Clubs in the French Revolution: The First Years* (1982).

Kennedy, Michael L. *The Jacobin Clubs in the French Revolution: The Middle Years* (1988).

Lefebvre, Georges. *The French Revolution*, 2 vols. (1962-1964).

Lyons, Martyn. *France Under the Directory* (1975).

Palmer, R. R. *The Age of the Democratic Revolution: A Political History of Europe and America, 1760–1800*, 2 vols. (1959-64).

Roberts, J. M. *The French Revolution* (1978).

Rudé, George F. *The Crowd in the French Revolution* (1959).

Rudé, George F. *The French Revolution* (1989).

Schama, Simon. *Citizens: A Chronicle of the French Revolution* (1989)

Soboul, Albert. *The French Revolution, 1787–1799* (1975).

Sydenham, M. J. *The First French Republic, 1792–1804* (1974).

Thompson, J. M. *Robespierre and the French Revolution* (1953).

Vovelle, Michel. *The Fall of the French Monarchy* (1984).

CHAPTER 15

Napoleon, France, and Europe

Time Line

1804	Napoleon's code of civil law takes effect
	Napoleon becomes emperor of the French
1805–1807	The War of the Third Coalition is fought
1806	Napoleon creates the Confederation of the Rhine and abolishes the Holy Roman Empire
	Napoleon establishes the Continental System
1812	Napoleon fights his unsuccessful Russian campaign
1813	Russia, Prussia, and Austria defeat Napoleon in the Battle of the Nations
1814	Napoleon abdicates and goes into exile on the island of Elba
1815	Napoleon returns to power, beginning the Hundred Days
	Napoleon is defeated at Waterloo
1821	Napoleon dies on Saint Helena

The history of France and Europe during the period from 1799 to 1815 is largely the story of Napoleon Bonaparte. A brilliant general in the cause of the French Revolution, Napoleon took power in 1799 and established the Consulate. In 1804, he took the title of emperor of the French. While Napoleon deprived the French people of political liberty, he provided them with an orderly and efficient system of government and confirmed or initiated a number of enduring legal, administrative, and educational reforms.

As a conqueror, Napoleon achieved his greatest military successes in the years from 1805 to 1807, defeating Austria, Prussia, and Russia. His ability and power gradually declined, however, and the disastrous invasion of Russia in 1812 marked the beginning of his fall. After abdicating in 1814, Napoleon returned to power for the period of the Hundred Days in 1815. Defeated at Waterloo in June 1815, he entered his final exile on the remote island of Saint Helena in the South Atlantic, where he died in 1821.

The Emergence of Napoleon

Napoleon Bonaparte (1769–1821) was born in Ajaccio, Corsica, into a family of the lesser nobility. In 1768, France had acquired Corsica from the Italian republic of Genoa; thus, Napoleon was a French citizen by birth. At the age of ten, he entered a military school at Brienne, France, and became a student at the military academy in Paris in 1783.

In 1785, at age 16, Napoleon was commissioned a lieutenant of artillery. When the revolution began, he became one of its most ardent supporters. In 1793, during the War of the First Coalition, a plan developed by Napoleon helped the French recapture Toulon, a naval base on the Mediterranean, from the British.. In October 1795, Napoleon's artillery dispersed a mob assaulting the National Convention. These achievements brought the young officer to the attention of the revolutionary leaders.

Napoleon married Josephine de Beauharnais (1763–1814), a widow six years older than he. Her contacts with leading figures in the government of the Directory helped advance her husband's career.

Napoleon's Early Military Successes

In 1796, at the age of twenty-seven, Napoleon received the command of the French army in Italy. He achieved a great success, defeating the Austrians and their Sardinian allies. Under the terms of the Treaty of Campo Formio, signed with the Austrians in October 1797, France annexed the Austrian Netherlands (Belgium), while Austria acquired most of the Venetian Republic. The Austrians agreed to recognize the independence of the Cisalpine Republic in northern Italy, which was in reality a French satellite. The treaty ended the War of the First Coalition (1792–1797) against France, although Great Britain continued fighting without allies. During 1798 and 1799, the French extended their control over Switzerland and most of Italy.

[handwritten: invaded]

Napoleon's Egyptian Campaign

[handwritten: Egypt   archeology]

In 1798, Napoleon invaded Egypt, hoping to threaten British control of the eastern Mediterranean and disrupt the British Empire. A significant byproduct of the Egyptian campaign was the discovery of the Rosetta Stone, which provided the key for deciphering ancient Egyptian hieroglyphics.

In July 1798, Napoleon's army won the Battle of the Pyramids near Cairo, defeating the Mameluke army. In August, however, a British fleet, commanded by Lord Horatio Nelson (1758–1805), destroyed a French fleet at Abukir Bay, near Alexandria. This British victory in the Battle of the Nile stranded the French army in Egypt. Leaving his army, Napoleon returned to France. The setback in Egypt did little to injure his prestige or popularity.

[handwritten: Russia ↔ G. Britain]

Beginning of the War of the Second Coalition (1798–1801)

[handwritten: → France (defeated)]

In late 1798, while Napoleon was still in Egypt, Russia formed a new alliance with Great Britain. Austria, Portugal, Naples, and the Ottoman Empire soon joined, beginning the War of the Second Coalition against France. Although Russia dropped out within a year, France suffered several defeats in Italy and Germany. These defeats, combined with continuing political and financial disorder at home, weakened the government of the Directory.

[handwritten: directory weakens]

Napoleon's Seizure of Power—The Consulate

In October 1799, Napoleon landed in southern France. With the help of two of the five directors and his brother, Lucien (1775–1840), who was the president of the Council of 500, Napoleon launched a conspiracy to seize power. On November 9, 1799, Napoleon overthrew the Directory. He was thirty years old.

[handwritten: overthrew the directory]

The Constitution of 1799

[handwritten: - new constitution → Consulate]

Having taken power, Napoleon directed the drafting of a new constitution, the Constitution of the Year VIII (Constitution of 1799), establishing the regime known as the Consulate. Napoleon ruled as first

[handwritten: dictatorship]

consul, with a term of ten years. There were two subordinate consuls who had no real authority.

After a decade of revolutionary upheaval, the French people wanted order and stability. In a plebiscite held in 1802, Napoleon was made first consul for life, with the right to designate his successor.

Napoleon's Defeat of the Second Coalition

While Napoleon was reorganizing France's government, he also took the offensive against France's enemies in the Second Coalition. In June 1800, he defeated the Austrians at Marengo in northwestern Italy and later in the year, defeated the Austrians again at Hohenlinden in Bavaria. In February 1801, Austria dropped out of the war, signing the Treaty of Lunéville.

The British continued the war, forcing the French armies in Egypt to surrender in the summer of 1801. France and Great Britain concluded peace in the Treaty of Amiens, signed in March 1802, which proved to be only a truce in the long conflict between Napoleon and his implacable British foe. Under the terms of the treaty, France kept almost all of its conquests in Europe and regained the colonies the British had taken.

The Napoleonic Empire

In 1804, Napoleon moved to solidify his power, declaring himself to be the hereditary emperor of the French. In 1805, he took the title of king of Italy, while his stepson, Eugène de Beauharnais (1781–1824), ruled as viceroy.

In 1809, Napoleon divorced Josephine, who had borne him no children, and the following year married Archduchess Marie-Louise (1791–1847) of Austria, the eighteen-year-old daughter of Francis I. In 1811, Marie-Louise gave birth to a son, whose father gave him the title of king of Rome.

Napoleonic Administration

Napoleon deprived the French people of political liberty and freedom of expression, which, he believed, served to encourage anarchy. On the other hand, he established a highly centralized administration that provided the French people with an efficient and orderly government.

Financial Reforms

Eliminating corruption and waste, Napoleon reorganized and centralized the assessment and collection of taxes. Various government bonds and other obligations that had fallen in value were called in and paid. These actions put the French government on a solid financial basis.

Centralized Government

To incease the central government's control of local affairs, Napoleon appointed a prefect to administer each of the country's eighty-three departments and a subprefect to administer each district. The system of prefects and subprefects represented an important part of Napoleon's effort to centralize authority in his government in Paris.

The Napoleonic Code   *civil code of law*

Under the Old Regime, the French legal system had been chaotic, giving rise to widespread protests. During the 1790s, the National Convention had begun the task of unifying the legal system, but much remained to be done.

In 1800, Napoleon appointed a commission of legal experts to draft a new code of civil law. This civil code went into effect in 1804 and was renamed the Napoleonic Code in 1807. By 1810, Napoleon's government had also enacted new codes of criminal and commercial law.   *equality*

The Napoleonic legal reforms reaffirmed the revolutionary principle of the equality of all citizens before the law and the abolition of privileges based on birth. Individuals were permitted to pursue occupations of their choice, and employment in the service of the state would be based on ability rather than on social position or wealth. The codes also reaffirmed the right to property acquired during the revolution and the end of the manorial obligations of the peasants, as well as the principle of freedom of religion.

In other ways, Napoleon's legal reforms were less progressive. The interests of the state took precedence over the rights of individuals, while men were granted greater authority over their wives and children. Penalties for political crimes were increased. These legal reforms were among Napoleon's most enduring achievements, and their influence spread beyond the borders of France, since they were instituted in lands the French conquered.

The Concordat of 1801

Napoleon was a child of the Enlightenment, and in his personal religious beliefs, he was a deist or perhaps an atheist. However, he recognized the importance of resolving the conflict between the French state and the Catholic Church that had developed during the revolutionary decade.

The Concordat of 1801 established a reconciliation with Pope Pius VII (r. 1800–1823) and governed relations between the French state and the Roman Catholic Church until its abrogation by the French in 1905. The concordat granted the Catholic Church special status as the religion of the majority of the French people, although it was not the established religion of the French state. The French government had the authority to nominate the bishops, who would then be invested in their offices by the pope. The bishops would appoint the priests. The system of electing the clergy established by the Civil Constitution of the Clergy was thus ended, and the French government exercised administrative control over the Catholic Church, as had been the case under the Old Regime. The pope regained control of part of the Papal States, which had come under French control earlier.

The pope agreed to accept the loss of church lands confiscated during the revolution, and the French government agreed to pay the salaries of the clergy. Napoleon's government also paid the salaries of Protestant pastors and rabbis, although this was not a provision of the concordat.

Reforms in Education

Napoleon established a new state-controlled system of elite secondary schools, the lycées, and several professional and technical schools, including the École Polytechnique, a famed engineering school located in Paris. All public educational institutions and many private ones came under the supervision of a government agency known as the University of France, established in 1806.

The Napoleonic Wars, 1805–1815

The War of the Third Coalition (1805–1807)

In 1803, Great Britain renewed the war against France. In 1805, Austria and Russia joined in the war against France, creating the Third Coalition. Prussia remained neutral at the outset.

Napoleon quickly advanced into Germany, beginning a great march of conquest across Europe. On October 17, 1805, the emperor defeated the Austrians at Ulm, located on the Danube in the south German state of Bavaria.

British Naval Victory at Trafalgar

Four days later, on October 21, the French suffered a major naval defeat, when Lord Nelson's British fleet smashed the combined French and Spanish navies near Cape Trafalgar off the southwest coast of Spain. The British eliminated French naval power for the balance of the war, and Napoleon had to suspend his plans to invade Great Britain.

French Victories on Land

On land, however, Napoleon's victories continued. Moving east from Ulm, he defeated a combined Austrian and Russian army at Austerlitz, north of Vienna, on December 2, 1805. Austria signed the Treaty of Pressburg at the end of December. Under its terms, France gained control of most of Austria's possessions in Italy, including Venice.

In July 1806, Napoleon organized a number of German states into a French satellite state known as the Confederation of the Rhine. This new state provided a buffer for France against both Austria and Prussia. In August, Napoleon ordered the dissolution of the Holy Roman Empire. The last Holy Roman emperor, Francis II (r. 1792–1806), now became the first emperor of Austria, known as Francis I (r. 1806–1835).

Napoleon's actions in Germany brought Prussia into the war against France. On October 14, 1806, however, Napoleon defeated the

Prussians at Jena, while, on the same day, another French army defeated a Prussian force at Auerstädt. Napoleon took the Prussian capital of Berlin in late October.

The Treaties of Tilsit

During the spring of 1807, Napoleon moved into East Prussia, defeating the Russians at Friedland on June 13. The emperor then met with Tsar Alexander I (r. 1801–1825) of Russia and King Frederick William III (r. 1797–1840) of Prussia. The rulers agreed on the terms of the Treaties of Tilsit, ending the War of the Third Coalition.

The Prussians and Russians recognized three of the French emperor's brothers—Joseph (1768–1844), Louis (1778–1846), and Jerome (1784–1860)—as the kings of Naples, Holland, and Westphalia, respectively. (Westphalia was a part of the Confederation of the Rhine.) Later, when Joseph became king of Spain, he was replaced as king of Naples by Marshal Joachim Murat (1767–1815), who was married to Napoleon's sister Caroline (1782–1839).

Prussia lost about half its territory, ceding some to Saxony and some to the newly created French satellite state, the Grand Duchy of Warsaw.

Russia gained a free hand to deal as it wished with the Ottoman Empire, although Napoleon refused to allow Alexander I to take Constantinople. The tsar promised to support the French emperor in his struggle against Great Britain.

The Continental System

Unable to defeat the British militarily, Napoleon established the Continental System in an effort to destroy the British economy. Created by the Berlin Decree of November 1806, the Continental System was expanded by the Milan Decree of 1807.

The Continental System was designed to make it impossible for the British to trade with the European continent. All European ports were ordered closed to British ships and goods, while French privateers were authorized to attack British ships and ships of neutral countries that cooperated with the British. In practice, the Continental System proved virtually impossible to enforce. Smuggling was widespread, and even the French violated the rules of trade.

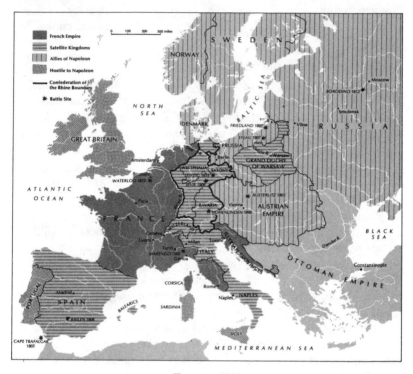

Europe, 1810

The Peninsular War

In late 1807, French troops moved into Portugal, which had failed to support the Continental System. To keep their lines of supply and communication open, the French also occupied Spain. In early 1808, Napoleon deposed Spain's Bourbon dynasty and installed his older brother Joseph as king of Spain.

When the Spanish people rose up in revolt against French domination, the British sent troops to Spain to support the insurgents. These troops were commanded by Sir Arthur Wellesley (1769–1852), who later became the Duke of Wellington. Possessing naval superiority, the British could reinforce this expeditionary force with ease. Continuing until 1814, the Peninsular War created a serious drain on France's military resources and served to encourage Napoleon's enemies elsewhere in Europe.

Conflict on Other Fronts (1808–1810)

In the spring of 1809, Austria renewed the war against France, invading Bavaria. Napoleon quickly defeated the Austrians at the Battle of Wagram (July 1809), however, and French forces occupied Vienna. Under the terms of the Treaty of Schönbrunn (October 1809), Austria ceded the Salzburg area to Bavaria, while the Grand Duchy of Warsaw acquired Austrian Poland. France annexed the Illyrian Provinces, Austrian territory along the northeastern coast of the Adriatic Sea.

On other fronts, the papacy's refusal to support the Continental System led to the French decision in 1808 to take Rome and imprison Pope Pius VII. France now annexed most of the Papal States.

In Scandinavia, Denmark (including Norway) became a close ally of France, while Napoleon recognized the French Marshal Bernadotte (1763–1844) as Sweden's crown prince. Bernadotte became King Charles XIV of Sweden in 1818.

In 1810, Napoleon's brother Louis, the king of Holland, protested against the emperor's determination to enforce the Continental System. Louis argued that ending Dutch trade with the British would ruin the country's economy. Napoleon responded by deposing his brother and annexing Holland.

French Colonial Losses

Even before Lord Nelson's great naval victory over the French at Trafalgar in 1805, Britain's naval power forced Napoleon to give up his plans to restore the French empire in America. While Napoleon compelled Spain to return the Louisiana territory to France, he decided to sell it to the United States in 1803. In the West Indies, the French colony of Haiti won its independence in 1804.

Napoleon's Russian Campaign

The Russians were increasingly dissatisfied with their position of subordination to France, and Tsar Alexander I refused to support Napoleon's Continental System. The French emperor responded by deciding to invade Russia.

Invasion of Russia

For his Russian campaign of 1812, the French emperor assembled a Grand Army of some 600,000 men. In late June 1812, the Grand Army entered Russia. By mid-August, the French had advanced some 300 miles, reaching Smolensk without having fought any major battles.

The Russians, under the command of Prince Mikhail Barclay de Tollay (1761–1818), continued to retreat, trading space for time. In September, Field Marshal Mikhail Kutuzov (1745–1813), who had replaced Barclay de Tollay, engaged the French at the Battle of Borodino, some 75 miles west of Moscow. Both sides suffered heavy casualties, and Napoleon failed to win a decisive victory over the Russians.

On September 14, the Grand Army entered Moscow. The Russians had abandoned the city, leaving it in flames. Napoleon remained in Moscow for five weeks, hoping that Alexander I would admit defeat and sue for peace. The tsar refused to do so.

French Retreat

On October 19, Napoleon began his retreat from Moscow. The Russian winter soon set in, aiding the Russian forces who harassed Napoleon's retreating army. Little of the Grand Army was left when the survivors regrouped near the Russian border in mid-December.

The Wars of Liberation (1813–1814)

In early 1813, Prussia made an alliance with Russia, and the Austrians joined in August. From October 16 to 19, the Russian, Prussian, and Austrian armies defeated Napoleon in the Battle of the Nations, fought near Leipzig in central Germany. Napoleon retreated across the Rhine back into France.

In November 1813, the Dutch revolted against French rule, while a British army, led by the Duke of Wellington, advanced from Spain and invaded southern France. In January 1814, Russian, Prussian, and

Austrian forces invaded France from Germany. On March 31, the allied armies entered Paris.

The Fall of Napoleon and the Hundred Days

On April 11, 1814, Napoleon abdicated. The allies allowed him to retain his title and gave him the island of Elba, located in the Mediterranean Sea off the west coast of Italy, on condition that he promise never to leave. The allies restored the Bourbon dynasty to the French throne with Louis XVIII (r. 1814–1824), a younger brother of Louis XVI, as king.

In early 1815, Napoleon left Elba and on March 1, landed on the Mediterranean coast of France with a small force. The restored Bourbon monarchy enjoyed little popular support, and the French army remained loyal to Napoleon. Troops sent out to apprehend him joined him instead. On March 20, Napoleon entered Paris in triumph, and the period of the Hundred Days began.

The Battle of Waterloo

Once again, the British, Russians, Prussians, and Austrians prepared for war. Napoleon decided to attack the allies in Belgium. At Waterloo on June 18, 1815, a British army commanded by the Duke of Wellington and a Prussian army commanded by Field Marshal Gebhard von Blücher (1742–1819) defeated Napoleon.

Following the Battle of Waterloo, the allies sent Napoleon into his final exile on the remote island of Saint Helena in the South Atlantic, where he remained until his death in 1821.

As France's ruler in the years after 1799, Napoleon deprived the French people of political liberty. But he confirmed a number of reforms achieved by the French Revolution—among them, freedom of religion and the principles of equality before the law and equality of opportunity—and made them permanent. Napoleon also introduced a number of reforms—including an efficient centralized administration, the Napoleonic Code, the Concordat of 1801, and a series of educational reforms—that became enduring features of French life.

Despite his undeniable genius as a military commander, Napoleon failed in his efforts to make France the master of Europe. In 1814–

1815, the statesmen of Europe met in the Congress of Vienna and sought to restore stability and order following a quarter of a century of turmoil.

Recommended Reading

Barnett, Corelli. *Bonaparte* (1978).

Bruun, Geoffrey. *Europe and the French Imperium, 1799–1814* (1938).

Connelly, Owen. *Blundering to Glory: Napoleon's Military Campaigns* (1987).

Connelly, Owen. *The Epoch of Napoleon* (1972).

Durant, Will and Ariel. *The Age of Napoleon* (1975).

Gates, David. *The Spanish Ulcer: A History of the Peninsular War* (1986).

Herold, J. Christopher. *The Age of Napoleon* (1963).

Holtman, Robert B. *The Napoleonic Revolution* (1967).

Horne, Alistair. *Napoleon: Master of Europe, 1805–1807* (1979).

Hutt, Max L. *Napoleon* (1965).

Lefebvre, Georges. *Napoleon,* 2 vols. (1969).

Markham, Felix. *The Bonapartes* (1975).

Markham, Felix. *Napoleon and the Awakening of Europe* (1954).

Parker, Harold T. *Three Napoleonic Battles* (1944).

Thompson, J. M. *Napoleon Bonaparte: His Rise and Fall* (1952).

CHAPTER 16

The Congress of Vienna and the Concert of Europe

Time Line

1814	The first Treaty of Paris establishes a lenient peace for France
1814–1815	The Congress of Vienna meets
1815	The Hundred Days end with Napoleon's defeat at Waterloo
	The Treaty of Vienna establishes a European territorial settlement
	The second Treaty of Paris imposes harsher terms on France

	Russia, Prussia, and Austria sign the Holy Alliance
	Great Britain, Austria, Prussia, and Russia sign the Quadruple Alliance
1818	The great powers meet in the Congress of Aix-la-Chapelle
1820–1821	The great powers meet in the Congresses of Troppau and Laibach
	The Greeks begin a revolt against Turkish rule
1822	The great powers meet in the Congress of Verona
1823	The United States issues the Monroe Doctrine
1829–1830	Greece gains independence from the Ottoman Empire
1830	Belgium secures independence from the Netherlands

After entering Paris in March 1814, the allies restored the legitimate Bourbon dynasty to the French throne, and Louis XVIII (r. 1814–1824) became king. In the first Treaty of Paris (May 1814), the allies offered France relatively lenient peace terms. However, following Napoleon's return to power during the Hundred Days in 1815 and his final defeat at Waterloo, the allies imposed harsher terms on France in the second Treaty of Paris (November 1815).

The other details of the peace settlement were determined by an international congress. The statesmen who met in this Congress of Vienna in 1814–1815 sought to reestablish a conservative order in Europe following the years of upheaval and war brought about by the French Revolution and Napoleon.

The First Treaty of Paris (May 1814)

Under the terms of the first Treaty of Paris, France lost all of its

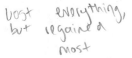
lost everything,
but regained
most

conquests of the revolutionary and Napoleonic periods but was permitted to retain its frontiers of 1792. France regained almost all of its colonies and was not required to pay an indemnity.

The Congress of Vienna

The Congress of Vienna began its deliberations in September 1814, and its sessions continued until June 1815.

Although a number of small states were represented, the four great powers that had joined to defeat France—Great Britain, Austria, Prussia, and Russia—expected to make the major decisions.   In their deliberations, the representatives of the great powers were influenced by several considerations.

1. The allied statesmen did not so much want to punish France as to insure that the French could not again embark on wars of aggression.

2. In addition, the statesmen sought to restore a balance of power, so that no one country could attempt to dominate Europe. France had a proper place in that balance; therefore, France should not be weakened excessively.

3. The principle of compensation was related to the balance of power. If one major state made gains, then the other major states should be compensated.

4. The principle of legitimacy involved the desire of the great powers to restore rulers and frontiers as they had existed prior to the wars of the French Revolution and Napoleon, insofar as that was possible and desirable.

5. Finally, the victorious allies expected to be rewarded for their efforts in defeating Napoleon and penalized countries that had cooperated with Napoleon.

The Major Statesmen at Vienna

Prince Klemens von Metternich (1773–1859), who served as Austria's foreign minister from 1809 to 1848, represented the interests of Emperor Francis I (r. 1806–1835) and acted as host for the Congress of Vienna. In recognition of his influence on the decisions of the congress and his active role in European affairs after 1815, the 1815 to 1848 period is called the Age of Metternich.

Metternich was firmly committed to the principles of conservatism. He regarded the new ideas of liberalism and nationalism as a threat to the survival of the Austrian Empire. He especially feared the spread of nationalism among the empire's subject nationalities. Metternich hoped the major powers would cooperate to maintain the conservative order, and he advocated intervention in any country where that order was threatened by the forces of change.

Viscount Castlereagh (1769–1822), the British foreign secretary from 1812 to 1822, generally shared Metternich's conservative views and strongly supported efforts to restore the balance of power.

Tsar Alexander I of Russia (r. 1801–1825) was in general agreement with his colleagues, although he also pushed for substantial territorial acquisitions, especially in Poland.

Prince Karl von Hardenberg (1750–1822) represented his king, Frederick William III (r. 1797–1840) of Prussia. He shared his colleagues' belief that the great powers should collaborate to maintain European peace and stability.

Charles-Maurice de Talleyrand (1754–1838), King Louis XVIII's foreign minister, found himself in the difficult position of representing the interests of his defeated country.

The Principle of Legitimacy

As a servant of the Bourbon king of France, Talleyrand was an ardent advocate of the principle of legitimacy. Not only was the legitimate Bourbon ruler restored to the French throne, but Talleyrand's influence led to the decision to restore Bourbons to the thrones of Spain and the Kingdom of the Two Sicilies, as well. In addition, the Congress of Vienna restored legitimate princely rulers in several other Italian states, including Sardinia-Piedmont, Tuscany, Modena, and the Papal States.

In Germany, however, the principle of legitimacy was ignored. The statesmen at Vienna had little desire to recreate the old Holy Roman

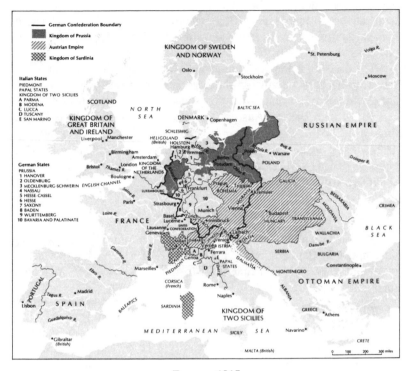

Europe, 1815

Empire or to restore the more than 300 states it had comprised. Instead, the Congress of Vienna created 39 German states, loosely joined in a new German Confederation.

The Conflict Over Poland and Saxony

Tsar Alexander I pressed his demand that Russia receive all of Poland. Prussia agreed to cede its Polish territory to the Russians on condition that it receive the German kingdom of Saxony as compensation.

Austria and Great Britain objected. Austria did not want to surrender its Polish territory and opposed both a further extension of Russian power into Europe and an increase of the power of Prussia, a potential rival of Austria's in German affairs. Like the Austrians, the British opposed an increase of Russian power, believing that an Eastern Europe dominated by Russia was as much a threat to the balance of power as was a Western Europe dominated by France.

The division among the victors gave Talleyrand the opportunity he sought to become an equal in the negotiations. He supported Austria and Great Britain, placing Metternich and Castlereagh in his debt.

Faced with British, Austrian, and French opposition, Russia and Prussia backed down, agreeing to accept less than they had initially demanded. Alexander I got a Russian-controlled kingdom of Poland, although it was smaller than he had wished, while Prussia acquired about two-fifths of Saxony.

The Territorial Settlement

Napoleon's return to power during the Hundred Days temporarily interrupted the deliberations of the Congress of Vienna, but the Treaty of Vienna was signed on June 9, 1815, nine days before Napoleon's final defeat at Waterloo.

Russia

In addition to acquiring more Polish territory, Russia retained Finland, which it had taken from Sweden in 1809. As compensation, Sweden retained Norway, which it had seized from Denmark, Napoleon's ally.

Prussia

In addition to acquiring two-fifths of Saxony, which had supported Napoleon, Prussia gained Swedish Pomerania and territory in the Rhineland in western Germany. Possession of the Rhineland brought Prussian power to the border of France to serve as a check on possible future French aggression.

The Netherlands

The Netherlands acquired the Austrian Netherlands (Belgium). The enlarged Kingdom of the Netherlands, bordering on France, would also serve as a check against future French aggression. For the same reason, the northern Italian state of Sardinia-Piedmont was strengthened by the acquisition of the republic of Genoa.

Austria

In compensation for its loss of Belgium, Austria acquired the northern Italian provinces of Lombardy and Venetia, which strengthened Austrian control over Italian affairs. Relatives of the Austrian emperor ruled the states of Parma, Modena, and Tuscany, while an Austrian archduchess was married to the Bourbon king of the Two Sicilies.

In addition to dominating Italy, Austria, the largest of the German states, dominated the German Confederation. Metternich was thus able to impose his repressive policies on the German states, just as he did in Italy.

Great Britain

The British, whose interests lay primarily outside of Europe, acquired a number of valuable colonial possessions. From the Dutch, they gained the Cape of Good Hope at the southern tip of Africa and the large island of Ceylon off the southeastern coast of India. In the West Indies, the British acquired several former French colonies, including Trinidad and Tobago. They also gained several other strategically located islands, including Helgoland in the North Sea and Malta in the Mediterranean.

The Second Treaty of Paris (November 1815)

Following Napoleon's final defeat at Waterloo, the allies imposed the second Treaty of Paris on France. Its terms were more severe than those of the first Treaty of Paris, but because of Talleyrand's influence, they were less harsh than they might have been. France was reduced to the borders of 1790. The French were required to pay an indemnity of 700 million francs to the allies and to accept allied military occupation of seventeen French forts for five years.

- 1790 land
- 5yr military forts
- pay 2 allies

The Holy Alliance and the Quadruple Alliance

In September 1815, the rulers of Russia, Prussia, and Austria signed the Holy Alliance, proposed by Tsar Alexander I. The three rulers pledged to observe Christian principles in both domestic and international affairs. While most of Europe's rulers ultimately signed the Holy Alliance, in practice it had little significance.

The Quadruple Alliance, signed by Great Britain, Austria, Prussia, and Russia in November 1815, was of greater importance. The four powers agreed to maintain the alliance that had defeated Napoleon and to meet periodically to discuss issues of mutual concern. This laid the basis for the Concert of Europe, the effort of the great powers to resolve international issues by consultation and agreement.

The Concert of Europe

The great powers hoped that the Concert of Europe would lead to the preservation of the balance of power and of the conservative order established at Vienna.

The Congress of Aix-la-Chapelle

In 1818, meeting in the Congress of Aix-la-Chapelle, the members of the Quadruple Alliance decided that France, which had paid its indemnity, should be freed of occupation. France rejoined the ranks of the great powers, and the Quadruple Alliance now became the Quintuple Alliance. Tsar Alexander I proposed that the great powers support existing governments and frontiers in Europe. Viscount Castlereagh, the British foreign secretary, rejected the proposal, marking the first break in the accord among the major powers.

The Congresses of Troppau and Laibach

In early 1820, a revolution broke out in Spain, where the army forced King Ferdinand VII (r. 1808–1833) to agree to rule in accordance with the liberal constitution of 1812, which he had previously ignored. In July 1820, a revolution also broke out in the Kingdom of the Two

Sicilies, where the army compelled King Ferdinand I (r. 1816–1825) to accept a constitution.

These revolutions were high on the agendas of the Congresses of Troppau and Laibach in 1820–1821. In the Protocol of Troppau, Russia, Prussia, and Austria asserted their right to intervene in other countries to oppose revolutions. Once again, the British objected to this interventionist policy.

The breach between the British and the three conservative powers widened at the Congress of Laibach, which authorized Austria to suppress the revolution in the Kingdom of the Two Sicilies, which it did in 1821.

The Congress of Verona

In 1822, the last of the congresses, the Congress of Verona, authorized France to intervene in Spain. With French support, King Ferdinand VII reestablished his absolute power.

George Canning (1770–1827), who became British foreign secretary in 1822, continued Britain's opposition to the policy of intervention. This opposition resulted, in effect, in Britain's withdrawal from the Quintuple Alliance.

British Opposition to Intervention and the Monroe Doctrine

British opposition to intervention made it impossible for the conservative powers of Europe to suppress the revolts in Spanish America, because they could not act effectively without the support of Britain's naval power. The British opposed intervention both because of principle and because they did not want any interference with their profitable trade with Latin America. Canning proposed that Great Britain and the United States join in a declaration against any European intervention in the Western Hemisphere.

The Americans, however, preferred to act independently. In the Monroe Doctrine, issued by President James Monroe (1758–1831) in December 1823, the United States announced its opposition to intervention and any further colonization by the European powers in the Western Hemisphere. The British endorsed the Monroe Doctrine, and both the

United States and Great Britain began to grant formal diplomatic recognition to the new Latin American republics.

Greek Independence

Revolution against Turkish rule broke out in Greece in 1821, and often brutal fighting continued for several years. By 1825, the Turks had almost crushed the revolt.

In Western Europe, sympathy for the Greeks mounted, in large part because of a sentimental regard for the contribution of the ancient Greeks to the development of Western civilization.

The Treaty of London (1827)

Great Britain, France, and Russia agreed in the Treaty of London of 1827 to demand that the Ottoman Empire recognize Greek independence and to use force, if necessary, to end the fighting. An allied fleet defeated a Turkish and Egyptian force at Navarino in October 1827.

The Treaties of Adrianople and London

In 1828, Russia declared war on Turkey, and Russian forces moved into the Turkish-controlled Danubian provinces of Moldavia and Wallachia (modern Rumania). Under the terms of the Treaty of Adrianople (1829), the Danubian provinces gained autonomy, as did Serbia, which the Turks had also ruled. Russia acquired territory at the mouth of the Danube River and in the Caucasus on the eastern coast of the Black Sea. The Turks agreed to permit Russia, France, and Great Britain to determine the future of Greece. In the Treaty of London (1830), the three powers recognized Greek independence. In 1832, Otto I (r. 1832–1862), the son of the king of Bavaria, was chosen as king of Greece.

Belgian Independence

In late August 1830, a revolt against Dutch rule broke out in Belgium. In November, a national congress declared Belgium's independence, and a liberal constitution was adopted in 1831. A German prince, Leopold of Saxe-Coburg, became Leopold I (r. 1831–1865), the first king of the Belgians. In 1839, the Netherlands formally recognized the independence of Belgium. Under the terms of the Convention of 1839, the major powers of Europe agreed to guarantee Belgian neutrality.

The conservative order established at Vienna in 1814–1815 prevailed throughout Central and Eastern Europe without serious threat until the outbreak of the revolutions of 1848. The balance of power established at Vienna remained fundamentally undisturbed until the unification of Germany in 1871, and no major war involved all of the major powers until the outbreak of World War I in 1914.

In Italy and Spain, the conservative powers succeeded in suppressing revolutions. However, Greece and Belgium, as well as the Latin American colonies of Spain and Portugal, made good their claims to independence. And in Great Britain and France, the conservative regimes that ruled in the years immediately following 1815 were able to forestall only temporarily the trend toward liberalization.

Recommended Reading

Artz, Frederick B. *Reaction and Revolution, 1814–1832* (1934).

Bernard, J. F. *Talleyrand: A Biography* (1973).

Bushnell, David. *The Emergence of Latin America in the Nineteenth Century* (1988).

Clogg, Richard, ed. *The Struggle for Greek Independence* (1973).

Kissinger, Henry. *A World Restored: Metternich, Castlereagh and the Problems of Peace, 1812-22* (1957).

Nicolson, Harold. *The Congress of Vienna: A Study in Allied Unity, 1812–1822* (1946).

Schenk, Hans G. *The Aftermath of the Napoleonic Wars: The Concert of Europe, an Experiment* (1947).

Woodhouse, C. M. *The Greek War of Independence: Its Historical Setting* (1952).

CHAPTER 17

Romanticism

Time Line

1781	Immanuel Kant publishes the *Critique of Pure Reason*
1790	Johann Wolfgang von Goethe publishes the first part of *Faust*
1798	William Wordsworth and Samuel Taylor Coleridge publish *Lyrical Ballads*
1812–1815	The Grimm brothers publish their collection of German folk tales
1819–1824	Lord Byron publishes *Don Juan*
1820	Percy Bysshe Shelley publishes *Prometheus Unbound*

	Sir Walter Scott publishes *Ivanhoe*
1830	Hector Berlioz's *Symphonie Fantastique* has its first performance
1831	Victor Hugo publishes *Notre Dame de Paris*
	Alexander Pushkin publishes *Boris Godunov*
1842	Nikolai Gogol publishes *Dead Souls*
1844	Alexandre Dumas publishes *The Three Musketeers*
1859	Alfred Lord Tennyson publishes *Idylls of the King*
1871	Giuseppe Verdi's opera *Aida* has its first performance
1876	The four operas comprising Richard Wagner's *Ring of the Nibelung* have their first performance

During the first half of the nineteenth century, the movement known as romanticism emerged as a dynamic expression of the creative energy of European civilization. While romanticism was a complex and diverse phenomenon, romantic thinkers, writers, artists, and composers were united in reaction against what they regarded as the Enlightenment's excessive emphasis on the supremacy of reason in human affairs. Instead, the romantics emphasized feelings and emotions, faith and intuition, and imagination and spontaneity. Many of the romantics rejected the Enlightenment's optimistic belief in the perfectibility of human beings and human society, although they continued to emphasize the importance and value of the individual and to promote individual freedom.

In their literary and artistic activity, the romantics rebelled against the formalism of eighteenth-century classicism and the rigid rules that classicism applied to the creative process.

The romantics also manifested a reverence for the past and an awareness of the emotional ties which joined the present with the past and gave a sense of order and stability to society and its institutions.

In particular, many romantics had a fascination for the culture of the Middle Ages, an age of faith, which stood in contrast to the eighteenth century age of reason.

Literature

Johann Wolfgang von Goethe (1749–1832) and Friedrich von Schiller (1759–1805)

In Germany, the late eighteenth century was a golden age. The works of two major writers of this period, Goethe and Schiller, were infused with the spirit of romanticism.

Born in Frankfurt, Goethe took up residence in 1775 in Weimar, a major center of German culture during the *Sturm und Drang* ("storm and stress") period in the late eighteenth century. In the romantically sensitive novel *The Sorrows of Young Werther* (1774), Goethe wrote of a young man involved in a tragic love affair who ends his life in suicide. In his poetic masterpiece *Faust,* Goethe retold the traditional German legend of the man who sold his soul to the devil in return for earthly knowledge and pleasure. The first part of *Faust* was published in 1790, and the work was completed in 1831, the year before the author's death.

A friend of Goethe, Schiller also resided in Weimar. He is best known for his dramas, which reflected his idealism and intense belief in the cause of human freedom. In *Die Räuber* ("The Robbers," 1781), Schiller delivered a powerful attack on political tyranny. The romantic heroes and heroines of his later dramas include William Tell, the Swiss fighter for freedom; Mary Queen of Scots; Joan of Arc; and Wallenstein, a great general of the Thirty Years' War.

Jakob (1785–1863) and Wilhelm (1786–1859) Grimm

The ranks of German romantic writers also include the Grimm brothers, Jakob and Wilhelm, who delved into the German past to collect traditional folk stories, which they published as *Grimms' Fairy Tales* (1812–1815).

Heinrich Heine (1797–1856)

Heine was a central figure in the revolutionary literary movement known as Young Germany. In his lyrical poetry, he reflected the romantics' concern for individual experience. Heine published several collections of his poetry, including the *Buch der Lieder* ("Book of Songs," 1827).

William Wordsworth (1770–1850) and
Samuel Taylor Coleridge (1772–1834)

The romantic era was a great age for English poetry. In 1798, Wordsworth and Coleridge published *Lyrical Ballads,* the first major work of English romantic literature. The volume contained Wordsworth's poem "Tintern Abbey."

While Wordsworth found inspiration in nature, Coleridge was fascinated by the mystical and exotic. "The Rime of the Ancient Mariner," a somber tale of a sailor burdened by a curse after killing an albatross, was his major contribution to *Lyrical Ballads.* Coleridge expressed the same fascination in his later poems, including "Christabel" and "Kubla Khan."

Lord Byron (1788–1824), Percy Bysshe Shelley (1792–1822), and
John Keats (1795–1821)

During their short lives, three other English romantic poets—Byron, Shelley, and Keats—gave free reign to the expression of their emotions. Byron and Shelley were ardent advocates of political liberty, and Byron died in Greece, where he had gone to help the Greek fight for independence. Perhaps the most popular of England's romantic poets, Byron is best known for *Childe Harold's Pilgrimage* (1812–1818), *The Prisoner of Chillon* (1816), and his masterpiece, *Don Juan* (1819–1824).

One of Shelley's most important works, *Prometheus Unbound* (1820), was inspired by *Prometheus Bound,* by the ancient Greek playwright Aeschylus. In Shelley's poem, Prometheus, who represents what is good in life, is locked in struggle with Jupiter, the symbol of tyranny and evil.

Keats wrote some of the most beautiful romantic poetry in the English language, including "The Eve of St. Agnes," the "Ode to a Nightingale," and the "Ode on a Grecian Urn," all published in 1820.

William Blake (1757–1827)

Blake was an accomplished painter and engraver in addition to being a poet. He demonstrated his imaginative, sensitive, and mystical genius in such poems as "The Lamb," "The Tiger," and "The Mental Traveler."

Alfred Lord Tennyson (1809–1892) and Robert Browning (1812–1889)

Two other English poets, Tennyson and Browning, are classified as writers of the Victorian period, although they expressed the romantic spirit in their work. In *Idylls of the King* (1859), Tennyson reflected his fascination with the Middle Ages in retelling the story of King Arthur and the knights of the Round Table.

Browning wrote several verse dramas and dramatic monologues, including "My Last Duchess" (1842).

Sir Walter Scott (1771–1832)

Scott holds a preeminent position among romantic British novelists. Inspired by a fascination with the Middle Ages and his native Scotland, he wrote more than thirty historical novels. *Ivanhoe* (1820), his best-known novel, is set in the twelfth century, in the time of King Richard the Lionhearted and the Crusades.

Honoré de Balzac (1799–1850), Alexandre Dumas (1802–1870), and Victor Hugo (1802–1885)

Balzac, Dumas, and Hugo emerged as major figures in French romantic literature. Balzac's early novels reflected his interest in the Middle Ages, but he soon turned his attention to his own time, writing in a more realistic fashion about the French bourgeoisie. His almost one hundred novels and stories, known collectively as *The Human Comedy*, present a broad analysis of the human character.

Dumas wrote exciting romantic tales, such as *The Three Musketeers* (1844) and *The Count of Monte Cristo* (1845), while Hugo is known for his novel *Notre Dame de Paris* (1831), set in the late Middle Ages in the time of King Louis XI. Hugo later turned to realism, writing *Les Miserables* (1862), a powerful story of the suffering human masses.

Alexander Pushkin (1799–1837) and Nikolai Gogol (1809–1852)

Pushkin and Gogol were the most prominent Russian authors of the early nineteenth century. Pushkin was the first major author to write in Russian, rather than in Slavonic, the language of the Russian Orthodox Church. The great-grandson of an African who served as a general in the army of Peter the Great, he turned to the national past for inspiration. *Eugen Onegin* (1825–1831), a novel in verse, and *Boris Godunov* (1831), a tragic drama, were based on the life and exploits of great figures of Russian history.

Regarded as the father of Russian realism, Gogol first won recognition with two volumes of stories based on his childhood in the Ukraine and published in the early 1830s. He then became a figure of controversy with his satirical drama *The Inspector-General* (1836). After emigrating to Italy, he wrote his most famous work, *Dead Souls* (1842), a bitter novel condemning serfdom.

Painting

During the first years of the nineteenth century, classicism continued to dominate European painting. Jacques-Louis David (1748–1825), who had gained prominence during the era of the French Revolution and Napoleon, remained the foremost classical painter. Gradually, however, romanticism began to take hold among Europe's artists.

Eugène Delacroix (1798–1863)

The French painter Delacroix used color and light to achieve dramatic effects. His flamboyant paintings manifested his rejection of classicism's insistence on restraint and order. In *The Massacre of Scio,* Delacroix depicted Turkish violence during the Greek war for independence, while in *Liberty Leading the People,* he painted a romantic celebration of the French revolution of 1830.

Landscape Painters

In France, Camille Corot (1796–1875) and other members of the Barbizon school, which flourished from about 1830 to 1870, painted romantic landscapes.

English romantic artists, including John Constable (1776–1837) and J. M. W. Turner (1775–1851), also became known for their landscapes.

Francisco Goya (1746–1828)

The Spanish artist Goya gained recognition both for his revealing portraits of the decadent Spanish Bourbons and for his powerful portrayals of the brutal French repression of the Spanish rebels against Napoleon in 1808. Paintings such as *The Third of May 1808* stand as powerful condemnations of war's cruelty.

Architecture

Architecture during the romantic period was dominated by the neoclassical and neo-Gothic styles, as well as by a fascination with the exotic. Inspired by ancient Greek and Roman architecture, the neoclassical style had won acceptance in the eighteenth century and remained popular in the romantic era. Romantic architects, reflecting the fascination with the Middle Ages that was characteristic of romanticism, promoted a revival of Gothic architecture. Following a fire in 1834, the reconstruction of the British Houses of Parliament in the neo-Gothic style began in 1840. Elsewhere, medieval Gothic cathedrals and churches were restored, including Notre Dame in Paris.

Other architects found their inspiration in the more exotic styles of the Orient, ranging from the Middle East and Persia to China. The Royal Pavilion in the seaside town of Brighton, built for Britain's prince regent, the later George IV (r. 1820–1830), is a memorable example of this style.

Music

Ludwig van Beethoven (1770–1827)

Beethoven was the major figure in the transition from classicism to romanticism in music. Born in Bonn in the German Rhineland, he moved to the Austrian capital of Vienna in 1792, remaining there for the rest of his life. His compositions include piano and violin sonatas, piano concertos, string quartets, and nine symphonies, as well as one opera, *Fidelio* (1803–1805), and one mass, the *Missa Solemnis* (1818–1823).

German Romantic Composers

Following Beethoven, Germany produced a host of romantic composers. Carl Maria von Weber (1786–1826), a pianist and composer, is recognized as the creator of the German romantic opera. Of his ten operas, *Der Freischutz* (1821) and *Oberon* (1826) are the best known. Franz Schubert (1797–1828) joined piano and voice in over 600 *Lieder* (poems set to music). Felix Mendelssohn (1809–1847) composed works for piano and violin, as well as chamber music and choral music. Of his five symphonies, the best known are the Scottish (1830–1842), the Italian (1833), and the Reformation (1830–1832). Robert Schumann (1810–1856) composed a wide variety of romantic music, including symphonies and piano concertos.

Richard Wagner (1813–1883)

German romantic music reached its culmination in the operas of Wagner, an ardent German nationalist who found inspiration in the epics of the Germanic past. The four operas known collectively as *The Ring of the Nibelung*——*Das Rheingold, Die Walküre* ("The Valkyries"), *Siegfried,* and *Götterdämmerung* ("The Twilight of the Gods")—had their first performance in Bayreuth in 1876.

Hector Berlioz (1803–1869)

Berlioz, France's major romantic composer, wrote the explosively emotional *Symphonie Fantastique,* which was first performed in Paris in 1830.

Giuseppe Verdi (1813–1901) and Giacomo Puccini (1858–1924)

The Italian Verdi was a prolific composer of romantic operas, including *Rigoletto* (1851), *La Traviata* (1853), *Il Trovatore* (1853), and *Aida* (1871). Another major Italian composer of romantic operas was Puccini, whose best-known work is *La Bohème* (1896).

Influences of Folk Music

Franz Liszt (1811–1886) was regarded by his contemporaries as Europe's greatest concert pianist. He composed a host of works for the piano, many of them inspired by the folk music of his native Hungary.

Traditional folk music also inspired the compositions of Mikhail Glinka (1804–1857) and Frédéric Chopin (1810–1849). The first of the Russian nationalist school of composers, Glinka is best known for two operas, *A Life for the Tsar* (1836) and *Russlan and Ludmilla* (1842). The latter was based on a poem by Pushkin. A Polish composer, Chopin wrote graceful works for the piano, including the concertos in E minor (1833) and F minor (1836).

Philosophy and Religion

Immanuel Kant (1724–1804)

Kant, a German philosopher, began the revolt against extreme rationalism in philosophy. A professor at the University of Königsberg in East Prussia, Kant wrote the *Critique of Pure Reason* (1781) and the *Critique of Practical Reason* (1790). While reason could neither prove nor disprove the existence of God, he argued, faith and intuition can lead one to an understanding of spiritual truths, including the existence of God, the immortality of the soul, and rewards and punishments after death.

G. W. F. Hegel (1770–1831)

Hegel, a professor at the University of Berlin, was Kant's most important follower. For Hegel, history represented the unfolding of God's plan for the world. He contended that change in history occurred as the result of a dialectical process, which involved a series of conflicts. In these conflicts, the established order (the thesis) encountered a challenge (the antithesis). Out of the conflict arose a new ordering of society (the synthesis), which represented a further step in the advance of human progress.

Pietism

In religion, many eighteenth-century Enlightenment intellectuals had embraced deism, which they regarded as the religious expression of rationalism. At the same time, however, millions of Christian believers were influenced by Pietism, which reaffirmed the importance of faith, emotional religious experience, and personal devotion to Jesus Christ.

Lutherans

During the seventeenth and eighteenth centuries, Pietism flourished among the Lutherans and Moravian Brethren of Germany. Philipp Spener (1635–1705), a Lutheran pastor, rejected religious formalism and urged his followers to develop a more intense personal religious faith.

Moravians

Count Nikolaus von Zinzendorf (1700–1760), a German Lutheran influenced by Pietism, offered the Moravian Brethren refuge on his estate in Saxony. The Moravian Brethren, also known as the Bohemian Brethren, were a small band of surviving followers of the early-fifteenth-century religious reformer John Hus. Like the pietistic Lutherans, the Moravians stressed personal piety rather than formal doctrine. Migrating to America, Zinzendorf established Moravian communities in Bethlehem and other towns in Pennsylvania. A number of Moravians migrated to the southern colonies, and an important

Moravian center was established in Salem (now Winston-Salem), North Carolina.

Quakers

In mid-seventeenth century England, George Fox (1624–1691) established the Society of Friends, popularly known as the Quakers. Like the German Pietists, Fox opposed religious formalism and emphasized the inner light of Jesus Christ that illumined the soul of the believer. Because the Quakers opposed war and the taking of oaths, they suffered persecution at the hands of the civil authorities. One of the best-known early Quakers was William Penn (1644–1718), the founder of the Pennsylvania colony.

Methodists

In the eighteenth century, John Wesley (1703–1791), an Anglican priest, founded the Methodist movement. Methodism opposed the formalism of the established Church of England and emphasized the development of personal piety, evangelism, and salvation through faith in Jesus Christ alone. The Methodists also worked to reduce social evils, campaigning against alcohol and the slave trade. John Wesley, his brother Charles (1707–1788), and other Methodist leaders, including George Whitefield (1714–1770) and Francis Asbury (1745–1816), won many converts in England and America. While Methodism began as a movement within the Church of England, it had become a separate denomination by the end of the eighteenth century.

The Catholic Revival

In the early nineteenth century, the romantics' emphasis on the mystical and supernatural led to a revival of traditional religious belief. Symbolic of this revival of religion was the pope's reestablishment of the Society of Jesus in 1814. The Jesuit Order had been suppressed in 1773 at the height of the Enlightenment. In France, the resurgence of traditional Catholicism received a powerful expression in *The Genius of Christianity* (1802), written by François René de Chateaubriand (1768–1848).

The Oxford Movement

In England, a group of Anglicans, known as the Oxford Movement, reasserted Catholic elements in the faith and practice of the Church of England. The Oxford Movement proved influential in the development of Anglo-Catholicism within the English church, although some of its leaders, including John Henry Newman (1801–1890), became converts to Roman Catholicism.

History

The romantics' sense of an organic union between the present and the past led to the writing of romantic national histories, which emphasized the uniqueness of a people's development and their historical mission. Major romantic historians included the Englishman Thomas Babington Macauley (1800–1859), the Frenchman Jules Michelet (1798–1874), and the Prussian Heinrich von Treitschke (1834–1896).

The romantic revolt against the extreme rationalism of the Enlightenment had an enduring impact on European culture. The romantics' love of nature and their willingness to break the bonds of artistic convention helped give birth to the movement of impressionism in painting later in the nineteenth century. Their emphasis on national traditions encouraged the growth of nationalism, the most powerful ideology to develop in Europe during the nineteenth century.

Recommended Reading

Ayling, Stanley Edward. *John Wesley* (1979).

Barbour, Hugh. *The Quakers* (1988).

Barzun, Jacques. *Berlioz and His Century: An Introduction to the Age of Romanticism* (rev. ed, 1982).

Barzun, Jacques. *Classic, Romantic, and Modern* (1961).

Bowra, C. M. *The Romantic Imagination* (1949).

Cassirer, Ernst. *Kant's Life and Thought* (1981).

Clark, Kenneth. *The Romantic Rebellion: Romantic Versus Classic Art* (1973).

Friedlaender, Walter F. *David to Delacroix* (1952).

Furst, Lilian R. *Romanticism in Perspective: A Comparative Study of Aspects of the Romantic Movement in England, France, and Germany* (2nd ed., 1979).

Hitchcock, Henry Russell. *Architecture: Nineteenth and Twentieth Centuries* (3rd ed., 1968)

LeBris, Michel. *Romantics and Romanticism* (1981).

Longyear, Rey M. *Nineteenth-Century Romanticism in Music* (3rd ed., 1988).

Löwith, Karl. *From Hegel to Nietzsche: The Revolution in Nineteenth-Century Thought* (1964).

Novotny, Fritz. *Painting and Sculpture in Europe, 1780–1880* (2nd ed., 1971).

Prawer, Siegbert, ed. *The Romantic Period in Germany* (1970).

Raynal, Maurice. *The Nineteenth Century: New Sources of Emotion from Goya to Gauguin* (1951).

Talmon, J. L. *Romanticism and Revolt: Europe, 1815–1848* (1967).

CHAPTER 18

Reform and Revolution in Great Britain and France

Time Line

1830	The French July Revolution overthrows King Charles X
1830–1848	The July Monarchy of King Louis Philippe in France
1830–1837	Reign of King William IV of Great Britain
1832	The British Parliament passes the Reform Bill of 1832
1837–1901	Reign of Queen Victoria of Great Britain
1839	The People's Charter is presented to Parliament for the first time
1846	The British Parliament repeals the Corn Laws
1848	The French February Revolution results in the overthrow of King Louis Philippe

Great Britain had emerged from the upheavals of the seventeenth century as a stronghold of constitutional monarchy and political liberty. Now, in the early nineteenth century, conservative rule gradually gave way to a movement for reform. The most important reform of these years was the Reform Bill of 1832, which redistributed seats in the House of Commons and granted the right to vote to most adult middle-class males. Nevertheless, the British ruling classes rejected the demands of the Chartist movement for full political democracy. In the area of trade policy, the British moved toward the adoption of free trade.

In France, the restored Bourbon kings, Louis XVIII and Charles X, gradually became more arbitrary in their exercise of power. The July Revolution of 1830 resulted in the overthrow of the Bourbons and established the rule of the citizen king, Louis Philippe. Although the July Monarchy of Louis Philippe was based on liberal principles, the king's government became increasingly more authoritarian in practice. Opposition to the king gradually intensified, culminating in the February Revolution of 1848.

Liberalism

In both Great Britain and France, the movement for reform in the years after 1815 was impelled by the ideology of liberalism.

In general, liberals opposed arbitrary government and advocated an expansion of political, economic, and religious freedom. In more specific terms, liberalism was primarily a middle-class movement that had relatively little concern for the economic and social problems of the masses. The middle-class liberals favored representative government, although in the early nineteenth century, relatively few liberals favored full democracy. They generally admired the British system of constitutional monarchy, under which the power of the monarch was limited and the prime minister and other cabinet ministers were responsible to the parliament. Liberals also favored the establishment of guarantees of civil liberties, including freedom of speech, the press, and assembly; freedom of religion; and freedom from arbitrary arrest and imprisonment.

Great Britain

Conservative Rule and Repression of Civil Unrest

For several years after 1815, the British ruling classes lived in fear of revolution. The country experienced a postwar economic depression, and mounting unemployment resulted in widespread hardship and unrest.

Lord Liverpool (1770–1828), a Tory, served as prime minister from 1812 to 1827, heading a reactionary cabinet that initially opposed demands for reform and sought to repress expressions of discontent.

The "Peterloo Massacre"

In August 1819, troops fired on a large crowd that had gathered at St. Peter's Fields in Manchester to hear speeches on parliamentary reform and the repeal of the Corn Laws. Eleven people were killed. The affair became known as the "Peterloo Massacre," in ironic contrast with the British victory over Napoleon at Waterloo in 1815.

The Six Acts

Following the Peterloo Massacre, Parliament adopted the Six Acts in December 1819. This repressive legislation restricted the freedoms of speech and assembly and other civil liberties, increased taxes on newspapers and fines for seditious libel, expanded the right of the police to search private homes, and provided for the speedy trial and harsh punishment of offenders against public order.

The Cato Street Conspiracy

In January 1820, following the death of King George III, the prince regent succeeded to the throne as George IV (r. 1820–1830). The following month, the government uncovered a plot to assassinate the entire cabinet. The leaders of the Cato Street Conspiracy, as it was known, were arrested and tried, and four were executed.

Tory Reform in the 1820s

Although Lord Liverpool remained prime minister until 1827, a younger group of Tory leaders gradually began to push for a program of moderate reform.

Criminal Codes

Robert Peel (1788–1850), who served as home secretary from 1822 to 1827, won parliamentary approval for a reform of the criminal codes, substantially reducing the number of capital crimes. Peel also reorganized the London police, who came to be known as bobbies in his honor.

Trade

William Huskisson (1770–1830), the president of the Board of Trade from 1823 to 1827, began the process of moving away from mercantilist regulation toward free trade by reducing tariffs on imports.

Religion

Religious restrictions were also removed. In 1828, Parliament repealed the Test Act, which had been enacted in the late seventeenth century. The Test Act barred Nonconformists from public office (see Chapter 7). In 1829, Parliament passed Catholic Emancipation, extending to Roman Catholics the right to vote and hold public office. Political restrictions against Jews remained in effect for several more years.

The Reform Bill of 1832

In the early nineteenth century, the British Parliament was far from democratic and not representative of the population. The House of Lords consisted of the hereditary nobility and the bishops of the Church of England. In addition, from time to time the king invoked his right to create new peers (noblemen), who acquired the right to sit in the House of Lords. The House of Lords could block the adoption of legislation passed by the House of Commons.

The House of Commons consisted mainly of prosperous country gentlemen (the gentry) and wealthy business and professional men. Only a small percentage of the adult male population met the property qualifications for voters. Many members of the House of Commons represented "rotten boroughs" (towns with very small populations whose voters could readily be bribed or otherwise influenced) or "pocket boroughs" (towns whose representatives in the House of Commons were selected by noble landowners). The new industrial towns were either completely without representation or seriously underrepresented.

Whig Support of Reform

From 1828 to 1830, the Duke of Wellington (1769–1852) served as prime minister. While the victor of Waterloo was a great national hero, he was a reactionary Tory and had no sympathy for reform. In 1830, however, the Tories lost the general election to the Whigs.

In 1831, the new Whig prime minister, Earl Grey (1764–1845), won the approval of the House of Commons for a parliamentary reform bill, but the Lords rejected it. When the Commons passed a second reform bill the same year, the Lords rejected it once again. Grey now appealed to the new king, William IV (r. 1830–1837), who promised to create enough new Whig peers to assure the Lords' passage of a reform bill.

The threat sufficed. In 1832, the House of Lords approved the third reform bill passed by the House of Commons.

Provisions of the Reform Bill of 1832

The Reform Bill of 1832 deprived 56 rotten and pocket boroughs of their 111 seats in the House of Commons, while 32 other small boroughs each lost one of their two members. The 143 available seats were then distributed to boroughs that had been either underrepresented or without any representation at all.

In addition to this redistribution of seats in the House of Commons, the Reform Bill of 1832 extended the right to vote to middle-class men. Property qualifications continued to bar most workers from voting. Nevertheless, the Reform Bill of 1832 represented the beginning of a decisive shift in political power from the landed aristocracy to the middle class.

Other Reforms

Abolition of Slavery

In 1833, the Parliament abolished slavery throughout the British Empire. This represented a victory for the abolitionists led by William Wilberforce (1759–1833).

Limitations on Work by Children and Women

A Factory Act adopted in 1833 placed restrictions on child labor in the textile industry. Children under the age of nine could not be employed in textile mills, while those between the ages of nine and thirteen could not work for more than nine hours a day. Work by children between the ages of thirteen and eighteen was limited to twelve hours a day. The Factory Act provided for a system of inspectors to make certain that the law was being observed. Later legislation placed further restrictions on work by women and children.

Municipal Councils

The Municipal Corporations Act of 1835 established a system of elected councils to govern most cities and towns.

Political Trends

During these years, British politics was experiencing change, as the two major political factions, the Tories and the Whigs, gradually evolved into modern parties, known as the Conservatives and Liberals, respectively.

In 1837, when King William IV died, he was succeeded by his niece, the eighteen-year-old Victoria (r. 1837–1901), whose reign proved to be the longest in English history. In 1840, Victoria married Albert of Saxe-Coburg-Gotha (1819–1861), a German prince. His untimely death in 1861 left her disconsolate.

The Repeal of the Corn Laws

The campaign for the repeal of the Corn Laws provided powerful evidence of the increased political power of the British middle class.

The Anti-Corn Law League, which was established in 1839, campaigned for the repeal of the Corn Laws (the tariff on wheat and other grains) and more broadly, for the introduction of free trade. The Corn Laws, which had been adopted in 1815, provided the great landowners with a protected market for their crops. The leaders of the Anti-Corn Law League included the prominent industrialists Richard Cobden (1804–1865) and John Bright (1811–1889).

The Anti-Corn Law League argued that reducing the price of food would improve the workers' standard of living, while reducing the cost of raw materials would increase the profits of industry. In addition, low food prices would make it easier for the industrialists to pay their workers lower wages.

Irish Famine

During the winter of 1845–1846, a severe famine struck Ireland following a failure of the potato crop. Starvation and diseases such as typhus and cholera took the lives of some 700,000 people. Hundreds of thousands of survivors emigrated, with many finding new homes in the United States.

Establishment of Free Trade

The Irish famine demonstrated the need for lower food prices, and in 1846 Parliament voted to repeal the Corn Laws. Repeal was a victory for Britain's urban dwellers, who for the first time comprised a majority of the population. In the following years, the British eliminated the remaining tariffs, establishing a free trade policy.

The Chartist Movement

Following the adoption of the Reform Bill of 1832, agitation developed for further parliamentary reform. In 1838, a group of working-class leaders drew up the People's Charter, which contained six demands:

1. Universal manhood suffrage.

2. The secret ballot in place of voting in public meetings.

3. The abolition of property requirements for members of the House of Commons.

4. The payment of salaries to members of the House of Commons.

5. The creation of equal electoral districts. (Members of the House of Commons should represent approximately the same number of people.)

6. Annual elections for the House of Commons.

The Chartists won support among many intellectual reformers, as well as from urban workers. In 1839, the Chartists presented to Parliament a petition setting forth their demands. However, the British middle classes were not yet prepared to share political power with the masses, and Parliament ignored the petition. Although Parliament also ignored Chartist petitions presented in 1842 and 1848, all the demands of the Chartists were ultimately enacted, except for annual elections for the House of Commons.

France

The Bourbon Restoration

From 1814 to 1830, France was ruled by the two kings of the restored Bourbon dynasty: Louis XVIII and Charles X. Both monarchs were younger brothers of King Louis XVI, who had been executed in 1793. (The supporters of the Bourbons regarded the young son of Louis XVI, who died in prison in 1795, as Louis XVII, although he never reigned.)

King Louis XVIII (r. 1814–1824)

Louis XVIII acknowledged the fact that the Old Regime could not be restored and believed it was essential to pursue a moderate course. As king, he sought to balance the interests of the old aristocracy, which had returned to France hoping for a restoration of their traditional position and privileges, with those of the liberal bourgeoisie, who had profited from the reforms of the revolutionary and Napoleonic eras.

The Charter of 1814

The French constitution, the Charter of 1814, provided for a two-house parliament. The king appointed the members of the Chamber of Peers, while the Chamber of Deputies was elected by property-qualified voters. The charter also contained guarantees of civil liberties, including freedom of religion, although Roman Catholicism was recognized as the religion of the state. The Napoleonic Code remained in effect, and the revolutionary redistribution of land confiscated from the church and the nobility was confirmed.

The Ultra-Royalists

The reactionary Ultra-Royalists, who represented the cause of the returned emigré nobility, did not accept this moderate settlement. The Ultras, as they were known, were led by the king's brother, the Count of Artois. Winning the 1820 elections for the Chamber of Deputies, the Ultras reduced voting rights and placed restrictions on civil liberties, including freedom of the press.

King Charles X (r. 1824–1830)

In 1824, the Count of Artois succeeded his brother, becoming King Charles X. The new king's actions quickly angered the bourgeoisie. In 1825, he reduced the interest on government bonds, held mainly by the bourgeoisie, from 5 to 3 percent in order to get money to compensate the aristocracy for the land they had lost during the revolution. In 1827, he disbanded the National Guard, whose members were drawn chiefly from the bourgeoisie.

When liberals and moderate royalists gained control of the Chamber of Deputies in 1827, Charles X sought for a time to govern in association with them. In 1829, however, he abandoned this policy and named the reactionary Prince of Polignac (1780–1847) as premier.

This enraged the liberals, who won a majority in the Chamber of Deputies in the May 1830 elections. Charles X and Polignac responded by enacting the Four Ordinances without parliamentary approval. These laws imposed further limitations on freedom of the press, dissolved the Chamber of Deputies, scheduled new elections, and restricted the electorate further in order to weaken the opposition.

The July Revolution

On July 27-29, 1830, the artisans and tradespeople of Paris, spurred on by the bourgeoisie, rose up in revolt against Charles X and Polignac. The king abdicated and sought refuge in Great Britain.

Some of the revolutionaries favored the establishment of a republic, but the liberals in the Chamber of Deputies, led by Talleyrand (1754–1838), Adolphe Thiers (1797–1877), and François Guizot (1787–1874), supported the creation of a constitutional monarchy. They proclaimed Louis Philippe, the Duke of Orleans, as king.

The July Monarchy: King Louis Philippe (r. 1830–1848)

The July Monarchy of the "citizen king" Louis Philippe ruled France from 1830 to 1848. Louis Philippe was a cousin of the deposed Charles X and the son of the revolutionary figure, Philippe Egalité (see Chapter 14). Prior to becoming king, Louis Philippe had carefully cultivated an amiable bourgeois image.

Reforms

Louis Philippe was known as "king of the French," rather than king of France, and the red, white, and blue revolutionary tricolor replaced the white and gold flag of the Bourbons. While Roman Catholicism was recognized as the religion of the majority of the French people, it was no longer the state religion. A revised version of the Charter of 1814 increased the electorate, but the property qualification for voters remained high.

Louis Philippe and his ministers believed that their primary duty was to support private property and its owners, promote prosperity, and maintain peace. During most of the 1830s, the most prominent figure in the government was Adolphe Thiers.

Economic Policies

France maintained high tariffs in order to protect industrialists from the competition of imported manufactured goods, especially from Great Britain, and to protect French farmers from the competition of imported grain. The government showed little concern for the needs of the urban poor, however.

End of the July Monarchy

From 1840 to 1848, François Guizot dominated the government. More conservative than Thiers, Guizot led the government in an increasingly more arbitrary direction. Opposition to the July Monarchy mounted and became more serious in the wake of a poor grain harvest in 1846 and an industrial depression that began in 1847. The political crisis reached a head in the February Revolution of 1848, which resulted in the overthrow of Louis Philippe and the proclamation of the Second Republic.

During the early nineteenth century, the British succeeded in averting possible revolution by carrying out a program of gradual reform. The most important of the reform measures, the Reform Bill of 1832, marked a decisive step in the shift of political power from the landed aristocracy to the middle class. This shift made possible the repeal of the Corn Laws in 1846 and the subsequent adoption of free trade. While Parliament ignored the demands of the Chartists for full political democracy, the impetus for reform continued, and by the early years of the twentieth century, the British had created a truly democratic political system.

In France, the events of the early nineteenth century revealed the difficulty the French experienced in trying to establish a workable system of government that could balance the interests of the bourgeoisie, whose importance had increased during the revolutionary and Napoleonic era, with those of the returned aristocracy. Moving in an increasingly more arbitrary direction in the years from 1814 to 1830, the restored Bourbon monarchy was overthrown. While the July Monarchy of Louis Philippe supported the interests of the bourgeoisie, it also gradually lost support and fell from power in the February Revolution of 1848.

Recommended Reading

Artz, Frederick B. *Reaction and Revolution, 1814–1832* (1934).

Breunig, Charles. *The Age of Revolution and Reaction, 1789–1850* (2nd ed., 1977).

Brock, Michael. *The Great Reform Act* (1973).

Bury, J. P. T. *Thiers, 1797–1877: A Political Life* (1986).

Cobban, Alfred. *A History of Modern France, vol. II, 1799–1871* (2nd ed., 1965).

Derry, John W. *A Short History of Nineteenth-Century England* (1963).

Droz, Jacques. *Europe Between Revolutions, 1815–1848* (1967).

Hobsbawm, E. J. *The Age of Revolution: Europe, 1789 to 1848* (1969).

Howarth, Thomas E. *Citizen-King: The Life of Louis-Philippe, King of the French* (1961).

Langer, William L. *Political and Social Upheaval, 1832–1852* (1969).

Longford, Elizabeth. *Queen Victoria: Born to Succeed* (1965).

Magraw, Roger. *France, 1815–1914: The Bourgeois Century* (1983).

Mansel, Philip. *Louis XVIII* (1981).

Pinkney, David H. *Decisive Years in France, 1840–1847* (1986).

Pinkney, David H. *The French Revolution of 1830* (1972).

Thomson, David. *England in the Nineteenth Century, 1815–1914* (1950).

Woodham Smith, C. V. *The Great Hunger: Ireland, 1845–1849* (1962).

Woodward, E. L. *The Age of Reform, 1815–1870* (2nd ed., 1962).

CHAPTER 19

The Conservative Order in Central and Eastern Europe

Time Line

1792–1835	Reign of Emperor Francis I of Austria
1797–1840	Reign of King Frederick William III of Prussia
1801–1825	Reign of Tsar Alexander I of Russia
1817	The German *Burschenschaften* hold the Wartburg celebration
1819	The German princes issue the Carlsbad Decrees
1825	The Decembrist Revolt breaks out in Russia
1825–1855	Reign of Tsar Nicholas I of Russia

1830	A revolt breaks out in Russian Poland
1831	Giuseppe Mazzini establishes Young Italy
1835–1848	Reign of Emperor Ferdinand I of Austria
1840–1861	Reign of King Frederick William IV of Prussia
1853–1856	The Crimean War is fought

During the years after 1815, conservative rule appeared firmly established in Central and Eastern Europe.

In Central Europe, the period from 1815 to 1848 is known as the Age of Metternich. Prince Klemens von Metternich (1773–1859), the Austrian chancellor, dominated not only the Hapsburg Empire but also the German Confederation and the Italian states. Metternich devoted his energies to the preservation of the conservative order and efforts to prevent the spread of the new ideologies of liberalism and nationalism.

To the east, in Russia, Tsars Alexander I and Nicholas I maintained the autocracy and expanded their territorial holdings. However, the decision of Great Britain and France to intervene in the Crimean War of the mid–1850s blocked the further expansion of Russian power at the expense of the Ottoman Empire.

Nationalism

In Central Europe, nationalism was the most powerful ideology in the early ninetenth century. In Germany and Italy, nationalism proved to be a unifying force, as the Germans and Italians came increasingly to acquire a sense of being one people. In contrast, nationalism promoted the disintegration of the Austrian Empire, as the various subject peoples of the Hapsburg emperor came to acquire consciousness of their own nationalities.

Johann Gottfried von Herder (1744–1803) was the great prophet of Central European nationalism. In his treatise *Ideas on the Philosophy of the History of Humanity* (1784–1791), Herder defined nationalism in terms of a people's language, literature, and history, which gave them a sense of identity. While Herder's was primarily a cultural nationalism, it had political implications. As Germans, Italians, and the subject nationalities of the Hapsburgs acquired a greater sense of peoplehood through an appreciation of their language, literature, and history, they also came to desire a state of their own.

Austria: The Multinational Empire

In Austria after 1815, Metternich strove to maintain the absolute monarchy of the Hapsburg emperors Francis I (r. 1792–1835) and Ferdinand I (r. 1835–1848).

Metternich's Policy

Metternich believed that the new forces of liberalism and, especially, nationalism presented a serious threat to the survival of the Austrian Empire. The Hapsburg empire was a multinational state, inhabited by Germans, Magyars (Hungarians), Poles, Ruthenians (Ukrainians), Czechs, Slovaks, Rumanians, Serbs, Croats, Slovenes, and others. In Metternich's view, any concessions to these national groups would begin a process that would inevitably result in the breakup of the empire. Furthermore, he believed, the introduction of liberal parliamentary government would provide the national groups with a new forum where they could fight their battles against one another and against their Hapsburg rulers. This, too, would weaken the monarchy.

The Development of Nationalism

Despite Metternich's efforts, liberal and nationalist ideas made some headway in the Austrian Empire in the years after 1815.

The Magyars

The threat to Hapsburg power was greatest in Hungary, where nationalism developed among the leaders of the Magyars. Some Magyar leaders, including Count Stephen Szechenyi (1791–1860), the greatest of the country's landowners, took a moderate approach, emphasizing the development of Magyar culture and the Hungarian economy. Others, such as the radical journalist Louis Kossuth (1802–1894), wanted Hungary to win its independence from Austria.

Other Subject Nationalities

Nationalism also emerged among other subject nationalities of the Hapsburgs, including the Czechs in Bohemia and the South Slavs (Serbs, Croats, and Slovenes).

The German Confederation

The Congress of Vienna had created a German Confederation of thirty-nine states. The Austrian Empire, the largest of these states, held the permanent presidency of the confederation. Although each state was in principle independent, Metternich exercised his control over German affairs to block the spread of liberal and nationalist ideas.

Prussia

Prussia, the second-largest German state, generally accepted its position of subordination to Austria. However, Prussia began to promote the commercial integration of the German states. In 1819, Prussia launched the *Zollverein* (customs union) and began to conclude treaties, which provided for reductions of tariffs and other barriers to trade, with neighboring German states. By 1834, most of the members of the German Confederation, with the notable exception of Austria, had joined the *Zollverein*.

The *Burschenschaften*

The greatest challenge to the conservative order in the German Confederation came from university students who had been imbued with liberal and nationalist ideals. Dreaming of constitutional government and national unity, these students organized associations known as *Burschenschaften*.

In 1817, a *Burschenschaft* at the University of Jena staged a celebration at Wartburg Castle (where Martin Luther had worked on his translation of the Bible) in commemoration of the three-hundredth anniversary of Luther's Ninety-five Theses and the fourth anniversary of the Battle of the Nations. Two years later, in March 1819, Karl Sand, a member of a *Burschenschaft*, assassinated August von Kotzebue, a reactionary journalist. Sand was tried and executed.

Metternich acted against what he regarded as dangerous agitation. In September 1819, he induced the German princes to issue the Carlsbad Decrees, which outlawed the *Burschenschaften* and restricted academic freedom.

While the forces of liberalism and nationalism were suppressed in Germany, they were not destroyed.

Italy

The Austrians remained dominant in Italian affairs after 1815 and strove to maintain reactionary rule throughout the peninsula. Relatives of the Austrian emperor governed the northern Italian states of Parma, Modena, and Tuscany, while an Austrian archduchess was married to the Bourbon king of the Two Sicilies. Lombardy and Venetia were an integral part of the Austrian Empire.

Reactionary Rulers

The northern Italian state of Sardinia-Piedmont was not directly controlled by the Austrians, but the Piedmontese kings of the House of Savoy were committed to reactionary policies. King Victor Emmanuel I (r. 1802–1821) was hostile to everything French and abolished most of the reforms established during the French occupation of his country, including freedom of religion and the Napoleonic civil and criminal codes.

Italian Nationalism

Despite the enforcement of reactionary policies, liberal and national ideas continued to influence many Italian radicals. The Carbonari ("charcoal burners") were the most active radical group in the years following 1815. They dreamed of freeing Italy from the tyranny of the Austrians and the Italian princes and of achieving national unity. The Carbonari launched abortive revolts in 1820–1821 and 1831.

Giuseppe Mazzini (1805–1872) and
Giuseppe Garibaldi (1807–1882)

The failure of these revolts discredited the Carbonari. Mazzini, who established the organization known as Young Italy in 1831, now emerged as the leading figure among Italy's revolutionary republicans. Mazzini's goals were the same as those of the Carbonari: eliminate Austria's domination of Italian affairs, overthrow the Italian tyrants, and unite Italy as a liberal and democratic republic. Garibaldi was Mazzini's best-known follower. Together, they led repeated unsuccessful revolts against the tyranny of the Austrians and the Italian princes.

Russia

Tsar Alexander I (r. 1801–1825)

During the early years of his reign, Tsar Alexander I showed some interest in proposals for reform. In 1808, he named Michael Speransky (1772–1839) to advise him on administrative reforms. Speransky drafted a proposal for constitutional government that included an elected legislative body. He also proposed a gradual abolition of serfdom. However, Speransky's projects proved too far-reaching for the tsar to consider.

Alexander I also carried out the traditional tsarist policy of territorial expansion. In 1801, he conquered part of northwestern Persia and also annexed Georgia in the Caucasus. During the Napoleonic wars, Russia absorbed Finland in 1809 and Bessarabia in 1812. The Congress of Vienna confirmed these gains and also granted the Russians additional Polish territory (see Chapter 16).

The Decembrist Revolt

Tsar Alexander I died in mid-December 1825. The late tsar's younger brother, the Grand Duke Nicholas, succeeded to the throne.

For several days, however, there was uncertainty about the succession. A group of younger army officers who had embraced liberal ideas staged a revolt in St. Petersburg. The leaders of this Decembrist Revolt called for reforms, including the introduction of a liberal constitution and the abolition of serfdom. The new tsar, Nicholas I, suppressed the revolt with little difficulty. In succeeding years, the example of the Decembrists served as an inspiration for Russian radicals.

Tsar Nicholas I (r. 1825–1855)

The Decembrist Revolt had terrified Nicholas I, and he exaggerated the revolutionary threat. In order to root out revolutionaries and suspected revolutionaries more effectively, he placed the secret police under his direct control as the Third Section of his chancery.

"Orthodoxy, Autocracy, Nationalism"

Count Sergei S. Uvarov (1786–1855), Nicholas I's minister of education from 1833 to 1849, promoted a program of Official Nationality, which was summed up in the words "Orthodoxy, Autocracy, and Nationalism." The principle of Orthodoxy involved increasing the control of the Orthodox Church over Russia's educational system and intellectual life and encouraging the non-Orthodox to convert, while the principle of Autocracy emphasized the absolute political authority of the tsar. The principle of Nationalism stressed the uniqueness of Russia—its language, religion, culture, and customs—which caused it to stand apart from the West. In practice, this led to discrimination against members of the non-Russian nationalities and to a policy of Russification, designed to compel them to adopt Russian culture.

Limited Reforms

While Nicholas I was a staunch reactionary, he did push through programs of reform that appealed to his understanding. He directed a reorganization of state finances, and he authorized Michael Speransky to prepare a systematic code of Russian law, which was published in 1833.

The Problem of Serfdom

Nicholas did nothing, however, about Russia's greatest national problem: serfdom. Well over 90 percent of the Russian people were serfs, who enjoyed virtually no personal freedom and lived in poverty.

Discontent mounted among the serfs, and more than seven hundred serf uprisings took place during Nicholas's reign.

Suppression of the Polish Revolt

In 1815, the Russians granted a constitution to Russian Poland that established a limited degree of Polish autonomy, although ultimate control remained in Russia's hands.

In November 1830, a revolt broke out in Warsaw and soon spread to the countryside. The Russians sent troops into Poland to suppress the revolt, and in February 1832, Nicholas issued the Organic Statute, which suspended the Polish constitution and declared Poland an integral part of the Russian Empire. The Russians also initiated a policy of Russification in Poland.

Intervention in European Revolutions

Apart from the Polish revolution of 1830, Russia escaped the revolutionary turmoil that affected much of Europe, especially in 1848. In 1830, Nicholas I was prepared to intervene to assist in the suppression of the revolutions in France and Belgium, but he did not do so. In 1849, however, he did provide assistance to Austria's new emperor, Francis Joseph, in suppressing the Hungarian revolt.

The Growth of Radicalism in Russia

Westerners and Slavophiles

Beneath the surface of repression in Russia, there were voices of dissent. During the reign of Nicholas I, two major schools of reformist thought developed: the Westerners and the Slavophiles. The Westerners contended that Russia should follow the example of Western Europe in its political, economic, and social development. The Slavophiles, in contrast, insisted on the uniqueness of Russian culture and rejected Western European models. They believed that rather than imitate the West, Russia needed to reform itself within the context of its own traditions. Both the Westerners and Slavophiles agreed in their opposition to the arbitrary rule of the tsarist bureaucracy, their advocacy of freedom of speech, and their calls for the abolition of serfdom.

Alexander Herzen (1812–1870)

Herzen emerged as Russia's most prominent radical during the reign of Nicholas I. He dreamed of a Russian peasant revolution and believed that the traditional village communes might provide the foundation for a new cooperative socialist society. Herzen left Russia in 1847 and spent the rest of his life in exile in Western Europe. There he established a Russian-language journal, *Kolokol* ("The Bell"), that was smuggled to intellectual dissidents in Russia.

The Decembrist Revolt, the debate between the Westerners and the Slavophiles, and the work of radicals such as Herzen helped give substance to the developing revolutionary movement in Russia.

Russian Expansion

The expansion of the Russian Empire continued during the reign of Nicholas I. In 1828, as a result of a war against Persia, Russia acquired part of Armenia in the Caucasus. A war against Turkey in 1828–1829 gave Russia additional territory along the Black Sea coast of the Caucasus, as well as land at the mouth of the Danube River. The Russians also continued their expansion in Central Asia and eastern Siberia.

The Crimean War (1853–1856)

Russia's continuing pressure on the declining Ottoman Empire, and in particular, Russia's claims to be the protector of the Orthodox Christian subjects of the Ottoman sultan, led to the outbreak of the Crimean War. In July 1853, the Russians occupied the Danubian principalities of Moldavia and Wallachia (later Rumania), and the Turks responded by declaring war in October. In March 1854, Great Britain and France declared war on Russia, and Piedmont soon joined the Allies. Prussia and Austria remained neutral.

British and French Intervention

The British and French intervened in the war primarily because they wanted to block any further expansion of Russian power and especially to prevent the Russians from acquiring control of the Turkish Straits, which would give the Russians access to the eastern Mediterranean. Napoleon III, the French emperor, also believed that an activist foreign policy would increase domestic political support for his regime.

During the war, the allies concentrated on efforts to take the Russian fortress at Sebastopol in the Crimea. The siege of Sebastopol included the famous and tragic charge of the light brigade at Balaclava in late October 1854. Here British cavalry units charged recklessly into a natural amphitheater where they were mowed down by cannon fire on three sides. Of the 700 who began the charge, only 195 survived. Following a siege of eleven months, Sebastopol fell to the allies in September 1855.

Treaty of Paris (March 1856)

Following the death of Nicholas I in March 1855, the new tsar, Alexander II (r. 1855–1881) sued for peace. Under the terms of the Treaty of Paris, Russia was compelled to return southern Bessarabia and the mouth of the Danube to the Turks. In the so-called Black Sea clauses, the Russians accepted the neutralization of the Black Sea, agreeing not to maintain any navy or coastal fortifications in the area. The Russians also renounced their claim to be the protector of Orthodox Christians in the Ottoman Empire. (In 1870, when the attention of Europe was distracted by the Franco-German War, the Russians unilaterally abrogated the Black Sea clauses of the Treaty of Paris.)

In the years after 1815, forces of change were gradually eroding the conservative order that appeared to dominate Central and Eastern Europe. In the Austrian Empire, liberal and nationalist ideas won an increasing number of adherents, both among the German-Austrians and the subject nationalities. In divided Germany and Italy, too, the ideologies of liberalism and nationalism were spreading. The explosion came in 1848, when revolutions swept the Hapsburg Empire and the German and Italian states.

Apart from the abortive Decembrist Revolt, the Russian tsars faced the threat of open revolution only in Poland, where it was easily suppressed. Beneath the surface of the repressive tsarist censorship and secret police, however, the Westerners and Slavophiles conducted their clandestine debate about the true nature of Russia, while a growing number of radicals dreamed about revolution and the dawning of a new socialist age.

Recommended Reading

Artz, Frederick B. *Reaction and Revolution, 1814–1832* (1934).

Breunig, Charles. *The Age of Revolution and Reform, 1789–1850* (2nd ed., 1977).

Carsten, F. L., et al., eds. *The Hapsburg Empire, 1835–1918,* 2 vols. (1982).

Hamerow, Theodore S. *Restoration, Revolution, and Reaction: Economics and Politics in Germany, 1815–1871* (1958).

Jelavich, Barbara. *Modern Austria: Empire and Republic, 1815–1986* (1987).

Kohn, Hans. *The Idea of Nationalism: A Study in Its Origins and Background* (1945).

Kraehe, Enno E. *Metternich's German Policy,* 2 vols. (1963, 1983).

Langer, William L. *Political and Social Upheaval, 1832–1852* (1969).

Lincoln, W. Bruce. *Nicholas I: Emperor and Autocrat of All the Russians* (1978).

Macartney, C. A. *The Habsburg Empire, 1790–1918* (1969).

Mack Smith, Denis. *Garibaldi: A Great Life in Brief* (1956).

Palmer, Alan. *Alexander I: Tsar of War and Peace* (1974).

Raeff, Marc. *The Decembrist Movement* (1966).

Riasanovsky, Nicholas V. *Nicholas I and Official Nationality in Russia, 1825–1855* (1959).

Salvemini, Gaetano. *Mazzini* (1957).

Seton-Watson, Hugh. *The Russian Empire, 1801–1917* (1967).

Shafer, Boyd C. *Nationalism: Myth and Reality* (1955).

Taylor, A. J. P. *The Habsburg Monarchy, 1809–1918* (1948).

Woodham Smith, C. V. *The Reason Why* (1954).

CHAPTER 20

The Agricultural and Industrial Revolutions

Time Line

1712	The Newcomen steam engine is used to pump water from a coal mine
1733	John Kay invents the flying shuttle
1764	James Hargreaves invents the spinning jenny
1769	Richard Arkwright patents the water frame
	James Watt patents a more efficient version of the Newcomen steam engine
1779	Samuel Crompton perfects the spinning mule

1784	Arthur Young establishes the *Annals of Agriculture*
1785	Edmund Cartwright patents a power loom
1793	Eli Whitney invents the cotton gin
1807	Robert Fulton's steamboat, the *Clermont*, goes into service on the Hudson River
1830	George Stephenson's locomotive, the *Rocket*, operates successfully on the Liverpool to Manchester railroad
1834	Cyrus McCormick patents the reaper
1836	Samuel F. B. Morse invents the telegraph
1840	Samuel Cunard begins regular transatlantic steamship passenger service
	Great Britain inaugurates the penny post
1856	Henry Bessemer develops the Bessemer converter
1859	The first commercially successful oil well is drilled in Pennsylvania
1866	The Siemens brothers develop the open-hearth process of steelmaking
	Cyrus Field lays the first successful transatlantic cable
1876	Alexander Graham Bell invents the telephone
1879	Thomas A. Edison invents the incandescent light bulb
1892	Rudolf Diesel patents the diesel engine
1899	Guglielmo Marconi transmits a wireless message across the English Channel

| 1903 | The Wright brothers make the first successful airplane flights |

The agricultural and industrial revolutions brought immense changes to the economy of Europe and ultimately, the world.

During the eighteenth and nineteenth centuries, the pace of the agricultural revolution quickened. The development of scientific agriculture, the introduction of new crops, the enclosure of agricultural land, and increasing mechanization expanded agricultural production and ended the specter of famine in Europe. Fewer farm workers were needed to produce food for Europe's growing population, and surplus agricultural labor migrated to the new industrial towns to find employment in the factories.

The industrial revolution, which began in Great Britain in the late eighteenth century, involved a number of elements, including the invention of power-driven machinery, the introduction of the factory system, and advances in the production of coal and iron and eventually, steel. In addition, the expansion of banking and credit facilities and the broader application of the principle of limited liability to business organization helped promote the process of industrialization. The industrial revolution was both accompanied and encouraged by contemporaneous revolutions in transportation and communications.

The Agricultural Revolution

The industrial revolution was preceded and accompanied by a revolution in agriculture, in which Great Britain led the way, as it would later do in the industrial revolution.

The Development of Scientific Agriculture

During the seventeenth and eighteenth centuries, science and technology were increasingly applied to British agriculture.

Influence of Tull and Townshend

Around 1700, Jethro Tull (1674–1741) developed a device that planted seeds in neat rows. Tull's seed drill replaced the less efficient method of scattering the seed. Viscount Townshend (1725–1767), an eighteenth-century aristocrat and statesman, urged Britain's farmers to plant clover, which would nourish the soil, and to practice crop rotation. Townshend also advocated the growing of turnips, which would both enrich the soil and provide food for livestock during the winter months. Townshend was such a fervent promoter of turnips that he gained the nickname "Turnip" Townshend. The increased cultivation of turnips ended the need for the mass slaughter of livestock at the onset of winter, and fresh meat gradually replaced salted meat in the British diet during the winter months.

Advances in Livestock and Agricultural Techniques

Later in the eighteenth century, Robert Bakewell (1725–1795) introduced the scientific breeding of cattle and sheep, while Arthur Young (1741–1820) became an effective publicist for the new methods of scientific agriculture, founding the periodical *Annals of Agriculture* in 1784.

Early in the nineteenth century, German agricultural scientists succeeded in extracting sugar from beets. The cultivation of sugar beets soon ended Europe's dependence on imported cane sugar. A few years later, Justus von Liebig (1803–1873) and other German chemists developed chemical fertilizers.

Inventions of Farm Machinery

The invention of the reaper, patented by Cyrus McCormick (1809–1884), an American, in 1834, represented a major step forward in the application of technology to agriculture. The combine, a harvesting machine that threshed the grain as it was reaped, was developed later in the nineteenth century.

New Crops

Scientific and technological advances in agriculture were accompanied by the introduction of new crops. The potato, which originated in the Western Hemisphere, had become the basic foodstuff of Ireland by the mid-eighteenth century, although many continental Europeans continued to believe that potatoes were poisonous. During the eighteenth century, peas and new varieties of beans were introduced into Great Britain from the Netherlands.

British advances in agriculture won only gradual acceptance on the European continent. Nevertheless, the agricultural revolution ultimately made it possible for Europe to feed its growing population.

The Enclosure Movement

The agricultural revolution in Great Britain was accompanied by an intensification of the enclosure movement, which had begun during the sixteenth century. Enclosure involved the efforts of landowning aristocrats and country gentry to enclose common land by building fences and stone walls and planting hedges, thereby ending the medieval practice of providing free access to grazing lands and woodlands. By the early years of the nineteenth century, almost all of England's agriculturally useful land had been enclosed. While peasants were supposed to receive their fair share of the enclosed land, they were often cheated in practice.

The enclosure movement resulted in an increase in the number of large and medium-sized farms, as well as an increase in the production of food and other agricultural products. At the same time, many peasants were reduced to the status of impoverished farm laborers. A growing number of these displaced peasants migrated to the industrial towns to find employment in factories.

The Industrial Revolution

Although the precise reasons for Great Britain's leadership in the industrial revolution cannot be fully explained, several elements helped make that role possible. First of all, Great Britain possessed ample resources of coal and iron, which were basic necessities for modern industry. In addition, British merchants had become wealthy as a consequence of their activities during the commercial revolution and thus had capital available for investment in the new industries. The British could also apply their mercantile experience to sell the products of their industries in the world market. Furthermore, the British government adopted policies designed to promote the interests of the country's merchants and industrialists.

The Cotton Textile Industry

The British cotton textile industry, centered in the area of Lancashire and its major industrial town, Manchester, was the first to experience the application of power-driven machinery on a wide scale.

Invention of Machinery

In 1733, John Kay (1704–1764), a Lancashire weaver, invented the *flying shuttle*, which enabled one weaver, rather than two, to operate a loom.

In the mid–1760s, James Hargreaves (d. 1778) invented a *spinning machine* that he called the *spinning jenny*, in honor of his wife. Although the spinning jenny made it possible for a single worker to spin a number of threads simultaneously, the thread produced was relatively weak.

The *water frame*, patented by Richard Arkwright (1732–1792) in 1769, produced a stronger thread, although it was coarser than that made by the spinning jenny.

In 1779, Samuel Crompton (1753–1827) perfected a spinning machine called the *mule*, which combined the best features of the spinning jenny and the water frame and produced thread that was both fine and strong.

The first *power loom* was patented by Edmund Cartwright (1743–1823) in 1785.

As the new textile machinery was placed in wider use, the demand for raw cotton grew. The problem of removing the seeds from the cotton, however, made it difficult to meet the demand. Then, in 1793, the American Eli Whitney (1765–1825) invented the *cotton gin*, an effective device for removing the seeds from the cotton fiber.

The cotton textile industry benefited from other inventions as well. Mechanical engineers studied the techniques used by watchmakers and developed *precision parts* that increased the operational efficiency of the new machines. The next step involved the development of *standardized, interchangeable parts* for industrial machinery. Eli Whitney, who operated an arms factory in Connecticut, made important contributions to this development.

In the 1780s, a *rolling press* was introduced for the printing of textiles, replacing the hand-operated plates that had previously been used.

French Technology

French inventors made significant contributions to the cotton textile industry. Count Berthollet (1748–1822), a chemist, developed a process for using chlorine to bleach cloth that reduced the time required for bleaching cloth from months to hours. Joseph-Marie Jacquard (1752–1834) developed a power loom capable of weaving intricate patterns.

The Factory System

The introduction of larger and more complex industrial machinery gradually resulted in the construction of factories, which replaced small workshops and cottage-based industries.

In England, some workers blamed machine industry for their low wages and unemployment. Between 1811 and 1816, angry mobs of workers assaulted factories and smashed machines. These Luddites, as they were known, were named for Ned Ludd, who had destroyed machinery a generation earlier.

Development of the Steam Engine

The invention and perfection of the steam engine provided a dependable and efficient source of power for the new industrial machinery.

About 1700, Thomas Savery, an English inventor, built a practical steam pump. A few years later, Thomas Newcomen (1663–1729) built a steam engine that was first used in 1712 to pump water from a coal mine. Although it was wasteful of fuel, the Newcomen steam engine met a need, and by 1760 about one hundred Newcomen engines were operating in Great Britain.

In 1769, James Watt (1736–1819) patented a more efficient version of the Newcomen engine. Watt's steam engine required substantially less fuel.

While most of the early steam engines were used to pump water, by 1800 several hundred steam engines powered machinery in cotton textile mills and other factories.

Coal, Iron, and Steel

The interrelationship among the steam engine, coal mining, and iron production was a central aspect of the early industrial revolution.

Coal

The steam engine was used not only to pump water out of coal mines but also to power ventilating fans that pushed fresh air into the mines, making it possible for the miners to work longer hours underground. Coal mining also benefited from the invention of the safety lamp, in which an oil flame burned behind a metal screen, reducing the danger presented by dangerous gases in the mines. These technological innovations led to a tremendous increase in British coal production.

Iron

The increased production of coal provided the fuel needed to power the growing number of steam engines. These steam engines, in turn, were also applied to the production of iron. The steam engine was an essential part of the blast furnace, which produced a purer and stronger iron. This stronger iron, in turn, made possible the manufacture of more efficient steam engines.

Steel

Even the best quality of iron lacked the strength and flexibility of steel, which is iron whose carbon content has been reduced by a process of intense heating. In the early nineteenth century, it was possible to manufacture steel, but it involved a costly process that was economically justifiable only in special circumstances.

In 1856, Henry Bessemer (1813–1898), an English inventor, developed the Bessemer converter, the first efficient method for the mass production of steel. At about the same time, an American inventor, William Kelly (1811–1888), developed a similar process.

A decade later, in 1866, William Siemens (1823–1883), a German-born inventor living in England, and his brother, Ernst Werner von Siemens (1816–1892), developed the open-hearth process of steelmaking. As a result of these inventions, the steel industry experienced a rapid growth.

The Revolution in Transportation

Roads and Canals

The revolution in transportation began with improvements in road construction and the expansion of canal systems. About 1815, John McAdam (1756–1836), a Scotsman, developed a durable road surface made of crushed stones cemented by stone dust and water. These macadam roads, as they were known, represented a marked improvement over the dirt roads then generally in use. Extensive canal systems were built in both Europe and America. In 1869, the great Suez Canal, linking the Mediterranean Sea with the Indian Ocean by way of the Red Sea, was opened to shipping.

Railroads

The development of the steam engine and improvements in the quality of iron led to the creation of railroads.

For several generations, horse-drawn carts, operating on wooden rails, had been used to move coal and iron. During the eighteenth century, iron replaced wood for both the rails and the wheels of the carts.

The next step was to develop a steam-powered locomotive to pull the carts. George Stephenson (1781–1848), a British inventor, was the first to develop an economically successful locomotive. In 1825, a Stephenson locomotive was put into operation on the world's first real railroad, running some forty miles from the coal fields around Darlington in northern England to the port of Stockton.   In 1830, Stephenson's famous locomotive, the *Rocket,* demonstrated its speed on the new Liverpool to Manchester railway, running twelve miles in fifty-three minutes.

A great boom in railroad construction began. In 1830, only a few miles of railroads were in operation. By 1870, European railway mileage totaled almost 900,000.

Steamships

Steam power was also applied to water transportation. In 1807, Robert Fulton (1765–1815), an American, introduced the first economically successful steamship, the *Clermont,* which operated on the Hudson River between New York City and Albany. In 1816, the first steamship crossed the English Channel, and three years later the *Savannah,* an American sailing ship equipped with auxiliary steam power, crossed the Atlantic in twenty-nine days. In 1833, the *Royal William,* a Canadian vessel, became the first ship powered entirely by steam to cross the Atlantic in a voyage taking twenty days.

In 1840, Samuel Cunard (1787–1865), a Canadian, inaugurated regular passenger service by steamship from the English port of Liverpool to Boston. The marine steam engine was still relatively inefficient, and the coal required for the voyage occupied about half the available space on the ship. While the cost of transporting passengers by steamship could be justified economically, freight continued to be carried by sailing ship. By the 1860s, a more efficient marine steam engine had been developed, while the screw propeller replaced the paddle wheel. Steamships soon operated on the seaways of the world, and the days of the great sailing ships came to an end.

Electricity and Petroleum

During most of the nineteenth century, the steam engine provided power for the industrial revolution. Gradually, however, a series of inventors made improvements in the electrical generator developed by Michael Faraday (1791–1867) in 1831. Nikola Tesla (1856–1943), an Austrian-born immigrant to the United States, developed a method for the long-distance transmission of electric power.

Thomas A. Edison (1847–1931)

In 1879, the American genius Edison developed the first successful incandescent electric light bulb. (Edison also invented the phonograph and the movie projector.) In 1882, he designed a plan for the construction of central electric power stations. The major urban centers of America and Europe soon became electrified, and electric light replaced kerosene and gas lighting. Electricity was used increasingly to power industrial machinery.

The Use of Oil for Power

The first commercially important oil well was drilled in Pennsylvania in 1859, and petroleum gradually began to be used instead of coal to power steam engines. In 1892, Rudolf Diesel (1858–1913), a German inventor, patented an engine that burned oil directly in its cylinders to produce power, instead of using it to make steam. Diesel engines were far more efficient than coal-burning steam engines, although they did not come into widespread use until after World War I.

The Automobile

The use of petroleum to power motor vehicles began in the 1880s, when the German inventor Gottlieb Daimler (1834–1900) used a gasoline motor to power a bicycle, thereby creating the first motorcycle. (Bicycles had come into widespread use in Europe during the 1870s.) Motorcycles did not come into general use, however, until after 1900. One of Daimler's associates used a gasoline engine in the world's first automobile, a vehicle with the engine in front, a clutch, gears, and a drive shaft. In 1885, Karl Friedrich Benz (1844–1929), another German inventor, developed a water-cooled internal combustion engine with electric ignition. During the 1890s, gasoline-driven trucks and buses appeared, and passenger cars soon followed.

Aviation

Aviation traces its origins back to the late eighteenth century, when the hot-air balloon was invented in France, but more than a century passed before aviation made further progress. In 1900, Count Ferdinand von Zeppelin (1838–1917), a German, built the first efficient dirigible, a powered balloon.

Others were experimenting with the possibility of flight with a craft that was heavier than air. In Germany, Otto Lilienthal (1848–1896) and his brother, Gustav (1849–1933), experimented with gliders. At Kitty Hawk, North Carolina, in December 1903, Wilbur (1867–1912) and Orville Wright (1871–1948) made the first successful flights in an airplane. Prior to World War I, however, the airplane was still in the early stages of its development.

The Revolution in Communications

Innovations introduced during the nineteenth century made rapid long-distance communication possible for the first time in human history.

The Telegraph

In 1836, Samuel F. B. Morse (1791–1872), an American, invented the telegraph and eight years later, in 1844, sent a message from Washington to Baltimore. In 1851, a telegraph cable was laid beneath the English Channel linking Great Britain with the continent. In 1866, soon after the end of the American Civil War, Cyrus Field (1819–1892), an American, laid the first successful transatlantic cable joining the United States and Great Britain.

Mail Delivery

In 1840, Great Britain introduced the penny post, creating the first modern postal system. The Universal Postal Union was established in 1874 to regulate the international delivery of mail.

The Telephone

In 1876, Alexander Graham Bell (1847–1922), an American, invented the telephone, and the Bell Telephone Co. was founded the following year. In 1884, telephone service began between New York and Boston, and by the 1890s, a telephone network was taking shape in Europe.

The Radio

During the 1890s, Guglielmo Marconi (1874–1937), an Italian inventor, began experiments in wireless telegraphy. In 1899, Marconi sent a message across the English Channel and in 1901, across the Atlantic Ocean. Radio, the wireless transmission of voices and music, developed on the eve of World War I, based largely on research undertaken by Sir John A. Fleming (1849–1945), an Englishman, and Lee de Forest (1873–1961), an American. Regularly scheduled radio broadcasting began in the years following World War I.

Banking, Credit, and Business Organization

During the industrial revolution, there was a great expansion of banking and credit as private banks lent increasing amounts of capital to assist the expansion of industry.

Limited Liability

The joint stock principle, which had earlier been applied to trading companies, soon began to be used for banks and industrial enterprises. Joint stock companies operated on the basis of limited liability. Investors purchased shares of stock in the company, thereby becoming part owners. The investors would share in the profits, if any, in proportion to the amount of stock owned. In the event the enterprise failed, the investors were liable only for the amount they had invested. Creditors of a bankrupt enterprise could not demand additional payments from them. By reducing the investors' risks, the principle of limited liability encouraged investment in new and untried ventures.

The Human Cost of Industrialization

·   While industrialization promoted the prosperity and wealth of both nations and individuals, the human cost was considerable. During the early stages of the industrial revolution, men, women, and children— many of them under ten years old—worked twelve to eighteen hours a day for very low wages in unsafe and unhealthy factories. The workers and their families lived in crowded slums, without adequate sewage facilities, a safe supply of water, and educational opportunities, and access to health care.

The industrial revolution spread gradually beyond Great Britain to the rest of Europe and North America and ultimately, to other regions of the world. Over the course of a few generations, the industrial revolution brought greater material changes to the lives of human beings than had occurred during all of recorded history up to that time.

Industrialization ultimately brought great improvements in the material standard of living to millions of people in the industrialized countries of Europe and America. In the first generation of the industrial revolution, however, miserable conditions prevailed in the factories and slums of the new industrial towns. These conditions brought the problem of poverty into sharp focus, promoting the growth of demands for reform.

Recommended Reading

Ashton, T. S. *Iron and Steel in the Industrial Revolution* (3rd ed., 1963).

Cameron, Rondo E. *France and the Economic Development of Europe, 1800–1914* (2nd ed., 1966).

Checkland, S. G. *The Rise of Industrial Society in England, 1815–1885* (1965).

Deane, Phyllis. *The First Industrial Revolution* (2nd ed., 1979).

Habakkuk, H. J. *American and British Technology in the Nineteenth Century* (1962).

Henderson, W. O. *Britain and Industrial Europe, 1750–1870* (3rd ed., 1972).

Henderson, W. O. *The Industrialization of Europe, 1780–1914* (1969).

Henderson, W. O. *The Rise of German Industrial Power, 1834–1914* (1975).

Himmelfarb, Gertrude. *The Idea of Poverty: England in the Early Industrial Age* (1983).

Hobsbawm, Eric. *The Age of Capital* (1988).

Landes, David S. *The Unbound Prometheus: Technological Change and Industrial Development in Western Europe from 1750 to the Present* (1969).

O'Brien, Patrick and Caglar Keyder. *Economic Growth in Britain and France, 1780–1914: Two Paths to the Twentieth Century* (1978).

Taylor, George Rogers. *The Transportation Revolution, 1815–1860* (1951).

Thompson, E. P. *The Making of the English Working Class* (1964).

Trebilcock, Clive. *The Industrialization of the Continental Powers, 1780–1914* (1982).

Usher, Abbott P. *A History of Mechanical Inventions* (rev. ed., 1954).

CHAPTER 21

Liberalism and Socialism

Time Line

1776	Adam Smith publishes *Wealth of Nations*
1789	Jeremy Bentham publishes *Principles of Morals and Legislation*
1798	Thomas Robert Malthus publishes *An Essay on the Principle of Population*
1817	David Ricardo publishes *The Principles of Political Economy and Taxation*
1825	The Count of Saint-Simon publishes *The New Christianity*
1826	Robert Owen establishes the socialist community of New Harmony, Indiana

1840	Louis Blanc publishes *The Organization of Work*
1848	John Stuart Mill publishes the first edition of *Principles of Political Economy*
	Karl Marx and Friedrich Engels publish *The Communist Manifesto*
1859	John Stuart Mill publishes *On Liberty*
1867–1894	The three volumes of *Das Kapital* ("Capital") by Karl Marx are published
1889	Eduard Bernstein publishes *Evolutionary Socialism*
1891	Pope Leo XIII issues the encyclical *Rerum Novarum*

During the early nineteenth century, the laissez-faire doctrine of classical liberalism won increasing support among the middle class, whose wealth and influence were increasing as a consequence of the industrial revolution. Laissez-faire appealed to the middle-class owners and managers of industry because it provided a justification for a free enterprise economy that produced increased profits for the middle class to enjoy.

Some sensitive liberals, however, were increasingly troubled by the hardships suffered by the workers. Retreating from strict laissez-faire doctrine. these liberals proposed state intervention to improve these conditions.

The socialists went even further, insisting that the poverty of the workers could be eliminated only by a radical transformation in the ownership of property, establishing some form of social ownership of the means of production.

Other reformers proposed a wide range of different solutions to the problem of poverty, including anarchism and Christian Socialism.

Classical Liberalism

At the heart of the ideology of liberalism was the belief in individualism and individual freedom. In the economic realm, this liberal belief expressed itself in the doctrine of laissez-faire. The economists who championed this doctrine are known as the classical economists.

Adam Smith (1723–1790)

The first major advocate of laissez-faire in the English-speaking world was Adam Smith, a professor at the University of Glasgow in Scotland. In *The Wealth of Nations* (1776), Smith argued that government attempts to regulate the economy, as the mercantilists had been doing, interfered with the operation of the natural laws that governed the economy (see Chapter 12).

Thomas Malthus (1766–1834) and David Ricardo (1772–1823)

The work of Malthus and Ricardo brought a further development of laissez-faire doctrine.

Malthus on Population

In *An Essay on the Principle of Population* (1798), Malthus contended that the population was increasing in a geometric ratio, while the food supply was increasing only in an arithmetic ratio. The inevitable result of population outstripping the food supply would be misery for most of humanity. Some slowing of population growth might result from war, famine, and disease. Malthus believed, however, that "moral restraint"—postponing marriage and practicing chastity until marriage—would serve as the most effective way of limiting population growth.

Ricardo on Wages

Influenced by Malthus's work, Ricardo set forth what came to be known as the Iron Law of Wages. In *The Principles of Political Economy and Taxation* (1817), he argued that wages would tend to hover around the subsistence level. In Ricardo's view, labor should be regarded like any other commodity whose price fluctuated in accordance with supply and demand. If the supply of labor was less than the demand for it, wages would increase. When wages rose above the subsistence level, workers would be encouraged to have more children, thereby enlarging the labor supply. In turn, if the supply of labor exceeded the demand, wages would decrease, causing workers to have fewer children, thus reducing the labor supply. Ricardo concluded that it was useless to raise wages in an effort to improve workers' lives, since higher wages would serve only to encourage them to have more children, thereby increasing the labor supply and forcing wages down once again.

The Retreat from Laissez-Faire

Jeremy Bentham (1748–1832)

The retreat from laissez-faire began with Bentham. Although Bentham believed in the fundamental validity of the doctrine of laissez-faire, he argued that in some instances the government should not be merely a passive policeman but should intervene on behalf of the disadvantaged.

Bentham developed the doctrine of utilitarianism in his *Principles of Morals and Legislation* (1789) and other writings. Central to this doctrine was the belief that every human practice and institution should be evaluated in terms of its utility, which Bentham defined as the amount of happiness it provides. In turn, he defined happiness as the presence of pleasure and the absence of pain.

For the most part, Bentham believed, the government could assure happiness (the most pleasure and the least pain) for the greatest number of people by permitting them the maximum possible amount of individual freedom. If, however, the pains suffered by the many exceeded the pleasures enjoyed by the few, then the government could justifiably intervene to redress the balance. In this way, Bentham began to develop the ideas that ultimately led to the creation of the twentieth-century welfare state.

John Stuart Mill (1806–1873)

Mill's thought represented a further evolution of liberal doctrine away from the doctrine of laissez-faire. He shared the liberals' belief in individual freedom, a belief he expressed in his eloquent essay *On Liberty* (1859). He was ahead of his time in advocating women's rights, including the right to vote, in *The Subjection of Women* (1869).

In his *Principles of Political Economy,* published in 1848 and in several subsequent editions, Mill expressed growing disagreement with the views of the classical economists. Concerned about economic and social injustice, he contended that society could and should exercise some control over the distribution of wealth. He believed that workers should have the freedom to form labor unions to promote their interests and that the government should adopt laws to restrict child labor and to protect women workers. He endorsed the establishment of universal suffrage, which would give workers a degree of influence over the actions of government. He also called for the creation of a system of state-supported elementary education, as well as the enactment of income and inheritance taxes to place limits on the concentration of wealth.

Socialism

While John Stuart Mill and some other liberals advocated a redistribution of wealth to benefit the disadvantaged, the socialists called for a fundamental change in the nature of property ownership itself. They urged that private ownership of the means of production, and perhaps also of the means of distribution, should be replaced by some form of community or state ownership. This social ownership of property, the socialists argued, would insure that property would serve the interests of all the people. The socialists also believed that people were—or could be educated to be—cooperative, rather than competitive, and that they should work together to promote their mutual well-being.

While the socialists agreed on these general principles, socialist thinkers offered a variety of proposals outlining their conceptions of what a socialist society would be like and how it could be brought into being.

Utopian Socialism

The socialists of the early nineteenth century are known collectively as Utopian Socialists.

Robert Owen (1771–1858)

Owen was one of the first Utopian Socialists to gain wide attention. After achieving an early success in the cotton textile industry, in 1799 Owen acquired part ownership of several textile mills at New Lanark in Scotland. He improved the conditions of health and safety in the mills, increased the workers' wages and reduced their hours, and provided them with decent housing. Owen made a substantial profit, thereby demonstrating that successful industrial capitalism did not require the exploitation of labor.

Owen's great dream, however, was to establish a socialist community. Selling his interest in the New Lanark mills, he went to America where he bought land in Indiana. In 1826, he established his community of New Harmony, where people would share both the ownership of property and the fruits of their labor. Within a few years, New Harmony failed. Owen returned to England and devoted the remaining years of his life to other reform projects.

The Count of Saint-Simon (1760–1825)

France produced a number of prominent Utopian Socialists. Saint-Simon expressed his ideas in a number of works, including *The New Christianity* (1825). Modern society, he believed, was shaped primarily by the nature of its industrial economy. Therefore, the focus of government should be on economic, rather than political, issues. Government should be directed by scientists and technicians who understood the operation of the modern industrial economy. This managerial elite would direct the economy so it would serve the interests of all the people. In this new society, all would willingly work for the benefit of society and all would be rewarded according to what they produced, although all workers would be assured that their needs would be met.

Charles Fourier (1772–1837)

Fourier urged the establishment of socialist communities known as phalanxes. Each of these largely self-sufficient phalanxes, he believed, should consist of about 1600 people who would work together in farm and workshop. Individuals would perform the type of work they most enjoyed and would change their jobs frequently in order to avoid boredom. Fourier hoped that philanthropists would come forward to subsidize the establishment of phalanxes, but none ever did. While no phalanxes were organized in France, a number were founded in other countries. None enjoyed an enduring success.

Louis Blanc (1811–1882)

In *The Organization of Work* (1840), Blanc proposed the use of competition to eliminate competition. The first step toward the socialist society of the future would involve political reform, including the creation of a French republic based on universal manhood suffrage and the establishment of a workers' party. As the number of industrial workers increased, the workers' party would ultimately win control of the government. The government would then nationalize the railroads, using the profits of the railroads, as well as tax revenues, to subsidize the establishment of what Blanc called a social workshop in each area of industry. These social workshops would be owned and managed by their workers, who would share in the profits. The workers would be happy and enthusiastic and would therefore produce better products at a lower cost than privately owned factories. The competition of the social workshops would thus drive privately owned factories into bankruptcy. These factories would then be acquired by their workers, who would convert them into social workshops. In time, all of industry would consist of cooperative social workshops. In this new socialist society, the principle of "from each according to his abilities, to each according to his needs" would prevail.

Auguste Blanqui (1805–1881)

Blanqui was an advocate of direct revolutionary action. He proposed that the working-class leaders in Paris should seize power by revolutionary violence. They would then establish a temporary dictatorship, eliminating private ownership of the means of production and distribution, reorganizing the economy so it would serve the interests of the workers, and reeducating the workers out of individualistic selfishness. Once these tasks had been accomplished, the dictatorship of the working-class leaders would end, and a democratic, socialist society would emerge.

Marxism

Karl Marx (1818–1883) was the most influential socialist thinker of the nineteenth century. Born in western Germany, the son of a successful attorney, Marx studied philosophy, earning his doctorate in 1842. While he had been a brilliant student, his reputation as a radical caused him to be denied a teaching position in the conservative universities of his native Prussia. Marx turned to journalism, working for a radical newspaper in Cologne in the Prussian Rhineland. In 1843, however, the newspaper was suppressed by the Prussian censors.

Moving to Paris, Marx became acquainted with French socialist thought and in 1844, began his collaboration with Friedrich Engels (1820–1895), another young German radical, the son of a successful manufacturer. Engels had spent some time in England working for his father. There he had studied conditions in the industrial city of Manchester and had written *The Condition of the Working Class in England* (1845). The collaboration between Marx and Engels continued until the former's death in 1883.

The Communist Manifesto

In 1848, Marx and Engels published *The Communist Manifesto,* setting forth the major ideas of what they regarded as "scientific socialism." Although Engels made significant contributions to its development, the ideology set forth in the *Manifesto* is known as Marxism.

The Marxist theory of revolutionary change was based on the ideas of the early-nineteenth-century German philosopher G. W. F. Hegel (see Chapter 17), who had developed the concept of the dialectic. In Hegel's view, the conflict between the existing order (the thesis) and a challenge to it (the antithesis) resulted in a new social order (the synthesis). Marxism also embraced the philosophical doctrines of materialism and determinism. Materialism is the belief that physical matter is the only reality. Therefore, in the view of the materialists, God does not exist. Marx was an atheist and denounced religion as "the opium of the people," since it distracted their attention from the hardships of their lives. Determinism is the belief that every act and event is the inevitable result of prior acts and events and is independent of human will.

Combining these philosophic concepts, Marx developed his doctrine of dialectical materialism or economic determinism. He believed that economic conditions provided the foundation of the social order. These economic conditions determined the nature of everything else in society, which Marxism described as the superstructure: family structure, the political system, religious and moral beliefs, the educational system, and social classes.

The existence of social classes, in Marx's view, led to a class struggle, which ultimately produced social change. Applying the concept of the dialectic, Marx outlined what he regarded as the inevitable course of historical development. The dominant feudal aristocracy, who derived their wealth and power from the ownership of land (the thesis), faced a challenge from the bourgeoisie, the middle class, who derived their wealth and power from commerce and industry (the antithesis). This class conflict led to the bourgeois revolution, which resulted in the creation of a new social order, dominated by the bourgeoisie (the synthesis).

This social order dominated by the bourgeoisie became, in turn, a new thesis and confronted an intensifying challenge presented by the proletariat, the industrial workers, who represented a new antithesis. The lower elements of the bourgeoisie, the small shopkeepers and artisans, would be unable to survive in an economic world dominated by the great capitalists and would gradually be forced into the proletariat.

The class conflict between the proletariat and bourgeoisie would become increasingly more intense, leading inevitably to the proletarian revolution. The proletariat would rise up, destroying the power of the bourgeoisie, much as the bourgeoisie had earlier destroyed the power of the feudal aristocracy.

Following the proletarian revolution, the leaders of the proletariat would establish their temporary dictatorship. The tasks of this dictatorship of the proletariat would include eradicating the last remnants of the bourgeoisie, reorganizing the economy by establishing the social ownership of the means of production and distribution so that the economy would serve the needs of the proletariat, and reeducating the proletariat so they would be willing to work in behalf of the interests of society rather than for individual gain.

In the new socialist society, since there would be only one class, the proletariat, there would in effect be no classes. Since there were no classes, there would be no exploitation of one class by another, there would be no class conflict, and harmony would prevail.

Spread of Marxism

Although *The Communist Manifesto* was published in 1848, Marxism had no impact on the revolutionary events of that year. In 1849, Marx left Paris and went to London, where he lived for the balance of his life. Marx continued to develop his ideas, writing extensively and publishing *Das Kapital* ("Capital"), his analysis and critique of the capitalist system, in three volumes from 1867 to 1894. (Engels completed the writing of *Das Kapital* following Marx's death in 1883.)

Marx also worked to promote the spread of his ideas. In 1864, the International Working Men's Association held its first meeting in London and embraced Marxism as its program. This First International made little headway in the decade prior to its collapse in 1873. The Second International was formed in 1889, and in the final years of the nineteenth century Marxism won increasing acceptance by socialist parties in several countries on the European continent.

Revisionism

In the late nineteenth century, some Marxists began to reevaluate Marxism in view of the fact that Marx's predictions were not being borne out by reality. In Germany, Eduard Bernstein (1850–1932) published *Evolutionary Socialism* (1889), noting that, despite Marx's predictions, the middle class was not becoming weaker, the condition of the industrial workers was improving, and capitalism showed no signs of collapsing. Bernstein's revisionism emphasized reform within the context of the existing order, rather than revolution, and the achievement of socialism through a democratic political process. Although the so-called orthodox Marxists denounced revisionism, the new doctrine won increasing support within the European socialist parties.

Anarchism

Like the socialists, the anarchists denounced capitalism for its exploitation of labor and favored the abolition of private property. The anarchists went further, however, and demanded the destruction of the state itself, which they regarded as an instrument of exploitation and oppression.

Pierre-Joseph Proudhon (1809–1865)

Proudhon is best known for *What Is Property?* (1840). He answered the question by declaring: "Property is theft." The people who do the work, he believed, should be the possessors of property, rather than the capitalists. He advocated the replacement of the state with a voluntary, cooperative society of peasants, shopkeepers, and artisans.

Michael Bakunin (1814–1876)

A Russian radical who spent many years in exile in Western Europe, Bakunin was an advocate of revolutionary violence. He believed that the revolutionary movement should be led by secret societies of committed radicals. Once these radicals had led the workers in the seizure of power, they should destroy the state and create a new social order based on a loose federation of autonomous communities.

Assassinations

Although the anarchists never led a successful revolution, they did carry out numerous acts of violence, including the assassinations of President Sadi Carnot of France (1894), Empress Elizabeth of Austria (1898), King Umberto I of Italy (1900), and President William McKinley of the United States (1901).

Christian Socialism

Some social and economic reformers found their inspiration in the teachings of the Christian religion. The Christian Socialists did not propose a specific ideology but instead advocated reforms, motivated by the Christian spirit of brotherly love, to benefit industrial workers and other disadvantaged groups.

Frederick Denison Maurice (1805–1872)

In the mid-nineteenth century, the Christian Socialist movement developed in the Church of England. Maurice, an Anglican priest and professor at Cambridge University, emerged as a major spokesman for Christian Socialism. In addition to promoting economic and social reform, he was active in efforts to advance educational opportunities for women and factory workers. These efforts led to the establishment of Queen's College for women in 1848 and the Working Men's College in 1854.

Pope Leo XIII and Catholic Social Concern

Pope Leo XIII (r. 1878–1903) expressed his concern about economic and social issues in his encyclical letter *Rerum Novarum* (1891), which was critical of both socialism and laissez-faire capitalism. He condemned socialism, especially Marxism, for its atheism, as well as for its opposition to the private ownership of property and the doctrine of the class struggle. The pope regarded laissez-faire capitalism as incompatible with the Christian faith because it regarded labor simply as one commodity among many.

Leo XIII insisted on the moral obligation of employers to pay their workers a living wage and defended the right of workers to form labor unions in order to improve their conditions.

Although the ideologies of liberalism and socialism took shape in the early and mid-nineteenth century, during the first generations of the industrial revolution, they continue to have a powerful impact on the world in the final years of the twentieth century. Regimes claiming to be guided by the principles of Marxism govern the Soviet Union, several Eastern European countries, China, and other states in Asia, Africa, and Latin America. In Western Europe, a number of countries have developed mixed economies, joining elements of both capitalism and socialism, while in the United States, public debate continues on the role of government in the economic and social spheres.

Recommended Reading

Beecher, Jonathan. *Charles Fourier: The Visionary and His World* (1986).

Cole, G. D. H. *A History of Socialist Thought,* 5 vols. (1953–1960).

Derfler, Leslie. *Socialism Since Marx: A Century of the European Left* (1973).

Harrison, John F. C. *Quest for the New Moral World: Robert Owen and the Owenites in Britain and America* (1969).

Heilbroner, Robert L. *The Worldly Philosophers* (5th ed., 1980).

Joll, James. *The Anarchists* (1965).

Laidler, Harry W. *A History of Socialism* (1968).

Lichtheim, George. *Marxism* (1961).

Lichtheim, George. *A Short History of Socialism* (1970).

McLellan, David. *Karl Marx: His Life and Thought* (1977).

Mack, M. *Jeremy Bentham* (1962).

Manuel, Frank. *The Prophets of Paris* (1962).

Matthews, Betty, ed. *Marx: A Hundred Years On* (1983).

Mazlish, Bruce. *James and John Stuart Mill* (1975).

Riasanovsky, Nicholas V. *The Teaching of Charles Fourier* (1969).

Rosenblum, Nancy L. *Bentham's Theory of the Modern State* (1978).

Spitzer, A. B. *The Revolutionary Theories of Louis-Auguste Blanqui* (1957).

Wolfe, Bertram D. *Marxism: One Hundred Years in the Life of a Doctrine* (1965).

CHAPTER 22

The Revolutions of 1848

Time Line

February 1848   A revolution in Paris results in the overthrow of King Louis Philippe and the proclamation of the Second Republic

March 1848   A revolution breaks out in Vienna, leading to Metternich's resignation

The Magyars approve the March Laws as a constitution for Hungary

King Charles Albert of Sardinia-Piedmont issues a constitution, the Statuto of 1848

The March Days mark the outbreak of revolution in Prussia.

April 1848	The Austrian government promises the Czechs a constituent assembly for the Kingdom of Bohemia
May 1848	The German National Assembly begins its deliberations in Frankfurt
June 1848	Radical workers in Paris rise up in revolt
	Austrian forces crush the Czech revolution
December 1848	Louis Napoleon Bonaparte wins election to the presidency of the Second French Republic
	Ferdinand I abdicates as Austria's emperor and is succeeded by Francis Joseph
March 1849	The German National Assembly completes its draft of a constitution for a united Germany
April 1849	The Hungarians proclaim the establishment of a republic
	King Frederick William IV of Prussia declines to accept the crown as Germany's emperor
August 1849	Austro-Russian forces crush the Hungarian revolt
November 1850	In the Humiliation of Olmütz, Prussia accepts Austria's demand for the reestablishment of the German Confederation

---

In 1848 widespread and growing discontent with reactionary rule resulted in a wave of revolutions in Europe. The revolutions of 1848 threw the conservative rulers off balance, and almost everywhere it appeared that the cause of revolution would triumph. It seemed that France would become a democratic republic, that Germany and Italy would achieve unity as liberal national states, that the Magyars of Hungary and perhaps other subject peoples of the Austrian Empire would gain their independence or at least a greater measure of self-rule,

and that Austria itself would achieve a liberal, constitutional govern-
ment.

As the months passed, however, the conservative rulers gradually
regained their confidence. When the revolutionary idealists manifested
their inexperience and divisions, the rulers began to reassert their
control.

By the early 1850s, the defeat of the revolutionary idealists ap-
peared complete, and almost everywhere the conservative order had
been restored. Nevertheless, despite the defeat of the revolutionary
idealists, their ideas lived on, and in the course of the next two decades,
Europe would be profoundly transformed.

Background of the Revolutions

Beneath the apparently tranquil surface of the conservative order
in Europe, discontent had been simmering for several decades. Then,
during the 1840s, economic problems intensified the discontent. The
European economies had not fully recovered from the depression of
1837, and in much of Europe the 1840s were appropriately called "the
hungry forties." Crop failures increased the misery of the masses, and
the workers in Europe's developing industries experienced continuing
hardships.

Western European Liberals

Workers and peasants did not, however, play the dominant role in
the revolutions of 1848. Instead, these revolutions were mainly liberal,
middle class, and urban. Western European liberals desired, above all,
to establish constitutional governments where the power of monarchs
would be limited by elected parliaments and guarantees of civil liberties. This was the liberal ideal that had taken shape during the Enlightenment and the French Revolution. Of the major countries of
Europe, only in France did many liberals favor the replacement of the
monarchy by a republic. Furthermore, only in France did many liberals
embrace the cause of democracy, which included, in particular, universal manhood suffrage. Elsewhere, liberals generally favored property
qualifications for voting.

Liberal Revolutionaries in Central Europe

In Central Europe—the Austrian Empire and the German and Italian states—the liberal revolutionaries also sought to promote the principle of nationalism. While the German and Italian liberals hoped to unify their people, in the Austrian Empire, the liberal leaders of the subject nationalities hoped to win independence from the Hapsburgs and to create separate national states.

The Revolution in France

The February Revolution

In France, discontent had been mounting against the increasingly arbitrary government of King Louis Philippe. On February 22, 1848, a large banquet was scheduled to be held in Paris by middle-class opponents of Louis Philippe and his chief minister, François Guizot (1787–1874). When the government attempted to prohibit the banquet, spontaneous rioting broke out in the streets.

On February 23, Louis Philippe responded to liberal demands and dismissed Guizot. Nevertheless, unrest continued among the city's workers, and the rioting intensified. In an attempt to avoid more bloodshed, Louis Philippe abdicated on February 24 and fled to England.

The Provisional Government

Following the king's abdication, the Chamber of Deputies formed a provisional government, and the Second Republic was proclaimed. The provisional government was split into two factions. The moderate republicans, whose aims were primarily political, were led by Alphonse de Lamartine (1790–1869), a statesman and poet. The socialists, led by Louis Blanc (1811–1882), regarded the republic as a means to an end: the creation of a socialist society.

Socialists Versus Moderate Republicans

In an attempt to placate the socialists and the workers of the capital, the provisional government placed Blanc in charge of establishing a system of national workshops to provide assistance to unemployed workers.

Although the socialists and other radical elements dominated Paris and drew support in other cities such as Lyons and Marseilles, the rural areas and small towns remained basically conservative. When elections for the National Assembly, which would draft a new constitution, were held in April, the moderate republicans won an overwhelming victory. In the wake of their electoral triumph, the moderate republicans in the provisional government ordered the national workshops to shut down.

Suppression of the June Days Revolt

In Paris, the workers responded to the closing of the national workshops by rising in a revolt, which lasted from June 23 to June 26. Acting on the orders of the provisional government, General Louis Cavaignac (1802–1857) crushed this June Days revolt.

Constitution of the Second Republic

In November 1848, the National Assembly completed the drafting of the constitution of the Second Republic. The constitution provided for a president and a one-house parliament, both to be elected by universal manhood suffrage.

Louis Napoleon Bonaparte (1803–1873)

In December 1848, Louis Napoleon Bonaparte, whose name stood for order, stability, and national glory, polled over 5 million votes and won the presidency. The combined votes for his opponents, including Lamartine, Cavaignac, and the socialist Alexandre Ledru-Rollin (1807–1874), totaled less than 2 million. From the beginning, Louis Napoleon desired to follow his uncle's example and establish a dictatorship.

The Revolutions in the Austrian Empire

The Revolution in Austria

In 1848, the Austrian Empire was ruled by the feebleminded

Ferdinand I (r. 1835–1848). Political authority was in the hands of a triumvirate, led by the reactionary Prince Metternich.

News of the February Revolution in France gave rise to revolutionary fervor in the Austrian capital of Vienna. On March 13, rioting broke out in the city. Responding to pressure from his opponents in the government, Metternich resigned and went into exile.

Abolition of Robot

In July 1848, an Austrian constituent assembly met and began to draft a constitution. The most enduring act of this assembly came in September, when it voted to abolish the *robot,* the system of obligatory peasant labor. The major source of the peasants' discontent had been eliminated, and they now ended their revolutionary activity.

End of the Revolution

As the revolutionary disturbances subsided, the Austrian government began to recover its confidence. At the end of October, troops loyal to the emperor regained control of Vienna. In early December, Prince Felix Schwarzenberg (1800–1852), who was now the leading figure in the imperial government, arranged for the abdication of Ferdinand I and his replacement by his eighteen-year-old nephew, Francis Joseph (r. 1848–1916). The government announced that the new emperor would not be bound by any commitments made by his predecessor.

Restoration of Centralized Government

In March 1849, the constituent assembly proposed the establishment of a decentralized system of government for the Austrian Empire, which might have satisfied some of the demands of the subject nationalities. Schwarzenberg rejected this proposal, however, and produced his own version of a constitution providing for a more highly centralized system. It was announced that, for the time being, Francis Joseph would rule without this constitution. In 1851, the constitution was suspended without ever having gone into effect. The old system of centralized government that had prevailed prior to 1848 was thus restored.

The Revolutions in Hungary and Bohemia

In 1848, the Austrian authorities were also confronted with revolutionary upheavals in Hungary and Bohemia.

Hungary

On March 3, 1848, the radical Magyar nationalist Louis Kossuth (1802–1894) demanded self-government for Hungary. In mid-March, the Magyars approved the March Laws, which established an elected parliament to replace the Hungarian diet and abolished serfdom. Faced with the revolution in Vienna, the Austrian government was forced to accept the March Laws, recognizing the virtual independence of Hungary.

Bohemia

Revolution also erupted among the Czechs in Prague, the capital of Bohemia. On April 8, the Austrian government promised the Czechs a constituent assembly for the Kingdom of Bohemia.

Other Revolts

Other anti-Austrian revolts broke out in Dalmatia, Galicia, Moravia, and Transylvania.

Suppression of Czech and Hungarian Revolutions

In early June 1848, the first Pan-Slav Congress met in Prague, urging Slavic solidarity against the Austrians and promoting the cause of independence for the subject nationalities in the Austrian Empire. Only a few days later, on June 17, Austrian forces commanded by Field Marshal Alfred von Windischgrätz (1787–1862) crushed the Czech revolution and established a military government in Bohemia.

In the autumn of 1848, the Austrians moved against the revolution in Hungary. Kossuth enlisted thousands of volunteers in his Home Defense army, which soon drove the Austrian forces from most of the country. In April 1849, the Hungarian diet declared Hungary's independence of Austria, established a republic, and elected Kossuth as its first president.

In June 1849, Emperor Francis Joseph accepted the offer of assistance made by Tsar Nicholas I of Russia. Some 100,000 Russian troops invaded Hungary, reinforcing the Austrian army there. On August 9, the combined Austro-Russian force defeated Kossuth's army in the Battle of Temesvar. Kossuth fled to Turkey, and Austrian control was restored over Hungary.

The Revolutions in Italy

Outbreak of the Revolutions

In early 1848, revolutions against both the princely rulers and Austrian domination swept the Italian states. In February, revolutionaries forced Ferdinand II (r. 1830–1859), the Bourbon ruler of the Two Sicilies, to grant a liberal constitution.

News of Metternich's fall on March 13 led to the outbreak of rioting in Milan, the capital of Lombardy, which Austria had annexed along with Venetia in 1815. The Milanese revolt of the Five Days from March 18 to March 22 forced the Austrians to withdraw from the city. On March 22, an anti-Austrian government, led by Daniele Manin (1804–1857), was proclaimed in Venice, the capital of Venetia.

In Sardinia-Piedmont on March 4, King Charles Albert (r. 1831–1849) of the House of Savoy granted his subjects a liberal constitution, the Statuto of 1848. Charles Albert also embraced the cause of Italian nationalism.

Suppression of the Revolutions

As early as May 1848, the revolution was suppressed in the Kingdom of the Two Sicilies. Then, in late July, an Austrian army commanded by General Joseph Radetzky (1766–1858) defeated the Piedmontese in the Battle of Custozza. Shortly thereafter, the Austrians restored their control over Lombardy.

Elsewhere in Italy, however, the revolutionary upheavals continued. In February 1849, revolutionaries, including Giuseppe Mazzini (1805–1872) and Giuseppe Garibaldi (1807–1882), proclaimed the establishment of the Roman Republic in the Papal States. In March, Piedmont renewed the war against Austria. Once again, the Austrians defeated the Piedmontese, this time in the Battle of Novara on March

23. King Charles Albert was now forced to abdicate in favor of his son, Victor Emmanuel II (r. 1849–1878).

In April 1849, Louis Napoleon Bonaparte sent French troops into action against the Roman Republic, as a part of his efforts to win support among French Catholics. The French took Rome at the end of June. In the meantime, the Austrians crushed the revolution in Tuscany in May and in Venice in August.

The German Revolution

Outbreak of the Revolution

As news of the French February Revolution spread through the German states, agitation mounted in the cause of liberal reform and national unification. In Berlin, the rioting of the March Days led Prussia's King Frederick William IV (r. 1840–1861) to initiate some liberal reforms, including abolition of censorship. He also announced his intention to summon an assembly to draft a Prussian constitution. This assembly met in May and continued its deliberations until autumn.

Elsewhere in Germany, liberal nationalists from several states agreed in March to convene a preliminary assembly (*Vorparlament*) to discuss the possibility of unifying Germany. This preliminary assembly decided to call for the election of a national assembly to draft a constitution.

The German National Assembly

Elected by universal manhood suffrage, the German National Assembly began its deliberations in Frankfurt on May 18, 1848.

One major issue facing the assembly was the question of whether Austria should be included in the new united Germany. Some of the more conservative delegates favored both including Austria and inviting the Hapsburgs to accept the German imperial crown. Others opposed the inclusion of Austria, arguing that the Hapsburgs would almost inevitably oppose a liberal constitution and pointing out that the Austrian Empire included large areas that were inhabited by non-Germans. The view of those who wanted to exclude Austria prevailed.

Collapse of the Revolution

The Prussian Constitution

While the National Assembly debated the nature of the new Germany, King Frederick William IV lost his initial enthusiasm for the revolution and began to suppress it in Prussia. With the support of his army, the king dissolved the Prussian constitutional assembly in December 1848. By royal decree, the king issued his own constitution for Prussia, which remained in effect until 1918. This constitution established a two-house parliament. The upper house consisted of the Junker nobility, while the lower house was elected under a three-class voting law that enabled the wealthiest 20 percent of the voters to elect two-thirds of its members. The king retained an absolute veto over legislation, along with the authority to suspend civil liberties and rule by royal decree.

"Humiliation of Olmütz"

In March 1849, the Frankfurt National Assembly completed its task of drafting a constitution and voted to offer the imperial crown of a united Germany to Frederick William IV. The king declined the offer. Instead of becoming Germany's emperor, the Prussian ruler attempted to form a Prussian-dominated federation of north German states. Austria opposed this project and forced the Prussians to give way in the Humiliation of Olmütz of November 1850. The Austrians then proceeded to reestablish the German Confederation.

By 1850, the revolutions had been suppressed and the conservative order had been restored. The changes brought about by the revolutions had been slight. In France, the arbitrary rule of Louis Philippe was replaced by that of Louis Napoleon. In the Austrian Empire, a young emperor, Francis Joseph, had replaced his mentally incompetent predecessor, Ferdinand I, and the traditional highly centralized government of the Hapsburgs had been reestablished. Obligatory peasant labor had been abolished, but that was among the few enduring changes that revolution had brought to Austria. In Italy, the Austrians assisted in the restoration of conservative governments, although Sardinia-

Piedmont retained its liberal constitution. In Germany, the Austrians reestablished the German Confederation.

Everywhere the revolutionary idealists had been defeated. But the revolutionary ideas of liberalism and nationalism lived on and continued to win adherents. And only a few years after the defeat of the revolutions of 1848, many of the goals of the revolutionaries had been achieved. Italy was unified in 1861. Hungary gained the right of self-government in 1867, while a united German Empire was proclaimed in 1871.

Recommended Reading

Bruenig, Charles. *The Age of Revolution and Reform, 1789–1850* (2nd ed., 1977).

Deak, Istvan. *The Lawful Revolution: Louis Kossuth and the Hungarians, 1848–1849* (1979).

Duveau, Georges. *1848: The Making of a Revolution* (1967).

Hamerow, Theodore S. *Restoration, Revolution, and Reaction: Economics and Politics in Germany, 1815–1871* (1958).

Hobsbawm, E. J. *The Age of Revolution: Europe, 1789 to 1848* (1969).

Langer, William L. *Political and Social Upheaval, 1832–1852* (1969).

McKay, Donald Cope. *The National Workshops: A Study in the French Revolution of 1848* (1933).

Merriman, John M. *The Agony of the Republic: The Repression of the Left in Revolutionary France, 1848–1851* (1978).

Namier, Lewis B. *1848: The Revolution of the Intellectuals* (1944).

Rath, Reuben J. *The Viennese Revolution of 1848* (1957).

Robertson, Priscilla. *Revolutions of 1848: A Social History* (1952).

Rudé, George. *The Crowd in History: A Study of Popular Disturbances in France and England, 1730–1848* (rev. ed., 1981).

Stearns, Peter N. *1848: The Revolutionary Tide in Europe* (1974).

Valentin, Veit. *1848: Chapters of German History* (1965).

Whitridge, Arnold. *Men in Crisis: The Revolutions of 1848* (1949).

CHAPTER 23

National Unification in Italy and Germany

Time Line

1849–1878	Reign of King Victor Emmanuel II of Piedmont, who becomes king of Italy in 1861
1852	Camillo Cavour becomes premier of Sardinia-Piedmont
1859	Piedmont and France defeat Austria; Piedmont annexes Lombardy
1860	Piedmont annexes Tuscany, Modena, Parma, and the Romagna
	Garibaldi and his Red Shirts land in Sicily

1861–1888	Reign of King William I of Prussia, who becomes German emperor in 1871
1861	The Kingdom of Italy is proclaimed
1862	Bismarck becomes minister-president of Prussia
1864	Prussia and Austria defeat Denmark
1866	Prussia defeats Austria in the Seven Weeks' War
	Italy annexes Venetia
1867	Prussia creates the North German Confederation
1870	France declares war on Prussia
	Italy annexes Rome
1871	Prussia and its German allies defeat France
	The German Empire is proclaimed
	Germany annexes Alsace and Lorraine

In 1848–1849, the liberal national idealists had been defeated in their efforts to unite Italy and Germany. By the early 1850s, the Austrians had reimposed their control over Italian and German affairs, and the German Confederation had been reestablished. Nevertheless, the desire for national unification remained strong in both Italy and Germany.

Leadership now passed into the hands of professional politicians. They possessed what the revolutionary idealists of 1848 had lacked: power and the will to use power, practical political experience, and a clear vision of their goals.

In Italy, Camillo Cavour, the premier of Piedmont, established a united Kingdom of Italy in 1861, while in Germany, Otto von Bismarck, the Prussian minister-president, created a united German Empire a decade later.

Although Cavour and Bismarck both unified their respective countries, they differed in political principles. Cavour was both a sincere liberal and a sincere nationalist who unified Italy as a liberal, constitutional state. In contrast, Bismarck was fundamentally a con-servative and a Prussian patriot, a loyal servant of the Hohenzollern king of Prussia. His primary objective was to enhance Prussia's power by establishing its dominance over Germany.

Italy

The failure of the Italian revolutionaries of 1848 largely discredited the republican idealists led by Giuseppe Mazzini (1805–1872) and Giuseppe Garibaldi (1807–1882), and it provided an opportunity for a political leader of another sort.

Divided Italy

Following the defeat of the Italian revolutions of 1848, Italy remained divided into three parts.

In the south, the Kingdom of the Two Sicilies was ruled by a king of the Bourbon dynasty. In the center, the pope governed the Papal States. In the north, several small states, including Tuscany, Modena, and Parma, were subject to Austrian domination. In addition, the northern Italian provinces of Lombardy and Venetia had been an in-tegral part of the Austrian Empire since 1815. Northern Italy also included the Kingdom of Sardinia-Piedmont, frequently referred to simply as Piedmont, ruled by the House of Savoy. While Piedmont retained its liberal constitution, the Statuto of 1848, the other Italian states had been restored to reactionary rulers.

Count Camillo Cavour (1810–1861)

Cavour, the unifier of Italy, proved to be one of Europe's most brilliant statesmen in the nineteenth century.

Youth and Early Career

Born into a family of the Piedmontese nobility, Cavour became a liberal while he was still in his teens. Although he planned to pursue a career as an army officer, his liberalism aroused the distrust of the royal authorities. Realizing that he could not expect to achieve success in a military career, Cavour resigned his commission. He traveled in France and Great Britain, increasing his admiration for their constitutional governments and progressive development.

Following the revolution of 1848, Cavour won election to the new Piedmontese parliament. He quickly proved his ability and was named minister of commerce and agriculture in 1850 and finance minister in 1851. King Victor Emmanuel II (r. 1849–1878) appointed him to the premiership in 1852.

Premier of Piedmont

As premier, Cavour carried out a program of liberal reform. These policies both reflected his sincere conviction and helped further the achievement of his initial goal: to unite northern Italy as a liberal constitutional monarchy ruled by the House of Savoy. A liberal Piedmont, Cavour believed, would discredit the tyranny of the reactionary Italian princes and Austria and would win the support of Italian nationalists, as well as the admiration of progressive elements in Great Britain and France.

Cavour's program included reforming the Piedmontese currency and state finances, and he succeeded in balancing the state budget. He promoted economic development, including the establishment of banks, the construction of railroads, the building of factories, the importation of machinery, and the development of the port of Genoa. Under Cavour's direction, Piedmont became a prosperous and progressive state.

Foreign Policy

Austria presented a major obstacle to the achievement of Cavour's plans. Realizing that Piedmont alone was not strong enough to defeat Austria, he sought to gain French assistance. In the mid–1850s, he sent a Piedmontese force to support the French and British in the Crimean War. Piedmont had no argument with Russia; its participation in the war was an obvious effort to curry favor with France and Great Britain.

Closer to home, Cavour offered assistance to the newly established Italian National Society. This secret organization operated in several northern Italian states, promoting revolts against the local pro-Austrian rulers.

In July 1858, Cavour met secretly with Napoleon III at Plombières in eastern France. The French emperor had a fondness for Italy, where he had lived during his youth, and he promised to send troops to aid Piedmont in a war against Austria. Piedmont would acquire the Austrian-ruled provinces of Lombardy and Venetia, and in return Cavour agreed to cede the Piedmontese provinces of Nice and Savoy to France.

The War Against Austria

In April 1859, Cavour provoked Austria into declaring war on Piedmont. As the Austrians pushed into Piedmont, a combined Piedmontese and French army counterattacked, driving the invaders back into Lombardy. Defeated at the battles of Magenta on June 4 and Solferino on June 24, the Austrians withdrew to their strongholds in Venetia.

Shocked by the bloodiness of the battles and fearful of a hostile reaction by French Catholics if Piedmont moved to annex the Papal States, Napoleon III decided to make a separate peace with Austria. Under the terms of the Peace of Villafranca of July 1859, Austria agreed to cede Lombardy to Piedmont. Austria, however, would retain Venetia. Furious at Napoleon's double-dealing, Cavour resigned as premier.

Piedmont's Annexations in Northern Italy

Piedmont's gains quickly proved far greater than Cavour had anticipated. In August and September 1859, revolutionary assemblies in Tuscany, Parma, Modena, and the Romagna, a part of the Papal States, offered to unite with Piedmont. Returning to the premiership in January 1860, Cavour carried out these annexations. Napoleon III acquiesced in Piedmont's gains in return for Piedmont's cession of Nice and Savoy to France.

Revolution in Southern Italy

In April 1860, a revolution broke out in Sicily in opposition to the reactionary policies of Francis II (r. 1859–1860), the new Bourbon ruler of the Kingdom of the Two Sicilies. This spread of revolution to the

The Unification of Italy

south was more than Cavour had anticipated and more than Napoleon III was prepared to support.

Garibaldi's Expedition

In May, Garibaldi sailed from the Piedmontese port of Genoa with his famous force of about 1,000 volunteers, the Red Shirts. Officially,

Cavour opposed Garibaldi's expedition, but he supported it secretly. Under the protection of British ships, the Red Shirts landed in Sicily. At the end of May, the Red Shirts and local recruits took Palermo, Sicily's major city.

In August 1860, Garibaldi's forces crossed the Strait of Messina to the Italian mainland. King Francis II fled, and on September 7, Garibaldi entered Naples, the capital of the Two Sicilies.

Annexation of the Papal States

Cavour had not expected the Red Shirts' rapid success, and he feared that Garibaldi might now attempt to seize Rome, which could lead France and Austria to intervene in defense of the pope. In an effort to restrain Garibaldi, Cavour decided to send Piedmontese troops into the Papal States. On September 18, the Piedmontese defeated papal troops at Castelfidardo on the Adriatic coast and quickly took control of most of the Papal States, although the pope retained possession of Rome. King Victor Emmanuel II then joined forces with Garibaldi, who agreed to the Piedmontese annexation of the Kingdom of the Two Sicilies.

Proclamation of the Kingdom of Italy

On March 17, 1861, an Italian parliament proclaimed the establishment of the kingdom of Italy, and King Victor Emmanuel II became king. Italy's liberal constitution was patterned after the Piedmontese Statuto of 1848. Italy's first capital was Turin, the capital of Piedmont, but the Italian capital was soon moved to Florence. Cavour did not long survive the creation of Italy, dying less than three months later at the age of fifty-one.

Annexation of Venice and Rome

In April 1866, Italy concluded an alliance with Prussia, which defeated Austria in the Seven Weeks' War during the summer. Austria ceded Venetia to the Italians.

After the kingdom of Italy was created in 1861, French troops remained in Rome to defend the pope's possession of the city and its surroundings. When the French withdrew these troops during the

Franco-German War of 1870, the Italians occupied and annexed Rome, which now became Italy's capital.

The annexations of Venetia and Rome completed the process of unification and marked the fulfillment of the Risorgimento, the great political and cultural revival of Italy during the nineteenth century.

Germany

The failure of the German revolutionaries of 1848 weakened the liberal nationalists and provided an opportunity for a political leader of another sort.

Divided Germany

Following the failure of the 1848 revolution, the German Confederation was reestablished as a loose union of the thirty-nine German states. Of these states, the most powerful were Austria, ruled by the Hapsburg dynasty, and Prussia, ruled by the House of Hohenzollern. Holding the presidency of the German Confederation, the Austrians dominated Germany much as they dominated Italy.

Otto von Bismarck (1815–1898)

Bismarck, like his Italian counterpart Cavour, proved to be one of nineteenth-century Europe's most brilliant statemen.

Youth and Early Career

Born into a family of the Prussian Junker aristocracy, Bismarck studied law and set out on a career in the Prussian civil service. He found the work of a bureaucrat unsatisfying, however, and resigned, spending the next several years as a gentleman farmer. In 1847, Bismarck was elected to the Landtag, the Prussian parliament.

In 1851, the Prussian king, Frederick William IV (r. 1840–1861), appointed Bismarck as Prussia's representative to the diet of the German Confederation, which met in Frankfurt. Witnessing Austria's domination of German affairs, Bismarck became convinced that Germany was too small for both Austria and Prussia. However, the Prussian government was not yet ready to challenge Austria and found

Bismarck's anti-Austrian attitude embarrassing. In 1859, Bismarck became Prussia's ambassador to Russia, and in 1862, he was named ambassador to France.

Minister-President of Prussia

The increasingly unbalanced King Frederick William IV dominated the Prussian government until he was declared insane in 1858. His brother became regent and then, when Frederick William IV died in 1861, succeeded to the throne as William I (r. 1861–1888).

William I introduced a program to strengthen the Prussian army. This program required a large appropriation, but the liberals in the Prussian Landtag demanded concessions from the king in exchange for their approval of new taxes. As the deadlock continued, Albrecht von Roon (1803–1879), the minister of war, suggested that Bismarck would be able to put the military reform program into effect, either with the support of the Landtag or against it, if necessary.

In September 1862, William I named Bismarck Prussia's minister-president. Addressing the Landtag, Bismarck presented his views forthrightly. The great issues of the day, he declared, would not be settled by parliamentary debate and majority vote. Instead, they would be settled by "blood and iron."

The Landtag continued to refuse to approve the new taxes. Acting unconstitutionally, Bismarck proceeded to collect the taxes anyway, and the military reform program was carried out.

The Schleswig-Holstein Affair

The Schleswig-Holstein affair provided Bismarck with an opportunity to begin the process of eliminating Austria from German affairs.

Schleswig and Holstein were two duchies located south of Denmark. The Danish king ruled the partly Danish-speaking and partly German-speaking duchies, although they were not a part of Denmark. In 1863, the Danish parliament annexed Schleswig, an action that infuriated German nationalists.

Prussian Alliance with Austria

Bismarck proposed a Prussian alliance with Austria to take action against Denmark. The Austrians accepted the proposal, and Prussia and

Austria went to war against Denmark in 1864. Denmark was quickly defeated and surrendered the two duchies. In the Convention of Gastein, signed in August 1865, Bismarck arranged for joint Austro-Prussian possession of the duchies, with Prussia occupying Schleswig and Austria occupying Holstein. This provided Bismarck with opportunities to provoke arguments with the Austrians.

Neutralizing Other Powers

Before moving against Austria, Bismarck sought to gain assurances of French, Italian, and Russian neutrality. Meeting with Napoleon III in October 1865, he hinted vaguely at the possibility that France might receive some territorial compensation in Belgium and Luxembourg or in the German Rhineland in the event of war between Prussia and Austria. The French emperor agreed to remain neutral. He underestimated Prussia's military power and expected a long war that Austria would ultimately win.

Turning to Italy, Bismarck formed an alliance with the Italians, which provided for the Italian acquisition of Austrian-ruled Venetia in the event of a Prussian victory over Austria.

Bismarck had already put Russia in his debt. In 1863, when a revolt occurred in Russian Poland, Prussia had supported the Russian suppression of the revolt, the only major European power to do so.

The Seven Weeks' War

Defeat of Austria

In the spring of 1866, Prussia accused Austria of violating the Convention of Gastein and proposed the abolition of the German Confederation. The Seven Weeks' War between Austria and Prussia began in June. The Prussian army decisively defeated the Austrians at the Battle of Königgrätz (Sadowa) in Bohemia on July 3.

Austrian Exclusion from Germany

In the Treaty of Prague, signed in late August 1866, Bismarck made a moderate peace with Austria. Prussia gained full possession of Schleswig and Holstein and also annexed the northern German states of Hanover, Hesse, Nassau, and Frankfurt. Austria agreed to the dissolution of the German Confederation and in effect, ceased to be an effective German power. Italy acquired Venetia.

The North German Confederation

With Austria excluded from German affairs, Prussia proceeded to establish the North German Confederation (1867), which united the German states north of the Main River under Prussian leadership.

The Independent South German States

While Prussia dominated the North German Confederation, to the south there were four independent states: the kingdoms of Bavaria and Württemberg, the grand duchy of Baden, and the duchy of Hesse-Darmstadt. Few Germans expected this division to remain permanent, and Bismarck himself wanted to absorb the south.

There were, however, several obstacles in the path of the extension of Prussian control over southern Germany. The south German states were largely Catholic in religion and had a relatively liberal political tradition. They were reluctant to be subordinated to the control of autocratic and militaristic Prussia, which was predominantly Lutheran. Furthermore, Napoleon III opposed a further increase in Prussian power. For centuries, France had benefited from a divided Germany, and the growth of Prussian power that had already occurred was to France's disadvantage. Bismarck believed it would be necessary to fight a war against France in order for Prussia to gain control of the south German states.

The Hohenzollern Candidacy

In 1868, a revolution in Spain began a series of events that ended with Prussia's defeat of France and the creation of the German Empire.

The Spanish revolution resulted in the overthrow of Queen Isabella, whereupon the Spanish began the search for a new monarch. Someone suggested the name of Prince Leopold of Hohenzollern-Sigmaringen, a south German Catholic relative of the Prussian king.

The French strongly opposed Leopold's candidacy. If he became Spain's ruler, a dynastic alliance might then come into being between

The Unification of Germany

Spain and Prussia. In the face of French protests, King William I of Prussia agreed to have Leopold's name withdrawn from consideration.

French Demands on Prussia

Not content with this diplomatic victory, the French made the mistake of making further demands. On July 13, 1870, the French ambassador to Prussia, Count Benedetti, met with William I in the town of Ems and asked the king for a formal guarantee that the Hohenzollern candidacy would not be renewed. Believing that the concessions he had already made to the French were sufficient, William I refused and later sent a report of his meeting with Benedetti to Bismarck in Berlin.

The Ems Dispatch

Bismarck edited the king's report of the conversation and released it. This so-called Ems Dispatch made it appear that King William I and Ambassador Benedetti had insulted each other. This angered Napoleon III, who responded by declaring war on Prussia on July 19, 1870.

Anticipating the possibility of war with France, Bismarck had already concluded alliances with the independent south German states. Now all of Germany, under the leadership of Prussia, went to war against France, the Germans' hereditary enemy.

The Franco-German War and the Proclamation of the German Empire

Mobilizing efficiently, the German armies invaded France. On September 2, Napoleon III and a large French army surrendered to the Germans at Sedan. In Paris, rebels proclaimed the establishment of the Third Republic, which sought to continue the war.

Completion of German Unification

On January 18, 1871, while the German siege of Paris was still in progress, King William I of Prussia was proclaimed German emperor before an assembly of German princes and other dignitaries in the Hall of Mirrors at the Palace of Versailles. The unification of Germany under the leadership of Prussia had been accomplished.

Annexation of Alsace and Lorraine

On May 10, 1871, France and Germany signed the Treaty of Frankfurt, ending the Franco-German War. The French ceded the provinces of Alsace and Lorraine to Germany and were also obliged to pay an indemnity of 5 billion gold francs ($1 billion). The German annexation of Alsace and Lorraine enraged the French and created an enduring obstacle in the path of peaceful relations between the two countries.

Although Cavour died soon after the creation of the kingdom of Italy, Bismarck served as chancellor of the German Empire until his dismissal by Emperor William II in 1890.

The unification of Italy and Germany brought a dramatic change in the European balance of power at the expense of Austria and France. Germany now became the most powerful state on the European continent, while Italy's position among the great powers had not yet been determined.

Recommended Reading

Albrecht-Carrié, René. *Italy from Napoleon to Mussolini* (1950).

Binkley, Robert C. *Realism and Nationalism, 1852–1871* (1935).

Craig, Gordon A. *Germany, 1866–1945* (1978).

Eyck, Erich. *Bismarck and the German Empire* (1950).

Hamerow, Theodore S. *Restoration, Revolution, Reaction: Economics and Politics in Germany, 1815–1871* (1958).

Holborn, Hajo. *A History of Modern Germany, vol. III, 1840–1945* (1969).

Kent, George O. *Bismarck and His Times* (1978).

Mack Smith, Denis, *Cavour* (1985).

Mack Smith, Denis. *Garibaldi: A Great Life in Brief* (1956).

Pflanze, Otto. *Bismarck and the Development of Germany, vol. I, The Period of Unification, 1815–1871* (1963).

Rich, Norman. *The Age of Nationalism and Reform, 1850–1890* (1970).

Taylor, A. J. P. *Bismarck: The Man and the Statesman* (1960).

Thayer, William Roscoe. *The Life and Times of Cavour*, 2 vols. (1914).

Whyte, Arthur J. *The Evolution of Modern Italy* (1950).

CHAPTER 24

The Advance of Democracy in Great Britain, France, and Italy

Time Line

1851	Louis Napoleon Bonaparte becomes French president for life
1852	Louis Napoleon Bonaparte establishes the Second Empire
1867	The British Parliament passes the Reform Bill of 1867
1868–1874	British Prime Minister William E. Gladstone heads his "Great Ministry"
1870	The French Third Republic is established

1871	The Paris Commune is suppressed
1874–1880	Benjamin Disraeli serves as British prime minister
1875	The French adopt constitutional laws for the Third Republic
1884	British farm workers win the right to vote
1886	The British Parliament rejects Irish home rule
1889	General Georges Boulanger challenges the French Third Republic
1894	A French army court-martial convicts Captain Alfred Dreyfus of treason
1900	The British Labor party is established
1903–1914	Giovanni Giolitti dominates Italian politics
1905	A Liberal government takes office in Great Britain
1911	The British Parliament Act of 1911 is adopted
1912	Italy adopts universal manhood suffrage

In the late nineteenth century, the cause of democracy advanced in Great Britain, France, and Italy.

In Great Britain, reform bills passed in 1867 and 1884 established close to universal manhood suffrage, while the Parliament Act of 1911 reduced the power of the aristocratic House of Lords. In addition to expanding voting rights, the reform programs of British governments during this period laid the foundations of the welfare state. The controversial issue of home rule for Ireland remained unresolved, however.

In France, Louis Napoleon Bonaparte subverted the Second Republic and created the Second Empire. Following the overthrow of Napoleon III in 1870, the French established the democratic Third Republic. France remained a deeply divided nation, however, and the leaders of the Third Republic did relatively little to promote economic and social reform.

Italy lagged considerably behind Great Britain and France in the process of democratization. In the years following the achievement of unification in 1861, political power was the monopoly of an upper-middle-class and upper-class oligarchy, and universal manhood suffrage was not established until 1912. Italy remained a poor country whose leaders responded to popular unrest with repression rather than reform.

Great Britain

The Reform Bill of 1867

During the generation after the passage of the Reform Bill of 1832, demands for further parliamentary reform mounted.

In the mid–1860s, Benjamin Disraeli (1804–1881), the Conservative Party leader in the House of Commons, decided that the Conservatives should push for the adoption of a new reform bill before their opponents, the Liberals, did.

A Conservative-dominated Parliament passed the Reform Bill of 1867. Some seats in the House of Commons were redistributed. More important, however, was the extension of the right to vote to most of Great Britain's urban workers.

Although Disraeli served briefly as prime minister in 1868, the parliamentary elections that year resulted in a Liberal victory.

Gladstone's "Great Ministry"

From 1868 to 1874, William E. Gladstone (1809–1898), the Liberals' leader, served as prime minister, heading his "Great Ministry."

Reform Program

The British Parliament enacted an extensive reform program. In 1870, competitive examinations were introduced for the civil service. The Education Bill of 1870 provided financial support to local school boards to operate free nonsectarian elementary schools. In addition, church-operated and other voluntary elementary schools continued to receive assistance from the state. The expansion of elementary education helped create a literate electorate.

In 1871, the workers' right to organize unions and to strike gained legal recognition, although the ban on picketing remained. The Ballot Act of 1872 introduced the secret ballot in British elections, while a reform of the judiciary was enacted in 1873.

Despite this reform program, Gladstone maintained the laissez-faire tradition of the Liberals and opposed state intervention in economic affairs.

Disraeli as Prime Minister

In 1874, the Conservatives won control of the House of Commons, and Disraeli became prime minister, holding office until 1880. He promoted a program known as Tory Democracy, designed to benefit the working classes and to win increased popular support for the Conservative party. The Conservatives were less committed to laissez-faire doctrine than were their Liberal opponents.

Labor and Housing Reforms

A series of laws passed in 1875 expanded the government's role in economic affairs. The Factory Act extended earlier legislation regulating working conditions, while the Public Health Act expanded the role of the state in urban sanitation. The Artisans' Dwellings Act authorized local authorities to carry out slum clearance programs and to construct public housing. Another law gave additional rights to labor unions and legalized picketing by striking workers.

The Reform Bill of 1884

During his second administration, from 1881 to 1885, Gladstone won the adoption of the Reform Bill of 1884, which extended the right to vote to most farm workers.

The Irish Question

The Irish question most concerned Gladstone during his second administration and his third (1886) and fourth (1892–1894) administrations, as well.

Home Rule

Since the adoption of the Act of Union in 1801, Ireland had been united with Great Britain and was governed by the British Parliament. Following the enactment of Catholic Emancipation in 1829, the number of Irish Catholics in the House of Commons grew considerably. These members became more outspoken in their demand for home rule under which Ireland would acquire its own parliament, although the British government would retain control over foreign policy. Irish home rule faced the strong opposition of the six predominantly Protestant counties of northern Ireland (Ulster) and many in Great Britain.

In 1886, Gladstone introduced a home-rule bill, but a coalition of Conservatives and anti-home-rule Liberals defeated it. A second home-rule bill, also sponsored by Gladstone, went down to defeat in 1893.

Conflict Between Ulster and Nationalists

In 1914, the Liberals finally succeeded in pushing an Irish home-rule bill through Parliament. It could not be enforced, however, because of opposition in Ulster, where the Protestants organized an illegal militia. In response, the Irish nationalists organized a militia of their own. By the summer of 1914, Ireland stood on the brink of civil war.

The Development of the Labor Party

During the late nineteenth century, Britain's labor unions grew in membership and began to have an impact on politics. In 1900, the unions joined with the Fabian Society and other groups to form the Labor Party.

The Fabian Society

Formed in 1883, the Fabian Society advocated a gradual approach to socialism, with the ultimate objective of establishing public ownership of the means of production and distribution. Among the major leaders of the Fabian Society were Sidney (1859–1947) and Beatrice Webb (1858–1943), the playwright George Bernard Shaw (1856–1950), and the writer H. G. Wells (1866–1946).

Growth of the Labor Party

In 1906, twenty-nine Laborites won seats in the House of Commons. As its popular support grew, the Labor Party ultimately replaced the Liberals as one of the two major political parties in Great Britain.

The Liberal Government

In the years after 1905, the Liberals dominated the government. Under the leadership of Prime Ministers Henry Campbell-Bannerman (1836–1908) and Herbert Asquith (1852–1928) the Liberals enacted an extensive reform program.

Economic Reforms

In an effort to retain the support of industrial workers, the Liberals enacted the Workmen's Compensation Act of 1906, expanding programs of aid to workers injured on the job. The Old Age Pensions Act of 1909 provided state-supported pensions for low-income citizens over the age of seventy.

The Parliament Act of 1911

In 1909, Chancellor of the Exchequer David Lloyd George (1863–1945) presented a budget calling for tax increases to support the new programs of social insurance and naval expansion. This "People's Budget" provided for higher income-tax rates for the wealthy and increases in inheritance taxes, as well as new taxes on the unearned increase in the value of land.

The refusal of the House of Lords to pass the budget led to a political crisis. Responding to the government's appeal, King George V (r. 1910–1936) agreed to create enough new Liberal lords to insure the passage of the Parliament Act of 1911. Faced with this threat, the Lords passed the bill.

Under the provisions of the Parliament Act of 1911, the House of Lords could no longer refuse to pass a money bill. Furthermore, the act provided that the House of Lords could not prevent the adoption of other legislation if the House of Commons passed it three times in a period of not less than two years. By weakening the power of the aristocratic House of Lords, the Parliament Act marked another step toward the creation of full political democracy in Great Britain.

Other Reforms

In 1911, the Liberal government won parliamentary approval for a bill providing for the payment of salaries to members of the House of Commons. The National Insurance Act, adopted the same year, established a system of health and unemployment insurance, financed by contributions from employers, workers, and the state. In 1912, a minimum wage law was passed.

The reform program of the Liberal government brought economic benefits to Britain's working people and helped move the country in the direction of a welfare state.

France

Louis Napoleon Bonaparte and the Second Republic

After winning the presidency of the Second Republic in December 1848, Louis Napoleon Bonaparte (1808–1873) set out to consolidate his support among the army, the middle class, the peasantry, and the Roman Catholic Church. In 1849, he sent French troops to Rome to help restore the authority of Pope Pius IX (r. 1846–1878) in the wake of the Italian revolutions of 1848. He also increased the influence of the Catholic Church in French education.

In December 1851, Louis Napoleon proclaimed himself president for life, and France's new constitution gave him ultimate authority. As head of the armed forces, he had the power to declare war and make peace. He also dominated the legislative process. The Council of State, whose members he appointed, drafted legislation, while the Senate, which he also appointed, could reject laws it judged unconstitutional. The Legislative Body, elected by universal manhood suffrage, could accept or reject legislation submitted to it but could neither initiate nor amend legislation. The government influenced elections for the Legislative Body by providing financial support to progovernment candidates and by using local officials to count the ballots.

Napoleon III (r. 1852–1870)

In late 1852, a plebiscite endorsed the reestablishment of the

Bonapartist empire, and on December 2, 1852, Louis Napoleon Bonaparte became Napoleon III. (The Bonapartists regarded Napoleon I's young son, who had died in 1832, as Napoleon II, although he had never reigned.) In 1853, the emperor married Eugénie de Montijo (1826–1920), a Spanish countess.

The Authoritarian Empire

From 1852 to 1860, Napoleon III was at the height of his power. The government maintained strict censorship of the press and prohibited the establishment of political associations.

Economic Programs

The emperor promoted economic expansion, and the prosperity of these years helped keep popular discontent at a minimum. The government established two investment banks, the Crédit Mobilier and the Crédit Foncier, to assist the development of railroads, public utilities, industry, and agriculture.

Aid to Workers and Peasants

The government also enacted measures to benefit the workers, including programs to improve housing and to construct hospitals and homes for the elderly. Private systems of social insurance for workers were encouraged, and labor unions received limited legal recognition.

Peasants were helped by the building and improvement of roads and canals, the draining of swamps, and the promotion of scientific agriculture and animal husbandry.

Public Works

Napoleon III initiated extensive programs of public works, which provided employment. The most famous of these projects involved the rebuilding of much of Paris under the direction of Baron Georges Haussmann (1809–1891).

The Liberal Empire

After 1860, several factors combined to cause Napoleon III to lose both popularity and his ability to control the government.

Domestic and Foreign Problems

In the economic sphere, the emperor's free-trade policy began to have a negative effect. In particular, the Cobden Treaty of 1860, which he negotiated with Great Britain, lowered French tariffs on imports of British manufactured goods, which now flooded the country to the detriment of French industry.

Napoleon III also suffered from the results of his inept intervention in Italy in 1859 (see Chapter 23).

The emperor sought to strengthen his position by making concessions. In 1860, he authorized both the Senate and the Legislative Body to discuss the speech from the throne and respond to it, and in the following year, the budgetary powers of the Legislative Body were increased.

Intervention in Mexico

In 1863, Napoleon III began his ill-fated intervention in Mexico, attempting to install the Austrian Archduke Maximilian (1832–1867), the brother of Emperor Francis Joseph, as the French puppet emperor. The United States protested but was unable to take effective action before the Civil War ended in 1865. In 1866, Napoleon III abandoned his efforts to create a French domain in Mexico. Mexican revolutionaries executed Maximilian the following year.

Political Concessions

Both the Maximilian affair and the Prussian defeat of Austria in 1866 further weakened Napoleon III. In 1867, he expanded the role of the Senate in the legislative process, and he agreed in 1868 to end press censorship and to permit political meetings to be held under government supervision.

Opposition to Napoleon III continued to mount, and in July 1869, he once again expanded the powers of the Legislative Body, granting it the authority to initiate legislation, and in December, he appointed a cabinet that represented a majority in the Legislative Body. In April 1870, the Senate became a true upper house, with the power to pass on legislation.

End of the Second Empire

The final crisis for the Second Empire came in the Franco-German War of 1870. At Sedan on September 2, the Germans captured Napoleon III. In Paris, radicals proclaimed the creation of the Third Republic.

The Paris Commune

While radicals dominated Paris and other major cities, the provinces were more conservative. In February 1871, monarchist candidates won a majority of seats in the new National Assembly.

The Third Republic also confronted a threat from radicals in Paris. On March 17, 1871, Adolphe Thiers (1797–1877), who headed the government, ordered the dissolution of the Paris National Guard. The radicals responded by electing a new city government, the Paris Commune.

Thiers decided to crush the Paris Commune. On May 8, the army began a bombardment of Paris, and on May 21, troops entered the city. During the following week, the army reestablished the government's control over the capital, taking about 20,000 lives in the process.

The Constitutional Laws

An attempt to restore the monarchy failed as a result of the rivalry between the Bourbon and Orleanist claimants to the throne, and in 1875 the constitutional laws for the Third Republic were adopted. These laws established a weak government, with authority centered in parliament. The parliament consisted of two houses, the Chamber of Deputies, elected by universal manhood suffrage, and the indirectly elected Senate. The executive functions of government were exercised by the cabinet, headed by a premier and responsible to the parliament. The president of the republic, elected by both houses of parliament for a term of seven years, had relatively little power. Their history since 1789 had taught the French that a strong executive was likely to seek to establish his arbitrary authority.

The government's effectiveness was further weakened by the multiparty system. Since no one party could command a majority in parliament, coalition cabinets were necessary. These coalitions often proved fragile as a result of disagreements among the parties and their leaders.

Anticlericalism

The Roman Catholic Church had generally supported the monarchist cause, and during the 1880s, the republican leaders promoted an anticlerical campaign, designed to reduce the church's influence in national life. The government established a system of free secular elementary schools to compete with schools controlled by the church. The Jesuit Order was expelled from France, and the name of God was removed from oaths.

The Boulanger Affair

In the late 1880s, the republic's survival was threatened by the emergence of General Georges Boulanger (1837–1891). A popular minister of war, Boulanger benefited from revelations of financial scandals involving a number of prominent republican politicians. In 1889, it appeared that Boulanger might attempt to carry out a coup d'état with monarchist and clerical support. He failed to do so, however, and instead fled the country. The Boulanger Affair discredited the monarchists and thus served to strengthen the republic.

The Dreyfus Affair

For several years around the turn of the century, France was torn apart by the Dreyfus Affair.

In December 1894, an army court-martial convicted Captain Alfred Dreyfus (1859–1935), a Jewish officer, of conveying secret information to the Germans, and he was sentenced to imprisonment in the penal colony of Devil's Island in French Guiana.

Some doubts remained about Dreyfus's guilt, however. In early 1896, Colonel Georges Picquart (1854–1914), the new head of the French intelligence service, developed evidence indicating that Major Ferdinand Esterhazy (1847–1923) was the guilty party, although he was promptly acquitted by a court-martial. It was also revealed that certain key documents used by the prosecution against Dreyfus had been forged.

A bitter conflict developed. On one level, the issue involved the question of Dreyfus's guilt or innocence. On another level, it was a conflict between the Dreyfusards, who supported both Dreyfus's innocence and the cause of the republic and anticlericalism, and the anti-Dreyfusards, who insisted on Dreyfus's guilt and supported the cause of the monarchists, the army, and the church. The anti-Dreyfusards were often openly anti-Semitic.

Zola's "J'Accuse"

In 1898, the novelist Émile Zola (1840–1902), a Dreyfusard, published a newspaper article entitled "J'Accuse" ("I Accuse"). Zola charged the army with forging the evidence that convicted Dreyfus and with deliberately suppressing evidence that would vindicate him. A new court-martial found Dreyfus guilty once again, although this time with "extenuating circumstances." The French president pardoned Dreyfus, and in 1906, the French supreme court invalidated the convictions handed down by the two courts-martial.

Renewed Anticlericalism

The victory of the Dreyfusards was a decisive defeat for the ultraconservative officers who dominated the French army and for the monarchists and the church, as well. The government now renewed its anticlerical campaign, adopting laws to exclude members of Catholic religious orders from teaching. In 1905, the government abrogated Napoleon's Concordat of 1801. Church and state were now separated.

French Socialism

Focusing their attention on the struggle against the monarchists and on the anticlerical campaign, the French republicans showed relatively little interest in the problems of the country's workers. In 1905, several socialist groups joined under the leadership of Jean Jaurès (1859–1914) and Jules Guesde (1845–1922) to form the United Socialist Party, which sought to represent the interests of the workers.

Italy

Italy After Unification

When the Kingdom of Italy was established in 1861, Victor Emmanuel II (r. 1861–1878), the Piedmontese king, became king of Italy. The Piedmontese constitution, the Statuto of 1848, was the model for the new Italian constitution. The two-house parliament consisted of the Senate, whose members included aristocrats and officials appointed by the king, and the Chamber of Deputies, which was elected by property-qualified voters. Executive authority was entrusted to a premier and cabinet, who were responsible to the parliament. While the political system was liberal, it was not democratic. In a population of 25 million, only about 500,000 possessed enough property to qualify as voters.

Economically, Italy was poor, overpopulated, and underdeveloped. It lacked raw materials and produced no coal or iron. This paucity of resources hindered the country's economic and social development. Some industrialization had occurred in northern Italy, but the region continued to lag behind most of the rest of Western Europe. In the south, impoverished and illiterate peasants lived in miserable conditions, reminiscent of medieval serfdom.

The Roman Question

Following the Italian seizure of Rome in 1870, Italian politics was troubled by the Roman Question, the conflict between the papacy and the Italian state. Pope Pius IX (r. 1846–1878) declared himself to be a "prisoner of the Vatican." He refused to recognize the Italian state and instructed Italy's Catholics not to participate in politics.

The conflict with the papacy continued until the negotiation of the Lateran accords in 1929 (see Chapter 31).

Political Developments

In the years following unification, Italy's governments were dominated by upper-middle-class and upper-class liberals from northern Italy who had been political allies of Cavour in the struggle for unification. The multiparty system made government by coalition necessary, and the coalitions were often unstable.

Economic and Political Unrest

Poor economic conditions led to considerable unrest. In 1893, serious peasant revolts broke out in Sicily and spread to other areas. Although socialist and anarchist organizations were outlawed in 1894, the unrest continued, reaching its culmination in riots that engulfed Milan and other northern Italian cities in the spring of 1898. During 1901 and 1902, Italy was swept by a great wave of strikes, which reflected both the continuing discontent of the workers and the spread of socialist and other radical ideas.

In 1900, an anarchist assassinated King Humbert I (r. 1878–1900), who had become king following the death of Victor Emmanuel II in 1878. Humbert was succeeded by Victor Emmanuel III (r. 1900–1946).

Giolitti's Premiership

During most of the period from 1903 to 1914, Giovanni Giolitti (1842–1928) held the premiership. In dealing with continuing unrest, Giolitti followed the policy of his predecessors, using repressive measures in an attempt to restore order.

The right to vote was gradually extended. In 1881, the voting age was reduced from twenty-five to twenty-one, and property requirements for voters were also reduced. In 1912, universal manhood suffrage was introduced.

During the decade prior to 1914, Italy experienced the fastest rate of economic growth in Western Europe. Nevertheless, neither the extension of the right to vote nor economic growth obscured the fact that Italy was a deeply troubled country.

In the late nineteenth century, Great Britain continued its reformist tradition, developing a more fully democratic political system and laying the foundations of the modern welfare state. While the new Labor party remained relatively weak in the years before 1914, its base of popular support gradually increased. The Irish question remained as Great Britain's most serious unresolved problem. The failure to enact Irish home rule left a legacy of hostility to trouble future generations.

In France, the democratic Third Republic replaced the Second Empire. France remained a deeply divided country, however. Monarchists and clericals rejected the republic, and France's political leaders were slow to enact economic and social reforms to meet the needs of the working masses.

In Italy, the political system gradually evolved toward democracy, but the country's stability was threatened by the unresolved Roman Question and unrest among peasants and workers.

Recommended Reading

Binkley, Robert C. *Realism and Nationalism, 1852–1871* (1935).

Blake, Robert. *Disraeli* (1967).

Bredin, Jean-Denis. *The Affair: The Case of Alfred Dreyfus* (1986).

Clark, Martin. *Modern Italy, 1871–1982* (1984).

Clough, Shepard B. *The Economic History of Modern Italy* (1964).

Cobban, Alfred. *A History of Modern France, vol. II, 1799–1871* (2nd ed., 1965).

Cross, Colin. *The Liberals in Power, 1905–1914* (1963).

Dangerfield, George. *The Strange Death of Liberal England* (1935).

Duff, David. *Eugénie and Napoleon III* (1978).

Elwitt, Sanford. *The Third Republic Defended: Bourgeois Reform in France, 1880–1914* (1986).

Ensor, R. C. K. *England, 1870–1914* (1936).

Ford, Colin and Brian Harrison. *A Hundred Years Ago* (1983).

Fremantle, Anne. *This Little Band of Prophets: The British Fabians* (1960).

Gilbert, Bentley B. *David Lloyd George: A Political Life: The Architect of Change, 1863–1912* (1987).

Hale, Oron J. *The Great Illusion, 1900–1914* (1971).

Hayes, Carlton J. H. *A Generation of Materialism, 1871–1900* (1941).

Hinton, James. *Labour and Socialism: A History of the British Labour Movement, 1867–1974* (1983).

Holton, Sandra S. *Feminism and Democracy: Women's Suffrage and Reform Politics in Britain, 1900–1918* (1986).

Horne, Alistair. *The Fall of Paris: The Siege and the Commune, 1870-71* (1966).

Kent, Susan K. *Sex and Suffrage in Britain, 1860–1914* (1987).

Loughlin, James. *Gladstone, Home Rule, and the Ulster Question, 1882-93* (1987).

Magnus, Philip. *Gladstone: A Biography* (1954).

Pelling, Henry. *The Origins of the Labour Party, 1880–1900* (2nd. ed., 1979).

Rich, Norman. *The Age of Nationalism and Reform, 1850–1890* (1970).

Seton-Watson, Christopher. *Italy from Liberalism to Fascism, 1870–1925* (1967).

Thompson, James M. *Louis Napoleon and the Second Empire* (1967).

Thomson, David. *England in the Nineteenth Century, 1815–1914* (1950).

Vicinus, Martha. *Suffer and Be Still: Women in the Victorian Age* (1972).

Williams, Roger L. *The French Revolution of 1870–1871* (1969).

Wright, Gordon. *France in Modern Times* (4th ed., 1987).

Yelling, J. A. *Slums and Slum Clearance in Victorian London* (1986).

CHAPTER 25

Autocratic Europe: Germany, Austria-Hungary, and Russia

Time Line

1855–1881	Reign of Tsar Alexander II of Russia
1861	Tsar Alexander II issues the edict of emancipation
1864	Tsar Alexander II establishes the zemstvos
1867	The Compromise of 1867 creates the Dual Monarchy of Austria-Hungary
1871	The German Empire is established
	Bismarck begins the *Kulturkampf*

1875	The German Social Democratic Party is established
1881	Tsar Alexander II is assassinated
1881–1894	Reign of Tsar Alexander III of Russia
1888	Emperor William I of Germany dies
1888–1918	Reign of Emperor William II of Germany
1890	Emperor William II dismisses Bismarck
1894–1917	Reign of Tsar Nicholas II of Russia
1898	The Russian Social Democratic Party is established
1901	The Russian Socialist Revolutionary Party is established
1903	The Russian Social Democrats split into two factions, the Bolsheviks and the Mensheviks
1904–1905	The Russo-Japanese War
1905–1906	Russia is swept by revolution
1905	Tsar Nicholas II issues the October Manifesto
1906	Tsar Nicholas II issues the Fundamental Laws

In the late nineteenth century, authoritarian government remained the pattern in Germany, the Austrian Empire, and Russia.

The constitution that Bismarck devised for the new German Empire in 1871 made some concessions to liberal opinion, but real power was exercised by the conservatives and above all, by the emperor. During the period prior to the outbreak of World War I in 1914, Germany's rulers refused to consider any real democratization of the country's political system.

In the Austrian Empire, Emperor Francis Joseph was forced to make concessions to the Magyars of Hungary. The desires of other nationalities remained unsatisfied, however, and their intensifying nationalism challenged both Francis Joseph's control of Austria and the Magyars' domination of Hungary.

In Russia, the tsarist autocracy appeared to be in firm control. While Alexander II abolished serfdom and introduced other reforms, his successors were totally committed to reactionary principles. A small but growing number of middle-class intellectuals embraced liberal or socialist ideas, however, and Russia's defeat by Japan resulted in the Revolution of 1905, which led to the establishment of an elected parliament. Nevertheless, the tsarist regime remained fundamentally authoritarian.

Germany

The Constitution of the German Empire

When the German Empire was created in 1871, Otto von Bismarck (1815–1898), Germany's chancellor (prime minister), devised a constitution that contained a combination of liberal and conservative features. Nevertheless, he made certain that ultimate control remained in the hands of the conservatives and Prussia.

The Parliament: Reichstag and Bundesrat

The lower house of the parliament, the Reichstag, was elected by universal manhood suffrage, a concession to the liberals. The Reichstag's consent was necessary for legislation. However, if the Reichstag failed to approve a new budget, the government could continue to operate under the old budget. This restriction of the Reichstag's budgetary authority strengthened the position of the country's conservative rulers.

The Reichstag's power was further limited by the upper house, the Bundesrat, whose members were appointed by the princely rulers of the German states. A thoroughly conservative body, the Bundesrat could prevent the passage of bills favored by the Reichstag. Furthermore, the state of Prussia alone had enough votes in the Bundesrat to block any amendment of the constitution.

Power of the Emperor

The power of the conservatives and Prussia was strengthened

further by the provision that the chancellor and the cabinet ministers were responsible only to the emperor. The emperor had the power to appoint the chancellor and the ministers, and he alone had the authority to dismiss them. From 1871 to his death in 1888, however, Emperor William I generally left the conduct of government to Bismarck.

The *Kulturkampf*

During the 1870s, the Iron Chancellor, as Bismarck was known, conducted a campaign against the Roman Catholics of Germany, known as the *Kulturkampf* ("the struggle of civilizations"). Bismarck distrusted the Catholics, believing they could not be loyal both to Germany and to the pope.

In 1872, the Jesuit Order was expelled from Germany, while other legislation dissolved all religious orders except those whose primary activity was caring for the sick. The May Laws of 1873, which applied only to the large state of Prussia, placed the education of the clergy under the supervision of the state and gave the state veto power over clerical appointments.

Germany's Catholics responded by voting in increasing numbers for the Catholic Center Party. In the late 1870s, Bismarck recognized the failure of the *Kulturkampf*. He now perceived what he regarded as an even greater threat than the Catholics: the emergence of the Social Democrats as a force in German politics.

Bismarck's Anti-Socialist Campaign

In 1875, several socialist groups, including the Marxists, joined to form the new Social Democratic Party. The Social Democrats, who advocated both socialism and the establishment of a republican form of government, made their primary appeal to the country's industrial workers.

In his campaign against the Social Democrats, Bismarck used a combination of repression and social welfare legislation designed to attract the workers to the support of the state. The antisocialist law, passed in 1878, banned socialist meetings, suppressed the party's newspapers, and restricted its fund-raising. Social Democrats remained eligible for election to the Reichstag, however. Bismarck's social welfare legislation was remarkably progressive. In 1883, a program of health insurance was enacted, and a program of accident insurance was adopted in 1884. In 1889, a system of old-age and disability pensions was approved.

Despite Bismarck's efforts, the votes polled by the Social Democrats continued to increase. In despair, Bismarck began to consider an abrogation of the constitution in order to abolish universal manhood suffrage.

The Reign of William II (1888–1918)

When Emperor William I died in 1888, he was succeeded by his son, Frederick III. The new emperor was already fatally ill and died after a reign of ninety-nine days.

The death of Frederick III brought William II to the imperial throne. Unlike his grandfather, William I, the young emperor was not content to leave the direction of affairs to Bismarck but wanted to rule in his own right. In 1890, he dismissed Bismarck.

Economic and Social Reforms

William II allowed Bismarck's antisocialist legislation to expire, but he expanded the program of social insurance in the hope that somehow the working class could be induced to abandon the Social Democrats and support more conservative parties. In 1891, the system of factory inspection was expanded, and a labor department was created the following year. A series of laws, passed between 1899 and 1903, expanded the programs of sickness and accident insurance and old-age pensions, while the Comprehensive Factory Act of 1908 placed restrictions on the employment of women and children. The Imperial Insurance Code of 1911 provided for a consolidation and further expansion of the social insurance programs.

Gains by Social Democrats

William II was no more successful than Bismarck had been in reducing support for the Social Democrats. In 1912, the last elections before the outbreak of war in 1914, the party polled over 4 million votes and elected 110 deputies to the Reichstag, where they were now the largest party. In fact, the Social Democrats and other parties favoring democratic reforms held a majority of seats in the Reichstag. Nevertheless, William II remained adamant in his refusal to appoint a chancellor and ministers who had the confidence of a Reichstag majority.

Economic Development

During the years from 1871 to 1914, Germany experienced tremendous economic growth. The country's industrial plant and railway mileage expanded, while its merchant fleet and foreign trade increased substantially. The expansion of industry was greatly faciliated by the availability of coal and iron, as well as by the country's growing population, which raised demand for the products of industry. Germany's population of 41 million in 1871 grew to 65 million by 1914. Germany became a close second to Great Britain in its level of industrial production and foreign trade.

Austria

Austria Following the Revolutions of 1848

Following the upheavals brought by the revolutions of 1848, the Austrian government reestablished the traditional system of centralized rule for the multinational empire, concentrating authority in the hands of German-speaking officials loyal to the Hapsburgs.

Attempts at Decentralization

Austria's defeat by Piedmont and France in 1859 weakened the prestige of the Austrian government. In an effort to regain popular support, Emperor Francis Joseph (r. 1848–1916) initiated an experiment in decentralization. The October Diploma of 1860 expanded the authority of the aristocratic assemblies in Hungary, Bohemia, and other provinces. These assemblies would also elect delegates to an imperial diet, which had limited powers. However, the Magyars of Hungary refused to participate in the new system and demanded the restoration of the March Laws of 1848 (see Chapter 22).

Resistance by Magyars

In the February Patent of 1861, Francis Joseph modified the October Diploma, establishing a parliament for the empire, known as the Reichsrat. The emperor would appoint the members of the upper house, while the lower house would be indirectly elected. The complex voting system was weighted in favor of the German-Austrian bourgeoisie and upper class. Once again, the Magyars refused to participate in the new political structure.

The Compromise of 1867: Dual Monarchy

In 1866, Prussia defeated Austria in the Seven Weeks' War (see Chapter 23). Just as in 1859, defeat weakened the prestige of the imperial government.

The Magyars, led by Francis Deák (1803–1876) and Julius Andrássy (1823–1890), pressed their demands against the Hapsburgs and, in 1867, Emperor Francis Joseph agreed to the Compromise of 1867 (the *Ausgleich* of 1867), which created the Dual Monarchy of Austria-Hungary.

The Compromise of 1867 divided the Hapsburg empire into two distinct units, the Austrian Empire and the Kingdom of Hungary. Austria was governed under a constitution based on the February Patent of 1861, while Hungary was governed under the March Laws of 1848, which had established a parliamentary government for Hungary during the revolution of that year.

Austria and Hungary operated for the most part as if they were two completely separate and independent countries, although joint ministries controlled foreign policy and military and financial affairs. Less formally, Austria and Hungary were bound together by the need to keep the minority nationalities under control.

Austria After 1867

Although Austria was in principle a constitutional monarchy, the emperor retained considerable authority. He could dissolve the parliament at will and had the power to legislate by decree when the parliament was not in session.

Electoral Reforms

In time, Austria developed a more democratic franchise. In 1907, universal manhood suffrage was introduced, along with the direct election of the members of the lower house of the Reichsrat.

Discontent Among Subject Nationalities

Extending the right to vote, however, did little to satisfy the minority nationalities in Austria, especially the Czechs and the South Slavs. Rather than becoming an effective instrument of government, the Austrian parliament provided the minority nationalities with an arena for attacking the Austrian government and each other.

Hungary After 1867

As king of Hungary, Francis Joseph had very limited authority. The Magyar aristocracy dominated both houses of the Hungarian parliament and made few concessions either to the Magyar peasants or the minority nationalities. In fact, they pursued a policy of Magyarization, seeking to force the minority nationalities to adopt the Magyar language and culture. The effect of Magyarization was the opposite of what was intended, since the minority nationalities—the Slovaks, Rumanians, and South Slavs—reacted to the arbitrary rule of the Magyars by becoming ever more conscious of their own nationality and more determined to gain rights of self-government.

Russia

The Reforms of Tsar Alexander II (r. 1855–1881)

After extricating Russia from the Crimean War in 1856, Tsar Alexander II turned his attention to Russia's most serious domestic problem: serfdom.

Emancipation of Serfs

In the Emancipation Edict of 1861, Alexander II abolished serfdom. Along with their freedom, the emancipated serfs acquired some land. The state compensated the landowners for the land they lost, while the peasants were required to reimburse the state in redemption dues extending over a period of forty-nine years. Title to the land was transferred not to individual peasants but to the village communes (mirs), which then distributed the land among their members and were responsible for paying the redemption dues.

In general, the land received by the peasants was insufficient to support their growing numbers, while the redemption dues placed a heavy financial burden on them. The freed peasants were often little better off than they had been as serfs, and peasant discontent and unrest continued.

The Rural Zemstvos

The emancipation of the serfs was followed by other reforms. A decree issued in 1864 established a system of elected rural assemblies, known as zemstvos. The district and provincial zemstvos were authorized to levy local taxes and to operate elementary schools and orphanages, to build and maintain roads and bridges, and to promote public and animal health. The zemstvos were elected under a three-class voting system, with private landowners, townspeople, and peasant communes all choosing representatives. The relatively small number of landowners and townspeople elected more representatives than the peasants. The zemstvos did important work in the Russian countryside, and they represented Russia's first experiment in representative government.

Other Reforms

Also in 1864, Alexander II decreed a reform of the legal and judicial system. The principle of equality before the law was proclaimed, and a new system of courts was established. The reform also provided for trial by jury and public trials.

An 1870 decree created municipal dumas. These elected councils in Russia's cities and towns gave the country's urban areas a system of self-government similar to that provided by the zemstvos in rural areas.

A reform of the army enacted in 1874 established the principle of universal liability for military service. The reform also reduced the term of service for draftees from twenty-five years to six years, with further reductions based on education.

Alexander II and Poland

At first, Alexander II pursued a moderate policy toward Poland.

Nevertheless, the Poles increased their nationalist agitation, and in 1863, a revolt against Russian rule broke out.

The Russians crushed the Polish revolt with a severity that brought diplomatic protests from Great Britain, France, and Austria, although Prussia extended support. Following the suppression of the revolt, the Russians intensified their efforts to promote the Russification of Poland.

Russian Expansion

During the reign of Alexander II, Russia continued its expansionist policies in Siberia and Central Asia. Acquiring the Maritime Provinces northeast of Manchuria, the Russians established the port of Vladivostok on the Sea of Japan. By the end of Alexander II's reign, Russian control extended over almost all of Central Asia north of Persia and Afghanistan, reaching from the Caspian Sea eastward to the border of China.

The Russians were less successful, however, in their efforts to expand at the expense of the Ottoman Empire (see Chapter 28).

Populism

The reforms of Alexander II served to increase demands for further reform. During the 1870s, middle-class radicals launched the Populist movement (the "going to the people" movement). Under the auspices of Land and Freedom, the major Populist organization, radicals went out into the countryside and attempted to organize the peasants as a revolutionary force. The uneducated Russian peasants generally failed to respond and often betrayed the radicals to the police.

Terrorism

In desperation, some radicals turned to terrorism, creating an organization known as the People's Will. The terrorists believed that acts of terrorism would force the regime to grant concessions. In fact, terrorism ultimately led to an intensification of repression.

As opposition mounted during the 1870s, Alexander II considered the possibility of further reforms. Responding to proposals made by Michael Loris-Melikov (1825–1888), the minister of the interior, the tsar agreed on March 13, 1881, to establish a representative council to advise the government on reform measures. Later the same day, terrorists assassinated Alexander II.

Tsar Alexander III (r. 1881–1894)

Tsar Alexander III was a determined autocrat who ruled Russia with an iron hand, rejecting all proposals for further reform.

While Vyacheslav Plehve (1846–1904), the head of the secret police, moved to crush the terrorist movement, Constantine Pobedonostsev (1827–1907), the procurator-general of the Holy Synod (the chief administrative official of the Russian Orthodox Church), placed renewed emphasis on the traditional formula of Autocracy, Orthodoxy, and Nationalism. Censorship was tightened, and controls over education were increased. In addition, efforts to promote the Russification of the country's ethnic and religious minorities were intensified. In particular, the government increased the economic and social restrictions on Russia's Jews, and tsarist authorities often encouraged peasants to conduct pogroms (anti-Jewish riots). The government also harassed Protestants in the Baltic provinces and Catholics in Poland.

Tsar Nicholas II (r. 1894–1917)

The last of the Romanovs to rule Russia, Nicholas II was as determined as his father had been to uphold the autocracy, although he lacked Alexander III's iron will and determination. His wife, the German-born Alexandra (1872–1918), exerted considerable influence over him.

Economic Development

The 1880s marked the beginning of Russia's industrial revolution. Railway mileage increased, and coal production mounted, as did the output of pig iron and steel.

Industry

Count Sergei Witte (1849–1915), who served as minister of finance from 1892 to 1903, played a central role in Russia's industrialization.

Witte put Russia on the gold standard, which attracted foreign investment, and furthered other policies designed to encourage industrialization. He also spurred the construction of the Trans-Siberian railroad, spanning the almost 5,000 miles between Moscow and the port of Vladivostok.

Agriculture

Despite the expansion of industry, Russia remained a predominantly agricultural country. As late as 1914, only 18 percent of the population was classified as urban. Russian agriculture continued to be backward, and rural poverty was so extensive that many peasant communes fell behind in their payment of redemption dues. Overpopulation served to intensify rural poverty, and migration to Siberia provided only slight relief.

The Growth of Radicalism

Despite the government's repression, radical movements continued to develop during the reign of Tsar Nicholas II.

Social Democrats: Mensheviks and Bolsheviks

In 1898, Russian Marxists, inspired by George Plekhanov (1857–1918), the father of Russian Marxism, organized an illegal party, the Russian Social Democratic Party. As Marxists, the Social Democrats sought to organize the increasing number of industrial workers as a revolutionary force. In 1903, the Social Democrats split into two rival factions, the relatively moderate Mensheviks (minority) and the hardcore revolutionary Bolsheviks (majority), led by Vladimir I. Lenin (1870–1924).

Socialist Revolutionaries

In 1901, a group of agrarian radicals, the political descendants of the Populists, established the illegal Socialist Revolutionary Party. Hoping to organize the peasants in the cause of revolution, the Socialist Revolutionaries looked forward to creating a new socialist Russia composed of peasant and worker communes.

The Union of Liberation

In 1903, middle-class liberals, many of whom had been active in the zemstvos, organized the Union of Liberation. Its goal was the establishment of a constitutional monarchy.

The Revolution of 1905

Russia's defeat by Japan in the Russo-Japanese War of 1904–1905 (see Chapter 27) discredited the tsarist government and encouraged the forces of discontent in Russia to come to the surface. The result was the Revolution of 1905.

Bloody Sunday

The first act of the revolution came on Bloody Sunday in January 1905, when troops fired on a large peaceful demonstration in St. Petersburg. Under the leadership of a Russian Orthodox priest, Father George Gapon, the demonstrators had gone to the Winter Palace to petition the tsar for reforms. In the aftermath of Bloody Sunday, a great wave of demonstrations and strikes swept the country. For the most part, the armed forces remained loyal to the tsar, although a famous mutiny occurred among the sailors of the battleship *Potemkin* in the Black Sea.

October Manifesto

Hoping to stem the tide of revolution, the government canceled the peasants' obligation to pay redemption dues. In addition, Tsar Nicholas II issued the October Manifesto of 1905, promising to grant a constitution, to provide guarantees of civil liberties, and to establish the Duma, an elected parliament.

Fundamental Laws

By the spring of 1906, the revolutionary upheaval began to subside, and the tsarist government recovered its confidence. In the Fundamental Laws, which served as the Russian constitution, Nicholas II restricted the powers of the Duma. The tsar retained control of financial affairs and foreign policy, as well as the authority to dissolve the Duma and to legislate by decree when the Duma was not in session. Cabinet ministers were responsible to the tsar, rather than the Duma. The tsar also created a conservative upper house, the Council of State, which would have to pass on legislation adopted by the Duma.

Political Parties

Political parties were now legal, and the Mensheviks, Bolsheviks, and Socialist Revolutionaries were no longer confined to clandestine activities. The middle-class liberals established two parties. The Union of October 17 (the Octobrists) took its name from the date of the October Manifesto and generally accepted the concessions the tsar had granted. The Constitutional Democrats (Cadets) urged further political reforms. In particular, the Cadets called for the establishment of a democratic constitutional monarchy on the British model, with the prime minister and other cabinet ministers being responsible to the Duma, rather than the tsar.

The Dumas Under Government Control

The first Duma, which was elected in 1906, expressed opposition to government policies and was soon dissolved. In 1907, the second Duma was elected. Proving to be even more hostile to the government than the first Duma, it, too, was quickly dissolved.

Following the dissolution of the first Duma, Prime Minister Peter Stolypin (1863–1911) attempted to conciliate the peasants by issuing, by decree, the Agrarian Reform Act of 1906. The law made it possible for peasants to withdraw from the village communes and to receive title to their land. The execution of this law over a period of years would have created an independent, landowning peasantry. The government hoped the landowning peasants would become a conservative force in society. Before the law could take effect on a broad scale, however, Russia was engulfed by war and revolution.

After the dissolution of the second Duma, Stolypin decreed a new electoral law, which increased the representation of the propertied classes. This made certain that the third Duma, elected in 1907, would be more conservative. The third Duma (1907–1912) served its full term, as did the fourth Duma (1912–1917). Nevertheless, at the outbreak of World War I in the summer of 1914, popular discontent was mounting, while the tsarist government remained adamant in its refusal to enact further reforms.

In Germany, Austria-Hungary, and Russia in the late nineteenth century, political power remained in the hands of conservatives. In all three countries, however, serious challenges to the existing order developed.

Germany retained its semidespotic political system, which Bismarck had established in 1871. While Bismarck failed in his campaigns against the Roman Catholics and Social Democrats, the German government functioned effectively during the almost two decades of his chancellorship. Under Bismarck's less capable successors, however, the stresses in German society became more evident. Although the imperial government remained adamant in its refusal to make concessions to those calling for democratic reforms, it appeared increasingly unlikely that the empire could survive for an extended period of time without fundamental political change.

The Compromise of 1867, which created the Dual Monarchy of Austria-Hungary, brought about a fundamental restructuring of the Hapsburg Empire. While the compromise satisfied the demands of the Magyars, the discontents of the other nationality groups, especially the Czechs of Bohemia and the South Slavs, became more intense. This nationalist unrest threatened the survival of the Dual Monarchy.

The late nineteenth century brought substantial changes to Russia. Tsar Alexander II abolished serfdom and introduced other reforms, while the Revolution of 1905 resulted in the establishment of an elected parliament. Despite the reforms, however, Russia remained a semi-autocracy. The growing middle class desired a more fully constitutional government, while the peasants and workers wanted relief from poverty. The unwillingness and inability of the tsarist government to undertake more far-reaching reforms increased the likelihood of revolutionary upheaval.

Recommended Reading

Balfour, Michael. *The Kaiser and His Times* (1964).

Carsten, F. L., et al., eds. *The Habsburg Empire, 1835–1918,* 2 vols. (1982).

Charques, Richard. *The Twilight of Imperial Russia* (1958).

Craig, Gordon A. *Germany, 1866–1945* (1978).

Crankshaw, Edward. *The Fall of the House of Habsburg* (1963).

Eyck, Erich. *Bismarck and the German Empire* (1950).

Haimson, Leopold H. *The Russian Marxists and the Origins of Bolshevism* (1955).

Hale, Oron J. *The Great Illusion, 1900–1914* (1971).

Hardy, Deborah. *Land and Freedom: The Origins of Russian Terrorism, 1876–1879* (1987).

Hayes, Carlton J. H. *A Generation of Materialism, 1871–1900* (1941).

Holborn, Hajo. *A History of Modern Germany, vol. III, 1840–1945* (1969).

Macartney, C. A. *The Habsburg Empire, 1790–1918* (1969).

Mosse, W. E. *Alexander II and the Modernization of Russia* (1958).

Rich, Norman. *The Age of Nationalism and Reform, 1850–1890* (1970).

Rogger, Hans. *Jewish Policies and Right-Wing Politics in Imperial Russia* (1986).

Rosenberg, Arthur. *Imperial Germany: The Birth of the German Republic, 1871–1918* (1964).

Seton-Watson, Hugh. *The Decline of Imperial Russia, 1855–1914* (1952).

Taylor, A. J. P. *Bismarck: The Man and the Statesman* (1960).

Taylor, A. J. P. *The Habsburg Monarchy, 1809–1918* (1948).

Ulam, Adam B. *Russia's Failed Revolutions: From the Decembrists to the Dissidents* (1981).

CHAPTER 26

Nineteenth-Century European Civilization

Time Line

1830–1842	Auguste Comte publishes *The Course of Positive Philosophy*
1838	Charles Dickens publishes *Oliver Twist*
1848	William Makepeace Thackeray publishes *Vanity Fair*
1853–1855	Count Arthur de Gobineau publishes the *Essay on the Inequality of the Human Races*
1857	Gustave Flaubert publishes *Madame Bovary*

1859	Charles Darwin publishes *On the Origin of Species*
1860–1896	Herbert Spencer publishes *Synthetic Philosophy*
1861	Ivan Turgenev publishes *Fathers and Sons*
1864	Pope Pius IX issues the *Syllabus of Errors*
1865–1869	Leo Tolstoy publishes *War and Peace*
1866	Feodor Dostoyevsky publishes *Crime and Punishment*
1872	Friedrich Nietzsche publishes *The Birth of Tragedy*
1874	The Impressionists hold their first group exhibition in Paris
1879	Henrik Ibsen publishes *A Doll's House*
1895	Wilhelm von Roentgen discovers X rays
1898	Marie Curie discovers radium
1900	Max Planck sets forth the quantum theory
1904	Anton Chekhov publishes *The Cherry Orchard*
1905	Albert Einstein proposes the theory of relativity

The nineteenth century was a productive period in European civilization. In science, Charles Darwin introduced the theory of evolution in the study of biology, while a new physics emerged to challenge the conclusions of the great seventeenth-century scientists. The idea of evolution proved particularly controversial, and an intense debate developed between the advocates of the evolutionary theory and the defenders of traditional religious doctrines. Philosophy took on a more pessimistic quality, while psychology developed as a serious field of study.

In literature, the movements of Realism and Naturalism emerged, while Impressionism and its successors produced a revolution in art.

Science and Religion

Darwin and the Theory of Evolution

During the nineteenth century, developments in biology had a powerful impact on Western thought. Charles Darwin (1809–1882), a British scientist who was fascinated by the world of plants and animals, advanced his theory of biological evolution.

In *On the Origin of Species* (1859), Darwin repudiated the theory of the special creation of each species, contending instead that all existing forms of life had evolved out of earlier forms. He also argued that life involves a constant struggle for existence, in which, as a result of a process of natural selection, the fittest survive. The organisms that survive because of their favorable characteristics then pass these characteristics on to subsequent generations. In time, an entirely new organism evolves. In *The Descent of Man* (1871), Darwin applied the concept of evolution to human beings.

Scientists accepted the fundamental validity of the theory of evolution, although some of Darwin's particular conclusions were subsequently disproved.

The Cult of Science

Huxley

Thomas Huxley (1825–1895), a British biologist, became a fervent advocate of the theory of evolution. His attacks on religious leaders who rejected the theory won him the nickname of "Darwin's bulldog."

For Huxley and those who thought as he did, science appeared to be revealing all the secrets of the universe. Through their understanding and application of science, human beings could continue their march of progress.

Comte

The cult of science was reflected in the doctrine of positivism, developed by the French thinker Auguste Comte (1798–1857). In *The Course of Positive Philosophy* (1830-42), Comte set forth his view that humanity had passed through two earlier stages in its history, the religious and metaphysical phases, and had now entered the third stage, the scientific or positive stage. In this third phase, humanity would be concerned with the scientific collection of information rather than with fruitless speculation about first causes, what had once been called God. In particular, Comte believed, the methods of science should be applied to the study of society. He introduced the term "sociology" to describe this study.

Religion

Scientific ideas, especially the theory of evolution, and the cult of science, the belief that science held the answers to all of humanity's questions, promoted the growth of a spirit of skepticism in religion. In addition, scholars brought the methods of scholarship to the study of the Bible and the early development of Christianity. This movement of the higher criticism, as it was known, challenged many traditionally accepted beliefs.

Strauss and Renan

David Friedrich Strauss (1808–1874), a German Lutheran scholar, in his *Life of Jesus* (2 vols., 1835-36), rejected the divinity of Jesus Christ, while later in the century, Ernest Renan (1823–1892), the French author of a *Life of Jesus* (1863), rejected the belief that Jesus had performed miracles or had been raised from the dead.

Protestant Reactions

Protestant Christians offered varying reactions to the new ideas. Some, known as Fundamentalists, continued to insist on the literal truth of the Bible and rejected any scientific or scholarly ideas that were inconsistent with biblical teaching. More liberal Protestants, the Modernists, accepted the teachings of science and the higher criticism and modified their religious ideas accordingly. Still others sought a compromise between science and religion, interpreting the Bible in figurative terms where it conflicted directly with the teachings of science.

Jewish Reactions

Science and scholarship had a similar impact on Judaism. While Orthodox Jews maintained their traditional religious beliefs and practices, the movement of Reform Judaism emerged as the Jewish equivalent of Modernism. A third movement, Conservative Judaism, sought to maintain what it regarded as the essentials of the Jewish tradition, while acknowledging the validity of modern learning.

Roman Catholic Reactions

The Roman Catholic Church reacted at first with hostility to the new political, economic, scientific, and religious ideas. Pope Pius IX (r. 1846–1878) presented the *Syllabus of Errors* in his encyclical letter *Quanta Cura* (1864). The pontiff condemned materialism, liberalism, freedom of speech, the separation of church and state, religious toleration, secular education, and civil marriage. In 1870, the First Vatican Council acted to strengthen the position of the pope as the head of the Roman Catholic Church by proclaiming the dogma of papal infallibility. According to this dogma, papal statements are free of error when the pope speaks *ex cathedra* (officially) on issues of faith and morals.

Pope Leo XIII (r. 1878–1903) proved more moderate than his predecessor. In addition to advocating economic and social reform (see Chapter 21), Leo XIII acknowledged the validity of much of the teaching of modern science and scholarship. In particular, he held that the theory of evolution was not inconsistent with the Catholic faith, and therefore the Genesis account of creation could be understood figuratively. Nevertheless, the pope did reaffirm traditional Catholic doctrine and promoted, in particular, the study of the thought of the medieval theologian St. Thomas Aquinas.

Social Darwinism

In his *Synthetic Philosophy* (10 vols., 1860–1896), the British thinker Herbert Spencer (1820–1903) sought to apply Darwin's theory of evolution to virtually every aspect of human society. He contended that in human society, just as in nature, life involves a struggle for existence as a result of which the fittest survive. The doctrine of Social Darwinism provided support for the economic practice of laissez-faire, which emphasized free competition and an absence of state intervention in the economy.

Racist Views

The theory of evolution was also used to defend doctrines of racial superiority. The white race dominated the world, the racists argued, because it was the fittest of the races and had triumphed in the struggle for survival.

In his *Essay on the Inequality of the Human Races* (1853-55), Count Arthur de Gobineau (1816–1882), a French writer, asserted the superiority of the white race and contended that within the white race, the Germanic "Aryans" were superior to Slavs and Jews.

Similar racist views were expressed by Houston Stuart Chamberlain (1855–1927), an English-born German writer. In his *Foundations of the Nineteenth Century* (1899), Chamberlain extolled the virtues of the Germanic race and denounced what he considered the racial inferiority of the Jews.

The New Physics

During the late nineteenth century, physicists began to question the mechanistic view of the universe that Sir Isaac Newton had set forth in the late seventeenth century (see Chapter 11). In Newton's view, the universe was a perfect and harmonious machine that operated in accordance with natural laws.

Atomic Theory

Nineteenth-century science promoted a revival of the atomic theory, the theory that all matter is composed of atoms. John Dalton (1766–1844), a British scientist, concluded that chemical elements were distinguished by the weight of the atoms that composed each element. About 1870, Dmitri I. Mendeleyev (1834–1907), a Russian chemist, devised the periodic chart showing the atomic weights of all known elements. Mendeleyev predicted the existence of three unknown elements. By 1886, all three had been identified.

Discovery of Electrons

During the 1890s, Joseph Thomson (1856–1940), a British physicist, and Hendrik Lorentz (1853–1928), a Dutch physicist, working independently of one another, demonstrated that atoms are composed of particles that Lorentz called electrons.

Discoveries in Radiation

In 1895, Wilhelm von Roentgen (1845–1923), a German physicist, discovered X rays. Marie Curie (1867–1935), the Polish-born wife of the French physicist Pierre Curie (1859–1906), discovered radium in 1898, and the Curies conducted important research into radioactivity.

Rutherford's Atomic Research

The atomic theory made further advances as a result of the work of Sir Ernest Rutherford (1871–1937), a British scientist who did basic research in radioactivity. Early in the twentieth century, Rutherford presented the view that each atom resembled a miniature solar system where the electrons revolved around the nucleus.

Planck's Quantum Theory

The idea also emerged that neutrons and electrons were not matter but positive and negative charges of electricity. In 1900, the German physicist Max Planck (1858–1947) set forth the quantum theory. Planck asserted that atoms absorb and emit energy in a series of discrete units, which he called quanta (singular quantum), rather than in a continuous flow, as traditional physics taught. The quanta were so small and were moving so rapidly that it was impossible to determine their exact position. One could state only the probability of their being in a specific place. The implication of the quantum theory was that objective scientific observation could not, in fact, reveal with certainty the ultimate secrets of nature.

Einstein's Theory of Relativity

In 1905, the German physicist Albert Einstein (1879–1955) proposed his theory of relativity. Einstein rejected Newton's belief that space, time, and motion are absolute. Instead, he argued, they are relative to one another and to the observer. Objects thus have not only the three dimensions of length, width, and depth, but also the fourth dimension of time. Einstein spoke of the space-time continuum.

Equivalence of Mass and Energy

Einstein also contended that mass is a variable, with the mass of a body depending on its rate of motion. A body's mass increases as its speed increases, with the speed of light providing a theoretical limit. In addition, Einstein proposed the idea of the equivalence of mass and energy, which he expressed in his famous formula $E = mc^2$. In this formula, E represents energy, while m is mass and c is the speed of light. According to this formula, if matter could suddenly be transformed into energy, only a small quantity of matter would be required to produce a great quantity of energy. This concept received a practical expression in the first atomic explosion in 1945.

Implications of the New Physics

The new physics did much to undermine the cult of science. Scientists were compelled to acknowledge the fact that they did not possess, nor could they hope to possess, absolute knowledge. They could speak of probability but not of certainty. This realization had implications that extended far beyond the realm of natural science. Summing up the implications of the discoveries of modern physics, Jacob Bronowski, a historian of science, remarked in *The Ascent of Man* (1973):

"One aim of the physical sciences has been to give an exact picture of the material world. One achievement of physics in the twentieth century has been to prove that that aim is unattainable. . . . There is no absolute knowledge. And those who claim it, whether they are scientists or dogmatists, open the door to tragedy. All information is imperfect. We have to treat it with humility. That is the human condition; and that is what quantum physics says. I mean that literally."

Philosophy and Psychology

Philosophy

While the nineteenth-century cult of science expressed an almost unbounded faith in human progress, philosophy sounded a more pessimistic note.

Schopenhauer

In *The World as Will and Idea* (1818), the German philosopher Arthur Schopenhauer (1788–1860) expressed the view that the dominant force in human existence, as in all animal life, is the will to survive, rather than reason, as the Enlightenment had believed. The world is the scene of strife and conflict where the strong devour the weak. The path to human happiness, Schopenhauer believed, involves an ascetic withdrawal from worldly concerns in order to escape this cruel competition.

Nietzsche

In works such as *The Birth of Tragedy* (1872), *Thus Spake Zarathustra* (1883-91), and *Beyond Good and Evil* (1886), the German philosopher Friedrich Nietzsche (1844–1900) exalted the will, believing that the assertion of the will provides life with a meaning. Nietzsche was vehement in his denunciation of Christianity and its "slave morality," which promoted such ideas as humility, pity, and altruism. Instead, he stressed the idea of the heroic leader, the superman, who was free of rules and restrictions, who desired to live at a more intense level of experience than ordinary humans, and who possessed a passion to dominate. Nietzsche presented an outspoken challenge to the fundamental values of Western civilization, but he offered little that was positive in their place. Clearly, European philosophy had moved far away from the optimistic, rationalist thought of the Enlightenment.

Psychology

In the late nineteenth century, the new science of psychology emerged to deal with the human mind.

Pavlov and Behaviorism

Ivan Pavlov (1849--1936), a Russian physiologist and psychologist, undertook research with dogs that led to his discovery of the conditioned reflex, which suggested that many responses are mechanical reflexes produced by subconscious stimuli. Pavlov and his followers established a school of psychological thought known as behaviorism, which emphasized the study of the human being as a physiological organism.

Freud and Psychoanalysis

In contrast to the behaviorists, Sigmund Freud (1856–1939), a Viennese physician, emphasized the importance of the unconscious mind in determining human behavior. Freud believed that human behavior is not fundamentally rational but is instead controlled by unconscious drives, especially the sex drive. In early childhood, he maintained, these drives were often suppressed, resulting in frustration and anger. In turn, this frustration and anger could cause neuroses. In an effort to cure his patients, Freud developed the system known as psychoanalysis, which enabled the patient to delve into his or her unconscious and discover the causes of neurotic behavior.

Literature, Art, and Music

Literature

The nineteenth century was the great age of the novel as a literary form. Many novelists strove, in particular, to present realistic portraits of society, giving rise to a movement known as Realism.

English Novelists

Major English novelists included William Makepeace Thackeray (1811–1863), Charles Dickens (1812–1870), and Thomas Hardy (1840–1928). In *Vanity Fair* (1848), Thackeray presented a fascinating portrayal of upper-middle-class London society at the beginning of the nineteenth century. In novels such as *Oliver Twist* (1838), *David Copperfield* (1850), and *Hard Times* (1854), Dickens demonstrated elements of both Romanticism and Realism. Dickens was critical of the bourgeoisie, whose influence was increasing in British life, and he also revealed the hardships endured by the urban workers during the first generations of the industrial revolution. Hardy's powerful realistic novels showed none of the sentimentality of Dickens. In such works as *The Return of the Native* (1878), *The Mayor of Casterbridge* (1886), *Tess of the D'Urbervilles* (1891), and *Jude the Obscure* (1895), Hardy expressed the view that human beings are ultimately the victims of fate.

French Novelists

Gustave Flaubert (1821–1880) and Anatole France (1844–1924) emerged as major French novelists. Flaubert's masterpiece, *Madame Bovary* (1857), is often described as the first great achievement of literary realism. Regarded in its time as a scandalous novel, *Madame Bovary* portrayed the despair leading to adultery of the wife of a small-town physician. Anatole France satirized both Christianity and bourgeois society in novels such as *Penguin Island* (1908) and *The Revolt of the Angels,* (1914).

Russian Novelists

For Russian literature, the nineteenth century was a time of particular genius. Leo Tolstoy (1828–1910) is best known for *War and Peace* (1865-69), an epic novel set in the time of Napoleon's invasion of Russia. In *Anna Karenina* (1875-77), Tolstoy presented a realistic portrayal of life in the Russian capital of St. Petersburg.

Other major Russian writers included Ivan Turgenev (1818–1883), Feodor Dostoyevsky (1821–1881), and Anton Chekhov (1860–1904). In *Fathers and Sons* (1861), Turgenev portrayed the conflict between the conservative older generation of Russians and the younger generation who had embraced the radical philosophy of nihilism. Dostoyevsky, a fervent Russian nationalist and a master of psychological analysis, set forth his mystical belief that humanity could be purified only through suffering in such powerful novels as *Crime and Punishment* (1866), *The Idiot* (1868), and *The Brothers Karamazov* (1879-80). Chekhov wrote realistic plays about the life of the provincial gentry in the years before World War I. Chekhov's better-known plays include *The Sea Gull* (1896), *Uncle Vanya* (1899), *The Three Sisters* (1901), and especially *The Cherry Orchard* (1904). Chekhov's plays were produced on the stage of the Moscow Art Theatre under the direction of Konstantin Stanislavsky (1863–1938).

Naturalism

The final years of the nineteenth century produced the literary movement known as Naturalism. Naturalistic writers focused their attention on social evils, often describing the seamy side of life in considerable detail. In France, Émile Zola (1840–1902) wrote about the social problems of an industrial society in such novels as *Nana* (1880), which dealt with prostitution, and *Germinal* (1885), which concerned the miserable lives of coal miners.

The Norwegian playwright Henrik Ibsen (1828–1906) attacked the values of bourgeois society. In *A Doll's House* (1879), Ibsen offered a powerful statement in support of women's rights, while *An Enemy of the People* (1882) told the story of a town rising up against a physician who revealed that the spa on whose waters the town depended for its prosperity were contaminated.

Art

Impressionism

In the late nineteenth century, a revolution in art was begun by the Impressionists, who held their first group exhibition in Paris in 1874. The Impressionists sought to reveal in their paintings immediate sense impressions of reality. Impressionism flourished especially in France in the work of such painters as Édouard Manet (1832–1883), Camille Pissarro (1830–1903), Edgar Degas (1834–1917), Alfred Sisley (1839–1899), Claude Monet (1840–1926), and Auguste Renoir (1841–1919).

Post-Impressionism

The freedom of artistic expression pioneered by the Impressionists encouraged the development of Post-Impressionism. Some Post-Impressionists, such as Paul Cézanne (1839–1906), emphasized formal structure, while others, such as Paul Gauguin (1848–1903) and Vincent van Gogh (1853–1890), experimented with the expressive possibilities of form and color.

Fauvism and Cubism

On the eve of World War I, the revolutionary developments in art continued in the work of Henri Matisse (1869–1954), a French artist, and the Spaniard Pablo Picasso (1881–1973). Matisse was the founder of a movement known as Fauvism, which was characterized by the use of bold and often discordant colors, while Picasso pioneered in the development of Cubism, which applied a geometric approach to the portrayal of the human figure.

Sculpture

In sculpture, Auguste Rodin (1840–1917), was the dominant figure of the late nineteenth century, introducing impressionistic elements into sculpture. His major works include *The Thinker, The Burghers of Calais,* and statues of the novelists Honoré de Balzac and Victor Hugo.

Music

Romanticism

The romantic tradition in music continued in the late nineteenth century in the work of several major composers, including the French composer Camille Saint-Saëns (1835–1921) and the Russian Peter Tchaikovsky (1840–1893), who presented both romantic and national themes in his work.

Nationalism

Other composers were heavily influenced by national traditions of folk music, including the Czechs Frederick Smetana (1824–1884) and Anton Dvorak (1841–1904), the Russian Nicholas Rimsky-Korsakov (1844–1908), the Norwegian Edvard Grieg (1843–1907), and the Finn Jan Sibelius (1865–1957).

Innovations

The late nineteenth century produced a series of important musical innovators. The French composer Claude Debussy (1862–1918) wrote sensitive music inspired by the Impressionist painters, while the German operatic composer Richard Strauss (1864–1949) was regarded as the chief heir of Richard Wagner. Igor Stravinsky (1882–1971), a pupil of Rimsky-Korsakov at the St. Petersburg conservatory, experimented with dissonance. Three of Stravinsky's ballets—*The Firebird* (1910), *Petrushka* (1911), and *The Rite of Spring* (1913)—received their first performances before the outbreak of World War I. Arnold Schoenberg (1874–1951), an Austrian composer, began the development of atonal music.

The late nineteenth century brought increasing diversity and uncertainty to European civilization. Science continued to reveal the secrets of the physical universe and in so doing, undermined faith in traditional religious beliefs. Yet science also revealed that it could not produce the ultimate answers to humanity's questions. In their repudiation of the view that humans are fundamentally rational beings, philosophy and psychology contributed further to the growing atmosphere of uncertainty.

Realism and Naturalism in literature, for their part, also emphasized the irrational elements in human nature, while innovative movements in art and music challenged and often defied traditional standards.

To describe European civilization in the late nineteenth century as a disintegrating civilization may be an exaggeration, but clearly its integrating elements were being eroded.

Recommended Reading

Barzun, Jacques. *Darwin, Marx, Wagner: Critique of a Heritage* (2nd ed., 1958).

Baumer, Franklin L. *Modern European Thought: Continuity and Change in Ideas, 1600–1950* (1977).

Cline, Barbara L. *The Questioners: Physicists and the Quantum Theory* (1965).

Gay, Peter. *Freud: A Life for Our Time* (1988).

Grana, Cesar. *Bohemian and Bourgeois: French Society and the French Man of Letters in the Nineteenth Century* (1964).

Hayes, Carlton J. H. *A Generation of Materialism, 1871–1900* (1941).

Hayman, Ronald. *Nietzsche: A Critical Life* (1980).

Himmelfarb, Gertrude. *Darwin and the Darwinian Revolution* (1959).

Infeld, Leopold. *Albert Einstein: His Work and Its Influence on Our World* (1950).

Irvine, William. *Apes, Angels, and Victorians: The Story of Darwin, Huxley, and Evolution* (1955).

Poliakov, Leon. *The Aryan Myth: A History of Racist and Nationalist Ideas in Europe* (1974).

Raynal, Maurice. *The Nineteenth Century: New Sources of Emotion from Goya to Gauguin* (1951).

Rewald, John. *The History of Impressionism* (4th ed., 1973).

Shattuck, Roger. *The Banquet Years: The Arts in France, 1885–1918* (1959).

Vidler, Alec R. *The Church in an Age of Revolution, 1789 to the Present Day* (1961).

CHAPTER 27

The Age of Imperialism

Time Line

1830	France begins its takeover of Algeria
1842	Great Britain acquires Hong Kong
1854	Commodore Matthew C. Perry "opens" Japan
1857	The Indian Mutiny results in the establishment of direct British rule over India
1860s	France begins its takeover of Indochina
1867	The British North America Act establishes the Dominion of Canada
1869	The Suez Canal is opened
1881	France acquires Tunisia

1882	Great Britain establishes a protectorate over Egypt
1885	The Congo Free State is established
1894–1895	Japan defeats China in the Sino-Japanese War
1896	The Ethiopians defeat the Italians at Adowa
1898	The British gain control of the Sudan
	The United States acquires the Philippines, Puerto Rico, and Hawaii
1899–1900	The Boxer Rebellion takes place in China
1902	The Boer War ends with the British takeover of the Orange Free State and the Transvaal
1904–1905	Japan defeats Russia in the Russo-Japanese War
1910	Japan annexes Korea

During the last quarter of the nineteenth century, there was a great surge of imperialist activity. The major European states, particularly Great Britain, France, and Germany, divided virtually all of Africa and much of Asia among themselves. This imperial expansion provided a dramatic manifestation of Europe's power and dynamism. By the end of the century, the United States and Japan had joined the ranks of the imperalist powers. As the imperialist powers increased their activity, rivalries intensified, increasing tensions among the powers.

Imperialism in the Early Nineteenth Century

During the first three-quarters of the nineteenth century, the European states showed relatively little interest in overseas expansion. When the Napoleonic wars ended in 1815, the only major overseas empires were those of Great Britain and the Netherlands.

Great Britain

Although the British had created a vast empire in the eighteenth century, they demonstrated little enthusiasm for further expansion. Only a few years earlier, the thirteen British colonies along the Atlantic seaboard of North America had rebelled against British rule and had gained their independence. The American Revolution suggested that the acquisition of colonies was ultimately an unproductive activity. Events after 1815 provided what seemed to be further evidence of this view, as Canada appeared for a time likely to follow the lead of the United States. British opponents of colonial expansion (the "Little Englanders") insisted that their government should focus its attention on domestic affairs.

The Netherlands

The Netherlands remained content with its profitable island empire in the East Indies, which had been acquired from Portugal in the early seventeenth century.

France, Prussia, and Austria

France, which had lost most of its overseas empire to the British in the eighteenth century, was too preoccupied with its domestic problems to devote much attention to overseas expansion in the early nineteenth century, while Prussia and Austria focused their attention on European issues.

Russia

Russia was the only European power to continue its expansionist policy throughout the nineteenth century, although Russian expansion was overland, rather than overseas. The Russians continued to press against the declining power of the Ottoman Empire and also moved into Central Asia and the Maritime Provinces on the Sea of Japan.

Renewed Interest in Expansion

During the 1870s, the European powers suddenly developed a new interest in overseas expansion. In Great Britain, the acquisition of additional colonies became an object of government policy and won wide support among the public. France achieved a measure of domestic political stability under the Third Republic and also began to look outward. In Germany and Italy, which had recently achieved their national unification, many regarded imperial expansion as evidence of national greatness.

Motives for Imperialism

A number of factors contributed to the drive for empire in the final decades of the nineteenth centuries.

Political and Psychological Factors

Political and psychological factors were particularly significant. During the late nineteenth century, competition among states for power and prestige intensified. While the possession of colonies offered a means to increase a country's military and economic power in relation to that of its rivals, the idea also came to be accepted widely that the possession of colonies was a sign of national greatness and vitality. Conversely, the failure to acquire colonies came to be regarded as a sign of national decadence.

Social Darwinism

Social Darwinists emphasized the idea of life as a struggle, with the stronger surviving at the expense of the weaker. Countries that failed to expand were seen as losing the struggle for survival. In addition, Social Darwinists believed that the advanced white race had an obligation to civilize the less developed peoples of the world.

Religious and Humanitarian Motives

Religious and humanitarian motives also contributed to imperialist policies. During the late nineteenth century, there was a great upsurge in Christian missionary activity by both Catholics and Protestants. These Christian missionaries sought not only to follow the command of

Jesus Christ to make disciples of all nations, they also believed in their mission to bring the advantages of European civilization to less advanced people. People motivated by religious and humanitarian impulses expected their governments to protect them.

The story of Dr. David Livingstone (1813–1873), a Scottish missionary, provides a good example of the joining of religious and humanitarian motives. Livingstone spent close to thirty years exploring Central Africa and gathering evidence on the activities of African and Arab slave traders. He and his supporters in the British antislavery movement believed that the British government should act to eliminate this slave trade.

Economic Motives

The growth of European industry led to demands for new sources of raw materials, as well as to a need for new markets for the products of industry. Furthermore, those who had accumulated fortunes from the profits of industry were often looking for new opportunities for the investment of their surplus capital. Others also had economic motives for supporting imperialist policies; among them, shipping companies and the manufacturers of munitions and other goods required by imperialist ventures.

Hobson and Lenin

Two early analysts of imperialism, J. A. Hobson (1858–1940) and V. I. Lenin (1870–1924), emphasized the importance of economic factors. In *Imperialism: A Study* (1902), Hobson argued that great financiers, who desired to increase their wealth through overseas investments, were the power behind imperialist policies. These financiers manipulated public opinion to win broad popular support for expansion and used their political influence to induce governments to acquire additional colonies.

Hobson's conclusions have been criticized by serious students of imperialism, as has the view advanced by Lenin in *Imperialism: The Last Stage of Capitalism* (1916): that capitalism must expand in order to survive. Once capitalist investment has saturated the domestic market, the capitalists are forced to seek overseas outlets for investment.

When capitalism can expand no further, Lenin insisted, it will collapse as a consequence of its internal contradictions.

Criticism of Economic Motives

While economic factors undeniably played a role in the development of imperialism, it is important to stress that they were by no means the only factors nor were they the most important. While some colonies possessed rich resources of raw materials, others had few or even none. Colonies inhabited by the impoverished peoples of Africa and Asia did not provide a sizable market for the products of European industry. And while some colonies offered substantial opportunities for investment, others did not. In the race for colonies, the imperial powers appeared more interested simply in the acquisition of territory than in the specific economic advantages that might be gained.

The British Empire
in the Early Nineteenth Century

In the early nineteenth century, the British controlled the most extensive empire in human history. Although they did not actively seek to expand their holdings during these years, the British consolidated their existing possessions.

The Western Hemisphere

In the Western Hemisphere, the British ruled Canada, a number of islands in the West Indies, British Honduras in Central America, and British Guiana in South America. In Canada, growing discontent with British rule led to greater self-government. The British North America Act of 1867 established the Dominion of Canada with extensive autonomy in domestic policy.

Africa

The British had acquired the Cape of Good Hope during the Napoleonic wars, and they also controlled a number of trading stations along Africa's coasts. During the 1820s, British settlers moved into the Cape Colony, where friction soon developed between them and the

Boers, the descendants of Dutch colonists who had settled at the Cape during the seventeenth century. In the Great Trek of 1835–1837, the Boers moved northward into the interior, where they established two independent republics, the Orange Free State and the Transvaal. In 1843, the British took control of Natal, to the east of Cape Colony.

Asia

India

The British had defeated France in the Seven Years' War (1756–1763), gaining control over India, which was administered by the British East India Company. In 1857, the Great Mutiny (also known as the Sepoy Rebellion) occurred, as Indian troops carried out a dramatic uprising against the British. The following year, the British government established its direct control over India.

China

When the Chinese government sought to prevent the British importation into China of opium from India, the British went to war against China in 1841. At the conclusion of the Opium War in 1842, the British annexed Hong Kong and compelled the Chinese to open five ports to foreign trade. In 1858, the Chinese were forced to open eleven additional ports.

Worldwide Outposts

The British also controlled a number of key strategic points around the world: Gibraltar at the western entrance to the Mediterranean Sea, the island of Malta in the central Mediterranean, Aden at the southern end of the Red Sea, Ceylon off the southeastern coast of India, and the great port of Singapore at the southern tip of the Malay peninsula. In the South Pacific, British possessions included Australia and New Zealand, which attracted many settlers from Great Britain and Ireland. Australia acquired rights of self-government as a dominion in 1901, while New Zealand gained dominion status in 1907.

Expansion of British Imperialism in Africa

Egypt

In 1875, Prime Minister Disraeli bought 44 percent of the shares in the Suez Canal Company from Egypt's ruler, the khedive. The purchase pleased British imperialists, who regarded the Suez Canal, which had been built by a French company and opened in 1869, as an essential link between Great Britain and India.

Although technically a possession of the Ottoman Empire, Egypt was in effect an independent state. The khedive had accumulated an enormous debt, borrowing heavily from European bankers, who demanded repayment. The sale of his Suez Canal shares provided him with only temporary financial relief, however, and at the end of the decade, the British and French established their joint control over Egypt's finances. Egyptian resentment of foreign intervention grew. In response, the British established a protectorate over Egypt in 1882, eliminating the French from Egyptian affairs.

South Africa

Cecil Rhodes (1853–1902)

In South Africa, Rhodes was the central figure in British imperialist activity. He had made a fortune in diamonds, which had been dis-covered at Kimberley in the Cape Colony in 1869. His great dream was the creation of a belt of British African possessions reaching from the Cape of Good Hope in the south to Egypt in the north. Pressing forward with this ambition, the British pushed their control northward into Bechuanaland, Southern and Northern Rhodesia, and Nyasaland.

The Jameson Raid

In 1886, gold was discovered in the Boer republic of the Transvaal. As prospectors moved in, tension mounted between the Boers and the British. In 1895, Dr. Leander S. Jameson (1853–1917) led an unsuc-cessful raid into the Transvaal. The Jameson Raid convinced President Paul Kruger (1825–1904) of the Transvaal that Rhodes, who was now prime minister of Cape Colony, was plotting to take over the Transvaal and its sister Boer republic, the Orange Free State.

Emperor William II of Germany sent a telegram to Kruger, congratulating him on his success in turning back the Jameson Raid. The British greatly resented this interference.

The Boer War

The Boer War broke out in 1899. Although the Transvaal and the Orange Free State put up a determined resistance, the war ended with a British victory in 1902. In 1910, the British united Cape Colony, Natal, the Transvaal, and the Orange Free State to form the Union of South Africa, a self-governing dominion.

West and East African Possessions

In West Africa, the British expanded their old trading stations into full-scale colonies, including Gambia, Sierra Leone, the Gold Coast, and Nigeria. In East Africa, British possessions included Kenya, Uganda, and British Somaliland, as well as the island of Zanzibar.

The French Empire
in the Early Nineteenth Century

In 1815, the French retained only a small part of their once substantial empire. In the West Indies, Guadeloupe, Martinique, and several other small islands remained under French control, as did French Guiana in South America. In Africa, the French operated several coastal trading stations. In Egypt and the Middle East, France exerted some influence.

In 1830, the French began the process of acquiring Algeria in North Africa. In 1843, they established a protectorate over Tahiti and soon moved to extend their control over other islands in the South Pacific. On the Asian mainland, the French began to move into Indochina during the 1860s.

French Imperialism in Africa

In the late nineteenth century, France succeeded in creating a huge empire in Africa. In North Africa, the French extended their control over Tunisia in 1881 and soon began the process of establishing a protectorate over Morocco. In addition, the French developed a number of colonies in French Equatorial Africa and in French West Africa. Major French West African colonies included Senegal, Guinea, and the Ivory Coast. France also acquired the large island of Madagascar off Africa's east coast, as well as French Somaliland on the Red Sea.

The Anglo-French Conflict Over the Sudan

The Sudan, located to the south of Egypt, became the object of a serious Anglo-French dispute in 1898.

In 1884, a British and Egyptian force commanded by General Charles Gordon (1833–1885) marched up the Nile River into the Sudan from its base in Egypt. Gordon's force was besieged at Khartoum by troops of the Mahdi, a Moslem religious leader. The ten-month siege ended in 1885 with the massacre of Gordon's army.

A decade later, in 1896, an Anglo-Egyptian force commanded by Lord Kitchener (1850–1916) advanced into the Sudan and defeated the Mahdi's followers at Omdurman in early September 1898. A few days later, at Fashoda on the Nile, Kitchener encountered a French force under the command of Major Jean Baptiste Marchand (1863–1934), who had moved into the Sudan from French Equatorial Africa.

During the ensuing Fashoda Crisis, tensions ran high between London and Paris, and for a time, war threatened. The crisis eased when the French decided to yield to the British. This French decision represented an important step toward the improvement of France's relations with Great Britain.

King Leopold II and the Congo

During the 1870s, King Leopold II (r. 1865–1909) of Belgium began the process of establishing an imperial domain in Africa. Acting as a private individual, rather than in his role as king, Leopold employed Henry Morton Stanley (1841–1904), an Anglo-American journalist and adventurer, to represent him in signing treaties with African chieftains in the Congo region of Central Africa.

In 1884–1885, an international conference held in Berlin autho-

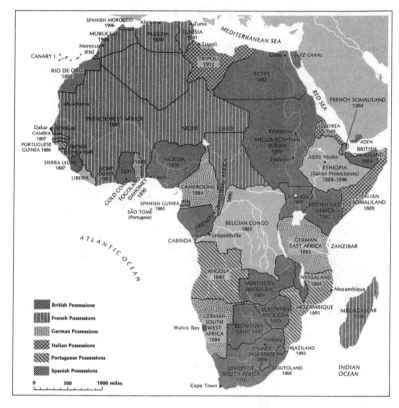

Imperialism in Africa, 1914

rized the establishment of the Congo Free State under the personal rule of Leopold II. The Congo became notorious for Leopold's use of forced labor in the production of rubber, ivory, and minerals. As international protests intensified, the Belgian government finally assumed control of the Congo in 1908.

Other Imperial Powers in Africa

Germany

Otto von Bismarck, Germany's chancellor from 1871 to 1890, had little interest in imperial expansion, believing that the newly united Germany should devote its attention to domestic and European matters. Nevertheless, Bismarck gradually gave way in the face of demands made by powerful interest groups that believed that colonies could provide economic benefits, as well as serving as a sign of Germany's status as a major power. In 1884, Germany acquired Togoland and the Cameroons in West Africa, as well as German Southwest Africa. In 1885, Germany established its control over German East Africa.

Italy

In contrast to Germany, Italy was relatively unsuccessful in its colonial endeavors in Africa. Seeking to create an East African empire, the Italians acquired Italian Somaliland in 1889 and Eritrea in 1890. In the mid–1890s, Italy began an abortive attempt to seize Ethiopia (Abyssinia), suffering a humiliating defeat in the Battle of Adowa in 1896. Ethiopia thus succeeded in maintaining its independence, as did the republic of Liberia in West Africa. Liberia was virtually an American protectorate, having been settled by freed American slaves earlier in the nineteenth century. After suffering a setback in East Africa, the Italians acquired Tripoli in North Africa from the Turks in 1912 (see Chapter 28).

Portugal and Spain

In the late nineteenth century, the Portuguese expanded their old coastal trading stations into the full-scale colonies of Portuguese Guinea and Angola in West Africa and Mozambique in East Africa. Spanish holdings included Rio de Oro and Rio Muni (Spanish Guinea) in West Africa. In the early years of the twentieth century, Spain established a protectorate over Spanish Morocco.

British Imperialism in Asia

In the late nineteenth century, India remained firmly under the control of Great Britain, although the British were concerned about Russian advances into Central Asia, north of India. The interests of Great Britain and Russia collided in Afghanistan, where tensions ran high for a number of years. Finally, in 1907, the issue was resolved with a Russian agreement to withdraw from Afghanistan (see Chapter 28). To the east of India, the British responded to France's moves into Indochina by annexing Burma in 1886.

Elsewhere in Asia, the British increased their control over the Malay peninsula, where they had established their presence in the eighteenth century. Great Britain and Germany agreed to partition New Guinea, north of Australia, in 1884, while the British and the Dutch partitioned Borneo in the East Indies in 1891.

French Imperialism in Asia

From the 1860s to the 1890s, the French extended their control over Indochina.

As the French expanded their Indochinese empire and the British moved from India into Burma, the possibility of conflict developed between the two major imperial powers. In 1896, however, Great Britain and France agreed to maintain Siam (modern Thailand) as an independent buffer state.

Imperialism in China

In the 1890s, China became a major theater of imperalist activity, as the decadent Manchu dynasty, which had ruled China since the seventeenth century, proved increasingly incapable of controlling the country.

Great Britain, which already held Hong Kong and possessed major commercial interests in China, developed a sphere of influence in the Yangtze River valley, while the French focused their attention on Kwangsi and Kweichow provinces in southern China, adjacent to Indochina.

Japanese Intervention

In 1894, Japan went to war against China, opening a new phase in the history of imperialism in that country.

The emergence of Japan as a major power was an unexpected event. In the seventeenth century, the Japanese had effectively isolated themselves from the outside world. That isolation continued until 1854, when an American naval expedition, commanded by Commodore Matthew C. Perry (1794–1858), compelled Japan to establish commercial relations with other countries.

Following this so-called "opening of Japan," the Japanese embarked on a remarkable program of westernization, modernizing their government, their economy, and their military and naval forces.

In the Sino-Japanese War of 1894–1895, Japan easily defeated China. Under the terms of the Treaty of Shimonoseki of 1895, the Chinese ceded the island of Formosa (Taiwan) to Japan. In addition, the Chinese recognized the independence of Korea, which would now be open to Japanese penetration. China also granted the Japanese a lease to the strategic Liaotung peninsula in southern Manchuria, including Port Arthur. Manchuria, too, would be open to Japanese penetration.

Russia, Germany, and France, fearing an advance of Japanese power in China, intervened. They forced Japan to agree to a nullification of Korean independence and the lease to the Liaotung peninsula.

Gains by European Powers

The Germans and Russians soon moved to take advantage of Japan's setback. In the late 1890s, the Germans occupied the Shantung peninsula, while the Russians acquired a lease to the Liaotung peninsula, as well as the right to build two railroads in Manchuria. The Chinese Eastern Railway in northern Manchuria would shorten the route of the Trans-Siberian Railroad from Moscow to Vladivostok in the Maritime Provinces, while the Manchurian Southern Railway would provide a link with Port Arthur in the Liaotung peninsula. France and Great Britain also expanded their interests in China.

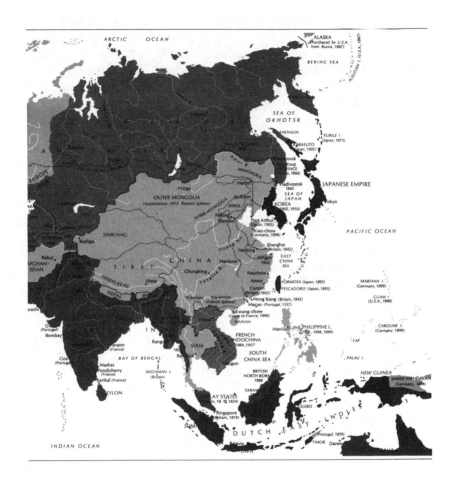

Imperialism in Asia, 1840–1914

The Boxer Rebellion

Intensifying antiforeign feeling in China resulted in the outbreak of the Boxer Rebellion of 1900. Some two hundred foreign missionaries and other civilians were killed, and in the summer of 1900, foreign legations in the capital city of Peking were besieged. An international expeditionary force was dispached to China to break the siege and suppress the revolt.

The Russo-Japanese War

Russian advances in northern China angered the Japanese. In addition to moving to create a sphere of influence in Manchuria, the Russians began to show some interest in expanding into Korea.

In February 1904, Japan went to war, executing a surprise attack on the Russian Far Eastern fleet anchored in Port Arthur. The Japanese defeated the Russians in the Battle of Mukden in February 1905 and three months later destroyed units of the Russian Baltic Sea fleet, which had been sent to the Far East, in the Battle of Tsushima Straits.

The Treaty of Portsmouth

President Theodore Roosevelt of the United States offered to mediate the Russo-Japanese conflict. Under the terms of the Treaty of Portsmouth of September 1905, Japan acquired the lease to the Liaotung peninsula. While northern Manchuria remained a Russian sphere of influence, the Japanese established their dominance in southern Manchuria. Russia ceded to Japan the southern half of Sakhalin island. In addition, Korea was now open to Japanese penetration, and Japan annexed Korea in 1910.

The New American Empire

In the late nineteenth century, the United States joined the ranks of imperialist powers. Alaska was purchased from Russia in 1867. In 1878, the United States acquired rights to a naval base at Pago Pago in the Samoan Islands in the South Pacific. In 1899, Samoa was partitioned between the United States and Germany.

Growing American interest in Hawaii led to its annexation by the United States in 1898, while the Spanish-American War of the same year resulted in the American acquisition of Puerto Rico, Guam, and the Philippine Islands. Cuba became, in effect, an American protectorate.

The growing role of the United States in world affairs was symbolized by its building of a two-ocean navy and the construction of the Panama Canal, which opened to shipping in 1914.

Americans focused their attention on the Pacific Ocean and East Asia, as well as the Caribbean and Central America, maintaining their traditional reluctance to become involved in European affairs.

During the late nineteenth century, the major European powers divided virtually all of Africa and much of Asia among themselves. One Asian power, Japan, joined the ranks of the imperialist states, waging a successful war against China and ten years later winning a surprising victory over Russia. Although imperial rivalries led to international tension, the Russo-Japanese War was the only military conflict among major powers to result from these rivalries. The United States also became a world power, with extensive interests in the Caribbean and Central America, as well as the Pacific.

Recommended Reading

Cady, John F. *The Roots of French Imperialism in Eastern Asia* (1954).

Edwardes, Michael. *The West in Asia, 1815–1914* (1967).

Esherick, Joseph. *The Origins of the Boxer Uprising* (1987).

Gifford, Prosser and William Roger Lewis, eds. *Britain and Germany in Africa: Imperial Rivalry and Colonial Rule* (1967).

Gifford, Prosser and William Roger Lewis, eds. *France and Britain in Africa: Imperial Rivalry and Colonial Rule* (1971).

Headrick, Daniel. *Tentacles of Progress: Technological Transfer in the Age of Imperialism, 1850–1940* (1988).

Henderson, W. O. *Studies in German Colonial History* (1962)

Hyam, Ronald. *Britain's Imperial Century, 1815–1914: A Study of Empire and Expansion* (1976).

Lewis, David L. *The Race to Fashoda: European Colonialism and African Resistance in the Scramble for Africa* (1987).

Morsy, Magali. *North Africa, 1800–1900: A Survey from the Nile Valley to the Atlantic* (1984).

Porter, Bernard. *The Lion's Share: A Short History of British Imperialism, 1850–1970* (2nd ed., 1984).

Rotberg, Robert I. *The Founder: Cecil Rhodes and the Pursuit of Power* (1988).

Thornton, A. P. *The Imperial Idea and Its Enemies: A Study in British Power* (2nd ed., 1985).

Westwood, J. N. *Russia Against Japan, 1904–1905: A New Look at the Russo-Japanese War* (1986).

CHAPTER 28

The Coming of the
First World War

Time Line

1890	Emperor William II of Germany dismisses Bismarck
1894	The Franco-Russian Alliance is signed
1904	The Anglo-French Entente is formed
1905	Germany provokes the First Moroccan Crisis
1907	The Anglo-Russian Entente is formed
1908	Austria's annexation of Bosnia and Herzegovina leads to the Bosnian Crisis
1911	Germany provokes the Second Moroccan Crisis
1912–1913	The Balkan Wars are fought
1914	Archduke Francis Ferdinand is assassinated at Sarajevo
	World War I begins

In European international relations, the 1870s and 1880s were truly the Age of Bismarck. During these decades, Bismarck's Germany dominated European diplomacy, establishing ties with Austria, Russia, and Italy and maintaining cordial relations with Great Britain. As a consequence, France remained isolated.

After Bismarck was dismissed as Germany's chancellor in 1890, his less capable successors let the ties with Russia lapse. Before long, France emerged at the center of a new diplomatic system. The French created an alliance with Russia, established an understanding with Great Britain, and succeeded in drawing Italy away from its ties to Germany and Austria.

As the alliance system divided Europe into armed camps, a series of international crises in the years after 1900 moved the powers closer to war.

The European Great Powers

In 1871, the ranks of the great powers included Germany, France, Great Britain, Austria, Russia, and Italy.

Germany

Otto von Bismarck (1815–1898), Germany's chancellor, regarded Germany as a satisifed power. He believed that Germany, having achieved its national unification, had no further territorial ambitions. Instead, it needed to consolidate its domestic institutions, promote its economic development, and maintain its position as the most powerful state on the European continent. The achievement of these goals required peace and stability in Europe, which, in Bismarck's view, could best be secured by isolating France.

France

France desired to regain the provinces of Alsace and Lorraine, which it had lost to Germany in 1871, but the French were too weak to challenge Germany without the assistance of an ally. For the time being, the French contented themselves with imperial expansion in Africa and Asia.

Great Britain

Great Britain sought to maintain its "splendid isolation" from the affairs of the European continent and to focus its attention on the far-flung British Empire. Britain's imperial interests in Africa and Asia conflicted especially with those of France and Russia.

Austria

Austria took essentially a defensive position, seeking to limit the growth of Slavic nationalism within its own borders and to the southeast in the Balkans. Slavic nationalism threatened Austria's survival.

Russia

Russia continued its traditional expansionist policies in an effort to advance its power both in East Asia and in the Balkans. The competing interests of Austria and Russia in the Balkans led to disputes between the two powers.

Italy

Italy sought opportunities to advance its claims to great-power status. Its efforts to build a North African empire led to disputes with France.

The Three Emperors' League (1872)

Bismarck's efforts to preserve European peace and stability by keeping France isolated achieved their first success in the formation of the Three Emperors' League (the *Dreikaiserbund*) in 1872. Germany's Emperor William I, Austria's Emperor Francis Joseph, and Russia's Tsar Alexander II pledged to cooperate in efforts to maintain peace and the status quo.

The Russo-Turkish War of 1877-78

Austro-Russian rivalry in the Balkans presented a serious threat to Bismarck's efforts to maintain Germany's ties with both Austria and Russia.

In 1876, a revolt against Ottoman rule broke out in Bulgaria. In suppressing the Bulgarian revolt, the Turks slaughtered thousands. The two small autonomous Balkan states of Serbia and Montenegro responded by declaring war on the Ottoman Empire. The Russians asserted their self-proclaimed role as the protectors of the Slavs and Orthodox Christians in the Ottoman Empire, going to war against Turkey in 1877.

Treaty of San Stefano (1878)

The Russians forced the Turks to accept the Treaty of San Stefano of March 1878. This treaty established the independence of Serbia, Montenegro, and Rumania and granted autonomy to a large Bulgaria, including most of Macedonia with access to the Aegean Sea. Bulgaria would be under Russian domination. The treaty awarded Batum and Kars and other Turkish lands in the Caucasus to Russia.

Threat of Anglo-Russian War

The Treaty of San Stefano substantially increased Russian power in the Balkans and thereby threatened Austrian interests in the region. While the Austrians protested Russia's gains, so, too, did the British, who feared the advance of Russian power toward the eastern Mediterranean. They sent units of their fleet to the Turkish Straits, which joined the Black and Aegean seas, and threatened to go to war against Russia.

The Congress of Berlin (1878)

In an effort to prevent a major war, Bismarck presented himself as an "honest broker" and invited the great powers to send representatives to a meeting in Berlin.

The Treaty of Berlin

The Congress of Berlin replaced the Treaty of San Stefano with a new treaty, the Treaty of Berlin (1878). This treaty confirmed the independence of Serbia, Montenegro, and Rumania, as well as the Russian acquisition of Batum and Kars. The size of Bulgaria was reduced. The northern area, Bulgaria proper, would be autonomous. To the south, Eastern Rumelia would be semiautonomous. Further to the south, the Turks would retain full sovereignty over Macedonia. (Eastern Rumelia united with Bulgaria in 1885.)

Austrian Gains

As compensation for the increase of Russian influence in the Balkans, Austria received the right to occupy and administer the Turkish provinces of Bosnia and Herzegovina, although the Austrians were not to annex them. The British gained the right to occupy the island of Cyprus in the eastern Mediterranean.

Bismarck intended this settlement as a compromise that would recognize Russian predominance in the eastern Balkans and Austrian control of the western Balkans. In reality, the settlement favored Austria by substantially reducing the gains made by the Russians in their war against the Turks.

The Dual Alliance (1879)

Austro-Russian conflict in the Balkans led to the collapse of the Three Emperors' League. In 1879, Bismarck concluded a secret defensive alliance with Austria. This Dual Alliance provided for mutual aid in the event either partner was attacked by Russia.

Revival of the Three Emperors' League (1881)

Bismarck hoped to restore the close relationship between Germany and Russia. In 1881, his efforts succeeded with the reestablishment of the Three Emperors' League. This association of the German, Austrian, and Russian rulers remained fragile, however, as a result of continuing Austro-Russian conflict over the Balkans.

The Triple Alliance (1882)

In 1881, the French established a protectorate over Tunisia in North Africa. This angered the Italians, who responded by seeking closer ties with Germany and Austria. In 1882, Italy joined Germany and Austria in a secret defensive alliance, the Triple Alliance. Bismarck now had ties with Italy as well as with Austria and Russia. In addition, Germany remained on good terms with Great Britain. France was thus more completely isolated than ever.

The Reinsurance Treaty (1887)

Continued Austro-Russian tension in the Balkans led to the Russian decision in 1887 not to renew the Three Emperors' League. However, the Russians wanted to maintain their relationship with Germany, and the two powers signed the Reinsurance Treaty of 1887. The treaty provided for benevolent neutrality in case either partner became involved in war unless Germany attacked France or Russia attacked Austria. Germany had no intention of attacking France. The provision that Germany would not be obliged to observe benevolent neutrality in the event of a Russian attack on Austria made the terms of the Reinsurance Treaty compatible with Germany's obligations under the Dual Alliance.

The Dismissal of Bismarck (1890)

In 1890, Emperor William II dismissed Bismarck as Germany's chancellor. Bismarck's successors proved far less capable than the Iron Chancellor had been, and Germany's international position quickly deteriorated.

In 1890, the Germans decided not to renew the Reinsurance Treaty with Russia, fearing it would be impossible to balance Germany's commitments to both Russia and Austria. The Germans believed that breaking the tie with Russia would pose no threat to Germany's interests since autocratic Russia and revolutionary, republican France were so ideologically antagonistic that an alliance between them was inconceivable. This belief proved to be mistaken.

The Franco-Russian Alliance (1894)

In the early 1890s, a diplomatic revolution began as long-isolated France and newly isolated Russia began to draw together. The rapprochement between France and Russia resulted in the signing of a secret military alliance in 1894. At the time, the Franco-Russian Alliance seemed directed primarily against Great Britain, the main rival of both France and Russia in the Mediterranean and Asia.

Deterioration of Anglo-German Relations

By the 1890s, Anglo-German relations became less cordial than they had been when Bismarck directed German policy. William II's telegram of support to President Paul Kruger of the Transvaal in 1896 angered the British (see Chapter 27), and they were alarmed by Germany's development of a high-seas fleet.

The Anglo-French Entente (1904)

Although colonial disputes contributed an element of tension to Anglo-French relations, the French believed that Germany, rather than Great Britain, posed the greater threat to France. In 1898, at the time of the Fashoda Crisis (see Chapter 27), Théophile Delcassé (1852–1923), the French foreign minister, urged the French government to give way to Great Britain in the Sudan. The French withdrawal from the Sudan marked the beginning of a reorientation of French policy.

During the Boer War, widespread international hostility to Great Britain convinced the British that isolation was dangerous. The first step in Britain's abandonment of isolation came in 1902, when the British signed an alliance with Japan. The Anglo-Japanese Alliance was directed primarily against the threat of Russian expansion in East Asia.

Anglo-French negotiations led to the conclusion of the Entente Cordiale in 1904. This diplomatic understanding dealt with colonial issues. The French recognized British dominance in Egypt, while the British agreed to support French claims to Morocco. The British and French also settled other differences in Africa and Asia and resolved a long-standing dispute about fishing rights in the North Atlantic off Newfoundland.

Following the conclusion of the Anglo-French Entente, the two countries began to consult on international issues of mutual interest.

Secret Italo-French Agreement (1902)

By the early 1900s, Germany's international position had deteriorated considerably. The Triple Alliance of Germany, Austria, and Italy remained in effect, but France actively sought to improve its relations with Italy. In 1902, Italy reached a secret agreement with France, promising to support French efforts to establish a protectorate over Morocco in exchange for French support of Italian ambitions elsewhere in North Africa. As Italy improved its relations with France, Austria became Germany's only reliable ally.

The First Moroccan Crisis (1905)

Emperor William II and his chancellor, Prince Bernhard von Bülow (1849–1929), attempted to improve Germany's diplomatic position. In 1905, the Germans provoked a crisis over Morocco, where the French were in the process of creating a protectorate. In March 1905, William II went to Tangier, where he declared that Germany had interests in Morocco and spoke in support of Moroccan independence. The Germans expected that Russia, which was being defeated by Japan, could not assist France, and they hoped that Britain would give France only token support. If these things happened, France's ties with Russia and Great Britain would be weakened.

The Algeciras Conference (1906)

The Germans pressed for an international conference to consider the status of Morocco. The conference met in early 1906 at Algeciras in southern Spain, near Gibraltar.

At Algeciras the Germans found themselves virtually isolated, securing only the support of Austria. Great Britain and Russia both supported France, as did Italy. France could now proceed with the establishment of its protectorate over Morocco.

Germany's belligerent attitude during the First Moroccan Crisis created an unfavorable impression and brought France, Russia, and Great Britain together more closely.

The Anglo-Russian Entente (1907)

The Russo-Japanese War of 1904-05 (see Chapter 27) created a difficult situation for France. Russia, France's ally, was at war with Britain's ally, Japan, while at the same time, France was working to achieve a diplomatic understanding with Great Britain. Nevertheless, the Anglo-French Entente was concluded, and the British supported France at the Algeciras Conference.

Japan's defeat of Russia reduced Britain's fears of Russian expansion in East Asia, although British and Russian interests continued to clash in Persia and Afghanistan.

With the encouragement of the French, London and St. Petersburg sought to resolve their differences. The Anglo-Russian Entente of 1907 recognized a Russian sphere of influence in northern Persia and a British sphere in the south. The Russians agreed to withdraw from Afghanistan, while both countries promised to respect the territorial integrity of Tibet. With these differences resolved, Britain and Russia could seek to collaborate in European affairs.

The Triple Entente

The Anglo-Russian Entente of 1907 completed the process of establishing the Triple Entente of France, Great Britain, and Russia. The Triple Entente faced the Triple Alliance of Germany, Austria, and Italy. The two power blocs were not as evenly balanced as that would suggest, however. As noted above, Italy was less than completely faithful to its alliance partners. In the years since Bismarck's dismissal in 1890, the diplomatic balance of power in Europe had shifted dramatically in France's favor.

The Bosnian Crisis (1908-09)

A series of international crises in the years after 1907 increased tension and uncertainty in Europe and contributed to the outbreak of war in 1914. With Austria as its only reliable ally, Germany could no longer seek to restrain Austria's activities in the Balkans as it had in the past. This increased the possibility that a crisis in the Balkans could escalate, thereby endangering the peace of Europe.

In September 1908, Alois von Aehrenthal (1854–1912), the Austrian foreign minister, met his Russian counterpart, Alexander Izvolsky (1856–1919), at Buchlau. In the Buchlau Agreement, the two statesmen agreed that Russia would support Austria's efforts to annex Bosnia and Herzegovina. In return, Austria would support Russia's efforts to gain the right to send its warships through the Turkish Straits.

Evidently the gains by Austria and Russia were intended to be simultaneous. However, in October 1908, Austria unilaterally proclaimed the annexation of Bosnia and Herzegovina. This action infuriated the Russians. Serbia was also angry, since the Serbs had hoped that they might one day be able to annex Bosnia and Herzegovina.

As the crisis mounted, Germany gave Austria its full support. The threat of war with both Austria and Germany forced the Russians to back down in the spring of 1909. The Bosnian Crisis thus ended with Russia's humiliation.

The Second Moroccan Crisis (1911)

In 1911, Germany renewed its objections to the establishment of a French protectorate over Morocco. The Germans sent a warship, the *Panther,* to the Moroccan port of Agadir, ostensibly to protect German interests. Tension eased when the French agreed to cede part of the French Congo to Germany in return for German recognition of the French position in Morocco.

Once again, Germany's belligerent diplomacy caused alarm. In 1912, the British navy began to concentrate its warships in the North Sea, while the French shifted the bulk of their navy to the Mediterranean. The British now had at least a moral obligation to protect France's northern coast in the event of war. The Entente Cordiale of 1904 had come close to being converted into a full alliance.

The Italo-Turkish War (1911–12)

In 1911, Italy went to war against the Ottoman Empire in an attempt to take control of Tripoli (Libya) in northern Africa. The Italians desired Tripoli both for reasons of national prestige and to compensate for the French acquisition of Morocco. The Italians easily defeated the Turks, and the peace treaty, signed in 1912, awarded Tripoli to Italy.

The First Balkan War (1912–13)

Italy's easy victory over the Turks encouraged the small Balkan states to press their demands against the Ottoman Empire. Under

Russian patronage, Bulgaria, Serbia, Montenegro, and Greece had formed the Balkan League. In 1912, the Balkan League went to war against Turkey. Under the terms of the Treaty of London (May 1913), the defeated Ottoman Empire lost all its territory in Europe except for the area immediately adjacent to the Turkish Straits.

As the First Balkan War drew to a close, both Austria and Russia intervened diplomatically. The Russians supported Serbia's demand for access to the Adriatic Sea, while the Austrians urged the creation of a new Balkan state, Albania, to contain Serbia's expansion. An international conference held in London in 1913 supported Austria's position. The establishment of Albania represented not only a setback for Serbia, but for Russia, as well. Once again the Russians had had to give way in the Balkans.

The Second Balkan War (1913)

Having been denied access to the Adriatic, Serbia demanded part of Bulgaria's share of Macedonia as compensation. Bulgaria, on the other hand, believed that its role in the First Balkan War entitled her to even more of Macedonia.

These disputes among the Balkan states resulted in the outbreak of the Second Balkan War in 1913. Serbia, Montenegro, Greece, Rumania, and Turkey joined to defeat Bulgaria. The Treaty of Bucharest (August 1913) forced Bulgaria to cede territory to Rumania, while Serbia and Greece gained most of Macedonia.

The crises in the Balkans had been serious, although they had not led to a general war. Nevertheless, the situation remained filled with danger. Russia's ambitions in the Balkans and the Turkish Straits had been frustrated. The Russians felt compelled to support Serbia more firmly in the future, while the Germans believed it was essential to back Austria.

The Sarajevo Crisis

On June 28, 1914, the final crisis began at Sarajevo, the capital of the Austrian province of Bosnia. A South Slav nationalist, Gavrilo Princip (1895–1918), assassinated Archduke Francis Ferdinand (1863–

1914), the heir to the Austrian throne, and his wife. A secret South Slav nationalist organization, Union or Death, also known as the Black Hand, had planned the assassination and had assisted Princip in carrying out the plot. Although the Serbian government was not directly involved, some Serbian officials were aware of the plot but took no action either to prevent its execution or to warn the Austrians.

The Outbreak of War

Austrian Demands on Serbia

Convinced that the Serbian government bore responsibility for the assassination, Austria was determined to settle accounts with Serbia, which had been encouraging nationalist unrest among South Slavs within the borders of the Dual Monarchy. The Austrians hoped to wage a limited war against Serbia and dispatched a stern ultimatum to the Serbian government on July 23. While Serbia did not accept all of Austria's demands, the reply was moderate enough to warrant further negotiations. However, determined to press forward against Serbia, the Austrians declared war on July 28.

The German "Blank Check"

Germany had earlier indicated its readiness to support Austria fully, issuing the so-called blank check to the Austrian government. Instead of trying to restrain the Austrians, the Germans appeared to be encouraging them to move against Serbia, whatever the risk of a general war might be.

Declarations of War

It was impossible for the Russians to accept another setback in the Balkans, and they were determined to back Serbia. On July 30, Tsar Nicholas II ordered a general mobilization of his armies. Germany responded by sending Russia an ultimatum, demanding an end to Russian mobilization. When the Russians refused, Germany declared war on Russia on August 1. The Germans asked the French government about its intentions in the event of a Russo-German war. France replied that it would "act in accordance with its interests." On August 3, Germany declared war on France.

The German general staff had established a plan for fighting a war on two fronts against both Russia and France. Assuming that Russia would mobilize slowly, this Schlieffen Plan called for a massive assault on France. When the French had been defeated, the Germans would then turn against Russia. The success of the Schlieffen Plan depended not only on rapid German mobilization but also on a speedy defeat of France. The Germans calculated that this objective could most readily be achieved by invading France by way of Belgium, even though this would involve a violation of Belgian neutrality, which the European powers had guaranteed by treaty in 1839. German troops invaded Belgium on August 3. Great Britain responded by declaring war on Germany the following day.

As dusk fell in London on August 4, 1914, Sir Edward Grey (1862–1933), the British foreign secretary, uttered an epitaph for the age that had ended: "The lamps are going out all over Europe; we shall not see them lit again in our lifetime."

During the Age of Bismarck from 1871 to 1890, Germany stood at the center of the European power balance, maintaining close ties with Austria, Russia, and Italy. Following Bismarck's dismissal from office in 1890, the balance began to shift in favor of France. The French formed an alliance with Russia in 1894 and a decade later, the Anglo-French Entente came into being. France also succeeded in drawing Italy away from its ties to Germany and Austria in the Triple Alliance.

In the early years of the twentieth century, international relations in Europe began to deteriorate as a result of a series of crises, focusing particularly on the Balkans, where Austro-Russian rivalry intensified. The last of these Balkans crises, the assassination of Archduke Francis Ferdinand at Sarajevo, led to the outbreak of the First World War.

Recommended Reading

Albertini, Luigi. *The Origins of the War of 1914,* 3 vols. (1952-57).

Berghahn, V. R. *Germany and the Approach of War in 1914* (1973).

Bosworth, Richard. *Italy and the Approach of the First World War* (1983).

Dedijer, Vladimir. *The Road to Sarajevo* (1966).

Fay, Sidney B. *The Origins of the World War*, 2 vols. (1928).

Fischer, Fritz. *Germany's Aims in the First World War* (1967).

Geiss, Imanuel. *German Foreign Policy, 1871–1914* (1976).

Geiss, Imanuel, ed. *July 1914: The Outbreak of the First World War* (1968).

Keiger, John F. V. *France and the Origins of the First World War* (1983).

Kennan, George F. *The Decline of Bismarck's European Order: Franco-Russian Relations, 1875–1890* (1979).

Kennedy, Paul M. *The Rise of the Anglo-German Antagonism, 1860–1914* (1980).

Lafore, Laurence. *The Long Fuse: An Interpretation of the Origins of World War I* (1965).

Langer, William L. *The Diplomacy of Imperialism, 1890–1902* (2nd ed., 1950).

Langer, William L. *European Alliances and Alignments, 1872–1890* (2nd ed., 1950).

Lieven, D. C. B. *Russia and the Origins of the First World War* (1983).

Schmitt, Bernadotte E. *The Coming of the War, 1914*, 2 vols. (1930).

Steiner, Zara S. *Britain and the Origins of the First World War* (1977).

Taylor, A. J. P. *The Struggle for Mastery in Europe, 1848–1918* (1954).

CHAPTER 29

The First World War

Time Line

1914   World War I breaks out in Europe

The Germans fail to take Paris; trench warfare begins in France

The Germans defeat a Russian offensive in East Prussia

The Ottoman Empire enters the war on the side of the Central Powers

1915   Italy enters the war on the Allied side

The British launch the Gallipoli campaign

Germany's campaign of unrestricted submarine warfare results in the sinking of the *Lusitania*

1916	The German offensive at Verdun and the Allied offensive on the Somme fail to produce breakthroughs
	The British and German fleets fight the Battle of Jutland
	David Lloyd George takes office as Great Britain's prime minister
1917	The United States enters the war on the Allied side
	Georges Clemenceau becomes premier of France
1918	President Woodrow Wilson announces the Fourteen Points
	Soviet Russia signs the Treaty of Brest-Litovsk
	Germany agrees to an armistice
1919	The Paris Peace Conference begins its deliberations
	The Germans sign the Treaty of Versailles

Despite its name, World War I was primarily a European conflict, fought over European issues.

The Allies of World War I included, first, the nations of the Triple Entente: France, Russia, and Great Britain. Serbia was also numbered among the Allies. Italy, Rumania, and Greece ultimately supported the Allied cause, as did the United States and Japan. Although the Japanese had no interests at stake in Europe, they hoped to acquire Germany's concessions in China, as well as the German-held islands in the North Pacific.

The Central Powers, Germany and Austria-Hungary, won the support of Bulgaria and the Ottoman Empire.

On the western front, the fighting in France quickly became stalemated between the invading Germans and the French and British defenders. On the eastern front, the Russians did relatively well against the armies of the Austro-Hungarian empire. By the end of 1916, however, the Germans had effectively ended Russia's ability to resist, although the Russians did not conclude a formal peace treaty with the Central Powers until March 1918.

Germany's campaign of unrestricted submarine warfare against Great Britain brought the United States into the war on the Allied side in April 1917. American participation in the war provided the French and British with what they most needed: manpower. In the summer of 1918, Allied offensives broke the stalemate in France. The Germans were forced to retreat, and the fighting ended with the signing of an armistice in November 1918.

The task of making the final peace settlement was in the hands of the Paris Peace Conference, which met in 1919–1920.

The War in the West, 1914–1917

On August 4, 1914, during the first week of the war, the Germans invaded Belgium. As the Germans advanced, the British Expeditionary Force (BEF) was sent to France.

Battle of the Marne

At the end of August, the Battle of the Frontiers resulted in a major German defeat of the French. A few days later, on September 5, 1914, the Germans crossed the Marne River at a point about twelve miles from Paris, but they lacked the strength to push on and take the French capital. The Battle of the Marne ended with the French turning back the German threat to Paris.

Stalemate on the Western Front

The front in France became stalemated, with the Germans controlling most of Belgium and a large section of northern France. The two sides dug trenches, which they protected with barbed wire and concrete pillboxes. Trench warfare continued in France for the better part of four years. Each side launched offensives, but the machine guns of the defenders mowed down the advancing infantrymen. In an attempt to achieve a breakthrough, both sides used heavy artillery. The Germans used chlorine gas for the first time at Ypres in April 1915. But neither artillery nor poison gas proved decisive.

Battle of Verdun

In February 1916, the Germans massed their armies and artillery in an assault on the French stronghold at Verdun. Failing to take Verdun, the Germans moved to the defensive in July, and the battle continued until December. By that point, the French had stabilized the front much as it had been at the beginning of the year. At Verdun, the French suffered some 540,000 casualties, while German losses exceeded 430,000.

Battle of the Somme

In July 1916, the British and French launched a great offensive on the Somme River. Along the thirty-mile Somme front, the Allies achieved a maximum advance of only seven miles. By the time the battle ended in November, British casualties totaled 400,000, while the French suffered 200,000 casualties. German casualties have been estimated at 650,000. During the battle, the British used tanks for the first time. But like heavy artillery and gas, tanks failed to produce a decisive breakthrough.

The Western Front in 1917

The war-weariness of the French required the British to assume greater responsibility for the front in France. During 1917, British offensives at Passchendaele in the Ypres sector and at Cambrai in Flanders proved both indecisive and costly.

After more than three years of fighting, neither the Allied nor the German armies had made any real gains and both sides had suffered tremendous casualties.

Changes in Political Leadership

In December 1916, British Prime Minister Herbert Asquith (1852–1928) stepped aside, giving way to a war cabinet headed by his fellow Liberal, David Lloyd George (1863–1945), the popular "Welsh

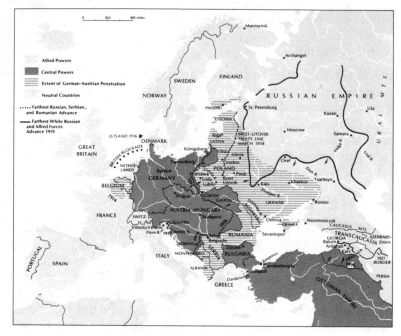

World War I

Wizard." In November 1917, Georges Clemenceau (1841–1929), the old "Tiger" of French politics, became premier, providing France with determined leadership.

The Eastern Front, 1914–1917

German Victories in East Prussia

When the war began in the summer of 1914, the Russians succeeded in mobilizing more rapidly than the Germans expected. Two Russian armies invaded East Prussia. The Germans inflicted crushing defeats on the Russians in the Battle of Tannenberg at the end of August and the Battle of the Masurian Lakes in early September.

The War in the East, 1914–1916

While the Germans were smashing the Russian invaders of East Prussia, the Russians scored some successes at the expense of Austria-Hungary. In order to relieve the pressure on their allies, the Germans pushed toward Warsaw in eastern Poland. By the end of 1914, the Russians held almost all of Galicia (Austrian Poland), while the Germans occupied about one-quarter of Russian Poland. Russia's industry was inadequate to meet the country's needs, and ammunition and military equipment were in short supply.

The German advance against Russia continued during 1915. By the end of the year, the Germans occupied most of Russian Poland and Lithuania. While the Russian offensives against the Austrians in Galicia achieved some success during 1915, they remained indecisive. In September 1915, Tsar Nicholas II took over the supreme command of the Russian army.

In June 1916, the Russians began a great offensive against the Austrians in Galicia. The Germans rushed in fifteen divisions and halted the Russian advance.

Prior to the Russian setback, Rumania entered the war on Russia's side in August, hoping to acquire the province of Transylvania from Austria-Hungary. By January 1917, however, Austro-German forces had defeated and occupied Rumania.

Defeat of Russia

By the end of 1916, the Germans had, in effect, defeated Russia, and the revolutions of 1917 ended any possibility that the Russians might continue fighting. The Treaty of Brest-Litovsk, signed in March 1918, ended the war between Russia and the Central Powers (see Chapter 30).

The Italian Front, 1915–1917

Although Italy was still technically allied with Germany and Austria under the terms of the Triple Alliance, Italy remained neutral when the war began. In an effort to win Italy's support, the Allies agreed to the secret Treaty of London of 1915, promising the Italians

Austrian and Turkish territory, as well as colonies in Africa. In May 1915, Italy entered the war on the Allied side.

Italy was unsuccessful in its war against Austria, and in the fall of 1917, the Austrians inflicted a humiliating defeat on the Italians in the Battle of Caporetto. The British and French had to rush troops in to help the Italians stabilize the front.

The Gallipoli Campaign

In November 1914, the Ottoman Empire entered the war on the side of the Central Powers, thereby closing the Turkish Straits to the Allies. The western Allies were thus unable to ship vital war supplies to the faltering Russians.

Winston Churchill (1874–1965), the British first lord of the admiralty, pushed for a campaign to open the straits. In February 1915, the British launched an amphibious invasion of the Gallipoli Peninsula at the southern end of the Dardanelles. However, the invasion failed as a result of errors in its planning and execution. In January 1916, the British withdrew.

While the Gallipoli campaign was in progress, Bulgaria entered the war on Germany's side in October 1915. Bulgaria had been at odds with Serbia since the Second Balkan War in 1913 and hoped to square accounts. Bulgarian forces helped Germany and Austria crush Serbia at the end of 1915.

The War in the Middle East

The Allies were able to make substantial gains at Turkish expense elsewhere in the Middle East. In the Caucasus, the Russians succeeded in turning back a Turkish offensive in early 1915. The Turks then began to deport and massacre the Armenians, whom they accused of aiding the Russians.

With the Turkish Straits closed to Allied shipping, the British hoped to open a route to Russia through Turkish-ruled Mesopotamia. In March 1917, the British seized Baghdad and soon took control of most of Mesopotamia.

Under the leadership of Colonel T. E. Lawrence (1888–1935),

known as Lawrence of Arabia, the British succeeded in stirring up revolts among the Arab subjects of the Turks. In 1917, the British invaded Palestine, capturing Jerusalem in December.

The War at Sea

Germany's much-vaunted high-seas fleet had little impact on the Allies during World War I. Their submarines, on the other hand, posed a serious threat.

Battle of Jutland

During the afternoon and evening of May 31, 1916, the British Grand Fleet battled the German fleet at the Battle of Jutland in the North Sea, off the coast of Denmark. The Germans inflicted substantially greater damage on the British than they suffered, but the battle proved indecisive. The Germans failed to break the British blockade, while the British failed to open the Baltic Sea route to Russia. Following the battle, however, the German surface fleet limited its activities to the Baltic and ceased to present any threat to the Allies.

Submarine Warfare

In February 1915, in an effort to starve out the British, the Germans declared a submarine blockade of the British Isles. In May, a German U-boat sank the British passenger liner *Lusitania* off the Irish coast, with the loss of 139 American lives. Vigorous American protests caused the Germans to reduce their submarine campaign.

During 1916, however, many German leaders urged the renewal of a campaign of unrestricted submarine warfare in an attempt to knock Great Britain out of the war. On February 1, 1917, the campaign began. The Germans were taking a calculated risk, hoping that the British would be forced out of the war before the United States could bring its power to bear in Europe.

United States Declaration of War

On February 26, the British liner *Laconia* was sunk without warning; two Americans died in the sinking. On March 1, the Zimmermann Telegram was revealed; in it, the Germans proposed an alliance with Mexico, promising to restore Texas, New Mexico, and Arizona to the Mexicans.

The United States declared war on Germany in early April 1917, but American troops were not present in large numbers on the front in France until almost a year later.

The End of World War I

In March 1918, the Germans launched a massive offensive in France in a final effort to win the war.

The Allied Advance

The British rushed in reinforcements, and some 2 million American troops, commanded by General John J. "Black Jack" Pershing (1860–1948), began to arrive in France. In April, the Allies established a unified command, headed by Ferdinand Foch (1851–1929), a French general.

In mid-July 1918, the French, British, and American armies began a counterattack that marked the beginning of the long offensive that ended the war. The Germans began to retreat along a broad front. On August 8, 1918, the Black Day of the German Army, British tanks scored a major breakthrough near Amiens.

Armistice

On September 30, Bulgaria signed an armistice. Turkey capitulated to the Allies on October 30, and Austria gave up on November 3. The armistice with Germany was signed at five A.M. on November 11, 1918, to go into effect at eleven A.M. World War I resulted in the loss of some 10 million military and civilian lives. Another 20 million were wounded.

The Paris Peace Conference

In January 1919, the peace conference began its deliberations in

Paris. Delegates representing some thirty-two nations attended. The main decisions, however, were made by the Council of Four: President Woodrow Wilson (1856–1924) of the United States, Premier Clemenceau of France, Prime Minister Lloyd George of Great Britain, and Premier Vittorio Orlando (1860–1952) of Italy. Neither Germany nor Soviet Russia was represented.

Wilson's Fourteen Points

A year earlier, in January 1918, President Wilson had presented his proposals for a peace based on principles of justice. In the Fourteen Points, he called for open diplomacy, freedom of the seas, free trade, and a reduction of armaments, and he urged self-determination for the subject peoples of the German, Austro-Hungarian, and Ottoman empires. In the fourteenth point, Wilson endorsed the creation of "a general association of nations." The League of Nations became the central part of Wilson's vision of the postwar world, and the Fourteen Points as a whole put the United States on a collision course with the European Allies.

French, British, and Italian Objectives

While Wilson sought to promote what he had earlier termed a "peace without victory," Clemenceau was determined to gain security for France against a possible future resurgence of German power. In addition, the French premier demanded substantial reparations from Germany to pay for the reconstruction of war-ravaged northern France. Lloyd George hoped to restore a continental balance of power so that Great Britain could devote its attention to its empire, while Orlando's primary objective was to gain as much territory as possible for Italy.

The Treaty of Versailles

The Paris Peace Conference produced five treaties for Germany, Austria, Hungary, Bulgaria, and Turkey. The most important was the Treaty of Versailles, the peace settlement with Germany.

The Rhineland

In drafting this treaty, a major controversy developed over French demands regarding the German Rhineland. Clemenceau wanted to separate the Rhineland from Germany in order to create a buffer state along the Franco-German border. Wilson objected, citing the principle of national self-determination. A compromise was reached, providing that the Allies would occupy the Rhineland for a period of fifteen years and that the Rhineland would be permanently demilitarized. In addition, in the Pact of Guarantees, the United States and Great Britain promised to come to the defense of France in the event of a future German attack. However, neither Great Britain nor the United States ever ratified this pact.

Alsace and Lorraine; the Saar

The Treaty of Versailles restored the provinces of Alsace and Lorraine to France. The treaty provided further that the coal-rich area of the Saar in western Germany would be placed under the control of the League of Nations for fifteen years. During this period, the coal of the Saar would be the absolute property of the French state. This was done to compensate France for the damage done during the war to the coal mines of northern France. At the end of the fifteen-year period, a plebiscite would determine the Saar's future. When the plebiscite was held in 1935, the people of the Saar voted to return to German control.

Poland

Germany suffered small territorial losses to Belgium and Denmark, but the most extensive territorial losses occurred in the east. The newly recreated Poland received a large piece of eastern Germany. In particular, the Polish Corridor was created to give Poland access to the Baltic Sea. The Polish Corridor separated East Prussia from the rest of Germany. The Germans greatly resented this as they resented the Allies' decision to make the port city of Danzig, at the head of the Polish Corridor, into a free city. Although Danzig was largely German in population, it was separated from Germany in order to provide Poland with a seaport that was not under German control.

Territorial Settlements, 1919–1926

German Disarmament and Reparations

The disarmament clauses of the Treaty of Versailles also caused resentment among the Germans. The German army was restricted to 100,000 men, to be raised by long-term enlistments, while the navy was reduced to the status of a coastal defense force. Germany was to be allowed no air force, no tanks, and no submarines.

Article 231 of the treaty became known as the war-guilt clause. Under its terms, Germany and its allies accepted the responsibility for causing the war. This provided the justification for requiring Germany to pay reparations to the Allies.

Signing of Treaty

When the drafting of the Treaty of Versailles was completed, a German delegation was summoned to Paris, where the treaty was signed in the Hall of Mirrors of the Palace of Versailles on June 28, 1919.

The Mandate System

Africa

The Treaty of Versailles deprived Germany of its colonies in Africa and the Pacific. The German colonies in Africa were assigned to Great Britain, the Union of South Africa, and France as mandates under the nominal supervision of the League of Nations. The mandate system was designed to protect the indigenous populations and to prepare them for independence, but in practice the system proved little more than disguised annexation.

The Pacific

Germany's islands in the North Pacific went to Japan as mandates, while Australia and New Zealand acquired Germany's island colonies in the South Pacific.

The Middle East

The Treaty of Sèvres, signed in August 1920, deprived Turkey of its Arab lands in the Middle East. France acquired Syria and Lebanon as mandates, while British mandates included Palestine, Transjordan, and Iraq.

The League of Nations

For Wilson, the most important issue at the Paris Peace Conference was the creation of the League of Nations, an association of states that would replace traditional power politics with a commitment to use peaceful means in the resolution of international disputes.

The Covenant of the League of Nations provided for the creation of an Assembly, representing all the members of the League; a Council, a smaller body with the major powers as permanent members along with several other members elected by the Assembly; and a Secretariat, which would be the League's administrative body. The Assembly, Council, and Secretariat would all be headquartered in Geneva, Switzerland. The Permanent Court of International Justice (PCIJ) operated under a protocol separate from the Covenant. Popularly known as the World Court, the PCIJ had its headquarters in the Dutch capital of The Hague.

At Wilson's insistence, the Covenant of the League was included as a part of the Treaty of Versailles and the other four peace treaties drafted at Paris. The United States did not join the League of Nations because of opposition in the Senate, which refused to ratify the Treaty of Versailles.

Conflict Over Italy's Claims

Italy's claims for territory at the expense of the former Austro-Hungarian Empire caused a major conflict at the Paris Peace Conference. Italy demanded and received the Trentino, a former Austrian possession with a large German minority, and Istria, with its seaport of Trieste. This area had also belonged to Austria. Although the population of Trieste was predominantly Italian, Istria itself was overwhelmingly Slovene, and on the basis of national self-determination, it should have been assigned to the new country of Yugoslavia.

Wilson resisted the Italian demand for Fiume, which was to be Yugoslavia's major seaport. The statesmen in Paris never resolved the Fiume question; it was left to be settled by direct negotiations between Italy and Yugoslavia (see Chapter 31). Italy's claims for territory in Africa and Asia Minor were not fulfilled.

Self-Determination in Eastern Europe

Wilson strongly supported the principle of national self-determination, although it proved difficult in practice to draw boundaries in areas where national groups were intermingled, which was generally the case throughout Eastern Europe.

Austria and Hungary

The end of the war brought with it the collapse of the Austro-Hugarian Empire. The Treaty of Saint-Germain, signed in September 1919, reduced Austria to the status of a small German-Austrian national state. The Treaty of Trianon, signed in June 1920, made Hungary a national state for the Magyars.

Czechoslovakia

The new country of Czechoslovakia was created entirely from territory taken from Austria and Hungary. Czechoslovakia was awarded the province of the Sudetenland, which had previously been a part of Austria, even though it was inhabited mainly by German-speaking people.

Yugoslavia

To the south, Yugoslavia emerged as the national state of the South Slavs, joining the formerly independent states of Serbia and Montenegro with territory lost by Austria and Hungary.

Rumania

The Treaty of Trianon awarded Rumania the province of Transylvania, which had a large Hungarian minority. In addition, Rumania took advantage of Russia's weakness to annex Bessarabia.

The Baltic Countries

Finland and the three small Baltic republics of Estonia, Latvia, and

Lithuania also profited from Russia's weakness and won their independence.

Poland

In addition to acquiring territory from Germany under the terms of the Treaty of Versailles, Poland gained Galicia from Austria under the terms of the Treaty of Saint-Germain. In 1920, the Poles waged a successful war against Russia and pushed their frontiers eastward.

Bulgaria

The Treaty of Neuilly, signed in November 1919, deprived Bulgaria of its outlet to the Aegean Sea, which was awarded to Greece. Bulgaria also lost territory to Yugoslavia.

World War I cost millions of lives and did immense physical damage. The war also brought the collapse of the German, Austro-Hungarian, Russian, and Ottoman empires.

The statesmen who met in the Paris Peace Conference faced many problems and produced an imperfect settlement. While the Germans condemned the Treaty of Versailles as unjust, it did not reduce Germany to the rank of a second- or third-rate power, as the history of the next quarter century would demonstrate. France, although victorious, emerged from the war in a seriously weakened state, unable to maintain the peace settlement without British and American support. Italy's failure to acquire the territory it demanded left the Italians in an angry and bitter mood.

Recommended Reading

Albrecht-Carrié, René. *The Meaning of the First World War* (1965).

Birdsall, Paul. *Versailles Twenty Years After* (1941).

Clements, Kendrick A. *Woodrow Wilson, World Statesman* (1987).

Ferro, Marc. *The Great War, 1914–1918* (1973).

Horne, Alistair. *The Price of Glory: Verdun 1916* (1963).

Link, Arthur. *Wilson the Diplomatist* (1957).

Marshall, S. L. A. *The American Heritage History of World War I* (1964).

Moorehead, Alan. *Gallipoli* (1956).

Schwabe, Klaus. *Woodrow Wilson, Revolutionary Germany, and Peacemaking, 1918–1919* (1985).

Taylor, A. J. P. *The First World War: An Illustrated History* (1963).

Tuchman, Barbara. *The Guns of August* (1962).

Weintraub, Stanley. *A Stillness Heard Round the World: The End of the Great War, November 1918* (1985).

Williams, John. *The Other Battleground: The Home Fronts—Britain, France and Germany, 1914–1918* (1972).

Wohl, Robert. *The Generation of 1914* (1979).

Zeman, Z. A. B. *The Gentlemen Negotiators: A Diplomatic History of the First World War* (1971).

CHAPTER 30

Soviet Russia Under Lenin and Stalin

Time Line

1917	The March Revolution leads to the abdication of Tsar Nicholas II
	The Provisional Government is established
	Soviets are elected in Petrograd and other Russian cities
	The Bolsheviks take power in the November Revolution
1918	The Soviet government dissolves the constituent assembly

	The Soviet government signs the Treaty of Brest-Litovsk
1918–1920	The Reds defeat the Whites in the Russian Civil War
1921	Lenin introduces the New Economic Policy (NEP)
1924	Lenin dies
	Joseph Stalin introduces the doctrine of socialism in one country
	The Union of Soviet Socialist Republics (USSR) is established
1928	Stalin initiates the first Five Year Plan
1934	The murder of Sergei M. Kirov marks the beginning of the Great Purge

---

World War I hastened the collapse of the tsarist regime. By the end of 1916, Russia was no longer able to sustain military operations against the Central Powers. The economy was in chaos, and the power of the government had all but evaporated.

In March 1917, Tsar Nicholas II abdicated. The new Provisional Government failed to establish its effective control over the country. In the November Revolution, Vladimir I. Lenin and the Bolsheviks took power, beginning their effort to create the world's first Communist society.

Following Lenin's death in 1924, Joseph Stalin gradually established his authority. In the Five Year Plans, which began in 1928, Stalin sought to reorganize the country's economy, eliminating capitalism and promoting the development of heavy industry and the collectivization of agriculture. Stalin's rule was also marked by the Great Purge, the dictator's attempt to eliminate any possible opposition to his absolute authority.

The March Revolution

National Collapse

For Russia, World War I was a devastating experience. Russia's backward agriculture and underdeveloped industry, transportation, and communications could not sustain a major war effort. In the autumn of 1915, Tsar Nicholas II (r. 1894–1917) took personal command of his army, leaving the government in the hands of his wife, the Empress Alexandra (1872–1918). She came increasingly under the influence of the unscrupulous Grigori Rasputin (1872–1916), a self-proclaimed holy man who supposedly had the mystical power to stop the bleeding of the imperial couple's hemophiliac son, Alexei. As Rasputin's power grew, the prestige of the tsarist regime suffered. In December 1916, a group of conspirators with close ties to the imperial family murdered Rasputin. The removal of one man, however, could not reverse the course of Russia's collapse.

End of Tsarist Regime

In early 1917, spontaneous strikes and demonstrations swept the Russian capital of Petrograd (formerly St. Petersburg). The unrest resulted from war-weariness, shortages of food and other goods, runaway inflation, and distrust of the government. Tsar Nicholas II dissolved the Duma (the Russian parliament), but most of its members remained in the capital. On March 12, the Duma elected a committee to represent its interests.

As the disturbances mounted, Tsar Nicholas II ordered troops to suppress the demonstrations. Disobeying their orders, the troops joined the demonstrators. On March 15, the tsar abdicated. After three hundred years of ruling Russia, the power of the Romanovs collapsed. (In 1917, Russia still used the Julian calendar, which, in the twentieth century, was thirteen days behind the Gregorian calendar. By the Julian calendar, the disturbances in Petrograd intensified in late February. For that reason, the revolution is often referred to as the February Revolution.)

The Provisional Government

The Duma committee now became Russia's Provisional Government, headed by Prince George Lvov (1861–1925), a liberal nobleman. Alexander Kerensky (1881–1970), a member of the Socialist Revolutionary Party, was the only socialist to serve in the liberal-dominated government. The Provisional Government promised reforms and announced plans for the election of a constituent assembly to draft a constitution for a democratic republic.

Creation of Soviets

In the meantime, workers, soldiers, and sailors in Petrograd, responding to a call issued by socialist leaders, elected the Soviet of Workers' and Soldiers' Deputies. ("Soviet" is the Russian word for council.) Although the Petrograd Soviet was controlled by members of the various socialist parties, it gave tacit support to the Provisional Government. Similar soviets were established in other Russian cities and towns.

Bolshevik Program

In April 1917, Vladimir I. Lenin (1870–1924), the leader of the radical Marxist group known as the Bolsheviks, returned to Petrograd from his exile in Switzerland. He presented his program, the April Theses, to his Bolshevik followers, urging them to push for a proletarian socialist revolution.

The Bolsheviks and other socialists called for "Peace, Land, and Bread": an end to the war, the confiscation of the land of the great landowners and its distribution to the peasants, and the seizure of food for the cities.

Policies of Provisional Government

While the Provisional Government recognized the peasants' need for more land, it also respected the rights of private property. Therefore, the government was not prepared to authorize the confiscation of land, nor was it willing to seize food to meet the needs of the cities.

The Provisional Government also wanted to continue the war against the Central Powers. In July 1917, the Russian army launched an offensive against the Austrians in Galicia. However, the offensive quickly collapsed.

The July Days

Even before news of the events in Galicia reached Petrograd, the July Days insurrection broke out in the capital. The July Days represented a spontaneous revolt against the unpopular Provisional Government. Most of the leaders of the Petrograd Soviet opposed the insurrection, believing it was premature. Although Lenin shared this view, the Bolsheviks nevertheless supported the July Days. When the insurrection was suppressed, Lenin had to flee to Finland to escape arrest. In the short run, the Bolsheviks were weakened by their support of the revolt. In the long run, however, this position won the Bolsheviks many new followers among the increasingly more radical workers, soldiers, and sailors of the capital.

In late July, Kerensky replaced Prince Lvov as head of the Provisional Government. The change in leadership did little to strengthen it.

The Kornilov Affair

In September 1917, General L. G. Kornilov (1870–1918), the commander of the Russian army, attempted to seize power and establish a military dictatorship. With the help of the Bolsheviks, who now controlled the Petrograd Soviet, the Provisional Government was able to turn back the threat. The Kornilov Affair served to weaken further the Provisional Government.

The November Revolution

In late October, Lenin ordered his followers to begin plans to overthrow the Provisional Government. On the night of November 6-7, the Red Guards, an armed force organized by the Petrograd Soviet, seized key strategic locations in the city. (By the Julian calendar, it was October 24-25, and even today the Soviets refer to the "Great Socialist October Revolution.")

On the morning of November 7, Lenin announced the establishment of a new regime, which bore the revolutionary name of the Council of People's Commissars. Lenin served as the council's chairman, while Leon Trotsky (1879–1940) became commissar for foreign affairs. Joseph Stalin (1879–1953) was commissar for nationalities.

In the other major cities and towns, the Bolsheviks also took control, although fighting continued in Moscow for several days. While the Bolsheviks had seized power with relative ease and little violence, their new government confronted immense problems.

Lenin

Youth and Early Career

The man known to history as Lenin was born Vladimir Ilyich Ulianov in 1870 in Simbirsk, a town on the Volga River east of Moscow. His father was the director of the elementary schools of the province. His older brother, Alexander I. Ulianov, was involved in a conspiracy to assassinate Tsar Alexander III. The plot was uncovered before it could be carried out, and Alexander Ulianov was executed in 1887.

Lenin attended the University of Kazan briefly but was expelled for participating in a student demonstration. He studied law on his own, and in the mid–1890s he passed the state law examination.

More interested in Marxism than the practice of law, Lenin became involved in radical activities in St. Petersburg. He was arrested and imprisoned and then exiled to Siberia. In 1900, he went into exile in Western Europe. There he published a Russian-language Marxist newspaper, *Iskra* ("The Spark"), which was smuggled into Russia.

Leader of the Bolsheviks

In 1898, a group of Russian Marxists established the Social Democratic Party (see Chapter 25). When the Russian Social Democrats met in London in 1903, Lenin and his followers, known as the Bolsheviks, split with the more moderate Russian Marxists, the Mensheviks. Lenin and the Bolsheviks insisted that party membership should be restricted to an elite group of committed revolutionaries. The Bolsheviks also believed the party should press for the proletarian revolution in Russia at an early date, rather than wait for Russian industrial capitalism to achieve a mature level of development.

Early Measures of the Bolshevik Regime

Following the November Revolution, Lenin and his followers sought to realize the Bolshevik vision of the new socialist society. The government urged the conclusion of an immediate peace. It called on the peasants to seize the landowners' land and the workers to take control of the factories.

Reform Laws

Regarding the Russian Orthodox Church as a reactionary institution, the Bolsheviks sought to destroy it. Church and state were separated; church property was seized, and many churches, monasteries, and convents were closed. Religious instruction was prohibited, and only civil marriage ceremonies had legal recognition.

The Bolsheviks replaced the Julian calendar with the Gregorian calendar and simplified the Cyrillic alphabet. Titles of nobility were abolished.

The Constituent Assembly

Prior to its overthrow, the Provisional Government had scheduled elections for a constituent assembly to be held in late November. Lenin's government decided to allow these elections to be held, but the results were disappointing for the Bolsheviks. Although the Bolsheviks had won increasing support in Russia's cities, the country remained overwhelmingly rural, and the Socialist Revolutionary Party had a large following among the peasants. Some 420 Socialist Revolutionaries were elected to the constituent assembly, while the Bolsheviks won only 225 seats.

In January 1918, the constituent assembly met in Petrograd. The

Bolsheviks dissolved it after only one session. Lenin also organized a secret police force, known by its Russian acronym as the Cheka, to combat counterrevolutionary activity. By dissolving the constituent assembly and establishing a secret police, Lenin began the process of creating a Bolshevik dictatorship to replace the autocracy of the tsars.

Treaty of Brest-Litovsk

Negotiations between Lenin's government and the Germans led to the signing of the Treaty of Brest-Litovsk in March 1918. Believing that it was impossible for Russia to continue the war, Lenin insisted that there was no alternative to accepting the harsh terms dictated by the Germans. In any event, he reasoned, the world revolution would soon engulf Germany, and the treaty would then be nullified.

The Treaty of Brest-Litovsk forced the Russians to give up Finland, Russian Poland, the Baltic area (Estonia, Latvia, and Lithuania), part of Belorussia and the Ukraine, and Transcaucasia. The treaty was nullified following Germany's defeat by the Allies later in 1918.

The Civil War

The November Revolution had been unexpected, catching the Bolsheviks' opponents off balance. By the spring of 1918, however, these opponents had recovered their poise and began their effort to topple Lenin's regime.

Reds Versus Whites

During the Civil War, the Bolsheviks—who began to call themselves Communists—had certain advantages. They dominated the heart of the country and had much of Russia's remaining industry under their control. Their lines of communication and supply were relatively short. Furthermore, Leon Trotsky, who now served as commissar for war, succeeded in creating an effective fighting force, the Red Army. On the other hand, the anti-Communist forces, known as the Whites, failed to coordinate their efforts. Furthermore, many Russians feared that a White victory would mean the restoration of the old order.

Nevertheless, the Whites took control of large areas of Russia. In

July 1918, as White forces approached the Ural Mountains town of Ekaterinburg, local Communists ordered the murder of the former tsar and his family to prevent their rescue by the Whites.

During 1919 and 1920, the Reds gradually defeated the major White commanders: Admiral Alexander Kolchak (1874–1920) in western Siberia, General Nikolai Yudenich (1862–1933) in the Baltic region, and Generals Anton Denikin (1872–1947) and Piotr Wrangel (1878–1928) in the Ukraine and northern Caucasus.

Allied Intervention

Allied intervention in the Civil War proved to be of limited significance. French, British, and American troops were sent to Russia to prevent the Germans from seizing stockpiles of raw materials, while the Japanese intervened in eastern Siberia. While the Allies provided some assistance to the White forces, they did not commit themselves fully to the effort to overthrow Lenin's regime. Nevertheless, the Soviets have never forgotten these Western invasions of Russia.

Soviet Territorial Losses

During the Civil War, the Soviets suffered some major setbacks. In the West, Finland and the Baltic states of Estonia, Latvia, and Lithuania gained their independence, while Rumania seized the province of Bessarabia. Independence movements failed, however, in the Ukraine and in Georgia and Armenia in the Caucasus. In 1920, Poland invaded Russia. Under the terms of the Treaty of Riga, signed in March 1921, Poland annexed western Belorussia and the western Ukraine.

War Communism

During the Civil War, the Soviet regime established a policy known as War Communism. The major industries, as well as banks and insurance companies, were nationalized. Private trade was prohibited, and the regime requisitioned food from the peasants in order to feed the cities. The Supreme Economic Council supervised the operations of the Russian economy.

The economy sank into deeper chaos. Agricultural and industrial production declined sharply, the transportation and communication systems collapsed, and the cities experienced increasingly more serious shortages of food and fuel.

The New Economic Policy

Soon after the Civil War, the mounting Russian discontent erupted. In February and March 1921, sailors mutinied at the Kronstadt naval base, near Petrograd. This was an especially shocking occurrence, since the Kronstadt sailors had long been ardent supporters of Lenin and the Communists.

Recognizing the need for changes, Lenin introduced the New Economic Policy (NEP) in March 1921. The NEP brought a partial restoration of capitalism, which Lenin justified as one step backward that would make possible two steps forward later.

Under the NEP, the state retained ownership and control of large industries, the so-called "commanding heights" of industry. The state also controlled transportation and foreign trade. Smaller industries were turned over to private operators and cooperatives, and private retail trade was permitted.

Believing that "it is easier for us to change our policy than it is to change the peasant," Lenin ended the requisitioning of food. A tax in kind, payable in grain, was levied on the peasants, who could then sell their surplus produce on the open market. This provided the peasants with an incentive to produce more. Peasants were also permitted to rent additional land and to hire labor.

Concessions were granted to foreign capitalists so that Russia could get the technical expertise it needed to carry out its economic recovery.

Under the New Economic Policy, the Russian economy revived. By 1927, it had generally regained the level of 1913.

The Soviet State

The Russian Soviet Federated Socialist Republic (RSFSR)

The constitution of 1918 established the Russian Soviet Federated

Socialist Republic, embracing the traditional heartland of European Russia, as well as Siberia and Central Asia. The indirectly elected All-Russian Congress of Soviets served as the republic's parliament, while executive authority was entrusted to the Council of People's Commissars.

The Union of Soviet Socialist Republics (USSR)

In 1924, a new constitution went into effect, creating the Union of Soviet Socialist Republics. This was a federation of the RSFSR with the Soviet republics of the Ukraine, Belorussia, and Transcaucasia. While the republics were permitted a degree of cultural autonomy, political control was exercised by the Communist party leaders in Moscow.

The Stalin Constitution (1936)

In 1936, the so-called Stalin constitution was adopted. The USSR remained a federation of states, which now numbered eleven republics. (There would later be fifteen.) A new national parliament, the Supreme Soviet, was established, consisting of two houses, the Soviet of the Union and the Soviet of Nationalities. The members of the Supreme Soviet were directly elected, with all citizens eighteen years of age and over granted the right to vote. The Council of People's Commissars continued to exercise executive authority.

The Stalin constitution also contained a bill of rights, which included the right to employment and the right of the elderly and disabled to care, along with guarantees of more traditional civil liberties.

Communist Party Rule

In the Soviet system, however, a wide gulf persisted between constitutional provisions and practical reality. Power remained in the hands of the leaders of the Communist Party. In theory, the work of the party was directed by a Central Committee, whose members were elected by a party congress that met every few years. In practice, however, the Political Bureau (Politburo), which consisted of the party's top leaders, dominated both the Communist Party and the Soviet state.

The Secret Police

The Soviet Union remained a police state. In 1922, the secret police, the Cheka, was reorganized as the GPU. In subsequent years, the Soviet secret police underwent a series of reorganizations, becoming in turn the OGPU, the NKVD, the MVD, and finally the KGB.

Stalin Versus Trotsky

In 1922, Lenin suffered the first in a series of strokes. He died in January 1924. Even before Lenin's death, a struggle for power began within the Soviet leadership. The chief rivals were Trotsky and Stalin.

Trotsky's Doctrine of Permanent Revolution

Trotsky, the commissar for war, was the second best-known Communist leader after Lenin. He was an advocate of the doctrine of permanent revolution, which taught that the revolution that had begun in Russia as a bourgeois revolution and had become a proletarian revolution would continue and turn into a world proletarian revolution. According to this view, the world revolution was necessary for the survival of Soviet Russia's socialist society.

Stalin's Doctrine of Socialism in One Country

Although Stalin was less well-known than Trotsky, he held several key positions in the Soviet leadership, including the posts of commissar for nationalities and general secretary of the Communist Party. Stalin used the latter position to develop support among the party rank and file.

As his rivalry with Trotsky intensified, Stalin proposed the doctrine of socialism in one country. Writing in *Problems of Leninism* (1924), Stalin contended that the Soviet Union could survive and develop its socialist society even if the world revolution did not occur in the near future.

Stalin's Victory

In his struggle against Trotsky, Stalin formed an alliance with two other ambitious men, Grigori Zinoviev (1883–1936), the leader of the Communist Party in Leningrad (formerly Petrograd) and the head of the Communist International (Comintern), and Lev Kamenev (1883–1936), the party leader in Moscow.

In 1925, the triumvirate of Stalin, Zinoviev, and Kamenev forced Trotsky to step down as commissar for war. In 1926, Trotsky and his supporters were expelled from the Politburo. In 1927, Trotsky was expelled from the Communist Party and exiled to Central Asia. Two years later, in 1929, he was exiled from the Soviet Union. Ultimately Trotsky went to Mexico, where he was murdered by a Stalinist agent in 1940.

As Trotsky appeared on the verge of defeat in 1926, Stalin ended his alliance with Zinoviev and Kamenev. The Left Bolsheviks, as Zinoviev and Kamenev and their followers were known, advocated the end of the New Economic Policy, forced industrialization, and a policy designed to compel the obedience of the peasants. Stalin now allied himself with the Right Bolsheviks, whose leaders included Nikolai Bukharin (1888–1938), a prominent party theoretician and the editor of *Pravda,* the official Communist party newspaper; Alexei Rykov (1881–1938), who had replaced Lenin as chairman of the Council of People's Commissars; and Mikhail Tomsky (1880–1936), the head of the trade unions. The Right Bolsheviks opposed a sudden ending of the NEP and forced industrialization and favored a conciliatory policy toward the peasants.

Zinoviev and Kamenev were soon isolated and expelled from the Communist Party. Stalin then ended his alliance with the Right Bolsheviks. By 1929, Stalin had established his dictatorial control.

The Five Year Plans

As Stalin moved toward establishing his unchallenged authority, he adopted the program of the defeated Left Bolsheviks. In 1928, he initiated the first in a series of Five Year Plans. These plans were designed to end the New Economic Policy, eliminate capitalism, and create a socialist economy; to promote the rapid development of heavy industry; and to collectivize agriculture. The collectivization of agriculture would accomplish two goals, increasing the productivity of agriculture and forcing the peasants to cooperate with the regime.

Industrialization

The entire Soviet economy was placed under the centralized direction of the State Planning Commission (Gosplan). Immense efforts were put forth in a campaign to develop the Soviet Union's industrial plant. In an effort to encourage productivity, efficient workers were rewarded with higher pay, better housing, and other benefits. The Stakhanovite award, named for Alexei Stakhanov, who mined an immense amount of coal in a single day, was presented to workers who exceeded their quotas. By 1940, the Soviet Union stood third in total industrial production behind the United States and Germany. However, the production of consumer goods and the construction of housing were neglected.

Collectivization of Agriculture

During the first Five Year Plan (1928–1932), the campaign to collectivize agriculture encountered intense resistance from the peasants, who did not want to surrender their holdings.

The state planned to establish two types of farms, collective farms (kolkhozes) and state farms (sovkhozes). Peasants joining a collective farm would pool their land to form a commune. An elected management committee would run the kolkhoz, and the peasants would share in its income. Peasants who worked on state farms would be paid regular wages, similar to those earned by factory workers. According to the plan, most farms would be kolkhozes.

To fight collectivization, many peasants burned their crops, smashed their equipment, and killed their livestock. In order to feed the cities, government agents seized food, leaving the peasants to starve. During the struggle over collectivization, some 5 or 6 million peasants died, most of them in the Ukraine and the northern Caucasus.

The regime denounced the resisting peasants as kulaks, peasant capitalists, and launched a campaign for the elimination of the kulaks as a class. Millions of peasants were sent to labor camps in Siberia and the Arctic region.

In order to accomplish the collectivization of agriculture, the regime made concessions to the peasants during the second Five Year Plan (1933–1937). Peasants on the collective farms would be allowed to have their own houses, a few head of privately owned livestock, and kitchen garden plots. They were allowed to sell surplus produce from their kitchen garden plots on the open market. With this compromise, a clear concession to capitalism in agriculture, the campaign for collectivization was pressed forward.

The third Five Year Plan was introduced in 1938 but was suspended following the German invasion of the Soviet Union in June 1941.

The Great Purge

In December 1934, Sergei M. Kirov (1888–1934), chief of the Communist Party in Leningrad, was assassinated. A popular Communist leader, he had challenged Stalin's policies. Stalin apparently instigated the murder, but the government blamed a conspiracy organized by the exiled Trotsky.

The secret police, now known as the NKVD, began mass arrests of party members and others. Between 1936 and 1938, three public trials of prominent Old Bolsheviks were held, involving more than fifty defendants. All were convicted, and almost all were promptly executed, including Zinoviev, Kamenev, Bukharin, and Rykov. A secret trial of the Soviet Union's top military commanders was held in the summer of 1937. Marshal Mikhail N. Tukhachevsky (1893–1937), the chief of the general staff, and seven other generals were executed. An extensive purge of the officer corps followed. Less prominent victims were sent to labor camps, which may have held as many as 10 million prisoners by 1939, when the Great Purge subsided.

The purge of prominent members of the Communist Party hierarchy and the military high command, however vicious, served to eliminate any possible rivals to Stalin. But the purge of millions of rank-and-file party members and ordinary Soviet citizens served no evident purpose apart from filling the citizenry with a sense of terror.

Soviet Foreign Policy

In the years immediately following the November Revolution, the Soviet leaders expected the world revolution would occur in the near future. In March 1919, they established the Communist International (Comintern) to further this goal; they placed little emphasis on traditional diplomacy as a means to foster the objectives of the Soviet state in international affairs.

The failure of the world revolution to materialize led the Soviets to return to the methods of diplomacy. From 1918 to 1930, Soviet diplomatic efforts were directed by Georgi Chicherin (1872–1936), the commissar for foreign affairs.

Diplomatic Relations

During 1920–1921, Soviet Russia established relations with several neighboring states, including Finland, Estonia, Latvia, Lithuania, Turkey, Persia, and Afghanistan. In 1922, the Soviets signed the Treaty of Rapallo, a treaty of friendship with Germany. By 1924, Chicherin had succeeded in establishing diplomatic relations with most of the Western European states, including Great Britain, France, and Italy. However, the United States did not extend diplomatic recognition to the Soviet Union until 1933.

Comintern Activities

While Chicherin sought to develop diplomatic relations with other countries, the Comintern continued its efforts to foment revolution against the governments of these countries. The activities of the Comintern thus interfered with Chicherin's efforts to conduct even the semblance of a normal foreign policy. Gradually, the Comintern was subordinated to serve the interests of the Soviet state. In the meantime, however, stresses developed in the Soviets' relations with the Western powers, and by the late 1920s the Soviets were almost as isolated diplomatically as they had been at the beginning of the decade.

By the time of the German invasion of the Soviet Union in June 1941, two basic Soviet realities had become apparent. The first was the reality of Soviet economic power. As a consequence of Stalin's Five Year Plans, the Soviets developed their heavy industry, although agriculture, the production of consumer goods, and the construction of housing were neglected.

The second Soviet reality was its totalitarian political system. The power of the Stalinist dictatorship was about as absolute as humanly possible. The dictator's use of terror forced the Soviet people into total submission, creating a society of isolated individuals incapable of any organized opposition.

Recommended Reading

Brovkin, Vladimir N. *The Mensheviks After October: Socialist Opposition and the Rise of the Bolshevik Dictatorship* (1987).

Carr, E. H. *The Bolshevik Revolution, 1917–1923*, 3 vols. (1951-53).

Carr, E. H. *Socialism in One Country, 1924–1926*, 3 vols. in 4 parts (1958-64).

Conquest, Robert. *The Great Terror: Stalin's Purge of the Thirties* (1968).

Conquest, Robert. *The Harvest of Sorrow: Soviet Collectivization and the Terror-Famine* (1986).

Deutscher, Isaac. *Trotsky*, 3 vols. (1954-63).

Ferro, Marc. *October 1917: A Social History of the Russian Revolution* (1980).

Ferro, Marc. *The Russian Revolution of February 1917* (1972).

Fischer, Louis. *The Life of Lenin* (1964).

Kennan, George F. *Russia and the West Under Lenin and Stalin* (1961).

Kuromiya, Hiroaki. *Stalin's Industrial Revolution: Politics and Workers, 1928–1932* (1988).

McDaniel, Tim. *Autocracy, Capitalism, and Revolution in Russia* (1988).

McNeal, Robert H. *Stalin: Man and Ruler* (1988).

Mandel, David. *The Petrograd Workers and the Fall of the Old Regime* (1983).

Mandel, David. *The Petrograd Workers and the Soviet Seizure of Power* (1984).

Mawdsley, Evan. *The Russian Civil War* (1987).

Nove, Alec. *Stalinism and After* (2nd ed., 1981).

Rassweiler, Anne D. *The Generation of Power: The History of Dneprostroi* (1988).

Reiman, Michael. *The Birth of Stalinism: The U.S.S.R. on the Eve of the "Second Revolution"* (1987).

Thompson, John M. *Revolutionary Russia, 1917* (2nd ed., 1989).

Ulam, Adam B. *Expansion and Coexistence: Soviet Foreign Policy, 1917-73* (1974).

Ulam, Adam B. *Stalin: The Man and His Era* (1973).

CHAPTER 31

Fascist Italy

Time Line

1926	The Italian government organizes thirteen syndicates
	Italy establishes a protectorate over Albania
1929	The Lateran Accord ends the conflict between the Italian state and the papacy
1931	Pope Pius XI criticizes Mussolini's regime in the encyclical letter *Non abbiamo bisogno*
1938	The Chamber of Fasces and Corporations replaces the Chamber of Deputies

Following World War I, the liberal politicians who ruled Italy offered few solutions to the nation's difficult economic and social problems. Benito Mussolini, the leader of the new Fascist movement, took advantage of the country's mounting chaos to force his way into the premiership in 1922. Once in office, he moved quickly to establish his dictatorship.

Mussolini promised to provide efficient and honest government for Italy, to deal with the country's problems, and to promote Italian influence and prestige in international affairs.

Postwar Italy

Italy was among the victorious Allies in World War I, but the Italian army had won little glory on the battlefield. While the Paris Peace Conference awarded Italy some territory from the dismembered Austro-Hungarian Empire, Italy's claims for Dalmatia, the Adriatic port of Fiume, and territory in the Near East and Africa were rejected. As a consequence, Italians had a sense of national frustration.

Fiume

In 1919, Gabriele D'Annunzio (1863–1938), a poet and extreme nationalist, led a force of war veterans in seizing Fiume. D'Annunzio ruled Fiume for slightly more than a year. Under the terms of the Treaty of Rapallo, signed by Italy and Yugoslavia in November 1920, Fiume became a free city.

Economic and Social Problems

The war exacerbated Italy's already serious economic and social problems. The country emerged from the war with a huge national debt, runaway inflation, and massive unemployment.

Between 1919 and 1921, social unrest mounted, as angry industrial workers seized factories and impoverished peasants occupied land owned by the great landlords. The factory owners' and landlords' fear of social revolution grew.

In this crisis situation, the liberal politicians who dominated the government failed to provide effective national leadership, while King Victor Emmanuel III (r. 1900–1946) proved weak and ineffective. The political drift led to two parliamentary elections and four premiers between June 1919 and March 1922.

Socialists and Popolari

The Socialist Party and the Popolari, the Catholic party, offered possible alternative leadership for the government. In November 1919, the Socialists won 160 seats, giving them a plurality in the Chamber of Deputies, the lower house of the Italian parliament.

At this time, however, the Socialist Party suffered from deep divisions. One faction of the party, inspired by events in Russia, wanted to join Lenin's new Communist International (the Comintern) and convert the party into the Italian Communist Party. Other Socialists favored a more moderate course. As a result of this internal conflict, the Socialists were unable to take advantage of what appeared to be an intensifying revolutionary situation. In 1921, the Italian Socialist Party split, with the radical faction becoming the Italian Communist Party.

The Popolari also made a strong showing in the November 1919 election, winning 103 seats in the Chamber of Deputies. While the Popolari were united in their support of the Catholic Church, the party was deeply divided on the critical issues of economic and social policy. The Popolari thus failed to offer a coherent program of reform to meet Italy's pressing needs.

Benito Mussolini (1883–1945)

The Italian political vacuum offered an opportunity to Benito Mussolini. Born in the Romagna, an area of central Italy with a long tradition of political radicalism, the young Mussolini followed the example of his blacksmith father and became a Socialist. He worked for a time as an elementary school teacher and then became a Socialist journalist. In 1912, he was named editor of *Avanti* ("Forward"), the chief newspaper of the Italian Socialist Party.

When war broke out in Europe in 1914, the Socialist Party opposed Italian intervention. Before long, Mussolini, who was more a lover of action than a truly committed Socialist, called for Italian participation in the war on the side of the Allies. Consequently, he lost the editorship of *Avanti* and was expelled from the Socialist party. He founded a new pro-interventionist newspaper, *Il Popolo d'Italia* ("The People of Italy"), which subsequently became the official newspaper of the Fascist movement.

After Italy entered the war in 1915, Mussolini enlisted in the army and served at the front, where he was seriously wounded.

The Fascist Movement

In 1919, Mussolini resumed his turbulent role in Italian politics, establishing the Fasci di Combattimento (combat groups) in the northern Italian city of Milan. The term "Fascism" is derived from the ancient Roman *fasces,* the bundle of rods surrounding an axe that was carried by Roman magistrates as a symbol of their authority.

Mussolini's Rise to Power

Mussolini was first and foremost an opportunist, more interested in power than in principles, and he was willing to change his positions on issues to meet the political needs of the moment. Although Fascism offered little in the way of a firm ideology or definite program, it did possess certain distinct characteristics. Fascism was intensely nationalistic, militaristic, and anti-Marxist. The Fascists denounced Marxism, with its emphasis on the class struggle, as a divisive force in national life. Fascism also repudiated liberal democracy, emphasizing the obligation of the individual to serve the state rather than the freedom of the individual. Mussolini talked in vague terms of economic and social reform, but he made few specific proposals. In addition, he used exciting words, speaking of youth, will, action, courage, sacrifice, victory. However dynamic the rhetoric, it was devoid of particular meaning. Above all, Fascism emphasized a cult of the leader and was designed to propel the movement's *Duce* ("leader"), Mussolini, into power.

Growth of the Party

Initially, the Fascist movement made little headway. During the labor and peasant unrest from 1919 to 1921, however, Mussolini portrayed Fascism as a bulwark against Communism, although the threat of a revolutionary seizure of power was, in fact, slight. A number of frightened industrialists and landowners began to provide the Fascists with financial support. Mussolini also won followers among disillusioned and frustrated Italians, including war veterans, the lower middle class, university students, civil servants, and army officers. In May 1921, Mussolini and thirty-four of his followers won election to the Chamber of Deputies.

Mussolini organized a Fascist party militia, the Black Shirts (*squadristi*), who terrorized Socialists, trade unionists, and other opponents. The clashes between the Black Shirts and their enemies resembled civil war.

The March on Rome

In late 1922, Mussolini decided to take direct action. He called on his followers to march on Rome, demanding that he be named premier. In the March on Rome of October 28, 1922, several thousand Fascists demonstrated in the capital. On October 30, King Victor Emmanuel III appointed Mussolini to the premiership.

The Consolidation of Mussolini's Power

Mussolini had to proceed cautiously at first. The cabinet he headed

was a coalition. Of its fourteen members, only four were Fascists.
Furthermore, there were only about three dozen Fascists in a Chamber
of Deputies of 535 members.

On November 23, 1922, in an effort to restore stability, the parliament granted the cabinet dictatorial powers for one year. Mussolini
used this authority to install Fascists in government posts and prevailed
upon the king to appoint Fascist senators, giving the Fascists a majority
in the upper house of parliament.

The Acerbo Law

In November 1923, as the cabinet's dictatorial powers were about
to expire, Mussolini pressured the parliament into approving a new
electoral law, the so-called Acerbo Law. This law provided that two-
thirds of the seats in the Chamber of Deputies would be allotted to the
party that polled the largest number of votes, with a minimum of 25
percent, in the parliamentary election. This would end the need for
coalition governments.

Electoral Victory

The Acerbo Law proved unnecessary, however. Using a combination of effective propaganda, intimidation, and fraud, the Fascists polled
65 percent of the votes in the April 1924 election, winning 375 seats in
the Chamber of Deputies. Mussolini now formed a new cabinet, composed entirely of Fascists.

The Murder of Matteotti

Giacomo Matteotti (1885–1924), a Socialist deputy, challenged the
legitimacy of the Fascist majority in the Chamber of Deputies. On June
10, 1924, he was murdered by a group of Fascists.

Although Mussolini denied any involvement in the murder, there
were calls for his resignation. In protest, anti-Fascist deputies staged a
dramatic withdrawal from the Chamber of Deputies. This so-called
Aventine Secession recalled an incident in ancient Roman history, when
the plebeians protested the domination of the patricians. The Aventine
Secession of 1924, however, had no useful effect. Once the anti-Fascist

deputies had withdrawn from the chamber, the Fascists would not let them return. The Fascists now had solid control of both houses of parliament.

Establishment of the Fascist Dictatorship

Mussolini moved to increase his dictatorial authority. Press censorship was tightened. All elected local government officials were replaced by podestas, who were appointed by the central government. Parliament granted Mussolini the authority to rule by decree. The Black Shirt militia was incorporated into the regular army. The secret police, known by its Italian acronym as OVRA, cracked down on political opponents of the Fascist regime. Opposition parties were eliminated, and Italy became a one-party state.

Nevertheless, Mussolini and the Fascists never fully succeeded in creating a truly totalitarian state. The *Duce* was unable to establish his dominance over the wealthy upper classes, the Catholic Church, and the army, and he often complained bitterly about his inability to secure complete obedience from the Italian people.

Fascist Economic Policy

Mussolini had pledged to restore order to Italy's economic and social life. Fascist economic policy emphasized regimentation, with strict controls over the economy, while at the same time the interests of the capitalists were protected.

Economic planning was instituted in an effort to promote increases in both agricultural and industrial production, and Italy strove to achieve economic self-sufficiency (autarky). This was an unrealistic goal, since a country as lacking in natural resources as Italy was could not hope to become self-sufficient.

The Fascist regime sponsored huge public works projects, which helped relieve the country's high rate of unemployment. The production of hydroelectric power was increased substantially, although Italy continued to be dependent on substantial imports of coal and oil.

The Battle of Wheat

The Battle of Wheat involved large-scale land-reclamation projects, undertaken in order to make more land available for agriculture. Marshlands were drained, including the Pontine Marshes near Rome. However, Italy continued to import much of its food.

The Battle of the Lira

Other efforts of the Fascist regime were less productive. The Battle of the Lira involved efforts to increase the value of the lira, Italy's unit of currency, in international exchange. Raising the value of the lira to an artificially high level served to make Italian products more expensive in the world market. As a consequence, Italy's exports declined.

The Corporate State

Mussolini's creation of the corporate state represented an attempt to create a new system, superior to both laissez-faire capitalism and socialism.

Syndicates

In 1926, the Italian government organized a series of syndicates for producers and workers in six major areas of the economy: agriculture, industry, commerce, sea and air transportation, land and inland waterway transportation, and banking. Another syndicate was established for professionals and intellectuals. The activities of the thirteen syndicates were directed by the new Ministry of Corporations, headed by Mussolini.

The old labor unions were abolished, and strikes and lockouts were banned. Labor-management relations were conducted within the structure of the syndicates, and disputes that could not be resolved by negotiation were submitted to compulsory arbitration. The Charter of Labor of 1927 reaffirmed the regime's support of private ownership of business and industry but insisted that the economy must serve the interests of the state.

Corporations

In 1934, Italian economic life came under further regulation with the establishment of a system of corporations. Syndicates in several areas of the economy were joined to form twenty-two corporations that embraced the entire economy. The corporations were directed by the National Council of Corporations, which was in charge of promoting Italy's economic development. The system generally supported the interests of the capitalists, rather than the workers, and it did more to promote bureaucratic red tape than economic efficiency and increased production. Despite Mussolini's promises, Fascism failed to provide economic prosperity for Italy.

Political Reorganization

In 1928, the system of syndicates became the basis for a reorganized Chamber of Deputies. The national councils of the thirteen syndicates were authorized to nominate a total of 800 candidates for the Chamber of Deputies, while cultural and charitable foundations could nominate an additional 200. The Fascist Grand Council would then select a list of 400 candidates from the list of 1000, although the Grand Council could also make its own nominations. The Fascist Grand Council consisted of about twenty high-ranking party leaders appointed by Mussolini, and he acted as its chairman. The Fascist Party thus came to dominate the Italian government much as the Communist Party dominated the political structure of the Soviet Union.

The Italian electorate could vote yes or no on the entire list of candidates and could not reject individual candidates. In 1938, the Chamber of Fasces and Corporations replaced the Chamber of Deputies, creating the capstone of the corporate state. The new chamber included the members of the Fascist Grand Council and the National Council of Corporations.

The Lateran Accord

In 1929, Mussolini found a solution to the Roman Question, the long conflict between the papacy and the Italian state, which resulted from Italy's seizure of Rome from the pope in 1870 (see Chapters 23 and 24).

The Lateran Accord of February 1929 consisted of three separate agreements. In a political treaty, the pope recognized Italy's possession of Rome. In return, Italy recognized Vatican City as an independent and sovereign state ruled by the pope. In a financial convention, Italy agreed to pay the papacy a substantial sum of money in settlement of any and all claims the papacy might have as a result of the Italian seizure of Rome.

The third agreement, the concordat, defined the relationship existing between the Roman Catholic Church and the Italian state. The Roman Catholic religion was recognized as the official religion of the state. Religious instruction in the Catholic faith would be compulsory in all public schools, and the religious marriage ceremony was recognized as valid in civil law. For its part, the state secured a veto power over the pope's appointment of Italian bishops, and the church agreed to refrain from involvement in political issues.

Relations between the Fascist state and the church remained generally good, although there were some conflicts. In 1931, a crisis developed when the Fascists sought to dissolve Catholic youth organizations, which competed with Fascist youth groups. In response, Pope Pius XI (r. 1922–1939) issued the encyclical letter *Non abbiamo bisogno,* which condemned the Fascists for their "pagan worship" of the state. Church and government officials reached a compromise that allowed the Catholic youth organizations to function with some limitations, and the tension eased.

Mussolini's Early Foreign Policy

The extreme nationalism of the Fascists expressed itself in a build-up of Italy's armed forces and a bellicose foreign policy. Mussolini's dream was to establish Italian dominance in the Mediterranean area, which he termed *mare nostrum* ("our sea"), thereby creating a modern version of the Roman Empire.

The Corfu Incident

The first major assertion of Italy's power came in 1923, when bandits murdered four Italians who were working for the League of Nations in marking the border between Albania and Greece. In response, Mussolini bombarded the Greek island of Corfu, which was then occupied by Italian troops. Negotiations resulted in a Greek agreement to pay Italy an indemnity, and the Italians withdrew from Corfu.

Negotiations with Balkan Countries

Mussolini's aggressive behavior in the Corfu incident evoked widespread international condemnation. For the next several years, he pursued a more moderate course. Negotiations with Yugoslavia led to a 1924 agreement providing for the Italian annexation of Fiume, while a 1926 treaty with Albania created a virtual Italian protectorate over that country.

Italy also moved to form what amounted to an association of nations discontented with the post-World War I peace settlement, signing treaties with Hungary in 1927 and Austria in 1930 and drawing Bulgaria into Italy's orbit through the 1930 marriage of an Italian princess to King Boris (r. 1918–1943).

The record of Mussolini's Fascist dictatorship was a record of failure. In domestic affairs, the Duce's only enduring success was the Lateran Accord of 1929, which resolved the Roman Question. Despite Mussolini's much-heralded creation of the corporate state, he failed to deal constructively with the country's serious economic and social problems. He also failed to provide Italy with effective and honest government. And he failed even to establish his full dictatorial authority.

In foreign affairs, Mussolini's bellicose policy ultimately led him into an alliance with Adolf Hitler, the German dictator. Italy's failures in World War II brought the collapse of the Fascist dictatorship, the death of Mussolini, and national ruin.

Recommended Reading

Cardoza, Anthony L. *Agrarian Elites and Italian Fascism: The Province of Bologna, 1901–1926* (1982).

Cassels, Alan. *Fascist Italy* (2nd ed., 1985).

Cassels, Alan. *Mussolini's Early Diplomacy* (1970).

Delzell, Charles F. *Mussolini's Enemies: The Italian Anti-Fascist Resistance* (1961).

Germino, Dante L. *The Italian Fascist Party in Power* (1959).

Kelikian, Alice A. *Town and Country Under Fascism: The Transformation of Brescia, 1915–1926* (1986).

Kirkpatrick, Ivone. *Mussolini: A Study in Power* (1964).

Lyttelton, Adrian. *The Seizure of Power: Fascism in Italy, 1919–1929* (2nd ed., 1987).

Mack Smith, Denis. *Mussolini* (1982).

Mack Smith, Denis. *Mussolini's Roman Empire* (1976).

Nolte, Ernst. *Three Faces of Fascism: Action Française, Italian Fascism, National Socialism* (1966).

Pollard, John F. *The Vatican and Italian Fascism, 1929-32: A Study in Conflict* (1985).

Segre, Claudio G. *Italo Balbo: A Fascist Life* (1987).

Seton-Watson, Christopher. *Italy from Liberalism to Fascism, 1870–1925* (1967).

Tannenbaum, Edward R. *The Fascist Experience: Italian Society and Culture, 1922–1945* (1972).

Wiskemann, Elizabeth. *Fascism in Italy: Its Development and Influence* (2nd ed., 1970).

CHAPTER 32

Germany from Weimar to Hitler

Time Line

1918	Emperor William II abdicates; a German republic is established
1919	The National Assembly adopts the Weimar Constitution
1923	French and Belgian troops occupy the Ruhr valley
	Germany experiences a catastrophic inflation
	The Beer Hall Putsch, led by Hitler and Ludendorff, fails
1924	The adoption of the Dawes Plan ends the Ruhr crisis

1925	Germany, France, Great Britain, and Italy sign the Locarno Pact
	Field Marshal Paul von Hindenburg wins the German presidential election
1926	Germany enters the League of Nations
1929	The Young Plan eases Germany's reparations burden
1930	The Reichstag election results in the Nazis becoming Germany's second-largest party
1932	Hindenburg defeats Hitler in the presidential election
	The July Reichstag election results in the Nazis becoming Germany's largest party
1933	Hitler becomes chancellor
	The Nazi Party becomes Germany's only legal political party
1934	A purge eliminates Hitler's opponents within the Nazi Party
	President Hindenburg dies; Hitler assumes the powers of the presidency
1935	The Nuremberg Laws deprive Germany's Jews of their rights as citizens

During the early 1920s, the new German republic survived threats from both the left and the right, as well as a catastrophic inflation. Later in the decade, however, the Weimar Republic began to enjoy a degree of political stability, as well as economic prosperity.

The Great Depression of the early 1930s proved the Weimar Republic's undoing. As the German economy spiraled downward, the Nazi leader Adolf Hitler won increasing support. In January 1933, Hitler became Germany's chancellor, and he moved quickly to establish his dictatorship. Opposition political parties were eliminated, the free trade unions were abolished, and Germany became a police state. Hitler also began a campaign to eliminate Germany's Jews from any significant role in national life.

Postwar Germany

On November 9, 1918, two days before the signing of the armistice, Emperor William II (r. 1888–1918) abdicated. The leaders of the Majority Social Democrats, the country's largest political party, proclaimed the establishment of a republic. Friedrich Ebert (1871–1925) took office as chancellor, heading a provisional government.

The abdication of the emperor and the end of the war came as a profound shock to the German people, who had not been told of the deteriorating military situation. Many Germans believed that the German army had never been defeated in the field but had instead been stabbed in the back by socialist and liberal politicians. The "stab-in-the-back" legend quickly entered the political mythology of German conservative nationalists.

The Spartacist Revolt

Left-wing radicals sought to take advantage of the confused situation that prevailed in Germany during the weeks following the armistice. In January 1919, Communists attempted to seize power in Berlin. Karl Liebknecht (1871–1919) and Rosa Luxemburg (1870–1919) led these Communists, who were known as Spartacists. (They took their name from Spartacus, who led a slave revolt in Rome in the first century B.C.) The government succeeded in suppressing the revolt, and both Liebknecht and Luxemburg were killed.

The German republic was able to overcome the threats from the Spartacists and other leftists because it secured the support of both the army and the free corps, volunteer units of former soldiers, which numbered about 400,000 at their peak. Consisting mainly of embittered nationalists, the free corps symbolized the intense frustration of many conservative nationalists in the postwar era.

The Weimar Constitution

In January 1919, the German voters elected a National Assembly to draft a constitution for the new republic. An overwhelming majority supported the parties most committed to a democratic republic: the Majority Social Democrats, the Catholic Center, and the Democrats.

The National Assembly met in Weimar, a provincial town that had been an important literary and cultural center in the late eighteenth century. Weimar stood as a symbol of a liberal Germany, in contrast to Berlin, which represented the Prussian tradition of authoritarianism and militarism.

The President

In one of its first acts, the National Assembly chose Friedrich Ebert as Germany's first president. The Weimar Constitution, approved in July, provided that future presidents would be popularly elected for a term of seven years and would be eligible for reelection. Article 48 of the constitution authorized the president to rule by decree in time of emergency.

The Parliament

The constitution established a two-house parliament. The lower house, the Reichstag, was elected by universal suffrage under a system of proportional representation, which allotted seats to the parties in direct proportion to the percentage of the votes they polled in the election.. This system assured representation to minor parties. However, it also served to encourage the development of a multiparty system, which made it impossible in practice for any one party to win a majority of seats in the Reichstag. As a consequence, Germany experienced a succession of unstable coalition governments. The cabinet and the chancellor were responsible to the Reichstag, although they were technically appointed by the president.

The upper house, the Reichsrat, consisted of representatives elected by the parliaments of the eighteen German states. It had the power to delay the passage of legislation but could not permanently block bills favored by the Reichstag.

Conservative Influence

While Germany became a liberal, democratic republic, many conservative nationalists remained in positions of influence, serving as higher civil servants, judges, military officers, and professors and teachers. These conservative nationalists were unsympathetic to the new republic, and their opposition to it increased as a result of the Treaty of Versailles.

The wartime Allies refused to listen to German pleas for modifications of the treaty, and Germany was forced to accept it in June 1919. Almost from the beginning, therefore, the Weimar Republic was associated in the minds of the German people with the peace treaty they regarded as the "Dictate of Versailles."

The Kapp Putsch

In March 1920, conservative nationalists, led by Wolfgang Kapp (1858–1922), attempted to take power in Berlin. Although the conservative leaders of the army had been willing to defend the government against the Spartacists, they refused to act against Kapp. The government called on the workers in Berlin to stage a general strike. Activity in the capital ground to a halt, and the revolt collapsed. The Kapp Putsch served as a symbol of the hostility of many conservative nationalists to the republic.

The Ruhr Crisis and the Great Inflation

In 1921, the Allied Reparations Commission set Germany's reparations debt at 132 billion gold marks (approximately $33 billion), to be paid over a period of years. Germany protested the amount as excessive and during 1922, began to fall behind schedule in making its reparations payments.

Occupation of the Ruhr

In response to the German default, French and Belgian troops occupied the Ruhr valley, a major industrial center in western Germany, in January 1923. If the Germans would not pay reparations, then they would be taken from Germany's current production.

Unable to resist by force, the German government called on the workers in the Ruhr to begin a campaign of passive resistance. The workers refused to perform any work in the factories and mines that could benefit the occupiers.

Runaway Inflation

When the Ruhr workers began their passive-resistance campaign in early 1923, the German government had to assume the responsibility for supporting them. This was a costly undertaking, and the German government got the money it needed by printing it. Inflation became catastrophic, and the German mark became literally worthless. In November 1923, when the Germans introduced a currency reform, the mark stood at 4.2 trillion to the dollar.

While this inflation benefited debtors and some industrialists, who were able to eliminate their indebtedness and take over small competitors, it destroyed the savings of the German middle class. Threatened with being reduced to the status of proletarians, the middle class became more hostile toward the republic and more sympathetic to right-wing nationalist movements.

Stresemann's Currency Reform

In August 1923, Gustav Stresemann (1878–1929), a leader of the German People's Party, took office as chancellor, heading a broad coalition. In November, Stresemann carried through a currency reform, which replaced the inflated mark with a new mark, with an exchange rate of one new mark for one trillion old marks. The German mark thus regained its prewar exchange value of 4.2 marks to the dollar.

The Policy of Fulfillment

While Stresemann served as chancellor for only three months (August-November 1923), he remained Germany's foreign minister until his death in October 1929, promoting what came to be known as the policy of fulfillment. This policy reflected his belief that if Germany fulfilled its obligations under the Treaty of Versailles and sought a reconciliation in particular with France, the Allies might then agree to a revision of the treaty.

The Dawes Plan

Ending passive resistance in the Ruhr, Stresemann urged a study of the reparations issue. In 1924, an international commission headed by Charles G. Dawes (1865–1951), an American banker, proposed the Dawes Plan. While the Dawes Plan did not reduce Germany's total reparations debt, it provided that in years when the German economy was strong, the Germans would pay a larger amount of reparations. When the German economy was weak, the amount of the payment would be reduced. The Dawes Plan also provided for foreign loans to help Germany get its economy back on its feet. Following the acceptance of the Dawes Plan, France and Belgium ended the Ruhr occupation in 1925.

The Locarno Pact

In October 1925, Stresemann; Aristide Briand (1862–1932), the French foreign minister; and Austen Chamberlain (1863–1937), the British foreign secretary, signed the Locarno Pact. Germany and France promised to respect their mutual frontiers, and in addition, the Germans agreed to accept the permanent demilitarization of the Rhineland, which had been imposed on Germany by the Treaty of Versailles. Great Britain and Italy served as guarantors of these commitments, pledging to intervene against any violator.

While there was no similar accord regarding the permanence of Germany's eastern frontiers, Germany signed arbitration treaties with Poland and Czechoslovakia.

Germany entered the League of Nations in 1926, receiving the permanent seat on the League Council that had originally been assigned to the United States.

The Young Plan

In 1929, the reparations issue received further consideration by an international commission headed by Owen D. Young (1874–1962), an American businessman. The Young Plan reduced Germany's total reparations obligation and extended the period for payment. The world depression soon hit Germany, however, and no further reparations payments were made after 1931.

The Young Plan was accompanied by an agreement to end the Allied occupation of the Rhineland in 1930, five years ahead of the date specified by the Treaty of Versailles. However, the permanent demilitarization of the Rhineland remained in effect.

German Dissatisfaction with Fulfillment Policy

Stresemann's policy of fulfillment did much to restore Germany's position in the European family of nations. Despite the agreements on reparations, however, the Germans continued to oppose having to pay any reparations at all. Furthermore, the Germans remained dissatisfied with their frontier with Poland and with the disarmament clauses of the Treaty of Versailles, which placed restrictions on Germany's armed forces (see Chapter 29).

Germany's Domestic Recovery

During the late 1920s, Germany experienced a remarkable recovery as its finances remained stable and the economy prospered.

In addition, Germany experienced improved political stability. In 1925, President Ebert died in office. Field Marshal Paul von Hindenburg (1847–1934), a hero of World War I, won the presidential election at the age of seventy-eight. Hindenburg was a conservative nationalist, but he was an honorable man who sincerely desired to abide by his oath to uphold the constitution. The election of Hindenburg may have helped strengthen the Weimar Republic by leading some of his fellow conservative nationalists to accept it.

The Great Depression

During 1930, the world depression struck Germany. Banks failed, foreign trade declined, factories closed, and millions of workers became unemployed.

In March 1930, President Hindenburg named Heinrich Brüning (1885–1970), a member of the Catholic Center Party, as chancellor. Brüning was unable to secure the support of a Reichstag majority, and Hindenburg invoked Article 48 of the constitution, which authorized him to rule by decree. In his attempt to deal with the depression, Brüning pursued a deflationary policy, reducing government expenditures in a time of declining tax revenues.

The 1930 Reichstag Election

The Reichstag election of September 1930 began the political crisis that resulted in Adolf Hitler's appointment to the chancellorship in January 1933. In this election, the extremist parties—the Nazis and the Communists—made substantial gains. Hitler's Nazi Party, which had won only 12 seats in the Reichstag in the 1928 election, suddenly became Germany's second-largest party, with 107 members in the Reichstag.

Nazi Supporters

The Nazis won their support primarily from the lower middle class and the peasantry. These voters were strongly nationalistic in their political views and feared that the depression would deprive them of their standard of living. In religion, most of the Nazis' supporters were Protestants. German Catholics remained firm in their support of the Catholic Center Party.

Attitude of Workers

Most of Germany's industrial workers continued to vote for the Social Democrats, which remained the largest party, with 143 seats in the Reichstag. However, many disgruntled industrial workers voted for the Communists, who elected 77 Reichstag deputies in place of the 54 elected in 1928.

Attitude of Big Business

There is little evidence to support the view that Hitler received substantial financial support from big business. The conservative upper classes generally regarded Hitler as an uneducated demagogue and gutter politician.

The Emergence of Adolf Hitler (1889–1945)

Adolf Hitler, the Nazis' dynamic leader, was primarily responsible for his party's success in taking advantage of the opportunity created by the depression.

Youth and Early Career

Born in Braunau, Austria, Hitler was the son of a minor official in the Austro-Hungarian customs service. A poor student, he dropped out of secondary school and in 1907, set off for the Austrian capital of Vienna with the ambition to become an artist. The art academy refused to admit him, however, because of what it regarded as his insufficient talent. He also failed to gain admission to architectural school because he lacked a secondary-school diploma.

Political Views

Hitler lived in Vienna for several years, working at odd jobs and absorbing the ideas of Austrian right-wing extremists. In 1913, he left Vienna and moved to Munich in southern Germany. He took with him the basic political ideas to which he would remain committed for the balance of his life. Central to Hitler's thought were his notions of race. He believed in the racial superiority of the Germanic peoples (the Aryan race) and in the inferiority of other races, especially Jews but also Slavs and blacks. Hitler also advocated the Pan-German ideology that was popular among many Austrian extremists. Pan-Germanism held the view that all Germans should be united in a single state. In addition,

Hitler was hostile to the ideology of Marxism, which emphasized the unity of the international working class rather than racial solidarity.

War Experience

Life in Munich proved no easier for Hitler than it had been in Vienna. When World War I broke out, Hitler enlisted in the German army. He served on the western front in France and was evidently a good soldier, winning the Iron Cross, although he was never promoted above the rank of corporal. When the war ended, Hitler was in a military hospital, recovering from a gas attack.

The Development of the Nazi Party

Following his discharge from the army, Hitler returned to Munich where he became involved with a small, ultranationalist political group. He soon became its leader, reorganizing the group as the National Socialist German Workers' Party, known as the Nazis. As the Nazis' absolute leader (*Führer*), Hitler developed his skills as an orator in speeches denouncing the Treaty of Versailles and playing upon the emotions and prejudices of the crowds he addressed. He attracted a small number of committed followers and organized some of them into a party militia, the storm troopers, also known as the SA or Brown Shirts. Ernst Roehm (1887–1934), a former major in the German army, served as the SA's leader. Other prominent Nazis who joined the party at this time included Rudolf Hess (1894–1987), who later became the party's deputy leader, and Hermann Goering (1893–1946), a wartime aviation ace who created Germany's new *Luftwaffe* (air force) in the 1930s.

The Beer Hall Putsch

The small Nazi Party first won national attention in the Beer Hall Putsch of November 1923, when the Ruhr crisis and the great inflation were at their height. Hitler and his Nazis joined with General Erich Ludendorff (1865–1937) and his conservative nationalist followers in an attempt to seize power in Munich. (The plot got its name because it was planned in one of Munich's beer halls.) Once they had taken

Munich, Hitler and Ludendorff planned to use the Bavarian capital as a base of operations against the republican government in Berlin. The support that Hitler and Ludendorff expected to receive from some conservative Bavarian politicians failed to materialize, however, and the police easily suppressed the revolt.

Following the collapse of the Beer Hall Putsch, Hitler and Ludendorff were tried for treason. In recognition of his services to Germany during the war, Ludendorff was acquitted. The conservative judges allowed Hitler to use his trial as a propaganda forum for his ideas. Hitler was convicted but sentenced to a term of only five years. He was released after nine months.

Mein Kampf

While he was imprisoned, Hitler wrote *Mein Kampf* ("My Struggle"). In addition to presenting a semifictionalized account of his life, Hitler expounded at length on his ideas of German racial superiority, German nationalism, anti-Semitism, and anti-Marxism. In addition, the Nazi *Führer* set forth his notions of what German foreign policy ought to be. In Hitler's view, Germany was a vigorous and growing country that needed living space (*Lebensraum*). He did not believe that Germany should seek this living space through the acquisition of colonies, since Germany's former colonies had been readily seized by the Allies during World War I. Instead, Germany should find living space in the east at the expense of Russia. Before Germany could move to the east, it would first be necessary to defeat France, since the French would not sit idly by while Germany expanded. Hitler also proposed that Germany should seek alliances with Great Britain and Italy. In his view, Germany's interests did not conflict with those of the British, whose interest was focused on their empire, or the Italians, who hoped to expand in the Mediterranean area.

Hitler also decided while he was in prison to abandon any attempt to seize power by revolutionary means. Instead, he would seek to develop a mass party that could achieve power through the electoral process. During the late 1920s, however, Hitler made little progress winning mass support, although he did expand the Nazi Party's organization throughout Germany. Dr. Joseph Goebbels (1897–1945) developed the party's propaganda, while Heinrich Himmler (1900–1945) organized a second party militia, the Elite Guard (SS).

Hitler's Rise to Power

Following the elections of September 1930, Chancellor Brüning remained in power, ruling by decree in cooperation with President Hindenburg. The economic situation continued to deteriorate, and by March 1932 unemployment was over 6 million.

In the spring of 1932, Hitler decided to challenge Hindenburg for the presidency. In an effort to block Hitler, the Social Democrats, Catholic Center, and other moderate parties supported Hindenburg for reelection. Hindenburg won, polling almost 20 million votes to Hitler's 13 million.

Papen's Chancellorship

Following his reelection victory, Hindenburg dismissed Brüning from the chancellorship and named Franz von Papen (1879–1969), a conservative nationalist, to the post. Like his predecessor, Papen ruled by decree in association with the president.

In July 1932, Papen called for Reichstag elections, hoping to increase his support. Instead, the Nazis emerged as the largest party, polling 37 percent of the vote and winning 230 seats in the Reichstag.

In a final effort to increase his support in the Reichstag, Papen called new elections for November 1932. Nazi strength dropped slightly to 196 seats, while the Communists won 100 seats. Failing to win popular support, Papen resigned in early December.

Hitler's Appointment as Chancellor

As Papen's successor, Hindenburg appointed General Kurt von Schleicher (1882–1934). Earlier, Schleicher had intrigued against Papen. Now Papen intrigued against Schleicher.

Behind the scenes, Hitler and Papen developed a scheme that led to Hitler's appointment as chancellor. Hitler possessed what Papen and the conservative nationalists lacked: a broad base of popular support. Papen and his allies believed, however, that Hitler did not have the ability to rule Germany. They expected to be able to use Hitler to destroy the democratic republic and replace it with a conservative, semiauthoritarian system such as had existed before 1918. Papen agreed to Hitler's demand for the chancellorship, expecting that he, as vice chancellor, would actually govern the country. Papen then convinced Hindenburg to dismiss Schleicher. On January 30, 1933, Hindenburg named Hitler to the chancellorship, with Papen as vice chancellor. Only two other Nazis served in the eleven-member cabinet, which consisted mainly of conservative nationalists.

The Creation of the Nazi Dictatorship

After taking office as chancellor, Hitler quickly outmaneuvered Papen and the conservative nationalists.

The Reichstag Fire

A new Reichstag election was scheduled for early March 1933. Only a few days before the election, on February 27, the Reichstag building was partially destroyed by fire. The Nazis may well have set the blaze, but they blamed the Communists, charging that the Communists were plotting to seize power. Hitler convinced Hindenburg to take strong action against the supposed Communist threat, and the president suspended freedom of speech and the press and other civil liberties.

March 1933 Election

The Nazis stepped up their harassment of their political opponents, and the March 5 election was held in an atmosphere of fear and intimidation. Polling 44 percent of the votes, the Nazis won 288 seats in the Reichstag. With the support of their conservative nationalist allies, who held 52 seats, the Nazis controlled a majority of the 647-member Reichstag. The Nazi majority was even more substantial, since none of the 81 Communist deputies were allowed to take their seats.

The Enabling Act

On March 23, 1933, the Reichstag passed the Enabling Act, which gave dictatorial authority to Hitler's cabinet for four years. Armed with full powers, Hitler moved to eliminate all possible centers of opposition. His policy is known as *Gleichschaltung,* which translates literally as coordination. In this context, however, it meant more precisely subordination; that is, subordinating all independent institutions to the authority of Hitler and the Nazi Party.

Consolidation of Nazi Power

In April 1933, the government abolished self-government in the German states by appointing governors responsible to the central government in Berlin. The states lost even more power in January 1934 when the Reichsrat, the upper house of the parliament, was abolished. The Reichsrat had represented the states.

In May 1933, the Nazis ordered the abolition of the independent labor unions. Both strikes and lockouts were prohibited, and a system of compulsory arbitration of labor-management disputes was established. All workers were compelled to join the German Labor Front, an agency of the Nazi Party, which was designed primarily to promote labor discipline rather than the interests of the workers.

During the spring of 1933, the Nazis moved to eliminate opposition political parties. In July, the Nazi Party became the only legal party.

Almost a year later, on June 30, 1934, Hitler carried out a purge that took the lives of a number of dissident Nazi leaders and other opponents. The exact number of victims has never been determined, although it probably exceeded one hundred. Ernst Roehm, the SA leader, was among these victims. The influence of the SA now declined, while that of Himmler's SS, which provided the executioners for the purge, increased. Himmler also controlled the Gestapo, the secret police created by the Nazis.

Following the death of President Hindenburg on August 2, 1934, Hitler abolished the office of president and assumed the president's powers. The members of the armed forces were now required to take an oath of allegiance to Hitler. This oath represented an important step in the establishment of Hitler's control over Germany's armed forces.

Nazi Anti-Semitism

Soon after taking power in 1933, the Nazis began a campaign directed against Germany's Jews, who numbered some 600,000, about 1 percent of the population. In April 1933, Jews were deprived of their positions in the civil service. Jews were also barred from the universities, and restrictions were imposed on Jewish physicians and lawyers. The Nazis organized a nationwide boycott of shops and other businesses owned by Jews.

The Nuremberg Laws

The campaign against the Jews was intensified following the adoption of the Nuremberg Laws of 1935. These laws defined a Jew as any person with at least one Jewish grandparent. Some 2.5 million Germans, in addition to the 600,000 who regarded themselves as Jews, were affected by this definition. The Nuremberg Laws deprived Jews of their rights as citizens, and Jews were barred from marrying non-Jews.

Crystal Night

In 1938, a Polish Jew assassinated a German diplomat in Paris. In response, the Nazis organized a campaign of mob violence known as the Crystal Night, which gained its name from the broken glass resulting from the destruction of synagogues and Jewish-owned businesses. Jews were now forced to wear a yellow star of David, and the German Jewish community was compelled to pay a large indemnity.

These measures against the Jews of Germany served as a prelude to the Holocaust of World War II, when the Nazis embarked on a campaign to exterminate the Jews of Europe (see Chapter 35).

The Nazis and the Christian Churches

The failure of German Christians, both Catholics and Protestants, to offer vigorous resistance to the crimes of the Nazis in general and to their persecution of the Jews, in particular, has been the subject of much historical controversy. Nevertheless, for German Christians the Nazi era was a time of pressure and persecution.

The Evangelical Church

The Nazis attempted to subordinate the Christian churches to their control. The major Protestant denomination, the German Evangelical Church, was forced to accept the direction of a handpicked national bishop. Dissenting Protestants established the Confessing Church under the leadership of Pastor Martin Niemoeller (1892–1984). He and other dissident churchmen were imprisoned in concentration camps.

The Catholic Church

In July 1933, the Nazi regime signed a concordat with the Vatican, pledging to maintain the traditional rights of the Catholic Church in Germany. Increasing violations of the concordat led to protests from Catholic leaders. In 1937, Pope Pius XI (r. 1922–1939) joined these protests, issuing the encyclical letter *Mit Brennender Sorge* ("With Burning Concern"). For the most part, however, both Protestant and Catholic leaders sought to avoid direct confrontations with the Nazi regime.

Nazi Economic Policy

Nazi regimentation extended to the economic sphere, although the property and profits of the capitalists were protected. In practical terms, the word "socialist" in the name of the Nazi Party did not refer to the nationalization of the means of production but rather to requiring the economy to serve the interests of the state.

Hitler succeeded in reducing unemployment by initiating public works projects, including the construction of superhighways (autobahns), and establishing the Labor Service to provide jobs for young workers who could not find employment in the private sector.

In 1936, the Four Year Plan was launched with the purpose of promoting economic self-sufficiency and of mobilizing the economy for war.

The Great Depression of the early 1930s resulted in the economic and political collapse of the Weimar Republic, Germany's post-World War I experiment in democracy. Adolf Hitler demonstrated his political skill in taking advantage of the opportunity provided by the depression. He developed his Nazi Party into a mass movement and used a combination of his popular support and behind-the-scenes intrigue to propel himself into power. Once he gained office, Hitler moved with ruthless determination to crush his opponents and establish his totalitarian dictatorship.

Recommended Reading

Allen, William Sheridan. *The Nazi Seizure of Power: The Experience of a Single German Town, 1930–1935* (1965).

Angress, Werner T. *Between Fear and Hope: Jewish Youth in the Third Reich* (1988).

Balfour, Michael. *Withstanding Hitler in Germany, 1933-45* (1988).

Bracher, Karl Dietrich. *The German Dictatorship: The Origins, Structure, and Effects of National Socialism* (1970).

Broszat, Martin. *Hitler and the Collapse of Weimar Germany* (1987).

Broszat, Martin. *The Hitler State: The Foundation and Development of the Internal Structure of the Third Reich* (1981).

Bullock, Alan. *Hitler: A Study in Tyranny* (rev. ed., 1962).

Conway, J. S. *The Nazi Persecution of the Churches, 1931–45* (1968).

Craig, Gordon A. *Germany, 1866–1945* (1978).

Dorpalen, Andreas. *Hindenburg and the Weimar Republic* (1964).

Engelmann, Bernt. *In Hitler's Germany: Daily Life in the Third Reich* (1986).

Eyck, Erich. *A History of the Weimar Republic*, 2 vols. (1962).

Flood, Charles Bracelen. *Hitler: The Path to Power* (1989).

Gordon, Sarah Ann. *Hitler, Germans, and the "Jewish Question"* (1984).

Haffner, Sebastian. *The Meaning of Hitler* (1979).

Hamilton, Richard F. *Who Voted for Hitler?* (1982).

Hayes, Peter. *Industry and Ideology: IG Farben in the Nazi Era* (1987).

Hoffmann, Peter. *German Resistance to Hitler* (1988).

Höhne, Heinz. *The Order of the Death's Head* (1969).

Lewin, Ronald. *Hitler's Mistakes* (1984).

Shirer, William L. *The Rise and Fall of the Third Reich: A History of Nazi Germany* (1960).

Speier, Hans. *German White-Collar Workers and the Rise of Hitler* (1986).

Spielvogel, Jackson. *Hitler and Nazi Germany: A History* (1988).

Stephenson, Jill. *Women in Nazi Society* (1975).

Taylor, Simon. *Prelude to Genocide: Nazi Ideology and the Struggle for Power* (1985).

Turner, Henry Ashby, Jr. *German Big Business and the Rise of Hitler* (1985).

Turner, Henry Ashby, Jr. *Stresemann and the Politics of the Weimar Republic* (1963).

Waite, Robert G. L. *The Psychopathic God: Adolf Hitler* (1977).

CHAPTER 33

Great Britain and France Between the Two World Wars

Time Line

1920–1924	France is governed by the right-wing National Bloc
1921	The Irish Free State is established
1922	David Lloyd George steps down as Great Britain's prime minister
1922–1923	Great Britain is governed by the Conservative prime ministers Andrew Bonar Law and Stanley Baldwin

1924	Ramsay MacDonald heads Great Britain's first Labor government
1924–1926	France is governed by a coalition of Radicals and Socialists
1924–1929	Stanley Baldwin heads a Conservative government in Great Britain
1926–1929	Raymond Poincaré heads a National Union ministry in France
1926	A coal miners' strike leads to a general strike in Great Britain
1929–1931	Prime Minister Ramsay MacDonald heads a minority Labor government in Great Britain
1931	The British Parliament passes the Statute of Westminster
1931–1935	Ramsay MacDonald heads the National Government in Great Britain
1932–1934	France is governed by a coalition of Radicals and Socialists
1934	The Stavisky scandal rocks French politics
	A National Union ministry, headed by Gaston Doumergue, takes office in France
1935	Pierre Laval becomes France's premier
1935–1937	Stanley Baldwin serves as Britain's prime minister
1936	King Edward VIII abdicates; George VI succeeds him
	Léon Blum's Popular Front government takes power in France

| 1937 | Neville Chamberlain becomes Britain's prime minister |
| 1938 | The Popular Front collapses in France |

Following World War I, both Great Britain and France confronted serious economic problems, which became even more intense during the depression decade of the 1930s. Nevertheless, both the British and the French maintained their democratic political systems.

For Great Britain, the prolonged economic crisis was particularly serious, as the British failed to regain their once dominant position in world trade. The most significant political development in Great Britain was the decline of the Liberal Party and the emergence of Labor as one of the major parties in the British two-party system. This political shift served to make the Conservatives the predominant party for most of the interwar years.

The British also confronted imperial problems, as demands for independence mounted in Ireland, Egypt, and India, and the dominions called for greater rights of self-government.

During the 1920s, the French economy made a better recovery than that of Great Britain, but the world depression of the 1930s hit France particularly hard. The political instability that had characterized the French Third Republic since its founding in 1870 became more serious following World War I.

Great Britain

Postwar Britain

World War I had been an exhausting experience, both physical and psychological, for Great Britain. The loss of more than 900,000 dead in the war was a profound shock for the British people.

The war had been costly in economic and financial terms, as well. British economic prosperity depended on foreign trade, but the war had disrupted Britain's trade links, which could not easily be reconstructed in a disorganized world. The national debt had increased by about 1,000 percent, and British finances were under a severe strain.

The 1918 Election

In December 1918, soon after the armistice, the British held a parliamentary election. David Lloyd George (1863–1945), the wartime prime minister, led his coalition into the campaign, calling for a new mandate to strengthen his position at the coming peace conference. Known as the Khaki Election because of the large number of soldiers who voted, this election was the first time women were able to vote. A law passed earlier in the year had extended the right to vote to all men over the age of twenty-one and to women over the age of thirty. The Lloyd George coalition won an overwhelming victory.

Economic Problems

By late 1920, Britain's brief postwar economic boom was over. By March 1921, the number of unemployed had risen to over 2 million.

Attempting to cope with the recession, the Lloyd George government increased unemployment insurance payments (the dole) and secured the adoption, in June 1921, of the Safeguarding of Industries Act, which imposed a tariff on some imports. This act represented a significant departure from Great Britain's traditional policy of free trade.

Despite the government's efforts, the recession persisted and deepened, especially in Britain's basic industries: coal, iron, steel, textiles, and shipbuilding.

Politics During the 1920s

The deepening recession cost Lloyd George much of his popularity, and in October 1922, the Conservatives withdrew from the coalition. Lloyd George resigned and Andrew Bonar Law (1858–1923), the Conservative leader, became prime minister. Parliamentary elections in November gave the Conservatives solid control of the House of Commons. A split in the Liberal Party between the factions led by Lloyd George and Herbert Asquith (1852–1928) helped the Labor Party become for the first time the second-largest party in the House of Commons.

Conservative Government Under Baldwin

In May 1923, Bonar Law left the prime ministership for reasons of health and was succeeded by Stanley Baldwin (1867–1947). Baldwin decided to support a broad program of tariffs to protect British industry from foreign competition and called an election on that issue.

The First Labor Government

In the parliamentary election of December 1923, the Conservatives lost their majority in the House of Commons, although they remained the largest party. Ramsay MacDonald (1866–1937), the leader of the Labor Party, took office as prime minister in January 1924, heading a minority government that depended on the support of the Liberals in the House of Commons. This first Labor government in British history lasted less than a year.

MacDonald extended full diplomatic recognition to the Soviet Union in February, hoping that increasing trade with Russia would help promote economic recovery. In August, a trade treaty was signed with the Soviets, and there was talk of a British loan to Russia. The Liberals opposed MacDonald on this issue, and he was forced to resign. A new election was called for October 1924, the second within a year.

The publication of the so-called Zinoviev Letter by the London *Daily Mail* hurt MacDonald's campaign. This letter, purportedly written by Grigori Zinoviev, the head of the Communist International, urged Britain's Communists to work harder on behalf of the proletarian revolution. Neither MacDonald personally nor his Labor Party were sympathetic to Communism, but they had endorsed closer relations with the Soviet Union. The election resulted in a major victory for the Conservatives.

Second Baldwin Government

Stanley Baldwin began his second term as prime minister and remained in office for the next five years, until 1929. Great Britain repudiated MacDonald's trade treaty with the Soviet Union and severed diplomatic relations in 1927, following charges of Soviet espionage.

The country's major problems involved the continuing economic and financial downturn, rather than foreign affairs. Unemployment remained high, and Britain's decision to return to the gold standard in May 1925 served to constrict the economy still further.

The general strike of 1926 confronted Baldwin's government with its greatest domestic crisis of the decade. Unresolved labor-management conflict in the coal industry resulted in a coal miners' strike in May 1926. The Trades Union Congress (TUC) then called a general strike in sympathy with the miners. For nine days, most of Britain's organized workers stayed away from their jobs. The workers expected the government to give way to their demands. When it did not, the general strike quickly collapsed. The coal miners ultimately returned to work on terms set by the mine owners.

A law passed in 1928 established equal rights for voting for men and women aged twenty-one and over.

Second MacDonald Government

The Conservatives lost the parliamentary election of May 1929, and for the first time in British history, the Labor Party held the largest number of seats in the House of Commons. But as in 1924, it was not a majority. MacDonald returned to the prime ministership, heading a minority Labor government with the support of the Liberals. Labor's success at the polls came primarily at the expense of the Liberals, who continued their decline to the status of a minor third party.

As prime minister from 1929 to 1931, MacDonald's policies did not differ markedly from those of his Conservative predecessor, although he did reestablish diplomatic relations with the Soviet Union.

MacDonald and the National Government

By 1930, the effects of the world depression were evident in Great Britain. Unemployment increased, and government tax revenues declined. In a report issued in July 1931, a committee of financial experts urged drastic reductions in government expenditures, especially a cut in the dole (unemployment benefits), in order to avoid an excessive budget deficit. This proposal infuriated much of MacDonald's own Labor Party, and the cabinet was deeply divided on the issue.

In August 1931, MacDonald resigned the prime ministership but quickly returned to office at the head of a coalition known as the National Government. The coalition had the backing of the Conservatives, some Liberals, and a few Laborites who supported MacDonald, and it won an overwhelming majority of seats in the House of Commons in the October 1931 election. While MacDonald continued to hold the prime ministership, Stanley Baldwin, the Conservative leader, was the dominant figure in the National Government.

Economic Retrenchment

Pursuing a policy of retrenchment, the National Government increased taxes in an effort to make up for the loss of revenue caused by the depression and cut government spending in order to avoid a budget deficit. Interest rates were lowered, and Britain abandoned the gold standard. The British pound fell in value from $4.86 to $3.49. Devaluation failed to stimulate exports significantly, while the decrease in the pound's value wounded British pride. In an attempt to provide a protected domestic market for British industry, protective tariffs were imposed on imports in Febuary 1932. This marked a definitive end to Britain's traditional free trade policy.

Uneven Reconomic Recovery

During the early 1930s, British unemployment fell from 3 million at the end of 1932 to 2 million at the end of 1934 and to 1.6 million at the end of 1936. However, economic recovery was uneven. New light industry, the building trades, and the armaments industry showed more improvement than heavy industry, textiles, and shipbuilding, which had once been the backbone of Great Britain's industrial might.

Return of Conservative Government

In May 1935, the British people celebrated the Silver Jubilee of King George V (r. 1910–1936). MacDonald retired from the prime ministership the following month, and Stanley Baldwin succeeded him. The new government was controlled by the Conservatives, although the term National Government continued to be used. Parliamentary elections increased the Conservatives' domination of the National Government.

The Crisis of the Throne

The death of King George V in January 1936 was followed by the accession of Edward VIII. The new king was unmarried, and rumors soon spread about his relationship with Mrs. Wallis Warfield Simpson, an American divorcée. The king indicated his intention to marry Mrs.

Simpson, but the government insisted that it was inappropriate for the monarch to marry a divorcée. In December 1936, Edward VIII abdicated and was succeeded by his younger brother, the Duke of York, who became King George VI (r. 1936–1952). The former king, who became the Duke of Windsor, went into exile and married Mrs. Simpson in June 1937.

Prime Ministership of Neville Chamberlain

Shortly after the formal coronation of George VI in May 1937, Baldwin retired from the prime ministership. Neville Chamberlain (1869–1940), his successor, was well equipped by temperament and experience to deal with domestic affairs. His misfortune was that he would be compelled to face difficult issues of foreign policy (see Chapter 34).

Imperial Problems

Ireland

In the Easter Rebellion of 1916, Irish nationalists carried out a revolt against British rule. While the British succeeded in suppressing the revolt, Sinn Fein (Gaelic for "We Ourselves"), led by Eamon de Valera (1882–1975), continued to agitate for independence. Violence grew in Ireland as special British forces, known as the Black and Tans, fought the Sinn Feiners.

An act of Parliament, passed in December 1919, partitioned Ireland into a predominantly Catholic south and a predominantly Protestant north, each with its own parliament. Continued protests by Sinn Fein led to a 1921 treaty establishing a virtually independent state in the south, the Irish Free State, also known as Eire. The six counties of Northern Ireland (Ulster) remained a part of the United Kingdom.

Egypt

In 1922, the British agreed to end their protectorate over Egypt. While Egypt was now independent in principle, the British continued to exert considerable influence over Egyptian affairs.

India

In India, two major nationalist movements emerged, the predominantly Hindu Indian National Congress, led by Mohandas K. Gandhi (1869–1948) and Jawaharlal Nehru (1889–1964), and the All-India Moslem League, led by Mohammed Ali Jinnah (1876–1948). In 1935, the British approved the Government of India Act, which provided for limited Indian self-rule.

The Dominions

Although the British dominions—Canada, Australia, New Zealand, and the Union of South Africa—were self-governing in their domestic affairs, Great Britain continued to control their foreign policy. Following World War I, there was growing sentiment in the dominions for autonomy. In 1926, the Imperial Conference decided in favor of autonomy for the dominions in foreign policy questions. According to the definition of the Imperial Conference, the dominions were "autonomous communities within the British Empire, equal in status, in no way subordinate one to another."

In 1931, Parliament endorsed this definition of dominion status in the Statute of Westminster, formally declaring that no act of the British Parliament would be binding in any dominion without its express consent.

France

Postwar France

For France, World War I had been a devastating experience. Of the 8 million men mobilized, some 1.4 million had been killed, while over 3 million more had been wounded.

France had also suffered immense physical destruction. For almost four years, northern France had been a battlefield. Hundreds of cities and towns had suffered severe damage, and factories, mines, and farmland had been devastated. The cost of reconstruction was immense.

Politics in the 1920s

The election for the Chamber of Deputies in November 1919 resulted in a victory for a coalition of centrist and rightist parties, the National Bloc, which dominated the French government until 1924. Aristide Briand (1862–1932) and Raymond Poincaré (1860–1934) were the leading figures in the government.

The National Bloc pursued a hard line toward Germany. When Germany defaulted on its reparations payments in 1922, France occupied the Ruhr (see Chapter 32).

On the left, the major event in the early 1920s was the split in the Socialist Party, which occurred in 1920. Left-wing Socialists formed the French Communist Party, which became increasingly subordinate to control from Moscow. The reorganized Socialist Party supported moderate, reformist policies.

The Left Cartel

In May 1924, a coalition of Socialists and Radicals, the Left Cartel (*Cartel des Gauches*), won the election for the Chamber of Deputies. Edouard Herriot (1872–1957), a leader of the Radicals, became premier. While tension with Germany eased, the Left Cartel proved as incapable as the National Bloc had been in coping with the problems of inflation, the national debt, and the unbalanced budget. The Left Cartel was troubled, in particular, by deep disagreements between the Socialists and the Radicals. The Socialists favored a tax on capital owned by the wealthy, increases in direct taxes, and lower interest rates on government bonds. Despite their name, the Radicals were relatively conservative on economic questions. They advocated budget cuts and modest increases in indirect taxes in an effort to cope with the government's financial problems.

As the deadlock between the Socialists and Radicals continued, inflation became more serious. Cabinet instability was worse than usual, and from April 1925 to June 1926, there were six cabinets.

Poincaré and the National Union Government

In an effort to restore some semblance of order to French politics and finances, the parliament granted extraordinary powers to a National Union ministry headed by Raymond Poincaré, which took office in July

1926. Poincaré, who had a reputation for financial expertise, won the support of the Radicals and the centrist and rightist parties for his program of cutting government spending and increasing taxes.

During the late 1920s, the French economy experienced a substantial recovery. There was a high level of employment, and the reconstruction of the war-devastated areas of the country was completed. However, subsequent events revealed that the recovery was only temporary.

Depression Politics

Poincaré's conservative successors governed France from 1929 to 1932. Without Poincaré's firm leadership, however, cabinet instability returned. This instability resulted from the multiparty system and the lack of discipline within parties.

As the great depression began to engulf the world, France appeared at first to be immune. The French economy possessed a good balance between industry and agriculture and did not feel an immediate impact from the economic downturn. By 1932, however, France was hit hard by the depression.

Return of the Left Cartel

The Left Cartel, the Radical and Socialist coalition, won a majority of seats in the Chamber of Deputies in the May 1932 election. Once again, as following the leftist victory in 1924, the Radical Edouard Herriot became premier. Having cooperated in order to win the election, the Radicals and Socialists continued to find it difficult to agree on policy. This discord led to continuing cabinet instability. From December 1932 to February 1934, five weak cabinets, all headed by Radicals, attempted to govern the country.

The Stavisky Scandal

In early 1934, scandal rocked the French political world. Serge Stavisky, who had cheated investors out of millions of francs, had allegedly been protected by a number of politicians, including several leading Radicals. Whether Stavisky committed suicide in order to avoid arrest or was murdered to prevent him from revealing his political connections has never been determined. In protest against the corruption and ineffectiveness of the Third Republic, ultra-right-wing political groups organized a great demonstration in Paris on February 6, 1934. The demonstration quickly turned into a riot when the demonstrators attempted to storm the Chamber of Deputies building.

National Union Ministry

In the wake of the Stavisky scandal, the Left Cartel collapsed and the parliament established a National Union ministry headed by Gaston Doumergue (1863–1937), a former president. The Doumergue cabinet was in power for most of 1934 and provided French political life with a degree of much-needed respectability. The National Union ministry did little, however, to cope with the intensifying economic crisis.

Laval's Premiership

During 1935, Pierre Laval (1883–1945) was the dominant figure in the French government, serving as premier from May until January 1936. The depression reached its lowest point, with total industrial production well below the 1913 level. Laval cut government expenditures and maintained the gold standard. While the index of industrial production showed a modest increase, other economic indicators failed to improve.

The Popular Front

The Popular Front, a coalition of Radicals, Socialists, and Communists, won a majority in the Chamber of Deputies in the May 1936 election. Although the Communists declined to take seats in the cabinet, they agreed to support the program of the Popular Front government headed by the Socialist leader, Léon Blum (1872–1950).

Reforms

The Popular Front carried out a number of reforms. Labor unions won the right to collective bargaining, and wages were increased by about 12 percent. The forty-hour workweek and paid vacations for workers were established. Compulsory arbitration of labor-management disputes was instituted. The Bank of France was nationalized, as was some of the armaments industry. Conflict between the Socialists and Radicals continued, however, and the Popular Front failed to produce any real solution to France's basic economic problems. In June 1937, Blum resigned. The Popular Front survived for another year until it fell apart in the spring of 1938.

Effects of Popular Front

When the Popular Front government was established, a great sense of hope had come to the workers of France, while conservatives had stood in fear of a revolution. Nothing happened to justify either the hopes or fears. In the long run, the failure of the Popular Front benefited the Communists, since it seemed to prove what they had been insisting: The only way to bring real change in France was to begin with a revolution that would completely shake up the country's economic and social structure. This attitude contributed to the emergence of a powerful Communist Party in France following World War II.

Daladier's Premiership

In April 1938, the Radical Edouard Daladier (1884–1970) became premier, heading a coalition of the Radicals with the centrist parties. Like Chamberlain in Great Britain, Daladier had to focus his attention on the deteriorating international situation.

The depression decade had a powerful negative impact on both Great Britain and France. In neither country was the government able to develop policies that led to a substantial economic recovery or a decrease in unemployment.

Despite economic problems and the decline of the Liberal Party and the emergence of Labor as one of the country's two major parties, Great Britain experienced general political stability. However, Great Britain failed to produce leaders of great stature.

France also lacked outstanding leaders, and the Great Depression undermined the already shaky political structure of the Third Republic. Cabinet instability became an increasingly familiar feature of the political scene. The experiment of the Popular Front from 1936 to 1938 proved a particular disappointment and left France more deeply divided than ever on the eve of World War II.

Recommended Reading

Ball, Stuart. *Baldwin and the Conservative Party: The Crisis of 1929–1931* (1988).

Branson, Noreen. *Britain in the Nineteen Twenties* (1976).

Branson, Noreen and Margot Heinemann. *Britain in the Nineteen Thirties* (1971).

Bryan, J., III and Charles J. V. Murphy. *The Windsor Story* (1979).

Cobban, Alfred. *A History of Modern France,* vol. III (1965).

Colton, Joel. *Léon Blum: Humanist in Politics* (1966).

Feiling, Keith. *The Life of Neville Chamberlain* (1946).

Graves, Robert and Alan Hodge. *The Long Weekend: A Social History of Great Britain, 1918–1939* (1941).

Greene, Nathanael. *From Versailles to Vichy: The Third French Republic, 1919–1940* (1970).

Harr, Karl G. *The Genesis and Effect of the Popular Front in France* (1987).

James, Robert Rhodes. *The British Revolution, 1880–1939* (1977).

Jarman, J. L. *A Short History of Twentieth-Century England* (1963).

Kitchen, Martin. *Europe Between the Wars: A Political History* (1988).

Middlemas, Keith and John Barnes. *Baldwin: A Biography* (1970).

Taylor, A. J. P. *English History, 1919–1945* (1965).

Thomson, David. *England in the Twentieth Century, 1914-63* (1965).

Wright, Gordon. *France in Modern Times: From the Enlightenment to the Present* (4th ed., 1987).

CHAPTER 34

The Coming of the Second World War

Time Line

1922	The Washington Conference produces an agreement on naval disarmament
1924	The adoption of the Dawes Plan ends the Ruhr crisis
1925	Germany, France, Great Britain, and Italy sign the Locarno Pact
1928	Over sixty nations sign the Kellogg-Briand Pact
1929	The Young Plan eases Germany's reparations burden

1931	Japan invades Manchuria
1933	Adolf Hitler withdraws Germany from the League of Nations and the Disarmament Conference
1935	Hitler denounces the disarmament clauses of the Treaty of Versailles
	Italy invades Ethiopia
1936	Germany remilitarizes the Rhineland
	The Spanish Civil War begins
	Germany and Italy form the Rome-Berlin Axis
1937	Japan attacks China
1938	Germany annexes Austria
	The Munich Conference awards the Sudetenland to Germany
1939	Hitler destroys Czechoslovakia
	Great Britain and France pledge to aid Poland
	Germany and Italy sign the Pact of Steel
	Germany and the Soviet Union sign a Nonaggression Pact
	Germany invades Poland

During the early 1920s, France's fear of a resurgence of German power contributed to tension in European international relations. This tension gradually eased, however, and an atmosphere of optimism prevailed during the second half of the decade. Nevertheless, few of the serious problems left by the peace settlement of 1919–1920 had been solved, and the 1930s proved to be a decade of intensifying crisis.

Soon after taking power in 1933, Adolf Hitler seized the initiative in foreign affairs and met remarkably little resistance from Great Britain and France. The French failure to resist Germany resulted in large part from their awareness of their own relative weakness. France believed it could act to contain Hitler only with the full support of the British. In Great Britain, however, there was a widespread belief that the Treaty of Versailles had been unduly harsh and that it should be revised in Germany's favor. In addition, in both of the Western democracies intense memories of the carnage of World War I created a powerful desire to do everything possible to avoid another conflict.

The French Search for Security

The French search for security in the face of a possible German resurgence was the central issue in European international relations during the 1920s. In their pursuit of security, the French established a new system of alliances, signing treaties with Belgium in 1920 and Poland in 1921.

The Little Entente

The Eastern European states of Czechoslovakia, Rumania, and Yugoslavia created the Little Entente in the early 1920s. The French then formed ties with the Little Entente states, signing alliances with Czechoslovakia in 1924, Rumania in 1926, and Yugoslavia in 1927.

Relations with Germany

In January 1923, French troops occupied the Ruhr valley, following the Germans' default on their reparations payments. In the mid–1920s, however, tensions between France and Germany eased. The Dawes Plan of 1924, an agreement on reparations, ended the Ruhr crisis, and the Young Plan of 1929 further reduced the conflict over reparations. In the Locarno Pact of 1925, Germany and France agreed to recognize the permanence of their frontiers, and Germany entered the League of Nations the following year. In 1930, the Allies ended their occupation of the Rhineland (see Chapter 32).

The Kellogg-Briand Pact

The signing of the Kellogg-Briand Pact of 1928, officially known as the Pact of Paris, suggested to many the dawning of a new age of international harmony. Some sixty countries ultimately signed this treaty, which bore the names of the American secretary of state and the French foreign minister, pledging to renounce war as an instrument of national policy. Events would soon demonstrate how little this noble renunciation meant.

Disarmament in the 1920s

The question of disarmament attracted considerable attention during the postwar decade.

The Washington Conference

The Washington Conference of 1921–1922 produced the Five Power Treaty, which limited capital ships (battleships) in a tonnage ratio of 5:5:3 for Great Britain, the United States, and Japan, and 1.67:1.67 for France and Italy. The Five Power Treaty slowed the naval race, even though it did not place any limits on lesser categories of ships.

The London Conference

At the London Conference of 1930, Great Britain, the United States, and Japan achieved limited agreements on the construction of cruisers, destroyers, and submarines, but France and Italy refused to participate in the accord.

The Geneva Conference

An international conference on the limitation of land armaments met in Geneva, Switzerland, in February 1932. By this point, the international situation had already begun to deteriorate, and the Geneva Disarmament Conference failed to produce any agreements prior to its collapse in 1933.

The Manchurian Crisis

In September 1931, Japan invaded Manchuria, a region of northeastern China. Charging Japan with aggression, the Chinese appealed to the League of Nations. When a League investigating committee condemned the Japanese use of force, Japan responded by withdrawing from the League of Nations. Having conquered Manchuria, the Japanese reorganized it as the puppet state of Manchukuo.

In the Manchurian crisis, the League of Nations faced and failed the first major test of its ability to take action against aggression. Many observers later regarded the Japanese takeover of Manchuria as the opening round of World War II.

In 1937, Japan attacked China proper, beginning a war that would continue until Japan's final defeat in 1945.

Hitler's Early Foreign Policy

A downturn in European international relations began soon after Adolf Hitler came to power in Germany in January 1933. At first, Hitler had to proceed with caution; Germany was not yet strong enough to risk provoking a strong response from Great Britain and France.

Charging that the World War I allies were not willing to treat Germany as an equal, Hitler withdrew Germany from both the League of Nations and the Geneva Disarmament Conference in October 1933. The German leader expressed his commitment to the cause of peace, however, and pledged to cooperate with other countries if they were prepared to recognize German equality.

Attempted Nazi Coup in Austria

In July 1934, Austrian Nazis attempted to seize power in Vienna. The attempt failed, although Engelbert Dollfuss (1892–1934), the Austrian chancellor, was killed. Kurt von Schuschnigg (1897–1977) took office as Dollfuss's successor. The strongest reaction to the events in Austria came from Benito Mussolini, the Italian dictator. Mussolini sent troops to the Austrian border and was prepared to intervene if necessary, believing that if Austria were joined with Germany, Italy's interests would be threatened. Hitler, however, denied any involvement with the events in Austria.

German Rearmament

In March 1935, Hitler moved more boldly, flouting the disarmament clauses of the Treaty of Versailles by reintroducing military conscription and proclaiming the existence of a German air force, both of which were prohibited by the treaty. The League of Nations condemned Hitler's actions in April.

The Stresa Front and the Anglo-German Naval Treaty

Concerned about Germany's intentions, British, French, and Italian representatives met at Stresa to discuss the possibility of joint action to contain Hitler. Nothing substantial came of this so-called Stresa Front, however. Instead, the British sought to win Hitler's agreement to a limitation of German naval expansion. The Anglo-German Naval Treaty of June 1935 provided that Germany would limit its navy to 35 percent of the British fleet. While this accord provided reassurances to the British, their acceptance of Germany's abrogation of the disarmament clauses of the Treaty of Versailles angered the French.

Italian Aggression in Ethiopia

In October 1935, Mussolini embarked on a war of aggression against Ethiopia. In the 1890s, Italy had attempted to conquer Ethiopia but had been defeated at the Battle of Adowa in 1896. Seizing Ethiopia would avenge that defeat.

League of Nations Action

In response to the Italian attack, Ethiopia's Emperor Haile Selassie (r. 1930–1974) appealed to the League of Nations, which branded Italy as an aggressor. The League also imposed limited economic sanctions on Italy, placing an embargo on the shipment of some goods to Italy. However, no embargo was placed on oil, which Italy desperately needed to continue its aggression. Having failed to take any effective action against Italy's aggression, the League of Nations, in effect, ceased to function. By May 1936, the Italians had completed their conquest of Ethiopia.

Remilitarization of the Rhineland

In March 1936, Hitler remilitarized the Rhineland, thereby violating the terms of both the Treaty of Versailles and the Locarno Pact.

The German dictator took a chance by moving his troops into the Rhineland. At this point, the French could have forced a German withdrawal. But Hitler was proved correct in his belief that the French—and the British, as well—were unlikely to take any action other than to protest.

The Spanish Civil War

In July 1936, a civil war broke out in Spain, marking a culmination of several years of unrest in that country.

Left-Right Conflict

In 1931, a Spanish republic had been proclaimed, replacing the monarchy of King Alfonso XIII (r. 1886–1931). While Spain's liberals and radicals supported the republic, it was vigorously opposed by conservative elements, including the landowners, industrialists, the army, and most of the Roman Catholic Church. Hostility between the republic's supporters and opponents intensified, and each side carried out acts of violence against the other.

In February 1936, the left-wing Popular Front won the parliamentary election. While relatively moderate elements controlled the republican government, ultraradical supporters of the Popular Front increased their violent attacks on conservative political leaders and the Catholic Church, provoking violent retaliation from the conservatives.

Nationalist Revolt

As Spain degenerated into increasing chaos, the leaders of the army launched a revolt against the republican government in July 1936. General Francisco Franco (1892–1975) soon emerged as the leader of the rebels, who were known as the Nationalists.

Great Britain and France joined in urging a policy of nonintervention in Spain, but Italy and Germany began providing aid to the

Nationalists, while the Soviet Union assisted the Loyalists, the supporters of the republic.

Franco's Victory

The Nationalists gradually increased their control of Spain. In early 1939, they captured Barcelona and Madrid, the last two Loyalist strongholds, and Franco became Spain's dictator. The victory of Franco and the Nationalists was generally regarded as a victory for Hitler and Mussolini and a defeat for the cause of the democracies.

The Rome-Berlin-Tokyo Axis

Anglo-French opposition to Italy's aggression in Ethiopia had enraged Mussolini and encouraged him to draw closer to Hitler, as did the fact that both Italy and Germany supported the Nationalist cause in Spain. In October 1936, Germany and Italy proclaimed the formation of the Rome-Berlin Axis. While this was not a formal alliance, it clearly indicated the shift in Italian foreign policy.

In November 1936, Germany and Japan signed an agreement known as the Anti-Comintern Pact, in which they pledged to cooperate in opposition to Communism and the activities of the Communist International (the Comintern). Italy joined the Anti-Comintern Pact in November 1937, thereby bringing the Rome-Berlin-Tokyo Axis into being. This represented the creation of a powerful bloc opposed to the maintenance of the international status quo.

German Annexation of Austria

In early 1938, Hitler moved against Austria. In mid-February, he summoned Austrian Chancellor Schuschnigg to his retreat at Bechtesgaden in the Bavarian Alps. He bullied the Austrian leader, forcing him to grant amnesty to imprisoned Austrian Nazis and to appoint Arthur Seyss-Inquart (1892–1946), an Austrian Nazi, as minister of the interior.

On March 9, Schuschnigg scheduled a plebiscite to give the Austrian people an opportunity to express their support of independence. This action enraged Hitler, who demanded that Schuschnigg postpone the plebiscite. In the face of mounting German pressure, Schuschnigg resigned. Seyss-Inquart became chancellor and invited German troops to enter Austria. On March 13, the German annexation (*Anschluss*) of Austria was proclaimed. A plebiscite in April produced an overwhelming majority in favor of the *Anschluss*. Once again, the Western democracies took no action.

The Czechoslovak Crisis

Sudeten German Demands

Soon after his absorption of Austria, Hitler turned his attention to Czechoslovakia, encouraging discontent among the German-speaking minority of the Sudetenland, located along the Czechoslovak border with Germany. In April 1938, the pro-Nazi Sudeten German party, led by Konrad Henlein (1898–1945), issued the Karlsbad program, demanding autonomy for the Sudetenland. When the Czechoslovak government refused to make concessions to the Sudeten Germans, Nazi-inspired demonstrations increased.

During the summer of 1938, the Czech crisis intensified. On September 7, acting on orders from Hitler, the Sudeten Germans broke off negotiations with the Czech government. On September 12, Hitler demanded the right of self-determination for the Sudeten Germans and threatened intervention in Czechoslovakia. The following day, Henlein called for the German annexation of the Sudetenland.

Chamberlain's Meetings with Hitler

In an effort to resolve the crisis, British prime minister Neville Chamberlain (1869–1940) proposed a meeting with Hitler. Chamberlain pursued a policy of appeasement, based on the mistaken belief that Hitler's demands were fundamentally just and that, if these demands were satisfied, Hitler would act as a responsible statesman and peace in Europe would be assured. Chamberlain's error was his failure to realize that Hitler's lust for conquest was incapable of being satisfied and that to give way in face of his demands would serve only to increase his appetite.

Berchtesgaden

On September 15, 1938, Chamberlain flew to Germany and conferred with Hitler at Berchtesgaden. During this meeting, Hitler demanded the German annexation of the Sudetenland. If this demand was not met, he threatened to go to war against Czechoslovakia.

Following this meeting, Chamberlain consulted with the French, convincing them to abandon their alliance with Czechoslovakia, and then began efforts to persuade the Czech government to give way to Hitler's demands. The French doubted the wisdom of Chamberlain's appeasement policy, but they were also concerned about France's relative weakness. They believed they had no choice but to follow Britain's lead. If they did not, and if war with Germany resulted, the French feared that the British would not support them.

Bad Godesberg

Chamberlain returned to Germany and met with Hitler on September 22 at Bad Godesberg on the Rhine. The British prime minister was shocked to discover that Hitler now had further demands. Germany's annexation of the Sudetenland would not be sufficient. Hitler insisted that Germany's forces enter the Sudetenland no later than October 1 and that the Czechs, when they withdrew, leave all their installations intact. In addition, the claims of Poland and Hungary against Czechoslovakia must be satisfied.

The Munich Conference

Czechoslovakia refused to give way to Hitler's demands, and for a few days, war seemed inevitable. In a final, desperate attempt to preserve peace, Chamberlain asked Hitler for another meeting. At Mussolini's suggestion, Hitler invited Chamberlain, Premier Edouard Daladier of France, and the Italian dictator to meet with him in Munich.

The Munich conference convened on September 29, 1938. Great Britain and France faced the choice of either sacrificing Czechoslovakia or risking war. They decided to sacrifice Czechoslovakia. The Munich agreement, signed in the early hours of September 30, granted Hitler's demand for the immediate annexation of the Sudetenland. The states-men at Munich did not consult Czechoslovakia, which had no choice but to accept the decision. Later adjustments gave the Teschen region of Czechoslovakia to Poland, while Hungary acquired southern Slovakia and Ruthenia.

Hitler's Destruction of Czechoslovakia

In mid-March 1939, Hitler destroyed what was left of Czechos-lovakia. Germany established its control over the western provinces of Bohemia and Moravia, while Slovakia became a separate puppet state. Hitler's action angered Chamberlain, who belatedly recognized that the German dictator's aggressive desires had no limits. Abandoning the policy of appeasement, Great Britain and France now pledged to come to the aid of Poland in the event of a German attack.

Mussolini's Conquest of Albania

Mussolini was jealous of Hitler's gains and sought to achieve a success of his own. On April 7, 1939, the Italians invaded Albania and soon conquered this small country. In May, Italy and Germany signed a full military alliance, which Mussolini dubbed the Pact of Steel.

The Polish Crisis and the Outbreak of War

German Demands on Poland

In April 1939, soon after his destruction of Czechoslovakia, Hitler ordered his military chiefs to prepare for an attack on Poland by September 1. Hitler began to make demands that he believed Poland would not accept: the return of the free city of Danzig to Germany, new access routes to East Prussia across the Polish Corridor, and improved treatment of the German minority in Poland.

As German pressure on Poland mounted during the spring and summer, Great Britain and France made a halfhearted attempt to form an alliance with the Soviet Union. On the one hand, the British and French wanted Soviet assistance in the event of war with Germany. On the other hand, the Western powers feared an expansion of Soviet power and Communism in Eastern Europe, and Poland was unwilling to allow Soviet troops into its territory. The Soviets, for their part, remained suspicious of the intentions of the Western powers.

German-Soviet Nonaggression Pact

As negotiations between the Soviets and the Western powers lagged, German-Soviet talks got under way. On August 23, 1939, Germany and the Soviet Union signed a Nonaggression Pact, which is often called the Hitler-Stalin Pact. A secret agreement accompanying the pact provided that, in the event of war between Germany and Poland, the Soviets would receive eastern Poland and a sphere of influence in Eastern Europe in return for their neutrality.

The Soviet commitment to remain neutral meant that Hitler did not face the danger of war on two fronts. With this threat removed, the German dictator could begin his war.

Declarations of War

On September 1, 1939, Germany invaded Poland. Two days later, on September 3, Great Britain and France fulfilled their guarantees of Poland and declared war on Germany. The Second World War had begun.

The outbreak of war in September 1939 marked the end of what has been called "the twenty years' truce."

The peace settlement following World War I had created much dissatisfaction, especially in Germany and Italy, while in Asia, Japan continued to harbor aggressive designs on China. Great Britain and France, the major European Allies of World War I, bore the primary responsibility for maintaining the post-World War I peace settlement. Their failure to cooperate in meeting this responsibility contributed to the outbreak of a new and greater world conflict. Nevertheless, when war came, it came as the result of the deliberate aggression of the Axis powers, Germany, Italy, and Japan.

Recommended Reading

Baer, George W. *The Coming of the Italian-Ethiopian War* (1967).

Baer, George W. *Test Case: Italy, Ethiopia, and the League of Nations* (1976).

Barnhart, Michael A. *Japan Prepares for Total War: The Search for Economic Security, 1919–1941* (1987).

Baumont, Maurice. *The Origins of the Second World War* (1978).

Gilbert, Martin and Richard Gott. *The Appeasers* (2nd ed., 1967).

Iriye, Akira. *The Origins of the Second World War in Asia and the Pacific* (1987).

Jacobson, Jon. *Locarno Diplomacy: Germany and the West, 1925–1929* (1972).

Kindermann, Gottfried Karl. *Hitler's Defeat in Austria, 1933–1934: Europe's First Containment of Nazi Expansionism* (1988).

Lafore, Laurence. *The End of Glory: An Interpretation of the Origins of World War II* (1970).

Luza, Radomir. *Austro-German Relations in the Anschluss Era* (1975).

Marks, Sally. *The Illusion of Peace: International Relations in Europe, 1918–1933* (1976).

Read, Anthony and David Fisher. *The Deadly Embrace: Hitler, Stalin, and the Nazi-Soviet Pact, 1939–1941* (1988).

Sontag, Raymond J. *A Broken World, 1919–1939* (1971).

Taylor, Telford. *Munich: The Price of Peace* (1979).

Thomas, Hugh. *The Spanish Civil War* (1961).

Thorne, Christopher. *The Approach of War, 1938–1939* (rev. ed., 1973).

Weinberg, Gerhard. *The Foreign Policy of Hitler's Germany: Diplomatic Revolution in Europe, 1933–1936* (1970).

Weinberg, Gerhard. *The Foreign Policy of Hitler's Germany: Starting World War II, 1937–1939* (1980).

Wiskemann, Elizabeth. *The Rome-Berlin Axis: A History of the Relations Between Hitler and Mussolini* (rev. ed., 1966).

Wyden, Peter. *The Passionate War: The Narrative History of the Spanish Civil War, 1936–1939* (1983).

CHAPTER 35

The Second World War

Time Line

1939	Germany invades Poland
	Great Britain and France declare war on Germany
1940	The Germans conquer Denmark and Norway
	The Germans overrun the Netherlands, Belgium, and Luxembourg
	Italy enters the war as Germany's ally
	France signs an armistice with Germany
	The German *Luftwaffe* begins the Battle of Britain

	The Italians invade Egypt and Greece
1941	The Germans send Rommel's Afrika Korps to North Africa
	The Germans overrun Yugoslavia and Greece
	Germany invades the Soviet Union
	The Japanese attack Pearl Harbor
	The Red Army defeats the Germans in the Battle of Moscow
1942	The Japanese take the Philippines and advance into Southeast Asia
	American marines land on Guadalcanal, beginning the island-hopping campaign in the Pacific
	American and British forces land in French North Africa
1943	Roosevelt and Churchill meet at Casablanca
	The Battle of Stalingrad ends in a German defeat
	German and Italian forces in Tunisia surrender to the Allies
	American and British troops invade Sicily and Italy
	Roosevelt, Churchill, and Stalin meet at Teheran
1944	The Western Allies launch the invasion of Normandy
	General Douglas MacArthur's troops land in the Philippines
1945	Roosevelt, Churchill, and Stalin meet at Yalta
	Germany surrenders

The last of the wartime Big Three conferences
meets in Potsdam

Japan surrenders

---

*The Second World War was truly a global conflict. During its first
years, from 1939 to 1942, the Axis powers—Germany, Italy, and
Japan—won a series of impressive victories in Europe, North Africa,
Asia, and the Pacific. Then the tide began to turn as the Allies, led by
the United States, Great Britain, and the Soviet Union, pushed forward
to victory.*

Hitler's March of Conquest, 1939–1940

The Polish Campaign

The Second World War began with Germany's attack on Poland
on September 1, 1939, and the British and French declarations of war
on Germany two days later. In their onslaught against Poland, the
Germans demonstrated the effectiveness of their *Blitzkrieg* ("lightning
war") technique, the use of tanks and airplanes to support the infantry.
In less than a month, Poland was crushed. In accordance with his pact
with Hitler, Stalin invaded Poland from the east on September 17. At
the end of the month, the Germans and Soviets partitioned Poland.

The Soviet Sphere of Influence

While the Soviets stood apart from the main conflict, they moved
to establish a sphere of influence in Eastern Europe.

On November 30, 1939, the Soviet Union began the Winter War
against Finland. While the Finns resisted with bravery and determination, they could not repel the overwhelming power of the Red Army.
When the war ended in March 1940, Finland was forced to cede some
16,000 square miles of territory to the Soviet Union, primarily in Karelia
near the Soviet city of Leningrad.

In the spring of 1940, the Soviets annexed the Baltic states (Estonia,

Latvia, and Lithuania). They also forced Rumania to cede the province of Bessarabia.

The Phony War

The war in the West during the winter of 1939–1940 became known as the Phony War. Hitler did not carry out his anticipated offensive against France, nor did the Anglo-French Allies move against Germany. From their experience in World War I, the French had concluded that in a future war the advantage would lie with the defense. They had built the Maginot Line, a line of fortifications along their frontier with Germany, and hoped to be able to repulse a German attack.

Hitler's Scandinavian Campaign

On April 9, 1940, the Germans invaded Denmark and Norway. This move into Scandinavia was designed to provide a secure route for the shipment of iron ore from neutral Sweden through Norway's coastal waters to Germany.

The Germans occupied Denmark almost immediately. In Norway, the Germans had the assistance of Vidkun Quisling (1887–1945), a pro-Nazi Norwegian, whose name quickly became a synonym for traitor. The British failed in their effort to relieve Norway.

Britain's failure in Scandinavia led to a debate in the House of Commons on Prime Minister Neville Chamberlain's conduct of the war. Facing considerable opposition, Chamberlain stepped down. On May 10, 1940, Winston Churchill (1874–1965) became prime minister. Earlier, in March, Paul Reynaud (1878–1966) had replaced Edouard Daladier (1884–1970) as France's premier.

The War in the West, 1940

On May 10, 1940, Hitler's long-awaited assault on Western Europe began, as the Germans overran Luxembourg and invaded the Netherlands and Belgium. The attack on the Low Countries outflanked the Maginot Line.

Surrender of the Netherlands and Belgium

Once again, the German *Blitzkrieg* proved irresistible. The Netherlands fell after five days. When Belgium surrendered at the end of May, a large Allied army was left stranded along the Belgian-French border near the English Channel. Between May 26 and June 4, the British succeeded in evacuating some 338,000 troops, two-thirds of them British, from the beaches of Dunkirk.

The Fall of France

On June 5, the Battle of France began. On June 10, Italy entered the war. When the war began, Italy, unprepared to fight a major war, had declared its nonbelligerency. Mussolini had grown jealous of Hitler's gains, however, and wanted to share in the spoils of victory.

On June 14, the Germans took Paris. The French government had fled south, and on June 16, after the French cabinet decided to seek an armistice, Premier Reynaud resigned. France's new government, headed by Marshal Henri Philippe Pétain (1856–1951), signed an armistice with the Germans on June 22.

The Vichy Government

Under the terms of the armistice, Germany occupied northern and western France. Unoccupied France was ruled by a collaborationist government, headed by Pétain, with its capital at Vichy in central France.

The Free French

On the eve of the French surrender, General Charles de Gaulle (1890–1970) went to London, where he established the Free French movement, a government-in-exile committed to continuing the war.

The Battles of Britain and the Atlantic

The Battle of Britain

After the fall of France, Great Britain stood alone in the struggle against Hitler's Germany.

The RAF Against the Luftwaffe

Hitler began planning for Operation Sea Lion, his invasion of England. In order for the Germans to launch this invasion, it would be necessary for the *Luftwaffe*, the German air force, to win control of the air space over the English Channel and southern England. During the first phase of the Battle of Britain, in August and September 1940, the *Luftwaffe* attempted to destroy Britain's Royal Air Force (RAF) and its bases. The RAF benefited from both the courage and determination of its pilots and from the newly invented radar warning system. The Germans suffered heavy losses.

The Bombing of British Cities

Frustrated in their effort to win control of the air, the Germans bombed London and other British cities in an effort to destroy industry and to weaken civilian morale. The effort failed.

Hitler's Diversion to Russia

Hitler was not unduly troubled by his failure in the Battle of Britain. By the late summer of 1940, the Nazi leader was already deeply involved in his planning for Operation Barbarossa, the invasion of the Soviet Union scheduled for the spring of 1941. He believed that the British might soon be forced to make peace on his terms. If they did not, they would have no choice but to surrender once the Soviets had been defeated.

The Battle of the Atlantic

The German submarine fleet in the North Atlantic presented a serious threat to Great Britain. The ability of the British to remain in the war depended on imports of food and war materials, but German submarines were sinking Allied shipping faster than it could be replaced.

American Aid to Great Britain

Following the fall of France, the United States increased its assistance to Great Britain. In September 1940, the United States gave fifty old American destroyers to the British in exchange for ninety-nine-year leases on British bases in the Western Hemisphere. The Lend-Lease Act of March 1941 authorized the President to provide aid to "any country whose defense the President deems vital to the defense of the United States." In September, American ships began to convoy British ships in the North Atlantic, and during September and October, German submarines sank one American destroyer and attacked two others.

Following the American entry into the war in December 1941, the United States stepped up its efforts in the Battle of the Atlantic.

Allied Victory in the Atlantic

The first turning point in the Battle of the Atlantic came in November 1942, the last month in which the Allied loss of ships exceeded new construction. The second came in May 1943, the first time the Germans lost more submarines than they were able to put into service.

Victory in the Atlantic made possible the unimpeded shipment of manpower and supplies from the United States to the European and Mediterranean theaters of war.

The War in the Mediterranean

North African Campaigns

Italian Failures in Africa

Italy's entry into the war endangered British control of the eastern Mediterranean. In September 1940, the Italians invaded Egypt from their colony in Libya, hoping to advance to the Suez Canal. The British drove the invaders back. Early in 1941, the British conquered Italy's East African Empire, occupying Italian Somaliland, Eritrea, and Ethiopia.

Rommel's Campaign

In order to stave off an Italian collapse in North Africa, the Germans, in early 1941, dispatched the Afrika Korps, commanded by Field Marshal Erwin Rommel (1891–1944), nicknamed the Desert Fox. In April 1941, Rommel's troops and their Italian allies renewed the attack, pushing the British back into Egypt. At this point, Hitler was committed in the Balkans and was preparing his assault on the Soviet Union. Reinforcements were not sent to Rommel, who was unable to follow up on his successful advance.

During late 1941 and early 1942, the British again moved into Libya. An Axis counterattack pushed them back, however, and by summer, Rommel had reached El Alamein, about sixty miles west of Alexandria, posing a serious threat to the Suez Canal. By this time, Hitler was deeply involved in a new offensive in Russia, and once again reinforcements were not sent to Rommel. In late October, Field Marshal Bernard Montgomery's (1887–1976) British Eighth Army counterattacked, forcing Rommel's forces to retreat.

Allied Victory in North Africa

On November 8, 1942, Anglo-American forces, commanded by General Dwight D. Eisenhower (1890–1969), carried out Operation Torch, the invasion of Morocco and Algeria in French North Africa. The German and Italian defenders were caught in a squeeze as Eisenhower's forces advanced from the west and the British pressed forward from the east. In May 1943, the remaining 250,000 Axis defenders surrendered in Tunisia.

The Invasion of Sicily and Italy

Downfall of Mussolini

Victory in North Africa led to the Anglo-American decision to invade Sicily and Italy. The invasion of Sicily in July 1943 was followed by the Italians' overthrow of Mussolini the same month. Conquering Sicily, the American and British armies invaded Italy at the beginning of September. The new Italian government surrendered on September 3. The Germans had anticipated the surrender, however, and quickly took control of about two-thirds of the country.

The Italian Campaign

For the Allies, the Italian campaign proved long and frustrating. The Allies did not take Rome until June 4, 1944, only two days before the invasion of Normandy. The war in Italy lasted until the spring of 1945, ending only a few days before the final German surrender.

Hitler's Balkan Campaign

Just as Mussolini's defeat in Egypt drew the Germans into North Africa, so, too, did Italian setbacks pull Hitler into the Balkans in early 1941.

Having watched Hitler's march of conquest in the spring of 1940, Mussolini decided to achieve some victories of his own, and in October 1940, he invaded Greece from bases in Italian-occupied Albania. The Greeks counterattacked, threatening to drive the Italians into the sea. To save Mussolini, in April 1941 the Germans overran Greece and Yugoslavia.

The Russo-German War

The Invasion of the Soviet Union

Early German Victories

On June 22, 1941, Hitler's armies invaded the Soviet Union, advancing on three fronts: toward Leningrad in the north, toward Moscow in the center, and into the Ukraine in the south. In mid-July, the Germans took Smolensk, the traditional gateway to Moscow, and the 900-day siege of Leningrad began in early September. In mid-September, the Germans captured Kiev, the capital of the Ukraine.

Soviet Counterattack

The deterioration of Japanese-American relations in the autumn of 1941 enabled the Soviets to move troops from the Manchurian border to the defense of Moscow. On December 6, 1941, Soviet forces led by Marshal Georgi Zhukov (1896–1974) counterattacked and drove the Germans back from fifty to one hundred miles before the front was stabilized in early 1942.

Campaigns of 1942 and 1943

Battle of Stalingrad

In the spring of 1942, the Germans launched a new offensive directed toward two objectives: the oil-rich Caucasus, lying between the Black and the Caspian seas, and the city of Stalingrad on the Volga River. While the Germans pushed into the Caucasus, they did not succeed in reaching the oil fields. At Stalingrad, the German attackers and Soviet defenders became engaged in one of the war's bloodiest battles. In early 1943, the remnants of the German Sixth Army surrendered.

Soviet Counterattack

In the early summer of 1943, the Germans launched their final offensive in the Soviet Union. A few days later, the Soviets counterattacked. By the end of the year, the Red Army had recaptured two-thirds of the Soviet territory the Germans had occupied.

The War in Europe During 1944 and 1945

The Air War Against Germany

By 1944, increased American aircraft production made it possible for the United States Army Air Force to put thousands of heavy bombers and escort fighters into the skies over Germany. The Americans specialized in daylight, high-altitude precision bombing, hitting at key targets, including facilities for the production of synthetic gasoline and rubber, aircraft factories, ball-bearing works, submarine bases, railroads, and electric power stations. The British Royal Air Force (RAF) concentrated on night area bombing.

Allied bombing did heavy damage to Germany's cities and economy. However, the bombing was not decisive. Victory over the Germans was not won by air raids but rather on the fields of battle.

The Normandy Invasion

By 1944, an Allied victory was in sight. In Italy, American and British troops continued their slow advance, while the Red Army pushed into the Baltic States, Poland, and the Balkans.

On D day, June 6, 1944, American, British, and Canadian forces commanded by General Eisenhower opened the Second Front in France. Operation Overlord, the invasion of Normandy, was the largest amphibious operation in history.

Attempted Assassination of Hitler

On July 20, 1944, German military and civilian opponents of the

Nazi tyranny attempted to kill Hitler. The *Führer* survived and ordered vicious reprisals against his would-be assassins.

Allied Advance in France

As Eisenhower's troops began to push toward Paris, other Allied forces carried out Operation Dragoon (earlier called Operation Anvil), landing August 15 on the coast of southern France between Marseilles and Nice, and began to advance northward through the Rhone valley.

Following the liberation of Paris on August 25, Allied troops pushed into the Low Countries and toward the Rhine River frontier between Germany and France.

The Eastern Front

On the eastern front, by mid-September 1944, the Red Army had advanced to a line running through the Baltic states to the Vistula River east of Warsaw, southward to the Carpathian Mountains, and into the Balkans as far as Sofia, Bulgaria. Germany's allies, Finland, Rumania, and Bulgaria, had dropped out of the war.

The Battle of the Bulge

It seemed that the European war might be over by the end of 1944, but this assessment proved to be optimistic. It discounted both the determination and the ability of the Germans to continue their resistance.

The Germans launched a powerful counterattack against the advancing Americans in the Ardennes Forest in Belgium in December 1944. In the Battle of the Bulge, the Germans pushed the Americans back, but they were not able to achieve a breakthrough.

The End of the European War

In mid-January 1945, the Soviets took Warsaw. The Red Army's advance continued, halting temporarily when it reached the Oder River about forty miles from Berlin during the first days of February.

In early March 1945, American troops captured the last remaining intact bridge across the Rhine at Remagen. Allied forces were now pouring into Germany. American and Soviet forces met on the Elbe on April 25, while on the eastern front, the Red Army moved through Hungary and into Austria, seizing Vienna on April 13.

At the end of April, Germany's armies in Italy surrendered. Italian partisans seized Mussolini, murdering him on April 28.

The Red Army entered Berlin on April 19, and Adolf Hitler committed suicide in his bunker beneath the city on April 30. His successor, Grand Admiral Karl Doenitz (1891–1980), surrendered to the Allies on May 7.

The Holocaust

When the Allies advanced into Germany in the final months of the European war, the enormity of the Holocaust—Hitler's attempt to exterminate the Jews of Europe—became evident. Hatred of the Jews had been at the center of the Nazi leader's thought (see Chapter 32), but few had imagined that he would attempt to carry this hatred to such extreme lengths.

Hitler entrusted what was euphemistically called the Final Solution of the Jewish Question to Heinrich Himmler (1900–1945), the head of the SS. The *Einsatzgruppen,* special SS murder squads, followed the advancing German army into the Soviet Union in 1941, rounding up and murdering Jews.

As the Final Solution gathered momentum, concentration camps, which had originally been established for German political prisoners, were converted into death camps, and new extermination camps were built. The SS rounded up Jews throughout Nazi-occupied Europe and shipped them to these camps, often in cattle cars. Auschwitz, located in Poland, was the most notorious of the camps, but there were others: Dachau in southern Germany, Buchenwald in central Germany, and Mauthausen in Austria, among them. The SS often found recruits among the local populations, especially in areas that had a powerful tradition of anti-Semitism, including the Baltic states, Poland, the Soviet Ukraine, and Rumania.

By war's end, the Germans had killed 6 million Jews, two-thirds of

Europe's Jewish population. Some 1.5 million of these victims were children.

The War Against Japan

Early Japanese Aggression

In the early 1930s, Japan seized Manchuria, and in July 1937, went to war against China. While the Japanese succeeded in conquering most of the coastal areas of China, their efforts to overrun the interior bogged down.

In early September 1940, Japanese forces occupied bases in the northern part of French Indochina. In the same month, Japan signed the Tripartite Pact, allying itself more closely with Germany and Italy.

American Economic Pressure on Japan

In an attempt to contain the Japanese threat and to aid China, the United States began to apply economic pressure on Japan. In late September 1940, President Roosevelt imposed an embargo on the shipment of scrap iron and steel to Japan.

In July 1941, the Japanese occupied the rest of French Indochina, which suggested that they were pressing forward in their efforts to create what they called the Greater East Asia Co-Prosperity Sphere. Roosevelt responded to Japan's action by freezing Japanese assets in the United States.

American economic sanctions confronted the Japanese with a dilemma. In order to get what it needed from the United States, Japan would have to cease its aggression. The alternative was for Japan to seize the oil resources of the Dutch East Indies, an action likely to evoke a strong American response.

Attack on Pearl Harbor

In October 1941, a prowar group led by General Hideki Tojo (1885–1948) took power in Japan. On December 7, Japanese aircraft attacked the American naval base at Pearl Harbor, Hawaii. The United

States declared war on Japan the following day. On December 11, Germany and Italy declared war on the United States.

Early Japanese Victories

The Japanese moved quickly to conquer Hong Kong, the Philippines, British Malaya with its great port at Singapore, British Burma, and the Dutch East Indies. Advancing into New Guinea, the Japanese threatened Australia. In addition, the Japanese seized the American possessions of Guam and Wake islands in the Central Pacific.

Battles of the Coral Sea and Midway

Two important naval battles took place in the Pacific in the spring of 1942. The Battle of the Coral Sea, fought on May 7 and 8, was the first naval battle in history in which the ships did not directly engage one another; all of the fighting was done by carrier-based airplanes. While the battle ended in a draw, it removed the Japanese threat to Australia.

The Battle of Midway, fought in the Central Pacific from June 3 to 6, resulted in an American victory, which eliminated the threat to Hawaii.

American Island-Hopping

In the Pacific, the Americans carried the war closer to Japan by a campaign of island-hopping. From the summer of 1942 to 1944, the names of Guadalcanal, Tarawa, Kwajelein, Eniwetok, and Saipan became permanently etched on the minds of a generation of Americans.

Return to the Philippines

On August 20, 1944, troops commanded by General Douglas MacArthur (1880–1964) landed in the Philippines. In late October, the Battle of Leyte Gulf was fought. The battle resulted in the destruction of most of what was left of Japan's naval power and gave the United States full control of the sea around the Philippines. The campaign in the Philippines ended with the fall of Manila to the Americans in February 1945.

Iwo Jima and Okinawa

American marines landed on Iwo Jima, in the Bonin Islands some 750 miles from Tokyo, on February 19, 1945. At the beginning of April, American army units invaded Okinawa in the Ryukyu Islands southwest of Japan. During this brutal battle, Japanese kamikaze (suicide) pilots crashed their planes into American ships.

The End of the War Against Japan

Possession of these islands enabled the United States to step up the air war against the Japanese home islands. American military planners believed, however, that Japan could be defeated only by an invasion, which was scheduled to begin about November 1, 1945. They estimated that this invasion would cost as many as 1 million American casualties.

The Atomic Bombs

Concern about heavy casualties was a major factor contributing to the American decision to use the atomic bomb against Japan. On August 6, 1945, the first atomic bomb was dropped on Hiroshima. On August 9, a second atomic bomb hit Nagasaki. The following day, Emperor Hirohito (r. 1926–1989) decided that Japan had no choice other than to surrender. He set one condition: He must be permitted to keep his throne.

Japanese Surrender

The Allies agreed to accept Hirohito's condition, and the news of Japan's surrender became public on August 14. The formal surrender documents were signed on September 2 on board the American battleship *Missouri* anchored in Tokyo Bay. The Second World War had ended.

Allied Wartime Diplomacy

During the war, the Allies held a series of conferences where they discussed military operations and their plans for the postwar world.

The Casablanca Conference

In January 1943, a few weeks following the Anglo-American invasion of French North Africa, Roosevelt and Churchill met at Casablanca in French Morocco. The two leaders agreed to demand the unconditional surrender of the Axis powers. In part, this decision resulted from a desire to reassure the Soviets that the Western powers would not attempt to make a separate peace with Hitler.

With victory in North Africa in sight, the two leaders agreed to move forward with an invasion of Sicily and Italy but not to abandon plans for the cross-Channel invasion of France favored by Roosevelt.

The Teheran Conference

In November-December 1943, Roosevelt and Churchill met with Stalin in Teheran, Iran. The three Allied leaders discussed the plans for the Second Front in Western Europe, scheduled for the spring.

At Teheran, Stalin made clear his determination to extend Soviet power in Eastern Europe following the war, while Roosevelt sought to overcome the Soviet leader's suspicions of the West in an effort to win his cooperation in the postwar world.

The Yalta Conference

In February 1945, Roosevelt, Churchill, and Stalin met at Yalta in the Soviet Crimea in the most important of the wartime conferences.

Soviet Agreement to Enter the War Against Japan

The atomic bomb had not yet been developed, and Roosevelt was concerned about the number of casualties the United States might suffer in an invasion of Japan. In response to Roosevelt's appeal, Stalin agreed to enter the war against Japan within three months following the defeat of Germany. In return, the Soviet Union would acquire the southern half of Sakhalin Island, which Russia had lost to Japan in 1905, the Kurile Islands, and a sphere of influence in Manchuria. In addition, the Soviets would receive an occupation zone in northern Korea.

Occupation of Germany

At Yalta, the three leaders agreed to add France as an occupying power in Germany, dividing that country into four zones of occupation instead of three. Churchill was anxious to encourage France's recovery of its status as a great power, hoping that France would contribute to the reestablishment of a balance of power in Europe.

Agreement on Voting in the UN

Agreement was reached on voting procedures in the Security Council of the new United Nations organization, with each of the Security Council's five permanent members (the United States, Great Britain, the Soviet Union, France, and China) to have a veto.

Disagreements on Poland

The question of Poland was the most difficult issue considered at Yalta. The United States and Great Britain maintained relations with the Polish government-in-exile located in London. The Soviets had broken relations with the London Poles after they refused to accept Moscow's demand to annex eastern Poland. When the Red Army entered Poland in 1944, the Soviets had established at Lublin a pro-Soviet, Communist-dominated government that agreed to Moscow's territorial demands.

At Yalta, Stalin agreed to permit a broadening of the Lublin government by adding to it representatives of the London Poles. The Polish government continued to be dominated by Communists, however, and the non-Communist representatives found themselves outnumbered and outmaneuvered. Stalin also promised to permit free elections in Poland, but they were never held.

While the Soviets annexed eastern Poland, the Poles were to be compensated by territory taken from Germany. No final commitments on this territorial compensation were made at Yalta, but the Soviets ultimately gave Poland the southern part of East Prussia—the Soviets annexed the northern part of the province—and German territory lying east of the line formed by the Oder and Neisse rivers (the Oder-Neisse Line).

Friendly Governments Versus Free Elections

The Big Three also agreed·on the text of the Declaration on Liberated Europe, pledging that postwar governments in the liberated countries of Europe would be established on the basis of free elections.

There was a basic incompatibility between the Soviet demand for friendly governments in Poland and other Eastern European countries and the Western Allies' demand for free elections. In most of Eastern Europe, and certainly in Poland, free elections would almost inevitably have led to the establishment of governments hostile to the Soviet Union. Stalin therefore got the friendly governments he wanted by imposing Communist-dominated regimes on countries occupied by Red Army troops. The Western powers protested Soviet actions, but Moscow ignored the protests.

The Potsdam Conference

New Participants: Truman and Attlee

On April 12, 1945, President Roosevelt died and was succeeded by his vice president, Harry S Truman (1884–1972). In mid-July 1945, Truman met with Churchill and Stalin in Potsdam, near Berlin, in the last of the wartime Big Three conferences. During the conference, Churchill was replaced by the newly elected British prime minister, Clement Attlee (1883–1967).

Decisions on German Occupation

By the time the Potsdam Conference met, the Americans, British, French, and Soviets had taken possession of their zones of occupation in Germany. The Potsdam Conference agreed that the occupation authorities in each zone should promote demilitarization, denazification, and democratization. On the controversial issue of reparations, the conference decided that each power should be permitted to remove property from its own zone, while the Soviets would also receive a percentage of capital equipment from the western zones.

The Potsdam Conference agreed to establish a four-power Allied Control Council to determine the policies to be executed in all of the four zones in Germany. In practice, however, the four powers failed to reach agreement on common policies, and thus each power proceeded to determine policy for its own zone.

The Second World War had far-reaching consequences. In Europe, the defeat of Germany created a power vacuum in Central Europe that made possible a great westward expansion of Soviet power. The growth of Soviet power, in turn, evoked an American response. The result was the Cold War.

In Asia, the defeat of Japan led to an increase of American influence, power, and reponsibility in the western Pacific and East Asia. Throughout Asia, and in Africa, as well, the war helped intensify nationalist movements, thereby hastening the disintegration of Europe's colonial empires.

The Second World War also brought many technological developments, especially the atomic bomb, which presented future generations with the specter of mass annihilation.

Recommended Reading

Beck, Earl R. *Under the Bombs: The German Home Front, 1942–1945* (1986).

Clark, Alan. *Barbarossa: The Russian-German Conflict, 1941-45* (1965).

Clemons, Diane Shaver. *Yalta* (1970).

Costello, John. *The Pacific War* (1981).

Feis, Herbert. *Churchill, Roosevelt, Stalin: The War They Waged and the Peace They Sought* (1957).

Hearden, Patrick J. *Roosevelt Confronts Hitler: America's Entry Into World War II* (1987).

Heinrichs, Waldo H. *Threshold of War: Franklin D. Roosevelt and American Entry into World War II* (1988).

Hilberg, Raul. *The Destruction of the European Jews* (1961).

Lyons, Michael J. *World War II: A Short History* (1989).

Marks, Frederick W., III. *Wind Over Sand: The Diplomacy of Franklin Roosevelt* (1988).

Mayer, Arno J. *Why Did the Heavens Not Darken? The "Final Solution" in History* (1989).

Mee, Charles L., Jr. *Meeting at Potsdam* (1975).

Mulligan, Timothy. *The Politics of Illusion and Empire: German Occupation Policy in the Soviet Union, 1941–1943* (1988).

Prange, Gordon W. *Pearl Harbor: The Verdict of History* (1986).

Prazmowska, Anita. *Britain, Poland, and the Eastern Front, 1939* (1987).

Salisbury, Harrison E. *The 900 Days: The Siege of Leningrad* (1969).

Schaffer, Ronald. *Wings of Judgment: American Bombing in World War II* (1985).

Snell, John L. *Illusion and Necessity: The Diplomacy of Global War, 1939–1945* (1963).

Stokesbury, James L. *A Short History of World War II* (1980).

Trevor-Roper, H. R. *The Last Days of Hitler* (6th ed., 1987).

Utley, Jonathan G. *Going to War with Japan, 1937–1941* (1985).

Weinberg, Gerhard L. *Germany and the Soviet Union, 1939–1941* (1954).

Wright, Gordon. *The Ordeal of Total War, 1939–1945* (1968).

CHAPTER 36

The Cold War

Time Line

1945	The United Nations is established
1946	Winston Churchill delivers his Iron Curtain speech
1947	Peace treaties are signed with Bulgaria, Finland, Hungary, Italy, and Rumania
	President Truman calls for American aid to Greece and Turkey
	The United States proposes the Marshall Plan
1948	A Communist dictatorship is imposed on Czechoslovakia
	The Soviets begin the Berlin Blockade

1949	The German Federal Republic and the German Democratic Republic are established
	The North Atlantic Treaty Organization (NATO) is created
	The Communists win the Chinese civil war
1950	North Korea invades South Korea
1953	An armistice ends the Korean War
1954	The Southeast Asia Treaty Organization (SEATO) is established.
1955	West Germany becomes a member of NATO
	The Soviets establish the Warsaw Pact
	The Baghdad Pact is established
	The Austrian State Treaty is signed
	The Geneva summit conference meets
1961	The Berlin Wall is built
1962	The Cuban missile crisis endangers world peace
1963	The United States and the Soviet Union sign the Nuclear Test Ban Treaty
1972	The United States and the Soviet Union sign the SALT I Treaty and the ABM Treaty
1979	The Soviet Union invades Afghanistan
1985	Mikhail Gorbachev becomes general secretary of the Soviet Communist party
1987	The United States and the Soviet Union sign the Intermediate Range Nuclear Force (INF) treaty

During World War II, the Allies were compelled to cooperate in order to defeat the aggression of the Axis powers. Once the defeat of the Axis was assured, the need for cooperation ended. Even before Germany's surrender in May 1945, the Western Allies—the United States and Great Britain—became alarmed by the expansion of Soviet power in Eastern Europe. As the Red Army advanced toward Germany, the Soviets established Communist regimes in the countries they occupied and refused to permit free elections.

Concerned about Soviet intentions, the Western powers moved to contain Soviet expansion. This clash between the Western powers and the Soviets resulted in the Cold War.

Origins and Development of the Cold War

The Founding of the United Nations

In April 1945, delegates from fifty nations met in San Francisco to draft the Charter of the United Nations (UN). The UN closely resembled the old League of Nations in its basic organization. All member nations were represented in the General Assembly, while the Security Council consisted of eleven (later increased to fifteen) members. The five great powers—the United States, the Soviet Union, Great Britain, France, and China—were permanent members of the Security Council with the right of veto. The other six members were elected for two-year terms by the General Assembly. The Secretariat, headed by the Secretary General, dealt with administrative matters. These UN agencies had their headquarters in New York, while the International Court of Justice met in The Hague, the capital of the Netherlands. The UN Charter also established several specialized agencies to deal with various political, economic, and social matters.

While the UN was intended to promote international cooperation in the cause of world peace, it quickly became a forum for the expression of increasing East-West antagonism.

The Soviets and Eastern Europe

As a consequence of its advance against Germany in the final months of World War II in Europe, the Soviets' Red Army came to dominate much of Eastern Europe.

The Soviet Bloc

Joseph Stalin (1879–1953), the Soviet dictator, used the power his army gave him to establish Communist dictatorships in Poland, Rumania, Bulgaria, and—slightly later—Hungary. Local Communists established themselves in power in Yugoslavia and Albania. In Czechoslovakia, a legitimate coalition government was created, although Communists held most of the important positions. Stalin thus accomplished his goal of making certain that the countries along the western frontier of the Soviet Union would have friendly governments.

The Iron Curtain

The Soviets refused to heed American protests, and East-West relations continued to deteriorate. In a speech at Fulton, Missouri, in March 1946, Winston Churchill (1874–1965), the former British prime minister, introduced a new term to the political vocabulary when he declared: "From Stettin in the Baltic to Trieste in the Adriatic, an iron curtain has descended across the continent."

East-West Relations in Germany

Following Germany's defeat in May 1945, the Americans, British, Soviets, and French took control of their occupation zones. Berlin, the former German capital lying within the Soviet zone some one hundred miles from the Western zones, was divided into four occupation sectors. The Western powers had access to their sectors by highway, railroad, and air routes through the Soviet zone.

The occupying powers established the Allied Control Council to determine the policies to be executed in their occupation zones. In practice, however, the four powers failed to reach agreement on common policies, and thus each power proceeded to determine policy for its own zone.

Consolidation of Western Zones

In early 1947, the American and British zones were merged for economic purposes, and the French joined their zone several months later. In this way, the Western powers took the first steps toward the establishment of a separate West German state.

Peace Treaties with Germany's Allies

The wartime Allies were never able to agree on a peace treaty with Germany. However, in February 1947, they signed peace treaties with Germany's allies: Bulgaria, Finland, Hungary, Italy, and Rumania.

U.S. Containment Policy

In early 1946, George F. Kennan (b. 1904), a member of the staff of the American embassy in Moscow, drafted a lengthy analysis of the Soviet Union and its expansionist policies. Recalled to Washington, Kennan played a central role in designing a policy to halt Soviet expansion, the policy he called containment. Kennan believed that only a policy of determined and continuing resistance could halt the advance of Soviet power.

The Truman Doctrine

The first step in implementing the new American containment policy came in response to an urgent appeal from the British. At the end of World War II, Great Britain had assumed a major responsibility in the eastern Mediterranean, providing assistance to the Greek government in its war against Communist rebels and to Turkey in its efforts to resist Soviet demands for a larger voice in the control of the Dardanelles. In February 1947, the British informed the United States that they no longer had the financial strength to continue this role. The United States would have to take over.

Appearing before a joint session of Congress on March 12, 1947, President Harry S Truman (1884–1972) called for the appropriation of $400 million for military and economic assistance to Greece and Turkey. The President also expressed what came to be known as the Truman Doctrine: "I believe that it must be the policy of the United States to support free peoples who are resisting attempted subjugation by armed minorities or by outside pressure." Congress quickly approved the President's appeal for aid to Greece and Turkey.

The Marshall Plan

The prospect of a total economic collapse of war-ravaged Europe increased fears that the Soviet Union might extend its power over the entire continent.

In June 1947, George C. Marshall (1880–1959), the American secretary of state, proposed a broad program of American assistance to help all of Europe recover economically. The Soviets refused to participate, evidently believing that the Marshall Plan was designed to weaken their hold on Eastern Europe.

The American Congress was initially reluctant to appropriate billions of dollars to promote economic recovery in Europe. Then, in February 1948, a Soviet-inspired coup in Czechoslovakia overthrew that country's coalition government and established a Communist dictatorship. Believing the Marshall Plan would help stop the advance of Soviet power, Congress approved it in April 1948. Between 1948 and 1952, the European Recovery Program (ERP), as the Marshall Plan was officially known, provided about $13 billion in American assistance for the economic revival of Western Europe.

The Berlin Blockade

As the Western powers proceeded with their plans for creating a separate West German state, the Soviets decided to apply pressure on the West where they could do so with the greatest ease, at Berlin.

The Airlift

On June 20, 1948, the Soviets cut off the highway and railroad routes between the Western occupation zones and Berlin, thereby initiating the Berlin Blockade. In response, the United States established the Berlin airlift, designed to provide the three Western sectors of the city with food, fuel, and other supplies.

Creation of Two German States

The Berlin airlift succeeded in meeting the needs of the Western sectors, and the Soviets decided against escalating the crisis. In May 1949, the Soviets ended the blockade, and the Western powers proceeded with their plans to establish the Federal Republic of Germany, which came into being in mid–1949. The Soviets responded by creating an East German state, the German Democratic Republic, in their zone.

The Establishment of NATO

Mounting East-West tension gradually led the Western powers to join in a military alliance.

The Brussels Pact

In March 1948, Great Britain, France, and the Benelux states (Belgium, the Netherlands, and Luxembourg) signed a treaty of alliance, the Brussels Pact. Also during 1948, the United States established a peacetime draft in order to increase the size of its armed forces.

The North Atlantic Pact

In April 1949, representatives of twelve nations met in Washington to sign the North Atlantic Pact. The twelve signers included the five Brussels Pact states plus the United States, Canada, Iceland, Denmark, Norway, Italy, and Portugal. Greece and Turkey joined in 1952, and West Germany was added in 1955. The North Atlantic Pact established the North Atlantic Treaty Organization (NATO) to coordinate the activities of the alliance.

The Cold War in Asia

The Communist Victory in China

Following the end of the war against Japan in 1945, China was torn apart by a civil war between the Nationalist (Kuomintang) government of Chiang Kai-shek (1887–1975) and the Communists, led by Mao Tse-tung (1893–1976). The United States provided Chiang with considerable financial and military assistance. But the Nationalist cause was weakened by widespread corruption and a devastating inflation.

The People's Republic of China

Mao's Red Army gradually extended its control over China. In October 1949, Mao proclaimed the establishment of the People's Republic of China (PRC), formed an alliance with Soviet Union, and initiated a campaign against American influence and power in East Asia. Chiang Kai-shek withdrew the remnant of his forces to the island of Taiwan.

The United States refused to recognize the PRC and instead maintained diplomatic relations with Chiang's government on Taiwan.

U.S.-Japanese Alliance

The United States began to develop Japan as its main ally in Asia. In 1951, the United States signed a peace treaty with Japan. The following year, the American occupation ended and the two nations signed a security treaty.

The Korean War

At the end of World War II, Japanese-ruled Korea was occupied by American and Soviet forces, with the line between the occupation zones established at the 38th parallel. In the south, the United States supported the creation of a government headed by Syngman Rhee (1875–1965), a conservative nationalist. In the north, the Soviets established a Communist government, led by Kim Il-Sung (b. 1912). Both occupying powers withdrew in 1949.

The Outbreak of War

On June 25, 1950, the army of North Korea attacked South Korea. The United States moved to support South Korea, taking advantage of a temporary Soviet absence from the UN Security Council to win that body's endorsement of American intervention. The Security Council's action made the Korean War officially a United Nations police action, although the bulk of the fighting was done by the Americans and South Koreans.

MacArthur's Advance

At first, the Korean War went badly as North Koreans poured across the 38th parallel. In August, the North Korean advance was halted at Pusan in the southeast corner of the country. In September, General Douglas MacArthur (1880–1964), the commander of the UN forces, carried out a brilliant landing at Inchon, behind the North Korean lines. Most of the North Korean army in the south was cut off and destroyed.

Although the United States had originally intervened in Korea in order to restore the dividing line of the 38th parallel, MacArthur's victory presented the prospect of using military force to unite all of Korea. The Chinese warned that they would intervene if the UN forces approached the Yalu River, the border between North Korea and China. The United States disregarded the warnings.

In late November, the Chinese intervened, and by December, had driven the UN forces out of North Korea. MacArthur finally succeeded in stabilizing the front near the 38th parallel.

Dismissal of MacArthur

When the Truman administration decided to wage a limited war in Korea and not attempt to reunify the country, MacArthur protested. In April 1951, Truman relieved MacArthur of his command. Under the leadership of General Matthew Ridgway (b. 1895), MacArthur's successor, UN armies smashed the Chinese and advanced northward, establishing a line roughly along the 38th parallel.

Signing of Armistice

In October 1951, armistice talks began at Panmunjom and continued until July 1953, when an armistice was signed. Under its terms, Korea remained divided at the 38th parallel.

The Cold War During the 1950s

The Rearmament of West Germany

The administration of President Dwight D. Eisenhower (1890–1969), which held office from 1953 to 1960, continued the effort initiated by Truman to reach an agreement to rearm West Germany and bring that country into the Western defense system. France's fear of a rearmed Germany stood as the main obstacle in the path of achieving this objective.

The European Defense Community

In October 1950, French Premier René Pleven (b. 1901) had proposed the creation of an integrated Western European army including West German troops. Complex negotiations on what came to be known as the Pleven Plan resulted in the signing, in May 1952, of a

Europe During the Cold War

treaty providing for the establishment of the European Defense Community (EDC). Even though the project had been originated by the French, the French parliament rejected the EDC treaty in the summer of 1954.

Agreement on West German Rearmament

Following the collapse of the EDC, negotiations among the

Western allies led to a British commitment to maintain several divisions on the European continent in order to provide reassurance to the French. The Western powers then agreed to permit the rearmament of West Germany, which became a member of NATO in 1955.

The Warsaw Pact

In May 1955, the Soviets established the Warsaw Pact. This military alliance of the Soviets with Albania, Bulgaria, Czechoslovakia, East Germany, Hungary, Poland, and Rumania formalized a system that already existed.

The American Alliance System

During the 1950s, the Eisenhower administration expanded the Western alliance system, which had begun with the creation of NATO in 1949.

SEATO

In September 1954, the United States sponsored the establishment of the Southeast Asia Treaty Organization (SEATO), the Asian equivalent of NATO. SEATO's members included the United States, Great Britain, France, Australia, New Zealand, the Philippines, Thailand, and Pakistan.

The Baghdad Pact (CENTO)

The creation of the Baghdad Pact in 1955 marked the completion of the American alliance system. Consisting of Great Britain, Turkey, Iraq, Iran, and Pakistan, the Baghdad Pact joined NATO and SEATO. Turkey, the easternmost member of NATO, was the westernmost member of the Baghdad Pact, while Pakistan, the westernmost member of SEATO, was the easternmost member of the Baghdad Pact.

In 1958, Iraq dropped out of the Baghdad Pact in the wake of an anti-Western coup. Since Baghdad was Iraq's capital, the alliance was renamed the Central Treaty Organization (CENTO).

The Geneva Summit

In March 1953, Stalin died, and control of the Soviet government passed into the hands of a more moderate collective leadership. Communist party chief Nikita Khrushchev (1894–1971) and Premier Nikolai Bulganin (1895–1975) spoke of "peaceful coexistence" between the Soviet Union and the West.

In 1955, the Soviet Union and the major Western allies, the United States, Great Britain, and France, reached agreement on the Austrian State Treaty. This accord ended the four-power occupation of Austria, which became a fully independent state committed to neutrality.

In July 1955, Eisenhower, British Prime Minister Anthony Eden (1897–1977), and French Premier Edgar Faure (1908–1988) met with Khrushchev and Bulganin in Geneva. This was the first meeting in a decade of the heads of the four governments, who conducted their talks in a cordial atmosphere. Following this summit meeting, there was talk of the "Spirit of Geneva," even though East and West had not reached any agreements on the major issues that divided them, notably German reunification and arms limitation.

The Berlin Crisis of 1958

In November 1958, Khrushchev began a campaign to solve the German question on terms favorable to the Soviet Union. He demanded that the Western powers agree to accept within six months the neutralization and demilitarization of West Berlin. If they did not, the Soviets would sign a separate peace treaty with East Germany and turn their rights in Berlin over to the East Germans. This would force the Americans, British, and French to deal with a government they did not recognize.

The Soviets acted in Berlin because West Berlin provided an easy escape route for dissatisfied East Germans. The flight of East Germans to the West created a crisis situation for the East German economy, which could not continue to sustain the loss of so much skilled labor.

When the Western powers refused to give way, Khrushchev let the six-month deadline pass. It remained apparent, however, that the Soviet leader was not prepared to accept the Berlin situation as it stood.

Nevertheless, the immediate crisis had passed by the spring of 1959, and in September Khrushchev visited the United States. Eisenhower and Khrushchev agreed to discuss Germany and other outstanding issues at a summit meeting to be held in Paris in the spring of 1960.

The U-2 Incident and the Collapse of the Paris Summit

Since 1955, American high-altitude U-2 spy planes had been carrying out surveillance operations over Soviet territory. On May 1, 1960, the Soviets succeeded in downing a U-2 and capturing its pilot. Khrushchev used this U-2 incident to break up the Paris summit meeting as it was about to convene in June. The summit had little likelihood of success, since neither side was prepared to give way on any of its established positions.

Crisis and Détente: East-West Relations from the 1960s through the 1980s

The Berlin Wall

In early 1961, Khrushchev renewed his pressure on the Western powers in Berlin. Then, on August 13, the Soviets and East Germans closed the border between East and West Berlin and began the construction of the Berlin Wall, which prevented the flight of East Germans to the West. While the Western powers protested the building of the wall, they took no other action, and the Berlin crisis gradually eased.

The Bay of Pigs

In 1959, Fidel Castro (b. 1927) overthrew the government of Fulgencio Batista (1901–1973), the American-supported Cuban dictator. Soon after Castro took power, strains developed in Cuban-American relations, and in January 1961, the United States broke diplomatic ties with Cuba.

The American Central Intelligence Agency (CIA) had begun training Cuban exiles for an invasion of Cuba. When President John F. Kennedy (1917–1963) took office in 1961, he approved the plan. On April 17, 1961, an exile force of 1,500 men landed at the Bay of Pigs on Cuba's southern coast. Within three days, Castro's forces crushed the invasion.   In December, Castro proclaimed himself a Marxist-Leninist and moved closer to the Soviet Union.

The Cuban Missile Crisis

Concerned about the possibility of American action against Cuba, Castro turned to the Soviet Union for aid. The Soviets provided the Cubans with airplanes and other conventional weapons and also began to construct missile launching pads for intermediate range missiles. The Cuban missile crisis, the most dangerous East-West confrontation of the Cold War, was about to begin.

U.S.-Soviet Confrontation

On October 22, 1962, Kennedy demanded that the Soviets dismantle the missile sites and remove the missiles. He also established an American naval quarantine to prevent Soviet ships from bringing additional offensive weapons to Cuba.

Negotiations and Settlement

Tense negotiations between Washington and Moscow brought an end to the Cuban missile crisis on October 28. Khrushchev agreed to dismantle the launching pads and remove the missiles, and Kennedy pledged not to invade Cuba. The United States agreed informally to pull its missiles out of Turkey, although this commitment was not a formal part of the agreement ending the crisis.

In the aftermath of the Cuban missile crisis, the Washington-Moscow hot line was established to facilitate speedy communication in the event of another crisis.

The Nuclear Test Ban Treaty

Following the resolution of the Cuban missile crisis, long-stalled American-Soviet negotiations resumed and resulted in the signing of the Nuclear Test Ban Treaty in July 1963. The treaty banned the testing of nuclear weapons in the atmosphere. Underground tests could continue. A number of other nations adhered to the treaty, although France and the People's Republic of China did not. These two countries were busy developing their own nuclear weapons.

Détente and East-West Treaties

Following the signing of the Nuclear Test Ban Treaty, the United States and the Soviet Union initiated efforts to promote a further reduction of tension in their relationship. This reduction of tension was referred to as détente.

The Outer Space Treaty

In January 1967, the United States, the Soviet Union, Great Britain, and fifty-seven other countries signed the Outer Space Treaty, banning weapons of mass destruction, as well as military installations, from outer space.

The Nuclear Nonproliferation Treaty

The United States, the Soviet Union, and sixty other nations signed the Nuclear Nonproliferation Treaty in July 1968. The treaty was designed to prevent the spread of nuclear weapons to nonnuclear countries. France, the People's Republic of China, and several other countries refused to accept the treaty.

SALT I and ABM Treaties

For several years, negotiations had been underway between the United States and the Soviet Union for a strategic arms limitation treaty (SALT). In May 1972, the Americans and Soviets signed the SALT I Treaty, agreeing to freeze the number of intercontinental ballistic missiles (ICBMs) at their existing levels for five years. However, no limit was placed on the number of warheads that could be carried by each missile. SALT I thus did little to end the arms race. The United States and the Soviet Union also signed the Antiballistic Missile (ABM) Treaty, agreeing to restrict the construction of antiballistic missile systems to two sites in each country. Other American-Soviet accords promoted increases in trade and scientific and cultural exchanges.

The SALT II Treaty

Further arms-limitation negotiations led to the signing, in mid–1979, of the SALT II Treaty, which placed limits on long-range missiles, bombers, and nuclear warheads. The treaty encountered strong opposition from American conservatives, who charged that the treaty favored the Soviets.

The End of Détente

In December 1979, the Soviet Union invaded Afghanistan in an effort to defend the pro-Soviet government against insurgents. President Jimmy Carter (b. 1924) responded to the Soviet action by imposing economic sanctions on the Soviet Union and declaring a U.S. boycott of the 1980 Moscow Summer Olympic Games. He also withdrew the SALT II Treaty from Senate consideration, though both sides continued to observe the obligations of the treaty. Nevertheless, by 1980, détente appeared to be at an end, and there was talk of a new Cold War.

Martial Law in Poland

President Ronald Reagan (b. 1911), who took office in 1981, pursued a hard line toward the Soviet Union. American-Soviet relations were strained further by events in Poland. In 1981, under pressure from Moscow, the Polish government imposed martial law in an attempt to destroy the challenge to its authority presented by Solidarity, an independent labor union. In protest, the United States imposed economic sanctions on Poland.

Korean Plane Incident

The atmosphere of the new Cold War was intensified in September 1983, when a Soviet fighter shot down a Korean Airlines 747 that had strayed over Soviet territory on a flight from Alaska to Seoul, South Korea. All 269 persons aboard the plane died. The Soviets insisted that the plane had been engaged in espionage.

Renewed Easing of East-West Tension

After Mikhail Gorbachev (b. 1931) took office as general secretary of the Soviet Communist party in March 1985, East-West tension began to ease. In late 1985, Reagan and Gorbachev held a cordial meeting in Geneva, Switzerland, agreeing to resume arms-limitation negotiations. The two leaders held their second summit meeting in Reykjavik,

Iceland, in October 1986, although no agreements on arms limitation were reached.

The INF Treaty

Continuing American-Soviet negotiations led to a third Reagan-Gorbachev summit in Washington in December 1987. The two leaders signed the Intermediate Range Nuclear Forces (INF) Treaty, which called for the scrapping, over a three-year period, of all American and Soviet missiles with a range of 315 to 3,125 miles. The INF Treaty was the first American-Soviet agreement to actually reduce the level of arms.

Continuing Issues of Disagreement

The United States and the Soviet Union continued negotiations in an effort to reach agreement on a reduction of conventional forces in Europe and long-range missiles. However, discord over American development of the Strategic Defense Initiative (SDI) continued. In addition, while Soviet forces withdrew from Afghanistan, the Americans and Soviets remained at odds over human rights in the Soviet Union and regional conflicts.

The Cold War conflict divided much of the world into two armed camps as the United States developed a global policy of containment in its effort to limit the expansion of Soviet power. Serious crises developed: at Berlin in 1948–1949 and again from 1958 to 1961, in Korea in the early 1950s, and in the Cuban missile crisis of 1962.

These crises did not lead to war, however, and gradually the two superpowers, the United States and the Soviet Union, sought a relaxation of tension—a détente—in their relationship. The Soviet invasion of Afghanistan in 1979 brought new strains to the East-West relationship, and there was talk of a new Cold War. Then, during the late 1980s, the United States and the Soviet Union renewed their arms-limitation negotiations, signed the INF Treaty, and sought ways to reduce the suspicion and distrust that had for decades marked their relationship.

Recommended Reading

Ambrose, Stephen E. *Rise to Globalism: American Foreign Policy Since 1938* (rev. ed., 1985).

Blair, Clay. *The Forgotten War: America in Korea, 1950–1953* (1987).

Davis, Lynn Etheridge. *The Cold War Begins: Soviet-American Conflict Over Eastern Europe* (1974).

Davison, W. Phillips. *The Berlin Blockade: A Study in Cold War Politics* (1958).

Divine, Robert A. *The Cuban Missile Crisis* (1971).

Divine, Robert A. *Eisenhower and the Cold War* (1981).

Feis, Herbert. *From Trust to Terror: The Onset of the Cold War, 1945–1950* (1970).

Gaddis, John Lewis. *The United States and the Origins of the Cold War, 1941–1947* (1972).

Gormly, James L. *The Collapse of the Grand Alliance, 1945–1948* (1987).

Halle, Louis J. *The Cold War as History* (1967).

Harbutt, Fraser J. *The Iron Curtain: Churchill, America, and the Origins of the Cold War* (1986).

Hastings, Max. *The Korean War* (1987).

Iriye, Akira. *The Cold War in Asia: A Historical Introduction* (1974).

Kuniholm, Bruce R. *The Origins of the Cold War in the Near East: Great Power Conflict and Diplomacy in Iran, Turkey, and Greece* (1980).

LaFeber, Walter. *America, Russia, and the Cold War, 1945–1980* (1980).

Levering, Ralph B. *The Cold War, 1945–1987* (2nd ed., 1988).

Mastny, Vojtech. *Russia's Road to the Cold War* (1979).

Paterson, Thomas G. *On Every Front: The Making of the Cold War* (1979).

Schaller, Michael. *The American Occupation of Japan: The Origins of the Cold War in Asia* (1985).

Thomas, Hugh. *Armed Truce: The Beginnings of the Cold War, 1945–1946* (1987).

Ulam, Adam B. *The Rivals: America and Russia Since World War II* (1971).

CHAPTER 37

The Western Democracies Since 1945

Time Line

1951	Conservative Winston Churchill becomes British prime minister
	The European Coal and Steel Community is established
1952	Britain's King George VI dies and is succeeded by Queen Elizabeth II
1955	Conservative Anthony Eden becomes British prime minister
1957	Conservative Harold Macmillan becomes British prime minister
	The Treaty of Rome creates the European Economic Community
1958	Charles de Gaulle becomes the first president of the Fifth French Republic
1963	Christian Democrat Ludwig Erhard becomes West Germany's chancellor
1966	The West German Christian Democrats and Social Democrats form a coalition government
1969	Social Democrat Willy Brandt becomes West Germany's chancellor
1974	Social Democrat Helmut Schmidt becomes West Germany's chancellor
1975	Francisco Franco, Spain's dictator, dies
1979	Conservative Margaret Thatcher becomes British prime minister
1981	Socialist François Mitterrand wins the French presidency
1982	Christian Democrat Helmut Kohl becomes West Germany's chancellor

When World War II ended in 1945, the prospects for Western Europe appeared dim. Millions of people had been killed, and property damage had been immense. Beneath the ruins, however, there lay the potential for a spectacular economic recovery that was well under way by the 1950s. This economic recovery was accompanied by a remarkable political resurgence and a largely successful movement for Western European integration.

Great Britain

World War II reduced Great Britain to the position of a second-rank power and left the country with serious economic and financial problems. The British depended on imports to feed themselves and to provide the raw materials consumed by the country's industries. The British were not able to sell enough manufactured goods in the world market to pay for these imports, and balance-of-payments problems continued to plague Britain's postwar governments.

The Attlee Labor Government

In July 1945, the Labor Party won a majority of seats in the House of Commons for the first time in history. Clement Attlee (1883–1967), the Labor Party's leader, became prime minister. The Labor government nationalized about 20 percent of the British economy, including the Bank of England, the coal industry, electricity and gas, civil aviation, and the railroads. Attlee's government also established the National Health Service to provide free medical care and extended government-sponsored social insurance programs to provide "cradle to the grave" protection.

The Return of Conservative Government

In 1951, the Conservatives returned to power, beginning a period of thirteen years of Conservative control of the House of Commons. Winston Churchill (1874–1965) once again became prime minister. Following Churchill's retirement in 1955, Anthony Eden (1897–1977) took office. While the Conservatives repealed Labor's nationalization of steel and long-distance trucking, they did not attempt to undo the other reforms of Attlee's government, and the welfare state remained intact.

In 1952, King George VI (r. 1936–1952) died and was succeeded by his daughter, Queen Elizabeth II.

Economic Problems

The Suez Crisis of 1956 (see Chapter 39) led to Eden's resignation in 1957. Harold Macmillan (1894–1986), the new prime minister, rebuilt the Conservatives' lagging support and led the party to an overwhelming victory in the 1959 parliamentary election. In 1963, Macmillan's government suffered a setback when French President Charles de Gaulle vetoed Britain's entry into the European Common Market. Macmillan had hoped that closer trade ties with Western Europe would promote British economic growth. (After de Gaulle left the French presidency, Great Britain entered the Common Market in 1973.)

Although Great Britain experienced some prosperity during the 1950s, the British failed to modernize their industry as rapidly as their competitors in the world market. Furthermore, British industry often lacked innovative management, and the economy continued to be hurt by labor-management conflict.

In 1964, the Labor Party returned to office, and for the next decade and a half, Labor and the Conservatives alternated in power. Although the British economy gradually improved, the old industries that had once provided the backbone of the country's industrial might—coal mining, shipbuilding, steel, and textiles—remained depressed. In an effort to place limits on budget deficits, the Conservatives instituted modest fees for some services provided by the National Health Service, while Labor, with its greater commitment to the welfare state, reduced or eliminated these fees when it was in power.

Thatcher's Conservative Government

In 1979, the Conservatives took control of the House of Commons. Margaret Thatcher (b. 1925) became prime minister, the first woman ever to hold that office and the first woman ever to head a major European government.

Economic Policies

Thatcher, the most conservative of Britain's postwar prime ministers, launched a campaign against "big government." In an effort to combat "stagflation," the combination of economic stagnation and a high inflation rate, she cut government spending, increased interest rates, and reduced taxes. She also sought to curtail the power of the labor unions. The results of what came to be called Thatcherism were mixed: Although the inflation rate dropped, unemployment increased to levels reminiscent of the depression years of the 1930s.

The Falklands War

In foreign policy, the Thatcher government encountered a crisis. Following years of unproductive negotiations, Argentina invaded the British-controlled Falkland Islands in the South Atlantic in April 1982. The British acted promptly to defend the Falklands and inflicted a sharp defeat on Argentina. This assertion of power produced a wave of popular support for the Thatcher government, which triumphed in the House of Commons election of 1983. Divisions in the Labor Party helped the Conservatives retain their hold on power, and they won another electoral victory in 1987.

The Irish Problem

Northern Ireland (Ulster) presented the British with a far more intractable problem than the Falklands war. In Northern Ireland, the Protestant majority had long enforced restrictions on the Roman Catholic minority. A Catholic civil rights movement began in 1968, while the radical Provisional Wing of the Irish Republican Army (IRA) initiated a campaign of terrorism in an effort to force the British out of Ulster and to unite it with the Republic of Ireland. Protestant organizations responded with a terrorist campaign of their own, while the British army attempted to restore and maintain order. Some twenty years after the beginning of this latest in a long series of Irish troubles, no solution appeared to be in sight.

France

The Fourth Republic

In 1946, the French established the Fourth Republic. Like the Third Republic, which had collapsed when France was defeated by Germany in 1940, the new regime concentrated authority in the parliament, while the executive was relatively weak. As in the past, the multiparty system necessitated the formation of coalition cabinets.

Cabinet Instability

General Charles de Gaulle (1890–1970), who had headed both the Free French movement during the war and France's postwar provisional government, opposed the new constitution. He believed that a system based on a strong parliament and a weak executive could not provide the country with effective government and angrily withdrew from an active role in political life.

As de Gaulle had feared, cabinet instability quickly became the main characteristic of government in the Fourth Republic.

Economic Recovery

Despite France's ineffective governments, the country made a good economic recovery and began to experience substantial growth. By 1960, industrial production had increased to two and a half times the 1938 level. France also experienced a significant postwar population growth, reversing the trend of the prewar years.

The Mendès-France Government

In the mid-1950s, Premier Pierre Mendès-France (1907–1982) sought to provide the Fourth Republic with strong leadership. He succeeded in ending France's involvement in the colonial war in Indochina (see Chapter 39) and began the process of ending French rule over Morocco and Tunisia in North Africa. When Mendès-France turned his attention to domestic problems, however, parliamentary wrangling increased, and he lost the premiership.

The Return of de Gaulle

The French regarded their North African possession of Algeria, with its population of over 1 million Frenchmen, as an integral part of France. In 1954, the Algerian National Liberation Front (FLN) began its struggle for independence, and soon a bitter colonial war was under way. The war in Algeria became an intensely divisive issue in French politics, and by 1958 it appeared that the government might enter into serious negotiations with the FLN.

Fearing a withdrawal from Algeria, army leaders began a revolt in Algiers, the Algerian capital, in May 1958. As France stood on the brink of civil war, the leaders of the Fourth Republic called on de Gaulle to take power.

Algerian Independence

De Gaulle established a new regime, the Fifth Republic, which increased the powers of the president and premier and reduced the authority of the parliament. After winning election to a seven-year presidential term in late 1958, de Gaulle acted to solve the Algerian problem. Although the army believed that de Gaulle would maintain French control over Algeria, the president was a realist. Nothing short of full independence for Algeria would satisfy the FLN, and de Gaulle agreed to this demand in 1962.

Foreign Affairs

In foreign affairs, de Gaulle promoted closer ties between France and West Germany, but he remained suspicious of the United States and Great Britain. In 1967, he pulled French forces out of NATO, although France remained a member of the North Atlantic alliance. De Gaulle wanted to establish a more independent role for France in international affairs, and he promoted the development of a French nuclear capability.

1968 Disturbances

De Gaulle focused his attention on foreign and military policy and tended to neglect domestic issues. Discontent gradually mounted, and serious unrest erupted in the spring of 1968. Beginning among the university students in Paris, the trouble soon spread to industry, as hundreds of thousands of workers went on strike.

For a time, de Gaulle's power seemed endangered, but he held on with the support of the army and the middle class. Following the defeat of some relatively minor constitutional changes in 1969, however, de Gaulle resigned.

The Pompidou and Giscard Governments

Georges Pompidou (1911–1974), who succeeded de Gaulle, and Valéry Giscard d'Estaing (b. 1926), who held the presidency from 1974 to 1981, worked to improve the economic situation of the French workers, thereby reducing the discontent that had contributed to the 1968 unrest. Pompidou and Giscard also promoted the cause of Western European integration.

The Mitterrand Government

In 1981, François Mitterrand (b. 1916), the leader of the Socialist Party, defeated Giscard's reelection bid. As president, Mitterrand nationalized several major banks that had not previously been nationalized. Other nationalizations increased the state's share in the ownership of French business and industry from 15 to 35 percent. Mitterrand also increased social benefits and encouraged wage increases in an unsuccessful effort to stimulate the lagging economy. After France was hit by a recession and the value of the franc dropped, Mitterrand adopted more cautious economic policies. The conservative parties regained control of parliament in 1986. During the 1988 presidential campaign, Mitterrand campaigned as a moderate and won a solid reelection victory.

West Germany

The Adenauer Government

When the German Federal Republic was established in 1949, Konrad Adenauer (1876–1967), the leader of the Christian Democrats, won the chancellorship. Adenauer remained chancellor until his retirement in 1963, thus serving longer than Hitler as Germany's leader.

The Adenauer years were the time of the West German economic miracle. Under the leadership of Ludwig Erhard (1897–1977), Adenauer's minister for economics, the economy recovered from the devastation of World War II and experienced remarkable growth. Encouraging private enterprise, Adenauer and Erhard developed a free market economy that quickly made the country one of the most prosperous in Western Europe.

The Adenauer chancellorship also produced a political miracle: the establishment of a stable democratic political system on the ruins of the Nazi dictatorship.

The Erhard Government

After Adenauer retired at the age of 87, Erhard became chancellor. Erhard lacked his predecessor's skills as a political manager, however, and stepped down in 1966. The new government was a coalition of West Germany's two major parties, the Christian Democrats and the Social Democrats. Willy Brandt (b. 1913), the Social Democrats' leader, served as vice chancellor and foreign minister. Following the 1969 parliamentary election, Brandt became chancellor.

The Brandt Government

Both as foreign minister and chancellor, Brandt pursued the policy known as *Ostpolitik* ("east policy"), designed to improve relations with the Soviet Union and the Communist states of Eastern Europe, including East Germany, while maintaining close ties with the West. In 1970, West Germany acknowledged the Oder-Neisse line as Poland's western frontier (see Chapter 35), while a 1972 agreement recognized the existence of two German states and established the bases for closer cooperation between them. Also in 1972, the two German states became members of the United Nations, and the Soviets pledged not to interfere with Western access to Berlin.

The Schmidt and Kohl Governments

In 1974, Brandt was succeeded in the chancellorship by a fellow Social Democrat, Helmut Schmidt (b. 1918). Moderate and capable, Schmidt emerged as a major leader of the Western democracies during his term of office, which ended in 1982.

The Christian Democrats now returned to power, with Helmut Kohl (b. 1930) serving as chancellor. In an effort to cut government spending, the Christian Democrats reduced appropriations for social programs, but they did not attempt to undo the welfare state. Kohl led his party to victory in the parliamentary elections of 1983 and 1987. In 1989, the extreme right-wing Republicans made a strong showing in local and state elections, introducing an element of uncertainty to the West German political scene.

Italy

Postwar Politics

In a 1946 plebiscite, the Italian electorate voted, by a narrow margin, to replace the monarchy with a republic. Postwar Italian politics were dominated by the Christian Democrats, whose leader, Alcide de Gasperi (1881–1954), served as premier from 1947 to 1953. The Christian Democrats never succeeded in winning a majority of seats in the Chamber of Deputies (the lower house of parliament) and had to govern in coalition with other parties. These coalitions were usually unstable and followed one another in rapid succession. Government instability was also promoted by the fact that after de Gasperi left office, the Christian Democrats failed to produce a strong leader who could hold the diverse party together.

"Opening to the Left"

During the 1960s, the Christian Democrats sought to establish a more stable coalition government in an alliance with the Socialists. This "opening to the left," as it was termed, also offered the prospect of promoting economic and social reforms that the more conservative wing of the Christian Democrats had opposed. While a series of

Christian Democratic-Socialist coalitions governed Italy from the 1960s to the 1980s, cabinet stability was not achieved, nor was a substantial reform program enacted.

Economic Recovery

Despite the general ineffectiveness of Italy's governments, the country experienced substantial economic growth. By 1960, Italy's industrial production was three and a half times greater than it had been in 1938, and industrial expansion continued during the 1960s. Italian automobiles, household appliances, and office equipment won large shares of the European market.

Communist Gains

During the 1970s, frustration with Italy's ineffective government mounted. Political terrorism increased, and acts of violence were committed by both neofascist groups and the leftist Red Brigades. Political instability and frustration also enabled the Communists to make significant electoral gains. The Italian Communist party had achieved a high degree of independence from Soviet control, and Enrico Berlinguer (1922–1984) proved to be an attractive and charismatic party leader. When the Communists won 35 percent of the votes in the 1976 election for the Chamber of Deputies, Berlinguer proposed what he called a "historic compromise": the establishment of a Christian Democratic-Communist coalition. The Christian Democrats refused, and the Communists began to lose some of their political momentum, especially after Berlinguer's death in 1984.

During the 1980s, the Christian Democrats held on to their position as Italy's largest party, and the country's political drift continued.

Spain and Portugal

Spain

Francisco Franco (1892–1975), Spain's dictator, owed much of his success during the 1936 to 1939 civil war to the support he received from the Axis dictators, Hitler and Mussolini. Nevertheless, he avoided the mistake of tying his fate to theirs during World War II. While the Franco dictatorship was widely unpopular in Western Europe after 1945, Franco's refusal to give full Spanish support to the Axis cause enabled him to survive.

Restoration of the Monarchy

After Franco's death in 1975, the Spanish monarchy was restored. Under the leaderhip of King Juan Carlos, a member of the Spanish Bourbon dynasty, Spain adopted a liberal constitution in 1976. During the next several years, Spain made a remarkably successful transition from dictatorship to pluralistic democracy.

Portugal

A similar transition occurred in Portugal, where Antonio Salazar (1889–1970) had exercised dictatorial authority from 1932 until he was disabled by a stroke in 1968. The dictatorship was maintained until 1974, when it was overthrown by an army revolt. In 1976, Portugal adopted a democratic constitution.

Western European Integration

Following World War II, Western Europe made remarkable progress in promoting economic integration.

The European Coal and Steel Community

In 1950, Jean Monnet (1888–1979), a French economic planner, convinced Premier Robert Schuman (1886–1963) to support a plan for the integration of the coal and steel industries of France and West Germany. Such integration would reduce French fears of a West German economic recovery.

Negotiations on the Schuman Plan, as the project became known, led to the establishment in 1951 of the European Coal and Steel Community (ECSC). The ECSC not only included France and West Germany, but Italy and the Benelux states (Belgium, the Netherlands, and Luxembourg), as well.

The European Economic Community

The success of the ECSC helped advance an even bolder proposal developed by Monnet. In 1957, the six members of the ECSC signed the Treaty of Rome establishing the European Economic Community (EEC), popularly known as the Common Market. The members of the Common Market committed themselves to eliminate trade barriers and to promote free movement of capital and labor. The success of the Common Market during the 1960s led to its expansion. Great Britain, Ireland, and Denmark joined in 1973, while Greece entered in 1981. In 1986, Spain and Portugal won admission.

The Council of Europe

Developments in the realm of Western European political integration have been more modest. In 1949, the Western European states organized the Council of Europe, an advisory body that meets in Strasbourg, France. Members of the Council of Europe, the so-called European parliament, were elected by the parliaments of the member states until 1979, when direct election was established. Direct election was intended to increase the European parliament's visibility and prestige. However, it remains an advisory body, since the member states are jealous of their political sovereignty.

As Western Europe moved into the final years of the twentieth century, the achievements of the almost half a century since the end of World War II were evident. Throughout Western Europe, democratic political systems were firmly entrenched, and even Spain and Portugal had made evidently successful transitions from dictatorship to democracy. A high degree of economic prosperity had been maintained, and the people of Western Europe had come to enjoy the highest standard of living in their long history. There were problems, including a general slowdown of economic growth, some serious economic weaknesses in Great Britain, and the failure to establish a truly workable system of government in Italy. Nevertheless, Western Europeans could take considerable satisfaction in what they had accomplished.

Recommended Reading

Beer, Samuel H. *Modern British Politics: Parties and Pressure Groups in the Collectivist Age* (1982).

Burridge, T. D. *Clement Attlee: A Political Biography* (1985).

Crozier, Brian. *DeGaulle* (1973).

Dönhoff, Marion. *Foe Into Friend: The Makers of the New Germany from Konrad Adenauer to Helmut Schmidt* (1982).

Douglas, Roy. *World Crisis and British Decline, 1929–1956* (1986).

Ehrmann, Henry W. *Politics in France* (4th ed., 1983).

Ellwood, Sheelagh M. *Spanish Fascism in the Franco Era: Falange Española de las Jons, 1936-76* (1987).

Harrison, Alexander. *Challenging De Gaulle: The O.A.S. and the Counter-Revolution in Algeria, 1954–1962* (1989).

Hartley, Anthony. *Gaullism: The Rise and Fall of a Political Movement* (1971).

Hiscocks, Richard. *The Adenauer Era* (1966).

Hull, Roger W. *The Irish Triangle: Conflict in Northern Ireland* (1976).

Kogan, Norman. *A Political History of Postwar Italy: From the Old to the New Center-Left* (1981).

Laqueur, Walter. *Europe Since Hitler: The Rebirth of Europe* (rev. ed., 1982).

Milward, Alan S. *The Reconstruction of Western Europe, 1945-51* (1984).

Nay, Catherine. *The Black and the Red: François Mitterrand, The Story of an Ambition* (1987).

Payne, Stanley G. *The Franco Regime, 1936–1975* (1987).

Postan, M. M. *An Economic History of Western Europe, 1945–1964* (1967).

Prittie, Terence. *Willy Brandt: Portrait of a Statesman* (1974).

Rioux, Jean-Pierre. *The Fourth Republic, 1944–1958* (1987).

Sampson, Anthony. *The New Anatomy of Britain* (1972).

Seale, Patrick and Maureen McConville. *Red Flag/Black Flag: French Revolution 1968* (1968).

Wiskemann, Elizabeth. *Italy Since 1945* (1971).

CHAPTER 38

The Soviet Union and Eastern
Europe Since 1945

Time Line

1947	The Soviet Union establishes the Communist Information Bureau (Cominform)
1948	A Communist dictatorship is imposed on Czechoslovakia
	Yugoslavia's Marshal Tito defects from the Soviet bloc
1953	Joseph Stalin dies; Georgi Malenkov becomes Soviet premier
	The Soviets suppress the East German revolt

1955	Marshal Nikolai Bulganin replaces Malenkov as premier
1956	Nikita Khrushchev denounces Stalin in a speech to the 20th Congress of the Soviet Communist Party
	Wladyslaw Gomulka becomes head of the Polish Communist Party
	The Soviets suppress the Hungarian revolution
1957	The Soviets launch *Sputnik I*
1958	Nikita Khrushchev becomes Soviet premier, succeeding Bulganin
	Boris Pasternak wins the Nobel Prize for literature
1960	Albania breaks with the Soviet Union
1963	Rumania begins to pursue a more independent course
1964	Leonid I. Brezhnev succeeds Khrushchev as general secretary of the Soviet Communist Party; Alexei N. Kosygin becomes premier
1968	The Soviets invade Czechoslovakia, ending Alexander Dubcek's reform efforts
1980	Solidarity, an independent trade union, is established in Poland
1981	General Wojciech Jaruzelski becomes head of the Polish Communist Party
1985	Mikhail Gorbachev becomes general secretary of the Soviet Communist Party
1989	The Polish government grants legal recognition to Solidarity

The Soviet Union emerged from World War II as one of the two super-powers, along with the United States. Although the Soviets had suffered immense losses of both lives and property, Soviet heavy industry continued to expand, and the country's armed might increased. The totalitarian political system remained intact, although after Stalin's death in 1953 his heirs made some efforts to reduce the repression. After taking office as general secretary of the Communist Party in 1985, Mikhail Gorbachev initiated a far-reaching reform program.

The Soviets took control of most of Eastern Europe at war's end. Despite the imposition of Communist governments in the so-called satellite states, however, nationalism remained a powerful force, and a number of challenges to Soviet domination emerged.

The Soviet Union

Stalin's Last Years

As Joseph Stalin's dictatorship moved into its final years, the Soviet Union remained a brutal police state. The expression of dissent was impossible, and intellectuals and artists were forced into a leaden conformity. Stalin's cult of personality grew, and his authority remained unchallenged.

Economic Policy

According to one estimate, World War II had cost the Soviet Union à third of its national wealth. The Soviets launched a new series of Five Year Plans designed to reconstruct the nation's economy and to promote its further expansion. Emphasis continued to be placed on the development of heavy industry, while the production of consumer goods and the construction of housing were neglected. Agricultural production lagged, and food shortages were a common feature of Soviet life. The Soviets also devoted much of their resources to the development of their military strength.

Death of Stalin

During late 1952 and early 1953, it appeared that Stalin might be on the verge of launching another great purge, repeating the horrors of the 1930s. The Soviet press reported charges that a group of physicians had conspired to kill a number of Soviet leaders. As the propaganda campaign intensified, Stalin died suddenly on March 6, 1953.

The Soviet Union Under Khrushchev

Although Georgi Malenkov (1902–1988) succeeded Stalin as premier, a collective leadership exercised power. The new leaders quickly brought a halt to the "Doctors' Plot" campaign and ordered the release of the accused. Lavrenti Beria (1899–1953), the ambitious head of the secret police, was dismissed and executed. Gradually, Nikita Khrushchev (1894–1971), the party secretary, emerged as the most influential of the country's new leaders. In 1955, he succeeded in replacing Malenkov with Marshal Nikolai Bulganin (1895–1975). Khrushchev then moved to solidify his own power, and by 1958 he was strong enough to take the premiership for himself. Nevertheless, Khrushchev was never able to wield the kind of unchallenged power that Stalin had.

Economic Policy

While the Soviet Union remained an authoritarian state, Khrushchev initiated a number of reforms. In the sphere of economic policy, although he did not abandon the traditional emphasis on heavy industry, Khrushchev encouraged the production of consumer goods and the construction of housing. He boasted that by 1970 Soviet per capita production would catch up with that of the United States. In fact, the expansion of the Soviet economy began to lag during the 1960s, and Khrushchev's boast was soon forgotten.

Agriculture

In an effort to increase agricultural production, Khrushchev consolidated collective farms into larger units and initiated the virgin lands program, beginning the cultivation of semiarid land, especially in Western Siberia and Central Asia. Although the program scored some early successes, a series of droughts soon turned much of the area into a dust bowl.

Space Achievements

The Soviets continued to invest much of their resources in the arms race and devoted increasing appropriations to space research. In the autumn of 1957, the Soviets launched *Sputnik I*, the first artificial earth satellite. In 1959, they succeeded in sending a rocket to the moon, and in April 1961, Yuri Gagarin (1934–1968) made the first manned orbital flight. The Soviets' space exploits greatly increased the international prestige of the Soviet Union, especially in the Third World.

"The Thaw"

In February 1956, Khrushchev delivered a powerful denunciation of Stalin's policy mistakes, crimes, and cult of personality in an address to the 20th Congress of the Soviet Communist Party.

Khrushchev rehabilitated many of Stalin's victims, some posthumously, and millions of prisoners were released from the Soviet Union's labor camps. Intellectuals and artists were permitted greater freedom of expression in what came to be called The Thaw. Works appeared in print that could not conceivably have been published in Stalin's time. One of the most notable was Vladimir Dudintsev's *Not by Bread Alone* (1957), an outspoken criticism of the Soviet bureaucracy.

Pasternak

The case of Boris Pasternak's great novel *Doctor Zhivago* soon revealed the limits of The Thaw. In *Doctor Zhivago,* Pasternak (1890–1960) celebrated the human spirit and did not attempt to conform to the ideological standards dictated by the Soviet Writers' Union.

Initially, the Soviet censors approved the publication of *Doctor Zhivago,* and a copy of the manuscript was sent to an Italian publisher. The censors then reversed themselves, declaring the novel unacceptable because of its rejection of the principles of the revolution. The Italian publisher refused to return the manuscript, however, and published an Italian translation in 1957. Translations in other Western languages quickly followed. Pasternak was awarded the Nobel Prize for literature in 1958. The Soviet authorities told Pasternak that if he left the country to accept the award, he would not be allowed to return. Pasternak spent the remaining years of his life in seclusion.

Foreign Policy

In foreign affairs, Khrushchev first sought a reduction of tension with the West and then pursued a more adventuristic policy, challenging the Western powers at Berlin and the United States in the Cuban missile crisis (see Chapter 36). In addition, Soviet relations with Communist China deteriorated.

Fall of Khrushchev

Opposition to Khrushchev gradually increased within the Soviet leadership, which criticized him for his failures in agriculture and foreign policy and also for his personal "rudeness." He was removed from his positions in October 1964. Alexei N. Kosygin (1904–1980) replaced him as premier, while Leonid I. Brezhnev (1906–1982) became general secretary of the Communist Party. Brezhnev gradually became the dominant figure in the Soviet regime, and in 1977 he assumed the additional title of president.

The Soviet Union from Brezhnev to Gorbachev

In economic affairs, the Brezhnev years were a period of increasing stagnation. Although more consumer goods and housing became available, the quality was often shoddy and shortages persisted. Agriculture remained particularly troubled, and the Soviets depended on grain imports from the United States and other Western countries.

Expulsion of Solzhenitsyn

For Soviet intellectuals and artists, the Brezhnev era was a time of renewed repression. The most famous case involved the writer Alexander Solzhenitsyn (b. 1918). Under Stalin, Solzhenitsyn had been imprisoned in a labor camp and his brief novel based on that experience, *One Day in the Life of Ivan Denisovich,* had been published in the Soviet Union in 1962. Solzhenitsyn ran into increasing trouble with the authorities, however, and permission to publish other works was denied.

Solzhenitsyn smuggled manuscripts to the West, where they were published, and he was awarded the Nobel Prize for literature in 1970. Like Pasternak, Solzhenitsyn was not permitted to leave the Soviet Union to accept the award. In 1974, *The Gulag Archipelago,* a long work on Soviet police terror and the labor camps, was published in the

West. Solzhenitsyn was expelled from the Soviet Union the following year.

Exile of Sakharov

Andrei Sakharov (1921-1989), a physicist and a key figure in the Soviet Union's development of the hydrogen bomb, also joined the ranks of the dissidents, calling for greater freedom of expression and a liberalization of the political system. In 1975, Sakharov was awarded the Nobel Peace Prize, but the authorities would not allow him to leave the country to accept it. Sakharov's contacts with Western journalists annoyed the regime, and he was sent into internal exile in the city of Gorky, which was off-limits to Westerners.

Jewish Emigration

The question of Jewish emigration from the Soviet Union became a serious issue during the Brezhnev years. In the 1970s, the Soviet regime permitted an increasing number of Jews to leave, although many continued to be denied exit visas. When American-Soviet relations deteriorated following the Soviet invasion of Afghanistan in 1979, Jewish emigration declined markedly.

Andropov and Chernenko

Following Brezhnev's death in November 1982, he was followed in quick succession by two men of his generation. Yuri Andropov (1914–1984) became seriously ill soon after taking over as general secretary and died in February 1984. Konstantin Chernenko (1911–1985) was already in declining health when chosen to replace Andropov and died in March 1985.

Mikhail Gorbachev (b. 1931)

The Soviet Politburo now turned to a younger generation of leaders, selecting Mikhail Gorbachev as general secretary. Gorbachev quickly introduced two new terms to the political vocabulary: *glasnost* and *perestroika*.

Glasnost

The policy of *glasnost* ("openness") sought to reduce the intellectual and cultural repression that had long characterized the Soviet system and had contributed to its stagnation. Gorbachev went far beyond Khrushchev's "Thaw" of the late 1950s. The reporting of news became more honest and less propagandistic, and restrictions on dissenters were reduced. *Glasnost* led, for example, to the decision to publish Pasternak's *Doctor Zhivago* and to permit Sakharov to return to Moscow.

Perestroika

Gorbachev's policy of *perestroika* ("restructuring") had implications for both politics and the economy. Gorbachev proposed reducing the direct involvement of the Communist Party leadership in the day-to-day governance of the country and increasing the authority of agencies of local government. In the economic realm, he sought to promote not only greater productivity in both industry and agriculture, but also to improve the quality of manufactured goods. *Perestroika* called for a decentralization of economic planning and controls, increased incentives, and greater private initiative than had been permitted in the past.

Political Changes

When his policies encountered opposition from a number of old-line bureaucrats and party officials, Gorbachev succeeded, in the autumn of 1988, in reshaping the Communist Party's leadership. He took the title of president for himself, removed several of his opponents from their positions, and demoted others. In 1989, for the first time in history, contested elections for the Soviet parliament were held, and a number of prominent Communists were defeated. While Gorbachev appeared serious in his determination to promote reform, he was equally determined to maintain the Communist Party's hold on power.

In foreign policy, Gorbachev sought improved relations with the Western powers (see Chapter 36) and pursued a reconciliation with China, visiting Beijing, the Chinese capital, in May 1989.

Eastern Europe

The Sovietization of Eastern Europe

The end of World War II brought with it a considerable extension of Soviet power in Eastern Europe. The Soviets reannexed the territory they had acquired as a result of Stalin's 1939 pact with Hitler (see Chapter 34): eastern Poland, the Baltic states (Estonia, Latvia, and Lithuania), and the Rumanian province of Bessarabia, as well as some Finnish territory. In addition, the Soviets imposed Communist-dominated governments on Poland, Rumania, Bulgaria, and Hungary. In Yugoslavia and Albania, local Communists took power, while Communists played the leading role in the coalition governing Czechoslovakia. The Soviets also controlled their occupation zone in eastern Germany and until 1955, an occupation zone in Austria.

In the late 1940s, as the United States initiated the Truman Doctrine program of aid to Greece and Turkey and the Marshall Plan (see Chapter 36), the Soviets moved to tighten their hold on Eastern Europe. In September 1947, they organized the Communist Information Bureau (Cominform) to serve as an instrument of control over the Eastern European Communist parties. The Soviets also removed from power Eastern European Communist leaders whom they suspected of being less than completely willing to accept Moscow's dictates. In February 1948, they imposed a Communist dictatorship on Czechoslovakia. Later the same year, the Soviets sponsored the creation of the Council for Economic Mutual Assistance (COMECON), a sort of Marshall Plan for the Soviet bloc. Instead of assisting the recovery of the Eastern European economies, however, the Soviets exploited them.

Tito's Defection

In March 1948, Marshal Tito (1891–1980), Yugoslavia's Communist dictator, defected from the Soviet camp. While Tito was a Communist, he was also a nationalist. His role in the Yugoslav guerrilla war against the Germans had brought him to power at war's end. Unlike other Eastern European Communist leaders, he did not owe his power to the Red Army. Refusing to obey orders from Moscow, Tito moved to improve Yugoslavia's relations with the Western powers.

Tito's revolt revealed the continuing strength of nationalism among the Eastern Europeans and suggested that the force of nationalism could create problems for the Soviets elsewhere among their satellites.

The East German Revolt

In 1949, following the creation of the German Federal Republic in the Western occupation zones, the Soviets established the Communist-dominated German Democratic Republic in their zone.

Mounting unrest in East Germany erupted in June 1953 when construction workers in East Berlin went on strike to protest the government's raising of work norms. The strike quickly spread to other East German cities, and the country appeared on the verge of open revolt against its Communist rulers. However, Soviet forces stationed in East Germany soon restored order.

Poland and Hungary

Following Stalin's death in 1953, the new Soviet leadership acted to improve relations with Yugoslavia's Marshal Tito, acknowledging his view that there were various paths to socialism and that it was not necessary for all Communist states to imitate the Soviet pattern. This, as well as Khrushchev's de-Stalinization campaign, had a powerful effect on the Eastern European Communist satellites.

In the autumn of 1956, long-smoldering resentments erupted in Poland and Hungary.

Poland's Deviation

The Polish Communist leaders removed their Stalinist party chief and replaced him with Wladyslaw Gomulka (1905–1982), a national Communist whom the Soviets had pushed aside in the late 1940s. Gomulka set out to develop a Polish path to socialism and to improve relations with the Roman Catholic Church, which continued to hold the allegiance of the vast majority of Poland's population.

For a time, it remained uncertain how the Soviets would respond to the events in Poland, but Gomulka succeeded in convincing them that Poland would remain a Communist state and would maintain its alliance with the USSR. Thus reassured, the Soviets agreed to let Poland pursue its new course. The Poles breathed a sigh of relief and spoke of "spring in October."

Hungary's Attempted Revolution

In Hungary, the outcome was less happy. Imre Nagy (1896–1958), a national Communist like Gomulka, became party leader in October 1956. Hungarian nationalism then exploded in a great popular revolution, which pushed Nagy further than he had originally intended to go. He announced that Hungary would reestablish a multiparty system. Almost inevitably, this would have ended the Communists' control of the government. In addition, Nagy indicated that Hungary would end its alliance with the Soviet Union and pursue a neutralist foreign policy.

In early November, the Red Army moved into Hungary. Nagy was removed and later executed. Janos Kadar (1912–1989) was installed as Hungary's new Communist dictator. During the revolt, some 200,000 Hungarians fled across the Austrian border, seeking refuge in the West.

While Kadar acted ruthlessly in his suppression of dissent, over the course of the next generation he gradually introduced reforms. While political power remained the monopoly of the Communists, Kadar permitted greater freedom of cultural expression and also allowed a degree of private economic enterprise that was unknown elsewhere in the Soviet bloc.

In May 1988, Kadar fell from power. Karoly Grosz (b. 1930), his successor, moved to democratize Hungary's political system and introduced reforms designed to revitalize the country's lagging economy.

Albania and Rumania

Like Tito in Yugoslavia, Enver Hozha (1908–1985), Albania's Communist leader, had achieved power on his own and thus owed little to the Soviets. Hozha's continued rigid adherence to Stalinist policies led to a break with Moscow in 1960. The Albanians then moved into the Chinese camp.

In 1963, Rumania refused to follow Soviet directives for its economic development and began to pursue a more independent course. In Moscow's view, Rumania should concentrate on agriculture and oil production; the Rumanians wanted to industrialize. While Rumania remained a rigid Communist dictatorship, it began to develop closer ties with the West.

The Crisis in Czechoslovakia

The most serious challenge to the Soviets during the 1960s came from Czechoslovakia. In January 1968, Alexander Dubcek (b. 1921), a national Communist, became head of the Czechoslovak Communist Party and initiated a reform program. Dubcek abolished censorship, allowing greater intellectual and cultural freedom and a more open discussion of political issues. He even considered permitting non-Communist political groups to exist. In foreign policy, Dubcek moved to improve relations with the West.

Fearing the spread of demands for reform to other Eastern European countries, Moscow began to pressure the Czechoslovak leaders to restrict the scope of reform. When the Czechoslovaks refused to do so, Soviet, East German, Polish, Hungarian, and Bulgarian troops invaded Czechoslovakia on August 21, 1968. Dubcek was forced out of office. His successor, Gustav Husak (b. 1913), restored tight Communist Party control over the country. Husak remained in power until December 1987, when Milos Jakes (b. 1922) succeeded him.

Renewed Crisis in Poland

During the 1960s, there were signs of renewed discontent in Poland, particularly over the failures of the government's economic policies, which resulted in serious food shortages and price increases. Protests led to Gomulka's resignation in 1970 and his replacement by Edward Gierek (b. 1913).

Despite the change in leadership, economic problems persisted and grew more serious, giving rise to increased discontent. In addition, there were growing demands for increased intellectual and cultural freedom.

In August 1980, shipyard workers in the Baltic port of Gdansk went on strike. As fear of violence increased, the government yielded to most of the strikers' demands and recognized their independent union, Solidarity, led by Lech Walesa (b. 1943). Gierek lost his post as head of the Communist Party and was succeeded by Stanislaw Kania (b. 1927).

The pressure for changes in Poland continued. In early 1981, Solidarity demanded a five-day workweek, while rebellious farmers organized a union of their own, Rural Solidarity. Poland's economic problems persisted, and food shortages led to rationing. As tension mounted, the Polish Communist Party replaced Kania with General Wojciech Jaruzelski (b. 1923). In December 1981, Jaruzelski declared martial law, outlawed Solidarity, and ordered the arrest of a number of its leaders, including Walesa.

Although Jaruzelski restored the control of the Communist Party, discontent persisted. In April 1989, the government extended legal recognition to Solidarity and promised that opposition groups would be represented in the new parliament. After Solidarity scored major gains in Communist Poland's first free elections later in the spring, the country's Communist leaders moved to share power with the union. Serious economic problems, including food shortages, shortages of consumer goods and housing, and rising prices, persisted, resulting in a steady decline in the standard of living of the Polish people.

Poland's problems were repeated throughout the Communist bloc, and as the twentieth century moved into its final years, the pressures for change were intensifying.

As the decade of the 1980s drew to a close, the Soviet Union appeared to be entering an entirely new period in its history. Gorbachev's policies of glasnost and perestroika, if they succeeded, would end the legacy of Stalinism: the demand for total intellectual and cultural conformity, the complete subordination of the Soviet government to the hierarchy of the Communist Party, and the emphasis on the development of heavy industry with a consequent neglect of consumer-goods production and housing construction.

Communist Eastern Europe also seemed destined for change. Reform in the Soviet Union, combined with the ever-present force of nationalism, would almost inevitably lead both to changes in the nature of the Communist system in the Eastern European states and to the development of new relationships between them and the Soviet Union.

Recommended Reading

Altshuler, Mordechai. *Soviet Jewry Since the Second World War: Population and Social Structure* (1987).

Ash, Timothy G. *The Polish Revolution: Solidarity, 1980-82* (1983).

Brzezinski, Zbigniew. *The Grand Failure: The Birth and Death of Communism in the Twentieth Century* (1989).

Byrnes, Robert F., ed. *After Brezhnev: Sources of Soviet Conduct in the 1980s* (1983).

Carrere d'Encaussé, Hélène. *Big Brother: The Soviet Union and Soviet Europe* (1987).

Cohen, Stephen F., et al., eds. *The Soviet Union Since Stalin* (1980).

Conquest, Robert. *The Pasternak Affair: Courage of Genius* (1962).

Crankshaw, Edward. *Khrushchev: A Career* (1966).

Dedijer, Vladirmir. *Tito* (1953).

Dornberg, John. *Brezhnev: The Masks of Power* (1974).

Dornberg, John. *Eastern Europe: A Communist Kaleidoscope* (1980).

Ellis, Jane. *The Russian Orthodox Church: A Contemporary History* (1986).

Feher, Ferenc. *Hungary 1956 Revisited: The Message of a Revolution* (1983).

Felkay, Andrew. *Hungary and the USSR, 1956–1988* (1989).

Golan, Galia. *The Czechoslovak Reform Movement: Communism in Crisis, 1962–1968* (1971).

Golan, Galia. *Reform Rule in Czechoslovakia: The Dubcek Era, 1968–1969* (1973).

Griffith, William E., ed. *Central and Eastern Europe: The Opening Curtain?* (1989).

Hazan, Barukh. *From Brezhnev to Gorbachev: Infighting in the Kremlin* (1987).

Jones, T. Anthony. *Perestroika: Gorbachev's Social Revolution* (1989).

Krisch, Henry. *The German Democratic Republic: The Search for Identity* (1985).

Nove, Alec. *The Soviet Economic System* (3rd ed., 1986).

Rywkin, Michael. *Soviet Society Today* (1989).

Seton-Watson, Hugh. *The East European Revolution* (3rd ed., 1956).

Shipler, David K. *Russia: Broken Idols, Solemn Dreams* (rev. ed., 1989).

Smith, Hedrick. *The Russians* (1976).

Syrop, Konrad. *Spring in October: The Polish Revolution, 1956* (1957).

Szajkowski, Bogdan. *Next to God—Poland: Politics and Religion in Contemporary Poland* (1983).

Werth, Alexander. *Russia: The Postwar Years* (1971).

Zinner, Paul E. *Revolution in Hungary* (1962).

CHAPTER 39

The End of European Empire

Time Line

1945	The Arab League is established
1947	India and Pakistan gain independence from Great Britain
1948	Israel declares its independence
1949	Indonesia gains independence from the Netherlands
1951	Libya gains independence
1952	A revolution in Egypt overthrows King Farouk and leads to the dictatorship of Gamel Abdul Nasser

1954	France withdraws from Indochina
1956	Tunisia and Morocco gain independence from France
	Egypt nationalizes the Suez Canal; Great Britain, France, and Israel attack Egypt
1957	The British West African colony of the Gold Coast gains independence, becoming Ghana
1958	Guinea gains independence from France
1960	Nigeria gains independence from Great Britain
	Most of France's African colonies become independent
	The Congo gains independence from Belgium
1961	Tanganyika gains independence from Great Britain
	The Union of South Africa withdraws from the British Commonwealth
1962	Algeria gains independence from France
	Uganda and Kenya gain independence from Great Britain
1965	Rhodesia issues its unilateral declaration of independence
1967	Israel defeats Egypt, Syria, and Jordan in the Six-Day War
1969	A military revolt in Libya leads to Muammar el-Qaddafi's coming to power
1970	Anwar el-Sadat succeeds Nasser as Egypt's leader
1971	Bangladesh gains independence from Pakistan

1973	Israel defeats Egypt and Syria in the Yom Kippur War
	The United States withdraws its troops from South Vietnam
1978	Israel and Egypt sign the Camp David accords

Following World War II, the spread of nationalism among the peoples of the Middle East, Asia, and Africa brought an end to the great empires of the European powers.

In the Middle East, the withdrawal of the British and French was followed by the decades-long conflict between the Arab states and Israel. In Asia, the Europeans recognized the independence of most of their former colonies by the early 1950s, although in Indochina the United States gradually replaced the French in the struggle against Ho Chi Minh. During the 1950s, the rising tide of nationalism engulfed black Africa, and by the early 1960s, a number of independent African states had come into being. In South Africa, however, there was a continuing struggle over the policy of apartheid (the separation of the races) enforced by the white-dominated government.

The Middle East

The Arab World

Between the two world wars, Arab nationalism emerged as a powerful force in the Middle East. Arab nationalism was directed primarily against the British and French, who dominated most of the area. Although the Arab states of the Middle East—Syria, Lebanon, Egypt, Iraq, Jordan, and Saudi Arabia—secured their independence, considerable distrust of the Western powers remained. In 1945, the Arab states organized the Arab League to promote cooperation among them, although behind the facade of Arab unity, differences persisted.

In North Africa, the former Italian colony of Libya became an independent monarchy in 1951. In 1969, a group of army officers seized power, and Colonel Muammar el-Qaddafi (b. 1943) soon emerged as Libya's strongman. Qaddafi used the income from Libya's rich oil reserves to buy arms from the Soviets and to aid terrorist activities in a number of countries.

In 1956, Tunisia and Morocco gained their independence from France, and following a bitter colonial war, the French acknowledged the independence of Algeria in 1962.

The Founding of the State of Israel

Following World War II, powerful pressures mounted for the establishment of a Jewish state in Palestine, which the British had acquired as a League of Nations mandate after World War I.

Zionism

In biblical times, Palestine had been the home of the Jewish people, and a desire to reclaim the Holy Land remained a part of the Jewish religious tradition. In the late nineteenth century, Theodor Herzl (1860–1904), an Austrian Jew, and others founded the modern Zionist movement, which actively sought the creation of a national home for the Jewish people in Palestine.

During World War I, the British issued the Balfour Declaration, pledging the establishment of such a national home. Faced with Arab opposition, however, the British did not fulfill this pledge, and they also restricted Jewish immigration into Palestine.

Israel's War of Independence

The World War II Holocaust brought the issue to a head. The Jews and their supporters demanded the establishment of a Jewish state in Palestine, while the Arabs remained adamant in their opposition. The British found themselves trapped between these competing demands.

In 1948, the British pulled out of Palestine, turning the problem over to the United Nations. The Jews proclaimed the establishment of the State of Israel, accepting the frontiers proposed by the UN in its effort to partition Palestine between the Jews and the Arabs. The Arab League refused to accept partition, however, and went to war against Israel.

Israeli Victory and Arab Refugees

The Israeli war of independence ended in 1949 with an Israeli victory. A number of Arabs were expelled from Israel, while others fled. The issue of the Palestinian refugees and their descendants would remain a troubling problem in the continuing conflict in the Middle East.

The Suez Crisis of 1956

In 1952, a revolution in Egypt overthrew King Farouk (r. 1936–1952). Gamel Abdul Nasser (1918–1970), an ardent Egyptian nationalist and advocate of Arab unity, soon established his dictatorship. Nasser developed an ambitious plan for Egypt's economic development, centered on the construction of a high dam at Aswan on the Nile River. Egypt received pledges of loans to help build the dam from the United States, Great Britain, and the World Bank.

Nationalization of the Suez Canal

When Nasser tried to play the two Cold War antagonists off against one another and secured arms and a loan from the Soviets, the United States responded in July 1956 by canceling American support for the Aswan high dam. Great Britain and the World Bank did the same. At the end of July, Nasser retaliated by seizing the privately owned Suez Canal Company. Although Nasser agreed to compensate the company's owners, the British and French were troubled by Egyptian control of the strategically important canal.

The Invasion of Egypt

Great Britain and France entered into a scheme with Israel, which feared an Egyptian attack. Acting in accord with London and Paris, Israel launched a preemptive strike against Egypt on October 29, 1956. Britain and France quickly moved into the canal zone, ostensibly to separate the antagonists but in reality to take control of the canal.

World opinion joined in condemnation of the British, French, and Israelis. Isolated diplomatically, they withdrew. Egypt paid the Suez Canal Company's stockholders $81 million for the canal, and the Soviets helped the Egyptians build the Aswan high dam.

The Suez Crisis of 1956 had settled little, and Nasser remained

implacably hostile toward Israel. The Middle East arms race intensified, as the Soviets supplied the Arab states with arms and the United
States aided Israel.

The Six-Day War

In 1967, a new Middle East crisis erupted. Egyptian, Syrian, and
Jordanian troops massed along Israel's borders. On June 5, Israel
attacked, beginning the Six-Day War. Catching their enemies off
balance, the Israelis occupied Egypt's territory east of the Suez Canal
(the Gaza Strip and the Sinai Peninsula), Syria's Golan Heights, and
Jordan's holdings on the West Bank of the Jordan River. On June 10,
an armistice was signed.

The Six-Day War humiliated not only the Arabs, but the Soviet
Union as well. The Soviets provided the Arab states with a new supply
of arms. In 1970, following Nasser's death, Anwar el-Sadat (1918–
1981) became Egypt's leader, and tension with Israel continued.

The Yom Kippur War

In October 1973, Egypt and Syria renewed their war against Israel,
beginning the so-called Yom Kippur War. This time the Israelis were
caught off guard, and they were pushed back.   Israel gradually
recovered its poise, however, and drove across the Suez Canal into
Egypt and advanced toward the Syrian capital of Damascus.

Golda Meir (1898–1978), Israel's prime minister, agreed to a
cease-fire, but the Israelis remained adamant in their refusal to give up
the territories they had occupied in 1967, insisting they were necessary
for Israel's security.

Arab Oil Embargo

Following the Yom Kippur War, the Arab oil-producing states
placed an embargo on the shipment of oil to the United States and
Western Europe in an effort to force them to put pressure on Israel to
make concessions. In addition, the Organization of Petroleum Export-
ing Countries (OPEC) began a round of increases in the price of

petroleum that helped spur an inflationary spiral in the industrialized countries.

Accords Between Egypt and Israel

Recognizing the negative impact that the continuing conflict with Israel had on Egypt's economic development, Sadat sought a normalization of relations between the two countries.

In September 1978, American President Jimmy Carter (b. 1924) invited Sadat and Israel's Prime Minister Menachem Begin (b. 1913) to meet with him at Camp David, Maryland. Carter succeeded in inducing the two leaders to sign the Camp David Accords, which established a framework for a peace treaty. In March 1979, Sadat and Begin returned to Washington to sign a formal peace treaty in which Israel agreed to return the occupied Sinai peninsula to Egypt. No agreement was reached, however, on an Israeli withdrawal from the Gaza Strip, the West Bank of the Jordan River, and the Golan Heights or the troublesome issue of the Palestinian refugees.

In October 1981, Egyptian nationalist extremists assassinated Sadat. Egypt's new president, Hosni Mubarak (b. 1928), continued the moderate foreign policy of his predecessor, and the peace settlement between Egypt and Israel remained intact.

Civil War in Lebanon

The question of the Palestinian refugees remained as a major obstacle in the path of a broader Middle Eastern settlement. Under the leadership of the Palestine Liberation Organization (PLO), headed by Yasir Arafat (b. 1929), the Palestinians demanded the return of the Israeli-occupied lands and the creation of a separate Palestinian state. Many Palestinians had taken refuge in Lebanon, creating a virtual state-within-a-state beyond the ability of the Lebanese authorities to control. In 1975, the Palestinians joined with the Lebanese Moslems in an attempt to overthrow the Christian-dominated government. As Lebanon sank deeper in the abyss of a vicious civil war, Syria moved in and established its military control over much of the country.

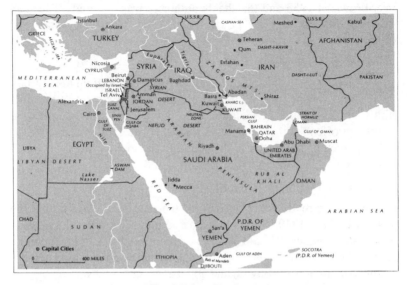

The Middle East, 1989

UN Intervention

Palestinian terrorism enraged the Israelis, who moved into southern Lebanon on several occasions to strike at PLO bases. In June 1982, the Israelis pushed deep into Lebanon. A cease-fire was arranged, and the United Nations organized an international peacekeeping force to establish a buffer zone between contending elements in Lebanon. Tension continued to run high in the area, however, as a result both of ongoing civil conflict in Lebanon and the uprising of Palestinians in the Gaza Strip and West Bank.

Iran

In 1951, Mohammed Mossadegh (1880–1967) became Iran's prime minister. He pursued an anti-Western policy, nationalizing the country's petroleum industry. Iran's ruler, Shah Mohammed Reza Pahlavi (r. 1941–1978), lost power and fled the country. With the support of a coup engineered by the American CIA, Mossadegh was overthrown in 1953 and the shah's authority was restored. The shah returned ownership of the petroleum industry to private hands and established close ties with the West.

The Shah's Regime

With American aid and oil royalties, the shah built up his military power and launched the White Revolution, which sought to promote Iran's industrial and agricultural development. The modernization campaign offended many of Iran's traditionalist Moslems, and it was accompanied by political repression and widespread corruption, which also increased opposition to the shah's regime.

Khomeini's Islamic Republic

In 1978, a revolt broke out against the shah's rule, and he left the country in early 1979. Power now passed into the hands of Ayatollah Ruhollah Khomeini (1902–1989), who proclaimed an Islamic republic. Khomeini was both an ardent Moslem and an ardent nationalist, strongly anti-American, anti-Soviet, and anti-Israeli in his views.

When the United States gave refuge to the exiled shah, who was dying of cancer, Iranians seized the American embassy in Tehran in November 1979, taking more than fifty Americans as hostages. Complex negotiations finally brought the release of the hostages in January 1981.

Asia

China

The victory of the Communists in 1949 reduced Western influence in China. While Mao Tse-tung (Mao Zedong, 1893–1976) formed an alliance with the Soviet Union and initiated a five-year plan, in imitation of the Soviet pattern of economic development, Sino-Soviet relations gradually cooled, and China moved to improve relations with the West. Following Mao's death in 1976, Deng Xiaoping (b. 1904?) emerged as the key figure in the government. Deng adopted reformist policies in an effort to promote China's economic development.

Japan

Following World War II, the United States established its occupation of Japan, with General Douglas MacArthur (1880–1964) serving as supreme commander. Under American tutelage, the Japanese drafted a democratic constitution establishing a parliamentary monarchy.

The Japanese undertook a remarkable development of their economy, and by the mid–1960s, Japan had become the world's third greatest industrial power, behind the United States and the Soviet Union.

India

In 1947, the British withdrew from their empire in the Indian subcontinent, and two independent states came into being, predominantly Hindu India and mainly Moslem Pakistan.

The establishment of the new India was largely the work of Mohandas K. Gandhi (1869–1948), known as the Mahatma (Great Spirit), and Jawaharlal Nehru (1889–1964). Soon after the achievement of independence, Gandhi was assassinated, and Nehru, the leader of the ruling Indian National Congress party, had to bear the primary responsibility for building the new state.

In international affairs, India pursued a neutralist course, seeking to avoid direct involvement in the East-West conflict.

Economic Problems

With a huge population of 350 million, most of whom lived in poverty, India required massive infusions of aid from more highly developed countries to advance its own economic development. Most of India's economic growth, however, was offset by the country's growing population.

Pakistan

The 70 million people of Pakistan emerged into independence in 1947 under the leadership of Mohammed Ali Jinnah (1876–1948), the head of the Moslem League, which had long sought the establishment of a separate Moslem state in the Indian subcontinent. Jinnah did not long survive the achievement of independence, dying in 1948.

In foreign policy, Pakistan adopted a pro-Western stance, joining both SEATO and the Baghdad Pact alliances during the 1960s (see Chapter 36). In later years, Pakistan adopted a more neutral posture.

Like India, Pakistan faced a host of problems, and economic underdevelopment increased political tensions. Pakistan's problems were compounded by the fact that the country was divided into two parts, with some 1,000 miles of Indian territory separating West Pakistan from East Pakistan. In 1971, East Pakistan rebelled and with India's help, won its independence, becoming the Republic of Bangladesh.

Bangladesh

In the years following its achievement of independence in 1971, the political and economic history of Bangladesh proved to be unhappy. Efforts to establish a workable form of representative government were uncertain at best, with military dictatorship alternating with civilian rule. Economically, the country remained desperately poor, overpopulated, and dependent on foreign aid for survival.

Indonesia

Following World War II, the Netherlands attempted to reassert its control over its rich empire in the East Indies. In 1949, however, the Republic of Indonesia gained independence under the leadership of Achmed Sukarno (1901–1970). Indonesia was rich in tin, oil, rubber, and other resources and faced a more promising economic future than many of the other newly independent Asian states.

Sukarno gradually increased his dictatorial power, establishing what he called a "guided democracy." Sukarno's decision to increase Indonesia's ties with Communist China intensified opposition to his rule. An army revolt in the autumn of 1965 led to Sukarno's ouster.

Other Asian Nations

Elsewhere in Asia, the United States recognized the independence of the Philippines, while Ceylon (which became Sri Lanka), Burma, Malaysia, and Singapore secured independence from Great Britain.

The British retained the crown colony of Hong Kong, although a treaty signed in 1984 provided for its restoration to China in 1997.

Southeast Asia: The Vietnam War

The Origins of the Vietnam Conflict

Following World War II, nationalist elements in Indochina began a guerrilla war in an effort to prevent the reestablishment of French imperialist control. What made Indochinese nationalism different from nationalism elsewhere in Asia was the fact that Ho Chi Minh (1890–1969), the leader of the Indochinese nationalists, was a Communist. Because Ho bore that label, the conflict in Indochina became a part of the Cold War.

The Viet Minh

By 1950, Ho had united the nationalists in the part of Indochina that would become known as Vietnam into a movement called the Viet Minh. Ho's forces succeeded in inflicting a series of defeats on the French, and the United States provided increasing support for the French cause. Despite this aid, the French stronghold of Dienbienphu fell to the Viet Minh in May 1954, and the French decided to withdraw from Indochina.

Geneva Accords

An international conference held in Geneva, Switzerland, in the summer of 1954 reached agreement on the Geneva Accords, which confirmed the division of Indochina into the three separate and independent states of Laos, Cambodia, and Vietnam and then further divided Vietnam at the 17th parallel. This separation of North and South Vietnam was supposed to be temporary, pending elections scheduled for 1956, which would determine the nature of Vietnam's government. Ho Chi Minh, who controlled North Vietnam, expected that these elections would give him control of the South, as well.

Start of U.S. Intervention

The United States began to provide assistance to South Vietnam and selected Ngo Dinh Diem (1901–1963), a fervent anti-Communist,

Asia, 1989

to lead the country. With American support, Diem refused to carry out the agreement to hold elections in 1956. In response, Ho Chi Minh renewed the war.

Increased American Involvement

During the 1960s, the United States increased its support of the Diem government in its struggle against the National Liberation Front (Viet Cong), guerrillas who were aided by North Vietnam. The American government viewed the situation in terms of the Cold War, regarding the war in Vietnam as part of the worldwide effort to contain the expansion of Communism and Soviet power, which were regarded as the same thing.

American Opposition to War

In 1965, the United States assumed the primary military responsibility in South Vietnam. As the ground combat intensified and the American bombing of North Vietnam increased, American losses mounted and popular opposition to the war grew in the United States.

The End of the Vietnam War

When Richard Nixon (b. 1913) became president in 1969, he regarded finding a solution to the problem of the Vietnam war as one of the main tasks of his administration.

The Paris Accords

Following long and complex negotiations, the United States, South Vietnam, North Vietnam, and the Viet Cong signed the Paris Accords in January 1973. The agreement provided for an immediate cease-fire and United States withdrawal of its remaining troops. In the spring of 1975, the North Vietnamese intensified their attacks on South Vietnam, and South Vietnamese resistance quickly collapsed. At the end of April 1975, North Vietnamese troops took the South Vietnamese capital of Saigon, and it was renamed Ho Chi Minh City. The long war in Vietnam had finally reached its end.

Africa

Decolonization in Black Africa

In black Africa south of the Sahara Desert, nationalism became a potent force during the 1950s.

The Gold Coast

The British West African colony of the Gold Coast gained independence in 1957 under the leadership of Kwame Nkrumah (1909–1972). It became the nation of Ghana.

Nigeria

The British colony of Nigeria, also in West Africa, secured independence in 1960. Nigeria was fortunate in possessing oil reserves, and it used the income from this resource to finance its economic development.

Tanzania, Uganda, and Kenya

In East Africa, Tanganyika, a British possession, became independent in 1961 under the leadership of Julius Nyerere (b. 1922). In 1964, the island colony of Zanzibar joined with Tanganyika to form the new country of Tanzania. Uganda gained independence from Great Britain in 1962.

In Kenya, another British East African possession, white settlers fought for several years against the terrorist Mau Mau organization. In 1962, however, Kenya became independent, and Jomo Kenyatta (1893–1978), a founder of the Mau Mau movement, became the country's first president.

Malawi and Zambia

In southern Africa, the British colonies of Nyasaland and Northern Rhodesia became independent in 1964, taking the names of Malawi and Zambia, respectively.

Former French Possessions

The French West African colony of Guinea gained its independence in 1958. Sekou Touré (1922–1984), Guinea's president, pursued a pro-Soviet foreign policy. France's other possessions in

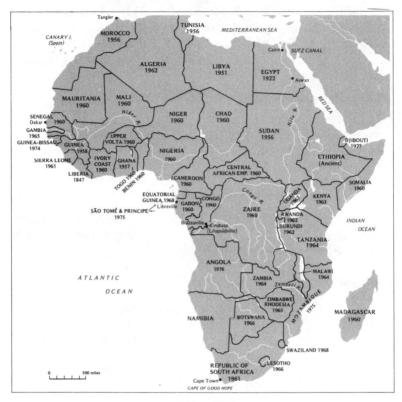

Africa, 1989

black Africa became independent in 1960. Unlike Guinea, they became members of the French Community and maintained close economic and cultural relations with France.

The Congo (Zaire)

Belgium hoped to maintain control over its rich colony of the Congo in Central Africa. The Belgians confronted mounting demands for independence, however, and abruptly withdrew in 1960. The new Republic of the Congo quickly sank into chaos, which persisted for several years.

In 1965, General Joseph Mobuto (b. 1930) seized power and established a dictatorship. Mobuto soon began to change names to erase the colonial past. The Congo became Zaire; its capital of Leopoldville became Kinshasa; and Mobuto Africanized his name, becoming Mobuto Sese Seko.

Angola and Mozambique

Of all the European colonial powers in Africa, Portugal held on to its possessions the longest, finally granting independence to Angola and Mozambique in 1975.

Southern Africa

In southern Africa, both the Union of South Africa and Rhodesia (formerly Southern Rhodesia) had sizable white populations, although in both cases they were small minorities.

Zimbabwe

In 1965, when the British attempted to secure equal political rights for blacks in Rhodesia, the white-dominated government issued a unilateral declaration of independence. The 250,000 whites feared they would be overwhelmed by the black majority, who numbered 6 million. Several years of controversy and conflict followed. Finally, in 1980, a government controlled by the black majority took power, and Rhodesia became Zimbabwe.

The Union of South Africa

Farther to the south, the Union of South Africa had been a self-governing dominion within the British Empire since 1910. Following World War II, the white minority in South Africa numbered about 4 million. These whites were primarily of British and Dutch ancestry. The latter, known as Afrikaners, became a majority of the white population in the post-World War II period and were determined to maintain white control, even though blacks and other nonwhites totaled some 18 million.

Apartheid

The Afrikaners' Nationalist Party imposed and maintained a system of rigid racial segregation known as apartheid. Blacks were compelled to live in separate townships and had little opportunity for higher education or occupational advancement. Black activists were imprisoned, often without trial, and strict censorship laws were enforced.

In the face of mounting pressure from Great Britain and other members of the British Commonwealth, the Union of South Africa pulled out of the Commonwealth in 1961, becoming the Republic of South Africa. The government remained firm in its determination to maintain apartheid.

The end of European empire did not bring stability to much of the Middle East, Asia, and Africa. In the Middle East, there was no resolution of the Arab-Israeli conflict, and the policies of both Libya and Iran also continued to contribute to international instability. In Asia, Japan succeeded in becoming both a viable democracy and an industrial giant, while China appeared to be making economic progress under a modified Communist system. Other Asian countries—South Korea, Singapore, and Malaysia, among them—were also advancing economically, but elsewhere in Asia, serious problems of overpopulation, poverty, and political instability persisted. Similar problems affected much of Africa, while in South Africa the conflict over apartheid was becoming more bitter.

Recommended Reading

Aroian, Lois A. and Richard P. Mitchell. *The Modern Middle East and North Africa* (1984).

Berger, Earl. *The Covenant and the Sword: Arab-Israeli Relations, 1948-56* (1965).

Burki, Shahid J. *Pakistan: A Nation in the Making* (1986).

Cable, James. *The Geneva Conference of 1954 on Indochina* (1986).

Calvocoressi, Peter. *Independent Africa and the World* (1985).

Cohen, Michael J. *The Origins and Evolution of the Arab-Zionist Conflict* (1987).

Cowan, L. Gray. *The Dilemmas of African Independence* (rev. ed., 1968).

Easton, Stewart C. *The Twilight of European Colonialism: A Political Analysis* (1960).

FitzGerald, C. P. *The Birth of Communist China* (1966).

Gardner, Lloyd C. *Approaching Vietnam: From World War II Through Dienbienphu, 1941–1954* (1988).

Gorni, Yosef. *Zionism and the Arabs, 1882–1948: A Study of Ideology* (1987).

Hane, Mikiso. *Modern Japan: A Historical Survey* (rev. ed., 1986).

Herring, George C. *America's Longest War: The U. S. and Vietnam, 1950-75* (1979).

Keddie, Nikki R. *Roots of Revolution: An Interpretive History of Modern Iran* (1981).

Knappert, Jan. *East Africa: Kenya, Tanzania and Uganda* (1987).

Moise, Edwin E. *Modern China: A History* (1986).

Morris, Benny. *The Birth of the Palestinian Refugee Problem, 1947–1949* (1987).

Muslih, Muhammad Y. *The Origins of Palestinian Nationalism* (1988).

O'Brien, Conor Cruise. *The Siege: The Saga of Israel and Zionism* (1986).

Peretz, Don. *The Middle East Today* (1988).

Sharabi, Hisham. *Nationalism and Revolution in the Arab World* (1966).

CHAPTER 40

Twentieth-Century European Civilization

Time Line

1913–1927	Marcel Proust publishes *Remembrance of Things Past*
1919	The Bauhaus is established in Weimar Germany
1920	H. G. Wells publishes *The Outline of History*
1922	John Galsworthy publishes *The Forsyte Saga*
	T. S. Eliot publishes *The Waste Land*
	James Joyce publishes *Ulysses*
1924	Thomas Mann publishes *The Magic Mountain*

1925	George Bernard Shaw wins the Nobel Prize for literature
1926	André Gide publishes *The Counterfeiters*
1928	D. H. Lawrence publishes *Lady Chatterley's Lover*
1929	Erich Maria Remarque publishes *All Quiet on the Western Front*
1942	Albert Camus publishes *The Stranger*
1943	Jean Paul Sartre publishes *Being and Nothingness*
1948	The World Council of Churches is established
1949	George Orwell publishes *1984*
1950	Simone de Beauvoir publishes *The Second Sex*
1958	John XXIII becomes pope
1959	Günter Grass publishes *The Tin Drum*
1962–1965	The Second Vatican Council meets
1978	John Paul II becomes pope

The two world wars of the twentieth century, with their accompanying horrors, did much to undermine the faith in the inevitability of human progress that was an influential legacy of the Enlightenment. Furthermore, while advances in science and technology greatly improved the material quality of life, they also increased the uncertainties and threats confronting humanity. As a consequence of these experiences of the twentieth century, philosophy and religion—and literature and the arts, as well—became increasingly more diverse in their consideration of the human experience in a troubled age.

Philosophy and Religion

Existentialism

Existentialism emerged as one of the twentieth century's most influential movements in philosophy. A complex movement, existentialism focused its attention on the helpless and alienated individual seeking his identity and salvation in an unreasonable and apparently meaningless universe.

Kierkegaard

An outgrowth of the revolt against reason that began in nineteenth-century philosophy, existentialism numbered the German philosopher Friedrich Nietzsche (see Chapter 26) and the Danish thinker Soren Kierkegaard (1813–1855) among its forerunners. While Kierkegaard wrote in the early nineteenth century, he did not win wide attention until after World War I. Deeply religious, Kierkegaard stressed the need for isolated human beings to make a leap of faith and establish a relationship with God. He believed, however, that the truths of the Christian faith are not revealed so much in doctrinal formulas and in the organized church as they are in the experience of human beings facing the crises of their lives.

Sartre

Jean-Paul Sartre (1905–1980), a French philosopher, novelist, and playwright, emerged as a significant spokesman for existentialism following World War II. *Being and Nothingness* (1943) is Sartre's major philosophical work, but he also expressed existentialist ideas in his novels, plays, and other writings. An atheist, Sartre believed that human existence has no transcendent significance and that it is, therefore, fundamentally absurd. This absurdity, however, means that human beings are free to make choices. In their choices, they can give meaning and purpose to their lives.

De Beauvoir

Simone de Beauvoir (b. 1908), a close friend of Sartre's, examined the existential dilemma in several novels, including *The Mandarins*

(1955). She also wrote *The Second Sex* (1950), a ground-breaking work on the condition of women.

Camus

The French novelist and playwright Albert Camus (1913–1960) is regarded as an existentialist, although he was more a literary man and moralist than a formal philosopher. Camus expressed existentialist views in his novels, including *The Stranger* (1942), *The Plague* (1947), and *The Fall* (1956). In *The Myth of Sisyphus* (1942), he set forth his concept of the absurdity of human existence. Although viewing the world as a place of absurdity, Camus nevertheless had great confidence in the human spirit. In *The Rebel* (1951), he extolled spiritual rebellion as a means for human beings to transcend their existential predicament.

Roman Catholicism

A new era in the history of the Roman Catholic Church began with the pontificate of Pope John XXIII (r. 1958–1963). In his 1961 enclyclical *Mater et Magistra* ("Mother and Teacher"), the pope strongly reaffirmed the commitment of the Catholic Church to the cause of economic and social reform and called for increased assistance to underdeveloped countries. John XXIII also endorsed religious ecumenism (improved relations with other Christian denominations). In his 1963 encyclical *Pacem in Terris* ("Peace on Earth"), the pope called on people of different religious and political persuasions to cooperate in promoting the cause of peace and social justice throughout the world.

Vatican II

Pope John XXIII initiated a movement for the renewal of the Catholic Church. To promote this renewal, what he called *aggiornamento* (bringing the church up-to-date), the pope convened the Second Vatican Council. Vatican II, meeting in four sessions from 1962 to 1965, was composed of archbishops, bishops, and other high-ranking churchmen from around the world. The council enacted a reform of the church's liturgy, introducing the use of vernacular languages in place of Latin and encouraging more active participation by the laity. It endorsed the ecumenical movement and promoted an improvement in relations with non-Christians, issuing a strong condemnation of anti-Semitism. Vatican II created a new atmosphere in the Catholic Church, where different points of view could more openly be expressed.

Pope Paul VI

Pope Paul VI (r. 1963–1978) supported the program of renewal introduced by Vatican II, although he maintained the traditional authority of the pope as head of the Catholic Church. In the controversial 1968 encyclical *Humanae Vitae* ("Of Human Life"), Paul VI reaffirmed the church's opposition to artificial contraception.

Pope John Paul II

Following Paul VI's death in 1978, John Paul I became pope, dying suddenly after a pontificate of only thirty-four days. The cardinals then elected the first non-Italian pope since the sixteenth century. Karol Wojtyla, who became Pope John Paul II, had been the cardinal-archbishop of Cracow, Poland. Elected at the age of fifty-six, John Paul II was the youngest man to become pope in over one hundred years.

John Paul II was a strong advocate of social justice and of ecumenism, although he pursued a moderately conservative course in governing the Catholic Church. He emphasized papal authority on matters of religious doctrine and practice, encouraged the traditional Catholic devotion to the Virgin Mary, and discouraged views and practices that he regarded as either excessively liberal or overly conservative. The pope reaffirmed the Catholic Church's requirement that the clergy be celibate and opposed the ordination of women to the priesthood. He was critical of liberation theology promoted by some Catholic radicals, especially in Latin America, and he condemned the traditionalist movement, which rejected many of the reforms instituted by Vatican II.

Protestantism

Barth

Neoorthodoxy emerged as one of the most important movements in Protestant Christianity in the twentieth century. Karl Barth (1886–1968), a Swiss theologian, was one of the most prominent neoorthodox thinkers. Barth rejected religious modernism and reaffirmed Reformation theology, emphasizing the word of God set forth in the Bible, the revelation of God in Jesus Christ, and the dependence of humanity on God. Barth's major writings include *Church Dogmatics* (4 vols., 1922–1962).

Tillich

Another powerful Protestant spokesman was Paul Tillich (1886–1965), a German theologian. For Tillich, God was ultimate truth, the "Ground of Being," and such traditional Christian doctrines as original sin, atonement, and immortality were not so much realities as symbols. Tillich's major works include *Systematic Theology* (3 vols., 1951–1963).

A growing ecumenical spirit among Protestants resulted in the establishment in 1948 of the World Council of Churches.

Literature

British Literature

Three British writers of the pre-World War I generation remained prominent in the postwar era: George Bernard Shaw (1856–1950), H. G. Wells (1866–1946), and John Galsworthy (1867–1933).

Shaw

The Dublin-born Shaw won popularity for a number of witty plays, including *Man and Superman* (1905) and *Pygmalion* (1913). *St. Joan* (1923) was among Shaw's successful plays produced in the 1920s. He won the Nobel Prize for literature in 1925.

Wells

Wells's popular prewar science fiction included *The Time Machine* (1895) and *The War of the Worlds* (1898). In the postwar era, *The Outline of History* (1920) won a wide readership, as did the futuristic novel *The Shape of Things to Come* (1933).

Galsworthy

Galsworthy, who won the Nobel Prize for literature in 1933, is best-known for his trilogy *The Forsyte Saga* (1922), which dealt with the decline of the English upper-middle class.

Lawrence

D. H. Lawrence (1885–1930) shocked his contemporaries with his frankness about sexuality. His novel *Sons and Lovers* (1913) appeared on the eve of World War I. *Lady Chatterley's Lover* (1928), Lawrence's best-known novel, was widely condemned as pornographic and was banned in the United States and Great Britain for many years.

Huxley

Aldous Huxley (1894–1963) is best known for his novel *Brave New World* (1932), which presented a grim picture of a future "ideal" society.

Eliot

The American-born T. S. Eliot (1888–1965) was among Britain's best-known poets, playwrights, and critics. In *The Waste Land* (1922), Eliot wrote of the barrenness of modern life. In his verse drama *Murder in the Cathedral* (1935), he told the story of the murder of Thomas à Becket, a twelfth-century archbishop of Canterbury.

Orwell

Among English writers of the post-World War II period, the satirist George Orwell (1903–1950) was among the most prominent. Orwell assaulted totalitarianism in his novels *Animal Farm* (1946) and *1984* (1949), which presented a vision of a sinister totalitarian society of the future.

French Literature

Gide

André Gide (1869–1951) demonstrated his ability as a keen observer of human nature in a series of novels, including *Lafcadio's Adventures* (1914) and *The Counterfeiters* (1926). Highly controversial, Gide was condemned both for his defense of homosexuality and his support of Communism, which he later repudiated. He won the Nobel Prize for literature in 1947.

Proust

Marcel Proust (1871–1922) presented a sharp psychological analysis of the old, decaying aristocracy and the new, ambitious bourgeoisie in the sixteen volumes of his novel *Remembrance of Things Past* (1913–1927).

Mauriac

François Mauriac (1885–1970), the winner of the Nobel Prize for literature in 1952, reflected his strong Catholic faith in a series of novels, including *The Desert of Love* (1925).

German Literature

Mann

Thomas Mann (1875–1955), who won the Nobel Prize for literature in 1929, is widely recognized as Germany's greatest twentieth-century writer. *The Magic Mountain* (1924), his best novel, is set in a sanitarium that served as a metaphor for what Mann regarded as the sickness of contemporary civilization. His other well-known works include *Buddenbrooks* (1901); *Joseph and His Brothers* (1933–1943), a series of four novels; and *Doctor Faustus* (1947). Strongly anti-Nazi, Mann left Germany in 1933.

Kafka

Franz Kafka (1883–1924), a German Jew living in Prague, wrote haunting novels and short stories dealing with the alienation of modern man. *Metamorphosis* (1912), a collection of stories, was published during Kafka's lifetime, but his major novels were published posthumously.

Hesse

The poet and novelist Hermann Hesse (1877–1962) also dealt with the theme of alienation in *Steppenwolf* (1927), his best-known novel.

Remarque

Erich Maria Remarque (1898–1970) is most famous for his powerful antiwar novel *All Quiet on the Western Front* (1929).

Böll and Grass

The horrors of the Nazi era and World War II exerted a powerful influence on postwar German literature. Heinrich Böll (1917–1985) criticized what he regarded as the degeneration of postwar German society in his novels and stories, including *The Lost Honor of Katharina Blum* (1975). In his first novel, *The Tin Drum* (1959), Günter Grass (b. 1927) confronted the viciousness of the Nazi years. His other novels include *Cat and Mouse* (1961) and *Dog Years* (1963).

Other Major Writers

Joyce

James Joyce (1882–1941), an Irish writer, achieved early recognition for *The Dubliners* (1924), a collection of short stories, and *A Portrait of the Artist as a Young Man* (1916), an autobiographical novel. In *Ulysses* (1922), Joyce broke new ground, experimenting with the stream-of-consciousness technique and long interior monologues. Criticized for obscenity, *Ulysses* was banned in several countries. Joyce continued his literary experimentation in the complex novel *Finnegans Wake* (1939).

Moravia

The Italian neorealist Alberto Moravia (b. 1907) is best known for his novels, including *The Women of Rome* (1947) and *Two Women* (1957), dealing with social alienation.

Art, Architecture, and Music

Painting

Henri Matisse and Pablo Picasso remained major artists in the years after World War I (see Chapter 26), while other artists developed the new movements of expressionism and surrealism.

Expressionism

Expressionism, which emphasized the artist's free expression of emotion, flourished in Germany in the years immediately prior to the outbreak of World War I. Georges Rouault (1871–1958), a French painter, is also regarded as an expressionist.

Surrealism

In the 1920s, the movement known as surrealism emerged. Influenced by Freudian psychology, the surrealists sought to portray subconscious fantasies. Max Ernst (1891–1976), a German painter, and the Spanish-born Salvador Dali (1904–1989) were among the best-known surrealists.

Modigliani

Amedeo Modigliani (1884–1920), an Italian painter, developed a unique style marked by the elongation of forms.

Sculpture

Twentieth-century sculpture moved away from the representation of reality toward more experimental styles.

Barlach

Ernst Barlach (1870–1938) introduced expressionism into German sculpture. His work, emphasizing bold and simple lines, conveyed a powerful sense of emotion.

Brancusi

Constantin Brancusi (1876–1957), a Rumanian, emphasized simplicity of form in his abstract shapes.

Epstein

The Russian-American sculptor Jacob Epstein (1880–1959), who lived in England for most of his career, produced massive and powerful figures, often inspired by personalities in the Bible, in stone and bronze.

Architecture

Twentieth-century architecture was characterized by an emphasis on function, rather than form, and by the use of structural steel and other modern construction materials, including concrete and glass. In addition, it tended to avoid decorative details that served no function.

The Bauhaus

In Germany, the Bauhaus was founded in Weimar in 1919, under the leadership of Walter Gropius (1883–1969). Ludwig Mies van der Rohe (1886–1969) became its head in 1930. The Bauhaus played a major role in the development of modern architecture prior to its dissolution after Hitler took power in 1933.

Le Corbusier

The Swiss-French architect Charles E. Jeanneret, better known as Le Corbusier (1887–1965), was one of the twentieth century's most innovative and influential architects. He is known for his dictum "a house is a machine to live in."

Music

The twentieth century produced a number of major composers, although few achieved the widespread popularity of their leading nineteenth-century counterparts.

Ravel

The French composer Maurice Ravel (1875–1937) wrote primarily piano and orchestral works. *Bolero* (1928) is his best-known composition.

Respighi

Ottorini Respighi (1879–1936), an Italian, composed romantic orchestral works, including the graceful *Fountains of Rome* (1917) and *Pines of Rome* (1924).

Bartok

Bela Bartok (1881–1945) found inspiration in the folk melodies of his native Hungary. He is best known for his compositions for piano, violin, and orchestra, as well as his choral works.

Hindemith

The German Paul Hindemith (1895–1963) wrote for the piano and other solo instruments and also composed orchestral and choral works.

Vaughan Williams and Britten

Among British composers, Ralph Vaughan Williams (1872–1958) and Benjamin Britten (1913–1976) are the best known. Vaughan Williams is widely regarded as the leading English composer of the early twentieth century. Influenced by English folk music, his compositions include song cycles, symphonies, and operas. Britten composed both instrumental and choral works, as well as operas.

Russian Composers

Igor Stravinsky remained active in the years following World War I (see Chapter 26). Other major twentieth-century Russian composers included Sergei Prokofiev (1891–1953) and Dmitri Shostakovich (1906–1975). A musical innovator, Prokofiev was inspired by traditional Russian folk music. His most popular work is *Peter and the Wolf* (1936). Shostakovich wrote symphonies and operas, as well as string quartets and concertos for violin, piano, and cello. His Fifth Symphony (1937) is particularly well-known.

In the late nineteenth century, Europeans often elevated their faith in science and technology to an almost religious level and expressed their belief in the inevitability of human progress. "Glory to man in the highest," the English poet Algernon Charles Swinburne proclaimed, "the maker and master of things."

The experience of the twentieth century has been a sobering one. Nevertheless, while the unbridled optimism so often expressed in the nineteenth century has proved unwarranted, so, too, is the intense sense of pessimism that has permeated so much of contemporary thought. The French writer Albert Camus made an eloquent statement of the intellectual temper of many in the twentieth century on the occasion of his acceptance of the Nobel Prize for literature in 1958. Expressing his sober belief in humanity's ability to prevail, Camus told his audience:

As the heir of a corrupt history that blends blighted revolutions, misguided techniques, dead gods, and worn-out ideologies, in which second-rate powers can destroy everything today, but are unable to win anyone over; in which intelligence had stooped to becoming the servant of hatred and oppression, our generation, starting from nothing but its own negations, has had to rees-

tablish both within and without itself a little of what constitutes the dignity of life and death. Faced with a world threatened with disintegration . . ., our generation knows that, in a sort of mad race against time, it ought to reestablish among nations a peace not based on slavery, to reconcile labor and culture again, and to reconstruct with all men an Ark of the Covenant. Perhaps it can never accomplish that vast undertaking, but most certainly throughout the world it has already accepted the double challenge of truth and liberty, and on occasion, has shown that it can lay down its life without hatred. This generation deserves to be acclaimed wherever it happens to be, and especially wherever it is sacrificing itself.

Recommended Reading

Arnason, H. H. *History of Modern Art: Painting, Sculpture, Architecture* (1969).

Barrett, William. *Irrational Man: A Study in Existential Philosophy* (1958).

Barzun, Jacques. *The House of Intellect* (1959).

Brée, Germaine. *Camus and Sartre: Crisis and Commitment* (1972).

Hughes, H. Stuart. *Consciousness and Society: The Reorientation of European Social Thought, 1890–1930* (1958).

Kaufmann, Walter A., ed. *Existentialism from Dostoevsky to Sartre* (1956).

Moore, Harry T. *Twentieth-Century French Literature* (1966).

Moore, Harry T. *Twentieth-Century German Literature* (1967).

Read, Herbert. *A Concise History of Modern Painting* (rev. ed., 1969).

Read, Herbert. *A Concise History of Modern Sculpture* (1964).

Salzman, Eric. *Twentieth-Century Music: An Introduction* (3rd ed., 1988).

Schilling, S. Paul. *Contemporary Continental Theologians* (1966).

Stromberg, Roland N. *After Everything: Western Intellectual History Since 1945* (1975).

Wohl, Robert. *The Generation of 1914* (1979).

Index